James Turner
Kevin Bedell

Struts

KICK START

SAMS

201 West 103rd Street, Indianapolis, Indiana 46290

Struts Kick Start

International Standard Book Number: 0-67232-472-5

Library of Congress Catalog Card Number: 2002107307

Printed in the United States of America

First Printing: December 2002

05 04 03 4 3 2

Trademarks

All terms mentioned in this book that are known to be trademarks or service marks have been appropriately capitalized. Sams Publishing cannot attest to the accuracy of this information. Use of a term in this book should not be regarded as affecting the validity of any trademark or service mark.

Warning and Disclaimer

Every effort has been made to make this book as complete and as accurate as possible, but no warranty or fitness is implied. The information provided is on an "as is" basis. The authors and the publisher shall have neither liability nor responsibility to any person or entity with respect to any loss or damages arising from the information contained in this book or from the use of the CD or programs accompanying it.

Executive Editor
Michael Stephens

Acquisitions Editor
Todd Green

Development Editor
Songlin Qiu

Managing Editor
Charlotte Clapp

Project Editors
Elizabeth Finney
Tricia Liebig

Copy Editor
Michael Henry

Indexer
Becky Hornyak

Proofreader
Carla Lewis

Technical Editors
David Barber
Chris Kenyeres
Ben Hanner

Team Coordinator
Lynne Williams

Multimedia Developer
Dan Scherf

Interior Designer
Gary Adair

Cover Designer
Gary Adair

Page Layout
Ayanna Lacey

Contents at a Glance

Table of Contents

Appendix

About the Authors

James Turner is the manager of Black Bear Software, LLC. He has more than 22 years of experience in the computer field and has worked for organizations that include MIT, Xerox, Solbourne Computer, BBN Planet, and Interleaf. He spent the last seven years managing and implementing e-commerce Web sites for companies including CVS, The Christian Science Monitor, and Woolworths UK. In addition, he is an active contributor to various Apache Jakarta projects and recently was the Release Manager for the Jakarta Commons Validator 1.0 release. Mr. Turner is also a well-published freelance journalist and technology writer who has written for publications including *The Christian Science Monitor*, *WIRED*, and *Web Developers Journal*. He lives in Derry, New Hampshire, in a 200-year-old colonial farmhouse along with his wife and son. James is also the author of *MySQL and JSP Web Applications: Data Driven Programming Using Tomcat and MySQL*, published in 2002 by Sams Publishing.

Kevin Bedell is an E-Business Systems Architect with Sun Life Financial in Wellesley, Massachusetts. His career has crossed a number of different fields including programming, consulting, IT management, network integration, and corporate finance and accounting. In the software development world, he worked for large and small companies including Oracle, Johnson Controls, and Sun Life Financial. He's a Sun Certified Java Programmer and has earned his MCSE certification from Microsoft. Kevin holds a BS in engineering from Michigan Tech and an MBA from the Crummer Graduate School of Business at Rollins College in Winter Park, Florida.

Dedication

James: To my parents, who let me buy that first TRS-80, so many years ago.

Kevin: To my family who are my greatest joy and biggest fans. And to the dedicated and growing group of open source developers and advocates who are truly changing the world.

Acknowledgments

This book wouldn't exist if it weren't for a dedicated group of individuals who have come together to create the Struts application framework itself. The work of getting Struts 1.1 ready for release was unglamorous, much of it downright tedious. Because of that, the authors would like to acknowledge the hard work of the entire Struts community, especially the core committers who are the lifeblood of the project.

A particular nod of thanks goes to Craig McClanahan, the originator of Struts, who continues to be one of the most active contributors. Several times during the writing of this book, he provided helpful direction on unclear or poorly documented areas of the Struts framework.

And finally, a thanks to our families, who had to endure our absence (mentally and sometimes physically) as we worked to get this book out under a fairly grueling schedule.

We Want to Hear from You!

As the reader of this book, *you* are our most important critic and commentator. We value your opinion and want to know what we're doing right, what we could do better, what areas you'd like to see us publish in, and any other words of wisdom you're willing to pass our way.

As an executive editor for Sams Publishing, I welcome your comments. You can email or write me directly to let me know what you did or didn't like about this book—as well as what we can do to make our books better.

Please note that I cannot help you with technical problems related to the *topic* of this book. We do have a User Services group, however, where I will forward specific technical questions related to the book.

When you write, please be sure to include this book's title and author as well as your name, email address, and phone number. I will carefully review your comments and share them with the author and editors who worked on the book.

Email: `feedback@samspublishing.com`

Mail: Michael Stephens
Executive Editor
Sams Publishing
201 West 103rd Street
Indianapolis, IN 46290 USA

For more information about this book or another Sams Publishing title, visit our Web site at `www.samspublishing.com`. Type the ISBN (excluding hyphens) or the title of a book in the Search field to find the page you're looking for. To go directly to the Struts Kick Start Web site visit `strutskickstart.com`.

Introduction

As the Java 2 Enterprise Edition (J2EE) platform has grown and spread (until it seems like it's now everywhere!), one of the fastest growing of the J2EE technologies has been JavaServer Pages (JSP). Nearly everyone developing Web-based applications with Java uses JSP now. The availability of free, open source JSP/servlet containers such as Tomcat from the Apache Jakarta project has accelerated this dramatically.

As JSP has matured and developers have become more experienced in it, there's been an explosion in the number of people using what are called *Web Application Frameworks* (or just *frameworks*). Frameworks help developers build applications faster and better by providing prepackaged starter kits for application development. New projects no longer begin with the question, "Should we use a framework?"—they begin with "Which framework should we use?".

Framework usage is taking off. Browsing the Google Web directory to the category `Computers > Programming > Languages > Java > Server-Side > Libraries and Frameworks` now lists almost 20 options for Web application frameworks!

Struts, from the Apache Jakarta project, is the king of these frameworks. It's arguably the best and most widely used framework of all. A groundswell is building behind it. The authors believe that soon a large percentage of *all* Web-based development done with JSP will use Struts.

And for good reason: Being the flagship framework from the Apache Jakarta project brings with it a lot of visibility and a huge user base. This user base means that Struts has been proven in a wide range of application environments, and such heavy usage means that it's debugged and ready for prime time. If you've chosen Struts for your project, congratulations on a great choice.

If you've chosen this book, congratulations again on a great choice! The authors are highly experienced developers who took it upon themselves to write the kind of book that *they* like: one that cuts through the fluff and gives you what you need to know to get moving quickly. This book is filled with ideas and tips and sample code and real advice. It doesn't just tell you how Struts works, it helps you learn quickly to use Struts well. You'll notice the difference.

Who Should Read This Book?

Among the books on Struts currently available, our goal was to write the book that was the most helpful in the least amount of time. This book is packed full of practical examples designed to get the point across quickly. If you're looking for a book that takes a leisure pace or tries to give you exhaustive coverage of every detail, look somewhere else. If you want to pick up the technology quickly and find sample code you can use as the basis for real applications, this book is for you.

If you're using Struts or JSP today, the value of this book is it's kick-start style and how you can work through only the chapters you need. As mentioned, the sample code and companion CD-ROM are of immediate value.

If you're new to the technology or just interested in learning, this book is a good choice as well. Because we cover the technology from a quick-start perspective, you'll find that we try to teach you what you need to know quickly, and don't dwell on material that's unimportant. We feel you can move fastest with this approach.

No matter what your needs are, the breadth of material covered will be useful. In addition to covering Struts itself, we present real-world examples of applications written using other important technologies such as JBoss, Apache Axis, Jakarta Torque, XDoclet, MySQL, and more. Copies of all these products are included on the companion CD-ROM, so you don't have spend all day downloading files.

What Do You Need to Bring to the Table?

This book provides a full introduction to Struts. However, it assumes that you already know at least some JSP. If you've never used JSP (or Java, for that matter), you need to get up to speed on those technologies first.

Because modern Web applications often have a SQL database behind them, examples are provided that use the MySQL database. If you know nothing about SQL, you need to spend extra time on that subject to get the most out of the examples.

More importantly, you should be reading this book if you want to design Web sites that are easy and fast to maintain and change. That's the promise of Struts. If you're designing only a simple one-page form, you probably won't see much initial benefit from using Struts. But if that site ever grows or if you're designing anything more complex, Struts gives you benefits both immediately and down the road.

What Does This Book Cover?

This book documents the Struts 1.1 release as of the 1.1-b2 beta and includes the latest features added in 1.1, including `DynaForms`, the Validator, and the Tiles tag library.

In addition to Struts, a number of other technologies are covered including JBoss, XDoclet, Apache Axis, Jakarta Ant, Cactus, and Jakarta Torque. A companion CD-ROM is provided that contains all code from the book plus copies of all these applications.

Specifically, this book

- Leads you through the process of installing and using Struts
- Explains the Model-View-Controller (MVC) design pattern and how Struts implements it

- Reviews and provides working sample code for all the Struts tag libraries
- Covers dynamic form handling and validation using `DynaForms` and the Validator
- Explains how to integrate Struts with Enterprise JavaBeans (EJB) servers and provides a detailed sample application based on Struts and JBoss
- Covers using Struts with Web services and provides a detailed sample application based on Struts and Apache Axis
- Discusses using Jakarta Ant to build and deploy Struts applications
- Reviews how to test Struts applications using JUnit and the Apache Cactus testing framework

Tools You'll Need

None of the technologies discussed in this book are platform-specific. You can make the presented Struts examples run on anything from a Windows 95 desktop machine to a Linux or Solaris server. Many of examples in the book are done under Windows, but they work equally well under other operating systems.

The application server you're using shouldn't matter either. All the examples are built using Jakarta Tomcat, but only because the authors assumed that everyone could get a copy of it and install it easily (a copy of Tomcat is included on the companion CD-ROM). Even so, people around the world are running Struts on all variety of application servers, including WebLogic, WebSphere, iPlanet, and many more.

All the applications, such as Struts, JBoss, Apache Axis, and MySQL, are included on the CD-ROM and are either open source or free for instructional use, so you won't need to purchase any additional software to run the examples or develop your own projects.

In addition to all sample applications and third-party tools used in the book, the CD-ROM also contains a copy of Sun's Java™ 2 Platform, Standard Edition, v 1.4.1 (also known as J2SE 1.4.1). Since the J2SE 1.4.1 is rather large, this may save you quite a bit of downloading time. You should note, however, that while Struts and Tomcat have been pretty well debugged for J2SE 1.4.1, we can't ensure that all the other applications provided on the CD-ROM have. In particular, JBoss 3.0.3 had a few documented issues with it. To be safe, all the sample code and third-party applications have been tested with Sun's J2SE v1.3.1.

How This Book Is Organized

This book is organized in a specific way to help you get the most out of it.

Chapters 1 through 5 of the book gives a high-level overview of Struts and introduces the Model-View-Controller design pattern behind Struts. The specifics of how Struts implements this design pattern are discussed with the goal of helping you understand how to better understand, design, and build Struts applications. A first Struts application is presented that covers each major function of Struts with an eye toward providing you a good base knowledge of how it works. You'll review JSP, Java servlets, and JSP tag libraries, and learn how they interact with Struts.

Chapters 6 through 10 are built around a sample financial application. This is introduced using a functional requirements specification that is followed by the specific implementation details behind the Model, View, and Controller components. Details of the `struts-config.xml` file are also covered. This sample application is designed to demonstrate each of the main pieces of the Struts framework.

Chapter 11 provides you with insight into how the Struts tag libraries are built by climbing inside and explaining a real sample tag from the inside out. Following that, Chapters 12–16 provide details on and sample code for all the Struts tag libraries, including Struts 1.1's new Tiles tags.

Chapter 17 provides a solid grounding on two important Struts technologies: `DynaForms` and the Validator. These technologies allow nearly codeless development of Web forms.

The book finishes with some advanced topics. Chapter 18 provides a set of best practices and a practical design pattern for integrating Struts with Enterprise JavaBeans, including a working sample application based on JBoss. Chapter 19 takes a similar look at integrating Struts with Web Services, including a detailed sample application using Apache Axis. Finally, Chapter 20 looks at building, deploying, and testing using Jakarta Ant and the Jakarta Cactus testing framework.

The Companion Web Site

In order to provide expanded information, the authors have created a companion Web site for this book: `http://www.strutskickstart.com`. We hope you'll check the site out and tell us what you think.

Conventions Used in This Book

This section describes the important typographic conventions and terminology used in this book. Features in this book include the following:

- Code lines, commands, statements, variables, and any text you see onscreen appears in a `mono` typeface.
- Placeholders in syntax descriptions appear in an *`italic mono`* typeface. Replace the placeholder with the actual filename, parameter, or whatever element it represents.
- *Italics* highlight technical terms when they're being defined.
- The ➥ icon is used before a line of code that is really a continuation of the preceding line. Sometimes a line of code is too long to fit as a single line on the page. If you see ➥ before a line of code, remember that it's part of the line immediately above it.
- The book also makes use of Notes, Cautions, and Tips. These special elements appear separately from the text and provide additional information about relevant topics.

NOTE

Notes are used to indicate that you might need additional information to understand the concept being discussed in the text. Because of its importance, it is given special treatment.

CAUTION

Cautions are used to make you aware of a potential pitfall associated with the subject being explained.

TIP

Tips are used to give you extra information that is not generally available. Often this information is something that the authors have learned from experience.

Updates and Corrections

For updates to this book, visit `http://www.samspublishing.com` or `strutskickstart.com`. From the home page, type this book's ISBN (0672324725) into the search window and click Search to access information about the book. If we discover any errors in the text, we'll post corrections at this page, too.

1 Struts in Context

IN THIS CHAPTER

The promise of Struts is this: Develop better software faster. There are two pieces to that contract. One is speed of development. If you begin a project using Struts, you've got a great running start. Struts provides an easy-to-use development model that builds in many of the things you'd otherwise develop yourself. If you begin a project without Struts, you're starting from scratch; it'll take you weeks to catch up to where Struts enables you to start. Using Struts saves you time—a lot of time.

The second piece of the contract is that Struts helps you deliver better software. Struts was built by a group of some of the best and most knowledgeable developers around. Then it was tested by literally hundreds (maybe thousands) of developers all over the world. When you have that many pairs of eyes on the code, you tend to find bugs pretty fast. Needless to say, by now Struts is a very solid framework, and it implements some of the best practices in software development there are.

The Parable of the Carpenter

Anyone who has been around the software integration business for a while can attest to one truism. The choices you make at the beginning of your project, when you're assembling the toolkit that will provide the foundation of your endeavor, are some of the most crucial.

Imagine you're building a house. You have a 2×4 that you want to nail to a beam. There are people out there who, lacking a hammer, would grab the nearest rock and start wailing away. Others, distrustful of store-bought hammers, would construct a forge and fashion their own hammer to their own precise specifications. Still other people might rush down to their local hardware store and buy the fanciest laser-leveled battery-powered auto-hammer they could get. Finally, a seasoned carpenter might take the trusty hammer that he knows like the back of his hand from his belt, and drive that nail straight and true.

The analogy holds true for software engineers. Some use the most primitive tools that can possibly get the job done. (You tend to find them still implementing Web sites using CGI scripts written in C, but the raw JSP crowd is rapidly joining their ranks.) Still others take the not-invented-here approach and create their own application infrastructure. You also find those who are enamored of the latest (and usually most expensive) buzzword-laden products. Finally, you find the veterans who have slowly developed an arsenal of trusted tools over time.

The advantage to using a toolset (or framework) is that you get the benefit of all the work that's been put into it by other people, just like you, solving problems just like yours. You usually get a huge step up because a lot of the gruntwork has already been done for you. You can probably learn an already existing database connection-pooling package faster than you can write your own, for example.

Struts is an example of such a framework. It was developed in response to an increasingly common problem in Web site development using Java. As a site grows in complexity, it becomes more and more difficult to manage the relationship between the various JSP pages, the backend business logic, and the forms and validations that move you around the site. As a result, many JSP sites end up looking like the Web equivalent of spaghetti code. Struts centralizes and standardizes this entire ball of wax.

But Struts is much more than just a framework that gets you started quickly. It's also a collection of best practices. Why build something on your own when some of the best JSP developers in the world (literally) have worked so hard to lay out a path for you to follow?

What Is Struts?

According to its creators, Struts is a "Web Application Framework." So, what does that mean? Let's look first at the *Framework* piece.

Frameworks

What's a framework?

The dictionary defines a framework as "A structure for supporting or enclosing something else, especially a skeletal support used as the basis for something being constructed." This perfectly describes Struts: a collection of Java code designed to help you build solid applications while saving time. It provides the basic skeleton and plumbing; you focus on the layout and look of each room.

Interestingly, the dictionary offers an alternative definition: "A set of assumptions, concepts, values, and practices that constitutes a way of viewing reality." This describes Struts as well—it's a way of looking at things. Struts saves you time by enabling you to view complex applications as a series of basic components: Views, Action classes, and Model components.

So, how does a framework save you time?

By using a framework, you don't have to spend time building your entire application. You can focus on coding the business logic and the presentation layer of the application, not the overhead pieces.

Using a framework also helps you encode best practices. The framework developers put a lot of thought into the best approaches to application building, so why rediscover them yourself?

Other benefits of using a framework are that it allows your code (at least in the case of Struts) to be highly platform independent. For example, the same Struts code that works under Tomcat on an old Windows NT machine should run using WebLogic Server on Linux or Solaris in production. In many cases, this can be accomplished without even recompiling. The same Web application (or `.war` file) simply can be copied from one host to another.

Another extremely important benefit—especially if you're relatively new to Web development—is that Struts gives you a place to start. Any developer will tell you that it's easier to take a basic application and modify it than it is to build something from scratch. This basic feature of Struts can save you days or weeks of planning and development.

Web Applications

Struts is for building Web applications.

By saying this, a couple implications are made. The first is that Struts is generally for building applications in which the client software is a browser.

The switch to building applications in which the client software is a browser is one of the greatest impacts of Internet technologies since 1995. Initially, this type of applications was primarily used on the Internet, and system users were generally using browsers. Toward the end of 1999 or so, it switched. Now all companies seem to want to build every application as browser-based.

This is due to the extremely compelling economics of the approach. It's cheaper for companies to deploy new applications to their internal users' desktops if the client software is a browser. If it's a client/server or other Win32-based client application written in Visual Basic or PowerBuilder, installing or upgrading the application requires software to be installed on the client machine's desktop. To install a new application if it runs in a browser simply requires sending the user a URL to point to.

Upgrades to Web-based applications are even easier to install. The end user does nothing at all! The next time the user comes to the site, he simply sees the latest version of the application!

So, whether your application is internal to your own organization or for use over the Internet, Struts can save you significant time building it when the client application is a browser.

The second implication of saying Struts is for building Web applications is a bit more formal. It's that Struts builds applications that are compliant Web applications, based on the Java Servlet specification (version 2.3 at the time of this writing). The Java Servlet specification is part of the larger J2EE (Java 2 Platform, Enterprise Edition) specification.

Being a compliant Web application (or Webapp, for short) implies, among other things, that Struts applications have

- A standard directory structure
- Certain standard configuration files (`web.xml` and so on)
- Dynamic functionality deployed as Java classes and .jsp pages
- A standard Web Archive (`.war` file) format for deployment

Although it's not required reading, it would be very useful to you as a Struts developer if you're familiar with (or at least have handy a copy of) the Java Servlet specification version 2.3 (or 2.2, depending on the application server you're using). This document will help you understand some of the formal Web application pieces of the framework. This is reviewed in more detail in the next chapter, so don't worry about reading the entire spec right now!

If you're unsure what a `web.xml` file is or why the directories always need to be named `WEB-INF`, details like this come from the Web application spec inside the Java Servlet specification.

Components of the Struts Framework

The Struts framework is based on two primary components: a Model-View-Controller architecture that makes it easy to build flexible applications and a set of JSP custom tags for building JSP pages.

Even though they're covered in more detail in the next chapter, let's take a quick look at these components right now.

Struts Model-View-Controller Architecture

Struts Model-View-Controller architecture simplifies building Web applications by providing a model into which you plug components. Take, for example, a simple application for updating a user's address information. In this case, the Model-View-Controller architecture might break the application into the following components:

Model:

> **Address.java**—A programming model of the user's address. `Address.java` would provide a simple way of setting and getting components of the user's address, and reading it from or storing it to a more permanent storage location (such as a database).

View:

> **AddressView.jsp**—A view to be used to display the user's information. `AddressView.jsp` would contain very little in the way of conditional logic; it simply takes the values in `Address.java` and displays them.

Controller:

> **AddressAction.java**—A controller to assist in validating the user's entries and choosing the right view to display the results. If errors are made in entering the data, `AddressAction.java` makes the decision to display an error page or send the user back to the original entry page.

Although this breakdown is simplified for illustration, you get the idea. The Model provides an internal representation of the data. The View doesn't make decisions, it simply displays data. The Controller determines what processing to perform and what steps to take next.

The Struts Tag Libraries

The Struts Tag libraries are used for creating View components.

One of the challenges of JSP development has traditionally been that programmers have a tendency to frequently use Java scriptlets in their pages. This makes the pages more complicated for an HTML designer to understand and maintain.

The Struts tag libraries provide a set of JSP custom tags that are generally understandable by both JSP developers and page designers. The custom tags have names like `<html:text>` and `<logic:iterate>`. You'll learn more about what these tags do in Chapters 12 through 16, which cover the tag libraries in detail, but for now understand that the Struts tag libraries provide a powerful set of functionality in a format designed to simplify developing pages (or *Views*, in Struts parlance).

State of Struts: Where Things Are Right Now

Struts has now reached a point where it is stable and mature enough for production applications. Many sites all over the world—both corporate internal applications and external Internet sites—are running production applications based on Struts.

Tomcat, the de facto standard for JSP/Servlet containers, now ships with a Struts-based administration application.

A groundswell is building behind Struts that's allowing it to emerge as the predominant framework for Web-based applications.

Struts Releases

Struts can be deployed in one of several versions. Understanding which version of Struts to use can save you significant time and heartache.

Although this might change from time to time, Struts generally has three releases active at any one time. They are

- **Stable Release**—This is the version of the code that can be counted on to be the most bug-free and production ready. It might lack current features, but it's generally the most stable.
- **Beta Release**—This version generally contains most of the latest features in a somewhat stable configuration. It's intended to work because the authors hope people will use it to provide feedback to them. Going production on the Beta Release should be considered risky, but might be the only option if a feature you need isn't in the Stable Release yet.
- **Nightly Build**—This is the version currently in use by the developers. If you want to use it, you must build it from source. You can count on at least parts of it not working.

Most production sites are built with the Stable Release, although more than a few go live on the Beta Release. As with any of the Apache Project applications, this changes as the technology continues to mature.

Other Applications That Are Available to Use with Struts

The community support behind Struts has been nothing short of amazing. A myriad of applications, tools, sample applications, and so on are now available. For a current list, you can check the Struts site, but here are some of the more notable contributions:

- **The Struts Console**—James Holmes contributed this outstanding application for managing Struts applications and configuration files. It can be used as a standalone Swing application or as a plug-in with JBuilder, NetBeans, or Sun Forte.
- **Adalon**—An "Internet Application Modeling Tool," according to the Synthis Web site. Adalon is a tool for performing business process design and Internet application design. Adalon can generate Struts code directly from its design.
- **StrutsTestCase for jUnit**—StrutsTestCase provides a jUnit extension that can be used to test code based on Struts.

This is merely a glimpse of what's currently available! The community support behind Struts is one of its greatest strengths.

Faces Behind the Code: Struts Development

In his insightful essay on Open Source development, "The Cathedral and the Bazaar," Eric Raymond described two development styles:

- The Cathedral—Development based on centralized control and management with careful planning of releases and tight control of the code.
- The Bazaar—Loose control of development with a large number of people offering their own input and contributions. Each person adds value where they can. The end result is faster development and much quicker isolation and fixing of bugs.

Raymond identifies Linux as the first great bazaar-style development project. Linux development went much further and much faster than anything before it.

Although there's a core of developers behind Struts, the speed and quality features of bazaar-style development are definitely at work. In the short time that Struts has been available, its development and user acceptance has been amazing.

The Core Developers

There have been many contributions to Struts, but a few of the contributors really stand out:

- **Craig McClanahan**—Craig was a contributor in the original Apache Jserv project, and then a core contributor to Tomcat. He was the original visionary behind Struts, one of its primary developers, and the chief architect of Struts as it stands today.

- **Ted Husted**—Ted has been a Struts committer since December of 2000, and built an early production site that launched in June of 2001. His ongoing development and support for the project has been outstanding.
- **James Holmes**—James is the author of the Struts Console, the previously mentioned application for managing Struts configuration files.
- **Cedric Dumoulin**—Author of Tiles and contributor to a number of other areas in Struts.

And there are many more. By the way, it's not too late for *you* to get involved. Whether as a developer, tester, tech writer (or in some other way that only *you* can dream of), feel free to get involved! You'll be a better Struts developer and make the product better for it. For more info, see the site.

Where Struts Is Going

What will the future bring? It's impossible to say for sure, but we believe it's possible to extrapolate at least a little.

Integration with JSTL

As the various applications servers adopt JSP 1.2, they can take advantage of the full power of the Java Standard Tag Library (JSTL). The main effect that this will have on Struts is to provide a much more powerful alternative to the Struts Tag Library that interoperates with non-Struts platforms.

As a result, you should expect to see the Struts tags gradually fall out of favor as time progresses.

Integration with JavaServer Faces

In addition to being a key Struts contributor, Craig McClanahan is also deeply involved in developing the JavaServer Faces specifications. Not surprisingly, Struts and JSF will become closely intermingled as time progresses.

Again, the main effect will be to de-emphasize the importance of the current Struts tags because the combination of JSTL and JSF (which work together) will make the proprietary Struts tags obsolete.

Struts Will Become More Widely Accepted

At the time of this writing, Struts was about to have its 1.1 release. This release is a major improvement over the previous one, both in features and code stability. As a result, it will become a more attractive platform for commercial applications development.

These things feed on themselves. As Struts becomes more popular, more people will contribute bug fixes and new features, which will in turn make Struts more popular. Certainly Struts will be the predominant applications framework inside the Jakarta community.

Conclusions

Struts is a "Web Application Framework" that helps you go further faster when developing applications for which the client is a browser. It enables you to build better applications by letting you take advantage of best practices put together by some of the best programmers in the world.

A *framework* is a collection of software and methods used to speed application development. Web application structure and format are formally governed by the Java Servlet and J2EE specifications.

The Struts framework is based on a Model-View-Controller architecture. The Model provides an internal representation of the data. The View displays data without incorporating significant business logic. The Controller determines what processing to perform and what steps to take next.

The Struts tag libraries are used to build Struts Views. The libraries' JSP custom tags provide a high level of functionality while making the Views more readable and easier to maintain.

Struts has matured and is now in wide use all over the world. The Struts user community has grown at a fantastic rate. Many complementary applications are now available for use with Struts and many dedicated developers have made contributions. Craig McClanahan has been the primary architect and visionary behind Struts.

The growing adoption of frameworks for development and of browser-based applications in general will continue to contribute to the rapid development and acceptance of Struts.

Get ready to go further faster. Welcome to Struts!

2

The Model-View-Controller Design Pattern: 'Model 2' JSP Development

IN THIS CHAPTER

- The Model-View-Controller Design Pattern
- The Origins of Model 1 / Model 2
- How Struts Implements the Model 2 Pattern
- Conclusions

Architecting great software takes skill, experience, and a lot of time. Of course, it goes much faster if you start with a significant amount of your code already written—especially if that code is based on architecture and designs that are time-tested and proven.

The goal of this chapter is to demonstrate how this principle is embodied in Struts. You'll also gain an understanding of the architecture and design patterns that Struts is based on. This will make you a better Struts developer and help you get up to speed faster.

In addition, you'll be presented a summary of the history and development of these design patterns. The perspective this provides will deepen your appreciation for the value that Struts adds to a development project. It will also help you recognize opportunities to reuse the patterns again in the future.

Specifically, in this chapter you will learn

- The MVC design pattern and how it speeds development and makes managing changes easier.
- What Model 1 and Model 2 JSP development are and where these terms originated
- How Struts implements the Model 2 pattern

The Model-View-Controller Design Pattern

A *design pattern* is a series of objects and object relationships that provide a proven, extensible solution to a particular software design problem. The Model-View-Controller (MVC) pattern is arguably the best known, most famous design pattern of them all.

MVC was originally developed in the late 1970s at the Xerox Palo Alto Research Center (PARC). It was originally built to manage the GUI and user interaction on some of the first window-based computers (another innovation from the PARC—in addition to Ethernet, local area networks, mice for input devices, and numerous other firsts).

The design problem that MVC solves is that of simplifying three primary functions that are common in many applications:

- Maintaining the data in a back-end store or remote system
- Building the end-user presentation layer
- Maintaining the conditional logic that decides which screens are presented to the user, what happens when errors occur, and exactly how and when the remote systems are updated

It is possible to combine all this processing into a single module and get a system to work. (In fact, a significant amount of early JSP development did exactly that!) Problems primarily occur when you try to perform maintenance on the code. In the case of JSP, this is compounded by the fact that the HTML designers who maintain the look and feel of the application are different people (and have different skill sets) from those who maintain the Java code that controls the processing.

MVC addresses this problem by separating the code into three distinct areas:

- Model components that maintain data in a back-end store or remote system
- Views that build the end-user presentation layer
- Controllers to maintain conditional logic that decides which screens are presented to the user, what happens when errors occur, and exactly how and when the remote systems are updated

MVC simplifies maintenance by keeping all this logic from becoming intertwined. It allows the details of each piece to be hidden from the others and reduces the coding linkages between them. This is how MVC provides a natural boundary between the people who write the Java and the people who maintain the HTML and presentation layer.

A good example of this is in how MVC can simplify exception processing. Imagine that after a user logs in, you send a request to a remote system to fetch the user's customer information. What do you do if the remote system is unavailable? In normal JSP processing, it's common to embed logic at the top of your JSP file to detect this and change what you display to the user when the problem occurs. Using MVC, you can pull this logic out of the JSP page altogether: You create a page dedicated to presenting the error message and have the Controller determine which page to send the user to. If the remote system is available, the user gets the first page. If not, the Controller sends him to the error page.

This approach to exception processing has multiple benefits. The first comes from the fact that, on many pages, multiple types of exceptions must be handled. Having a single JSP page that detects all possible errors and presents a different message when each error happens can become complicated fast. Moving that logic into a Controller makes things easier to maintain: The logic is maintained in the Controller, and only the presentation is maintained in the JSP file.

Of course, another primary benefit of pulling the exception logic out of the main JSP pages is that it makes maintaining the JSP pages easier!

These benefits really extend to all forms of conditional processing. Here are some other examples:

- If different Views are required depending on what data is retrieved from a database or remote system (for example, products on sale versus products not on sale), the Controller component can make the decision about which page to present. This keeps the logic out of the JSP page itself.
- If your site changes based on either the time of day or the day of the week, that logic is easy to implement in the Controller. You simply have the Controller check the date and forward the user to the appropriate page.
- Sometimes a data entry process can span several pages, some of which are optional. An example of this is signing up for insurance: You need to be shown the data entry pages for dependents only if you choose family coverage. In cases like this, MVC makes it easy to control the flow of pages that are shown to the user. Trying to embed this logic into the JSP pages makes things much more complex.

THE ORIGINS OF THE MVC DESIGN PATTERN

It is widely agreed that the MVC pattern was originally popularized in Smalltalk-80. MVC was used to manage the GUI relationship in some of the earliest window-based GUIs that were developed at the Xerox PARC.

In researching the origins of the MVC pattern, I came across an archived posting from the Usenet group `comp.lang.smalltalk` from 1994. The posting read, in part:

I thought you might be interested in a 'bit of history' on origin of the Model-View-Controller paradigm.

Prof. Trygve Reenskaug is generally cited as being the creator of the MVC concept. He worked with the Smalltalk group at Xerox PARC as a visiting scientist in 78/79. During this stay at Xerox PARC he developed the MVC. I know him well and have talked to him about this. He confirms it, although stating that it was a collaborative effort at Xerox PARC.

[...]

Regards,

Carl

Carl P. Swensson, Senior Systems Eng.

I then looked up Prof. Reenskaug's current home page on the Internet. In his biography, he lists the creation of "Model-View-Controller, the world's first reusable object oriented framework, in 1979" as one of his career accomplishments.

I traded e-mails with Prof. Reenskaug while writing this book. He described his initial thoughts on MVC like this:

My first idea was to separate presentation from information because the information structure is reasonably stable while the way we need to see it and manipulate it varies with the task. (This idea stems from around 1970 when I first became interested in distributed systems.)

Prof. Reenskaug is now a Professor Emeritus from the University of Oslo in Norway. More recently, he contributed to the development of the Unified Modeling Language (UML) versions 1.4 and 2.0. The Object Management Group (`http://www.omg.org`) has honored him with a special award for his many contributions to the field of object-oriented design.

The Origins of Model 1 / Model 2

In documentation and general discussions surrounding Struts and MVC architectures for JSP processing, you'll frequently run across the terms *Model 1* and *Model 2* processing. Understanding where these terms came from will give you a better understanding of Struts and the design goals behind it. (As an added benefit, you'll also know what these people are talking about!)

The JSP Specification Version 0.92

Way back in the dark ages of JSP processing (October 7, 1998 to be exact) Sun Microsystems released the JSP 0.92 specification. A number of early container providers adopted this standard and put out JSP/servlet containers based on this version of the specification.

In this version of the specification, there was an overview that included a "JavaServer Pages Access Model(s)" section. In fact, there were only two models—appropriately named Model 1 and Model 2. Little did the authors of this document realize that the names they gave these two models would last long after the document itself was no longer available!

Model 1 described JSP processing as it was most commonly being done at that time. It showed the HTTP request being sent directly to a JSP file. All processing was done directly in the JSP (or in the beans it interacted with) and the HTTP response came directly from this JSP file.

Model 2 was different. It indicated that a servlet, rather than a JSP file, should receive the initial HTTP request. The servlet was to handle the processing tasks required for the request, and then store the information in a bean. The bean was then to be passed to the JSP file, which would pull information from it and render the HTTP response.

MVC and *Model-View-Controller* don't appear anywhere in the specification, but Model 2 was clearly based on the MVC architecture that is behind Struts today.

JavaWorld, 1999

At JavaWorld in December 1999, Govind Seshadri presented an article that clearly identified Model 2 as being the MVC architecture. This article was published on the JavaWorld site and is still there as of this writing (`http://www.javaworld.com/javaworld/jw-12-1999/jw-12-ssj-jspmvc_p.html`).

In this article, Seshadri outlines how the Model 2 (or MVC) architecture is the best approach for development because it provides a clean separation of tasks between page designers and Java developers.

Enter Craig McClanahan, Jakarta Tomcat, and Struts

In March of 2000, Craig McClanahan launched the Struts project as a subproject of the Apache Jakarta project. Craig had been active in the Tomcat project and with Apache JServ (an early Java servlet implementation) before that.

Craig has been, without question, the leading architect and visionary behind Struts. His dedication and contributions to the open source Java community have been invaluable and critical to the success of both Tomcat and Struts.

How Struts Implements the Model 2 Pattern

Struts implements the Model 2 (or MVC) design pattern by providing an overall framework for development. This framework provides a variety of system services in addition to managing the HTTP request and response flow.

This frees the developer to focus on building discrete components and assembling them into an application using the Struts configuration file. This component approach simplifies development, debugging, and maintenance. It also provides natural boundaries for breaking the project between developers and HTML designers—although there will still be a requirement for them to work closely together.

To begin with, it's important to look at how to implement MVC as a Web application in general.

MVC Architecture for Web Applications

Implementing the MVC design pattern using a Web application is a pretty natural fit given the underlying request/response cycle of the HTTP protocol. The basic ideas are altogether independent of Struts.

Figure 2.1 provides a graphical illustration of how this works.

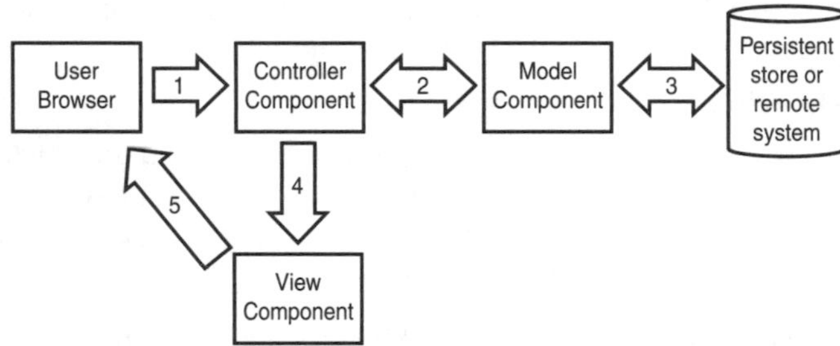

FIGURE 2.1 A MVC architecture diagram for a Web application.

Figure 2.1 shows the MVC pattern implemented for a Web application. Processing proceeds as follows:

1. The client browser issues an HTTP request to the application.
2. The Controller component receives the request. It then begins making decisions on how to proceed with processing based on the business rules encoded in it.
3. The Model components perform the actual interaction with the persistent data stores or remote systems that they manage interaction with.

4. Based on the results of processing and the data returned from the Model components, the Controller determines the View component that should be used to render the user display. Data is prepared for the View object to render.

5. The View component chosen renders the HTTP response to be sent to the user.

The following sections provide some details to the Model, View, and Controller elements that make up the MVC architecture. These sections provide information about Model, View, and Controller component design in general, as well as specific information about their implementations in Struts.

Model Components

Model components generally represent a business object or physical back-end system. For example, in a system that allows users to log in and maintain personal information, there might be a Model component that represents a User.

The User Model component would likely provide methods to access and modify the user's personal information such as his name, password, and so on. The specifics of the design would be driven by the application, but the critical ideas are

- Model components are used to access information from databases or remote systems for presentation to users.
- Model components should be designed to hide the implementation details for accessing that information.

Let's examine the first point: providing information for presentation. Model components provide access to the information from which the user presentation is built. Model components may store this information directly or simply provide convenient access to it.

In an application built using only a servlet container such as Tomcat, the Model component may simply be a Java bean providing a business view to some JDBC logic that maintains the information in a database. The rest of the application interacts with the Model component to read or write the information; only the Model component interacts with the database.

In an application built with the front-end using JavaServer Pages and the back-end accessed via Web services, Model components would be used to provide a business representation of the back-end system. The rest of the application would still access information through the Model, but only the Model would access the Web service.

It would be similar in a system in which an EJB server managed the back-end. Model components would manage access to the EJBs. In some designs, the Model components themselves may be EJBs.

This approach would be the same if the Model components managed access to a remote system. For example, in a system providing stock quotes, there might be a Model component that provides a programming representation of a stock quote. When accessed, the Stock Quote Model component would manage the access to the remote system providing the actual stock quote information.

One of the strengths of MVC should be pretty obvious now: the flexibility of model components! The idea of building a programming interface that hides the details of some back-end data store (or remote system) is extremely powerful and flexible.

It's also pretty well established. In the early 1970s (even before the original MVC ideas were developed at the PARC), Professor David Parnas published his influential work on what he termed *information hiding* in the article "On the Criteria to Be Used in Decomposing Systems into Modules," for the journal *Communications of the Association for Computing Machinery*. In it, he wrote:

We have tried to demonstrate by these examples that it is almost always incorrect to begin the decomposition of a system into modules on the basis of a flowchart. We propose instead that one begins with a list of difficult design decisions or design decisions which are likely to change. Each module is then designed to hide such a decision from the others.

Using these same ideas, Struts Model components hide implementation details for the remote systems and databases they interact with.

View Components

In MVC, the View components focus on just that: creating the presentation layer that the user views. They should contain little in the way of business logic or complex analysis.

Using the HTTP request/response model of a Web application, View components are almost always those components associated with the response. More specifically, View components in JSP and Struts are the JSP files that render the HTML to be sent to the user.

A primary advantage of JSP is its ability to combine HTML, JSP tags, and even Java scriptlets to build dynamic pages (or Views). But although this makes JSP easier and more flexible than just using servlets, it can be a challenge for HTML designers who need to build and maintain the look and feel of the pages.

It can be too easy for a Java developer to overuse java scriptlets and embed conditional business logic and looping directly in the JSP. This makes the HTML designers' job even more difficult. In fact, the embedding of scriptlets into JSP files is one of the primary criticisms of JSP.

MVC addresses exactly this problem. By segregating complex processing into the Model and Controller components, MVC allows the JSP files themselves to be smaller and simpler. This simplifies and speeds development, testing, and maintenance for both Java developers and HTML designers.

Struts takes this approach even further. In addition to providing the MVC architecture, it also provides a whole series of custom JSP tags that are used for constructing View components. These tags (with names such as `<html:text>` and `<logic:iterate>`) give both Java developers and HTML designers the ability to build functionality with tags that would otherwise require the use of scriptlets.

To summarize, Struts Views are part of an MVC framework that simplifies the creation of JSP pages through 1) separating complex logic and Java scriptlets from JSP pages and moving them to Controller and Model components; and 2) providing a series of custom tags to extend the functionality that can be accomplished without requiring the use of Java scriptlets.

Controller Components

Controller components direct all the action. Whenever the user submits a form, it's the controller that processes it. If the user asks for another page, the controller decides what to show her. The Controller component also collects the data from the Model components so that the View components have something to display.

In Struts, a Controller component performs several primary activities:

- Validates that the data entered by the user was valid
- Makes decisions about which Model components need to be accessed or updated and manages these activities
- Collects the data that the View component will need for display
- Makes decisions about how to recover when errors occur in processing the request or response
- One of the most important activities is deciding which View component should be displayed to the user

Conclusions

In this chapter, we covered the basics of the Model-View-Controller (MVC) design pattern, its history, and how it is implemented in Struts. We also covered the origins of the terms *Model 1* and *Model 2* JSP development. Struts is based on Model 2.

The Model-View-Controller design pattern is a time-proven architecture for building software that manages interaction with users (using Views), implements business rules that are dependent on user input (using Controllers), and relies on data that exists in a remote database or system (accessed using Model components). MVC originated at the Xerox PARC in the late 1970s, although its roots go back even further.

The terms *Model 1* and *Model 2* originated in the JSP 0.92 specification. The primary characteristics of Model 1 are

- HTTP requests are posted directly to `.jsp` files.
- The logic for directing program flow, for accessing databases and remote systems, and for building user displays are all embedded directly in JSP files.

The primary characteristics of Model 2 are

- HTTP requests are posted to Java servlets.
- The logic for directing program flow (Controllers) and for accessing databases and remote systems (Models) are implemented in Java servlets and classes. All user displays (Views) are built using JSP files.

Struts implements the MVC design pattern and is based on Model 2. Struts implements MVC using

- Model components that provide a programming model of back-end databases and remote systems and services
- View components that use JSP and Struts custom tags to build pages for user presentation
- Controller components that implement the business logic that defines the program flow

3

Hello World!: A First Struts Application

IN THIS CHAPTER

- Hello World! Application Requirements
- Applying the Model-View-Controller Pattern
- The View Component: The HTML Form and the Form Bean
- `MessageResources` and `Application.properties` Files
- The Struts Form Bean: `HelloForm.java`
- Data Validation and `ActionErrors`
- The Controller Component: `HelloAction.java`
- The Model Component (`HelloModel.java`)
- Passing Data to the View Using Attributes: `Constants.java`
- Tying It All Together: The `struts-config.xml` File
- Conclusions

This chapter provides a rapid introduction to Struts by building a complete—although basic—application from scratch. The goal of this chapter is to enable a competent developer to quickly grasp all the basics of how to build Struts applications.

The chapter continues the longstanding tradition of developing a first program in a new language that simply prints `Hello World!`. This enables developers to quickly grasp the fundamentals of how the program works without forcing them to think too much about the application requirements. To demonstrate some of the important features of Struts, however, the application built here will have a few additional features.

Development of a sample application will be covered including:

- Application requirements
- Using the Model-View-Controller pattern to design a solution using Struts
- The View component: The HTML form and the form bean
- `MessageResources` and `Application.properties` files
- The Struts form bean: `HelloForm.java`
- Data validation and using `ActionErrors`
- The Controller component: `HelloAction.java`
- The Model component: `HelloModel.java`
- Passing data to the View using attributes: `Constants.java`
- Tying it all together: `struts-config.xml`

Hello World! Application Requirements

The requirements of this application are very basic. They are as follows:

- Enable the user to enter a name to say Hello! to and output the string `Hello <name>!`.
- Don't let the user submit the entry form without entering a name. If he does, provide an error message to help him fill the form out correctly.
- To add more Controller functionality (and have a bit more fun), the application should not allow the user to say hello to people they're "not allowed" to talk to.
- To demonstrate Model components, the application should use a Model component to save the name entered for later.

This basic application provides a little bit of functionality in all three of the Model, View, and Controller components.

Applying the Model-View-Controller Pattern

The Struts Model-View-Controller architecture will be a good fit for this application. Here's how it will work:

- The Model component will be a Java bean that has basic set/get methods for reading and writing the name entered by the user. In this case, there also will be a method to save the data. In a more complex application, the Model may be a front for an EJB or Web service.
- The View will be a single JSP file that presents information to the user. In addition, the View will also include a Struts form bean. A form bean is a regular Java bean with a couple of additional methods included to allow input resetting and validation.
- The Controller component will be a Struts `Action` class. `Action` classes are the basic controller components in Struts. The `Action` class will coordinate the action in the application including making sure that the user doesn't try to say hello to the wrong people. The `Action` class also decides which View component to show the user.

In addition to the Model, View, and Controller components, the Struts configuration file (`struts-config.xml`) will be needed to determine how these components fit together.

The following basic ideas provide a quick view of the strengths of Struts:

- The Struts framework enables you to break the application functions into components quickly and easily.
- A configuration file (`struts-config.xml`) enables you to assemble the application from components. This simplifies the development process.
- The framework provides a way to think about the application. That is, it provides a mental framework as well as a physical framework. Understanding the Struts Model-View-Controller framework will help you speed development because you'll be able to quickly break down complex applications into a series of simpler components.

The View Component: The HTML Form and the Form Bean

For this application, the best place to start is with the View component. The View in this case is made up of a JSP file and a Struts form bean.

Figure 3.1 shows the HTML form for this application. This is the only HTML page in the application.

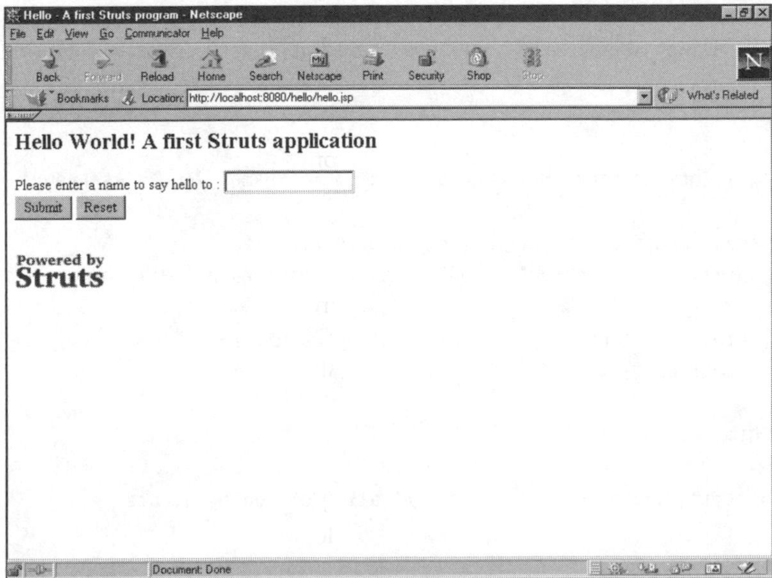

FIGURE 3.1 The Hello World! application.

Listing 3.1 shows the JSP file used to create this HTML page. (This book assumes that you have a basic understanding of Java and JSP, so the discussion around Listing 3.1 will focus on the Struts portions of the file.)

LISTING 3.1 The JSP File for the Hello World! Application (`hello.jsp`)

```
<%@ page contentType="text/html;charset=UTF-8" language="java" %>
<%@ taglib uri="/WEB-INF/struts-bean.tld" prefix="bean" %>
<%@ taglib uri="/WEB-INF/struts-html.tld" prefix="html" %>
<%@ taglib uri="/WEB-INF/struts-logic.tld" prefix="logic" %>

<html:html locale="true">
  <head>
    <title><bean:message key="hello.jsp.title"/></title>
    <html:base/>
  </head>
  <body bgcolor="white"><p>

    <h2><bean:message key="hello.jsp.page.heading"/></h2><p>

    <html:errors/><p>

    <logic:present name="ch03.hello" scope="request">
       <h2>
         Hello  <bean:write name="ch03.hello" property="person" />!<p>
       </h2>
    </logic:present>

    <html:form action="/HelloWorld.do?action=gotName" focus="username" >

      <bean:message key="hello.jsp.prompt.person"/>
      <html:text property="person" size="16" maxlength="16"/><br>

      <html:submit property="submit" value="Submit"/>
      <html:reset/>

    </html:form><br>

    <html:img page="/struts-power.gif" alt="Powered by Struts"/>

  </body>
</html:html>
```

The first thing you notice in the JSP file are the Struts custom tags; for example, `<html:form>` and `<bean:message>`. The Struts custom tags provide features that are either unavailable in standard JSP or that help tie the JSP page into the rest of the Struts framework. The Struts tags are built using standard JSP custom tag functionality. (More information about JSP custom tags will be provided in Chapter 5, " JSP, Taglibs, and JSTL: Extending Java onto the Page.")

The second thing you might notice is that none of the text on the HTML page is actually *in* the JSP file. Instead, there are property names such as `hello.jsp.title`. This is how Struts handles localization and internationalization (referred to as *i18n* because there are 18 letters between the *i* and *n* in the word *internationalization*) of your application.

For now, just understand that the text you see on this HTML page is put there by the Struts `<bean:message>` tags. For example, the line

```
<bean:message key="hello.jsp.prompt.person"/>
```

prints the prompt in the form. The `key` values for these tags are defined in one or more property files. There is one properties file for each locale for which your application needs to present localized text. More on this follows in the next section.

Now let's get back to the Struts tags. The most important function they provide is to tie the Struts View components to the rest of the framework. They enable you to access and present the data passed in from the Controller and Model components. Details on all the tags will be provided in other chapters, but we'll look at some of the more important ones here.

To begin with, the lines

```
<%@ taglib uri="/WEB-INF/struts-bean.tld" prefix="bean" %>
<%@ taglib uri="/WEB-INF/struts-html.tld" prefix="html" %>
<%@ taglib uri="/WEB-INF/struts-logic.tld" prefix="logic" %>
```

identify and load the Struts tag library definitions. These lines indicate we are using the Struts `bean`, `html`, and `logic` tag libraries. This is standard JSP syntax to load the tag libraries and make the tags available for use in the file.

There are a number of HTML tags in this file, including `<html:errors>`, `<html:form>`, and `<html:text>`. Let's look at these three:

- `<html:errors>`—This tag is used to access and present the results of Struts' data validation. Errors detected by other portions of the framework are accessible to the View component via this tag.

- `<html:form>`—This tag is used for all HTML form processing in Struts; it ties the form fields to properties in Struts form beans. It also ties the fields into Struts' automatic form validation. Form beans (to be covered shortly) are Java beans that transfer the values entered in a form to the Controller component (that is, the Struts `Action` class). Each form field will be tied to a corresponding property in the form bean.

- `<html:text>`—This tag is used inside an `<html:form>` tag. It ties a text field in the form to a property in the form bean. In this case, the line

  ```
  <html:text property="person" size="16" maxlength="16"/>
  ```

  ties this form field to the person property in the form bean. Upon submission of the form, the data in the field (or `null` if the field is empty) will be stored in the form bean using the `setPerson()` method.

NOTE

The description of how the `person` field is populated into the form bean is valid only for a normal Struts form bean. A second type of form bean, called a `DynaFormBean`, handles data posting differently. This will be covered in more detail in Chapter 17, "`DynaForms` and the Validator."

There are two Struts bean tags in the file—the `<bean:message>` and `<bean:write>` tags:

- `<bean:message>`—This tag is used to output locale-specific text from a `MessageResources` bundle.

- `<bean:write>`—This is a general-purpose tag that's used to output property values from a bean. `<bean:write>` is a commonly used tag that provides a great deal of power and flexibility in presenting data. Here, the tag writes the value of the `person` property of the bean named `ch03.hello` to the JSP output.

Finally, our first application uses a single logic tag:

- `<logic:present>`—This tag renders its output only if a bean is present and available to the JSP page. It is one of a number of tags that allow for conditional presentation based on logic or substring pattern matching. Its opposite tag is `<logic:notPresent>`. This tag renders the output inside it only if a bean named `ch03.hello` is present and available in the request scope.

MessageResources and Application.properties Files

The hello.jsp file uses the <bean:messages> tag to display a banner title and data entry prompt. Listing 3.2 presents the file where the actual text is stored.

LISTING 3.2 The Application.properties File for Hello World!

```
; Application Resources for the "Hello" sample application
;
; Update History:
;
; Date      Whom   Action
; ========  ====   ======
; 06/01/02  kmb    Creation
;

; Application Resources that are specific to the hello.jsp file

hello.jsp.title=Hello - A first Struts program
hello.jsp.page.heading=Hello World! A first Struts application
hello.jsp.prompt.person=Please enter a name to say hello to :

; Validation and error messages for HelloForm.java and HelloAction.java

ch03.hello.dont.talk.to.atilla=I told you not to talk to Atilla!!!
ch03.hello.no.person.error=Please enter a <i>PERSON</i> to say hello to!
```

You can see that some of the properties are used in the hello.jsp file, but others are accessed from Java classes as well. Comments have been added for organization.

Also, the properties themselves have been named in a way that makes them easier to manage. For example, all properties accessed from the hello.jsp file follow the naming pattern hello.jsp.foo.bar. When you have a large application with numerous tags, this makes understanding the file much easier.

The Struts Form Bean: HelloForm.java

When a user clicks the Submit button on an HTML form built with Struts, the data from that form is populated into a Java bean called a form bean.

A form bean has properties that match up with all the fields on the form. When the form is submitted, the bean properties are automatically populated. In addition, form beans provide support for automatic data validation and resetting of the bean property values. Listing 3.3 presents the file HelloForm.java, it's the form bean that's used to process the form data in our hello.jsp file.

LISTING 3.3 The Struts Form Bean for Hello World! (`HelloForm.java`)

```
package ch03.hello;

import javax.servlet.http.HttpServletRequest;

import org.apache.struts.action.ActionError;
import org.apache.struts.action.ActionErrors;
import org.apache.struts.action.ActionForm;
import org.apache.struts.action.ActionMapping;

/**
 * Form bean for Chapter 03 sample application, "Hello World!"
 *
 * @author Kevin Bedell and James Turner
 */
public final class HelloForm extends ActionForm {

    // --------------------------------------------------- Instance Variables

    /**
     * The person we want to say "Hello!" to
     */
    private String person = null;

    // ----------------------------------------------------------- Properties

    /**
     * Return the person to say "Hello!" to
     *
     * @return String person the person to say "Hello!" to
     */
    public String getPerson() {

        return (this.person);

    }

    /**
     * Set the person.
     *
     * @param person The person to say "Hello!" to
```

LISTING 3.3 Continued

```
     */
    public void setPerson(String person) {

        this.person = person;

    }

    // -------------------------------------------------------- Public Methods

    /**
     * Reset all properties to their default values.
     *
     * @param mapping The mapping used to select this instance
     * @param request The servlet request we are processing
     */
    public void reset(ActionMapping mapping, HttpServletRequest request) {
        this.person = null;
    }

    /**
     * Validate the properties posted in this request. If validation errors are
     * found, return an <code>ActionErrors</code> object containing the errors.
     * If no validation errors occur, return <code>null</code> or an empty
     * <code>ActionErrors</code> object.
     *
     * @param mapping The current mapping (from struts-config.xml)
     * @param request The servlet request object
     */
    public ActionErrors validate(ActionMapping mapping,
                                 HttpServletRequest request) {

        ActionErrors errors = new ActionErrors();

        if ((person == null) || (person.length() < 1))
            errors.add("person", new ActionError("ch03.hello.no.person.error"));

        return errors;
    }
}
```

As you can see, a standard Struts form bean is nothing but a simple Java bean with methods added for input validation and to reset the properties to default values. (The two methods (`validate()` and `reset()` are actually not required; they override empty stubs in the base `ActionForm` class.) Struts `DynaFormBeans` are different and are covered later.

NOTE

The statement: "...must provide bean properties (set/get methods) for each field on the form" is not strictly true. There are some situations where this is not possible.

If an HTML form presents a table with a variable number of rows, for example, the number of fields will vary depending on the number of rows presented. There are also situations where the fields displayed on an HTML form might be completely dynamic. In that case, there might be no way to predict how many fields will be displayed in a form or what their field names might be.

Struts can handle these cases by allowing for the posting of arrays of values or by using `DynaForms`. A discussion of these components is beyond the scope of this chapter and will be presented in Chapter 17, "`DynaForms` and the Validator."

Data Validation and `ActionErrors`

Creating data validation logic is an important and time-consuming part of any application. Fortunately, Struts provides an easy-to-use, powerful way of handling this for you.

This functionality is broken into two pieces:

- Providing an easy-to-use method of capturing error information as it is discovered
- Making that information available to the View component in a manner that makes it easy for the View component to access and display the information as needed

The Struts framework provides two classes to assist you with this:

- `ActionError`—This class is used to represent a single validation error.
- `ActionErrors`—This class provides a place to store all the individual `ActionError` objects you create. As you create `ActionError` objects, you simply stuff them into the `ActionErrors` holder and continue processing.

These two classes solve the problem: The `ActionError` classes make it easy to capture errors when it's convenient in your code. The `ActionErrors` class stores them and makes them easily available to your JSP files.

The Hello World! application has been defined to have two different types of errors: basic data/form validation errors and business logic errors. The requirements for the two types are

- Form validation—In the data entry form, make sure that the user doesn't submit the form with the `person` field empty.
- Business logic—Enforce a rule that the user can't say hello to a person he isn't allowed to talk to. (Because Atilla the Hun has such a bad reputation, let's make him the person we won't speak to.)

NOTE

The reason the errors are broken into these two types is purely for demonstration purposes. It enables us to show error handling in both the form bean and in the `Action` class (which will be introduced in the next section).

In practice, it's not uncommon to break validation into these two categories. Do whatever makes sense for your application.

The first type of validation (data/form validation) is done in the form bean. This is demonstrated by the following code segment from `HelloForm.java`:

```
public ActionErrors validate(ActionMapping mapping,
                             HttpServletRequest request) {

    ActionErrors errors = new ActionErrors();

    if ((person == null) || (person.length() < 1))
        errors.add("person", new ActionError("ch01.hello.no.person.error"));

    return errors;
}
```

If the `validate()` method returns the `ActionErrors` object empty, Struts assumes there are no errors and processing moves to the `Action` class. If `ActionErrors` contains any `ActionError` elements, the user is redirected to the appropriate page to correct the errors.

If processing is redirected for the user to correct the data entry, the `ActionErrors` object carries the individual `ActionError` elements back to the View for display. The View component can access the `ActionErrors` either directly or through the `<html:errors>` tag.

Validation can be enabled or disabled on a page-by-page basis through settings in the Struts configuration file (`struts-config.xml`).

The Controller Component: HelloAction.java

It's finally time to go over the Action class—the center of all the action! The Action class for the Hello World! application follows in Listing 3.4.

LISTING 3.4 The Struts Action Class for Hello World! (HelloAction.java)

```
package ch03.hello;

import javax.servlet.RequestDispatcher;
import javax.servlet.ServletException;
import javax.servlet.http.HttpServletRequest;
import javax.servlet.http.HttpSession;
import javax.servlet.http.HttpServletResponse;

import org.apache.struts.action.Action;
import org.apache.struts.action.ActionError;
import org.apache.struts.action.ActionErrors;
import org.apache.struts.action.ActionForm;
import org.apache.struts.action.ActionForward;
import org.apache.struts.action.ActionMapping;

import org.apache.struts.util.MessageResources;

import org.apache.commons.beanutils.PropertyUtils;

/**
 * The <strong>Action</strong> class for our "Hello" application.<p>
 * This is the "Controller" class in the Struts MVC architecture.
 *
 * @author Kevin Bedell
 */

public final class HelloAction extends Action {

    /**
     * Process the specified HTTP request, and create the corresponding HTTP
     * response (or forward to another web component that will create it).
     * Return an <code>ActionForward</code> instance describing where and how
     * control should be forwarded, or <code>null</code> if the response has
     * already been completed.
     *
     * @param mapping The ActionMapping used to select this instance
```

LISTING 3.4 Continued

```
     * @param actionForm The optional ActionForm bean for this request (if any)
     * @param request The HTTP request we are processing
     * @param response The HTTP response we are creating
     *
     * @exception Exception if business logic throws an exception
     */
    public ActionForward execute(ActionMapping mapping,
                                 ActionForm form,
                                 HttpServletRequest request,
                                 HttpServletResponse response)
    throws Exception {

        // These "messages" come from the ApplicationResources.properties file
              MessageResources messages = getResources(request);

        /*
         * Validate the request parameters specified by the user
         * Note: Basic field validation done in HelloForm.java
         *       Business logic validation done in HelloAction.java
         */
        ActionErrors errors = new ActionErrors();
        String person = (String) PropertyUtils.getSimpleProperty(form, "person");

        String badPerson = "Atilla the Hun";

        if (person.equals(badPerson)) {
            errors.add("person",
               new ActionError("ch03.hello.dont.talk.to.atilla", badPerson ));
                  saveErrors(request, errors);
                  return (new ActionForward(mapping.getInput()));
        }

        /*
         * Having received and validated the data submitted
         * from the View, we now update the model
         */
        HelloModel hm = new HelloModel();
        hm.setPerson(person);
        hm.saveToPersistentStore();

        /*
```

LISTING 3.4 Continued

```
         * If there was a choice of View components that depended on the model
         * (or some other) status, we'd make the decision here as to which
         * to display. In this case, there is only one View component.
         *
         * We pass data to the View components by setting them as attributes
         * in the page, request, session or servlet context. In this case, the
         * most appropriate scoping is the "request" context since the data
         * will not be nedded after the View is generated.
         *
         * Constants.HELLO_KEY provides a key accessible by both the
         * Controller component (i.e. this class) and the View component
         * (i.e. the jsp file we forward to).
         */

            request.setAttribute( Constants.HELLO_KEY, hm);

        // Remove the Form Bean - don't need to carry values forward
        request.removeAttribute(mapping.getAttribute());

        // Forward control to the specified success URI
        return (mapping.findForward("SayHello"));

    }
}
```

This is the biggest file so far in the application, so let's take it a step at a time and not go too deep for now.

How the `Action` Class Works

To begin with, the `Action` class gets its name from the fact that it is a class that extends the base class:

```
org.apache.struts.action.Action
```

Thus, the name *Action class.*

The primary method that must be written in an `Action` class is the `execute()` method. The framework calls this method after the form bean is populated and validated correctly. This is great because the `Action` class can assume that the form bean has passed it data that's approved by at least a basic level of validation.

Here's the signature of the execute() method in any Action class:

```
public ActionForward execute(ActionMapping mapping,
                             ActionForm form,
                             HttpServletRequest request,
                             HttpServletResponse response)
    throws Exception {
```

This is the same every Action class. As you can see, the four parameters passed into an Action class are

- ActionMapping mapping—The ActionMapping provides access to the information stored in the configuration file (struts-config.xml) entry that configures this Action class.
- ActionForm form—This is the form bean. By this time, the form bean has been prepopulated and the validate() method has been called and returned with no errors (assuming that validation is turned on). All the data entered by the user is available through the form bean.
- HttpServletRequest request—This is the standard JSP or Servlet request object.
- HttpServletResponse response—This is the standard JSP or Servlet response object.

It's also important to point out that the execute() method in an Action class must return an ActionForward object. ActionForward objects will be discussed in more detail in Chapter 8, "The Controller: Directing the Action," but for now understand that they represent the View chosen to display the results of the Action.

The Action class uses an execute() method to accomplish its work. It is passed a form bean containing data from the View and an ActionMapping containing configuration information, along with the standard JSP request and response objects.

Accessing the Locale-Specific Text in MessageResources

Now let's review the first section of code in the execute() method:

```
// These "messages" come from the ApplicationResources.properties file
MessageResources messages = getResources(request);
```

This section of code loads a copy of the MessageResources that were defined in the Application.properties file that you saw earlier. Now the Action class has full access to all the locale-specific text needed for the application.

Business Logic–Level Validation

The next section of code performs the business logic validation that was discussed earlier:

```
/*
 * Validate the request parameters specified by the user
 * Note: Basic field validation done in HelloForm.java
 *       Business logic validation done in HelloAction.java
 */
ActionErrors errors = new ActionErrors();
String person = (String) PropertyUtils.getSimpleProperty(form, "person");

String badPerson = "Atilla the Hun";

if (person.equals(badPerson)) {
    errors.add("person",
       new ActionError("ch03.hello.dont.talk.to.atilla", badPerson ));
          saveErrors(request, errors);
          return (new ActionForward(mapping.getInput()));
}
```

At times there is a need to perform data validation based on more complex logic than is appropriate to put in a form bean. This is a relatively simple example.

In other situations, validation might be based on information retrieved from a Model component. For example, having to type your mother's maiden name on a "Forgot My Password" form requires that the maiden name be retrieved from a user account Model component.

More on accessing Model components is covered in the following section.

Interacting with Model Components

In the next section of code, the Controller component directs interaction with the Model component:

```
/*
 * Having received and validated the data submitted
 * from the View, we now update the model
 */
HelloModel hm = new HelloModel();
hm.setPerson(person);
hm.saveToPersistentStore();
```

Here the Controller creates a new Model component, sets a value in it, and calls a method to save the data to a persistent store. This is common way that Controller components will interact with a Model.

This is a very simple example. In other situations, a controller component might

- Read data back from the model for display by the View
- Interact with more than one Model component
- Choose the View component (`ActionForward`) to display based on information retrieved from a Model

The `HelloModel.java` component itself will be presented later in this chapter. Model components are discussed in more detail in Chapter 9, "Model Components: Modeling the Business."

Passing Data to the View Component

The `Action` class passes information to the View component using standard JSP/Servlet `setAttribute()` and `getAttribute()` method calls.

The following is the code fragment from `HelloAction.java` that passes data to the View:

```
/*
 * If there was a choice of View components that depended on the model
 * (or some other) status, we'd make the decision here as to which
 * to display. In this case, there is only one View component.
 *
 * We pass data to the View components by setting them as attributes
 * in the page, request, session or servlet context. In this case, the
 * most appropriate scoping is the "request" context since the data
 * will not be needed after the View is generated.
 *
 * Constants.HELLO_KEY provides a key accessible by both the
 * Controller component (i.e. this class) and the View component
 * (i.e. the jsp file we forward to).
 */

request.setAttribute( Constants.HELLO_KEY, hm);

// Remove the Form Bean - don't need to carry values forward
request.removeAttribute(mapping.getAttribute());
```

This code actually accomplishes two things:

- Sets the HelloModel instance as an attribute on the request to be passed to the View component.
- Removes the form bean from the request object. In this case the form bean is not needed, so it is discarded.

In some situations, the form bean attribute should not be removed. For example, if completing a process in your application requires several data entry pages, you might want to have only a single form bean that, by the end, will hold all the data entered in each of the steps.

Forwarding to the Appropriate View Component

The final step in this Controller component is to forward control to the view chosen to display the results of the action:

```
// Forward control to the specified success URI
return (mapping.findForward("SayHello"));
```

The ActionForward SayHello is defined in the struts-config.xml file.

The Model Component (HelloModel.java)

In the previous section, you saw how the Action class interacted with the Model component HelloModel.java. In Listing 3.5, let's take a look at the HelloModel.java file itself.

LISTING 3.5 The Struts Model Component Hello World! (HelloModel.java)

```
package ch03.hello;

/**
 * <p>This is a Model object which simply contains the name of the person we
 * want to say "Hello!" to.<p>
 *
 * In a more advanced application, this Model component might update
 * a persistent store with the person name, use it in an argument in a web
 * service call, or send it to a remote system for processing.
 *
 * @author Kevin Bedell
 */
```

LISTING 3.5 Continued

```
public class HelloModel {

    // --------------------------------------------------- Instance Variables

    /**
     * The new person we want to say "Hello!" to
     */
    private String _person = null;

    // ----------------------------------------------------------- Properties

    /**
     * Return the new person we want to say "Hello!" to
     *
     * @return String person the person to say "Hello!" to
     */
    public String getPerson() {
        return this._person;
    }

    /**
     * Set the new person we want to say "Hello!" to
     *
     * @param person The new person we want to say "Hello!" to
     */
    public void setPerson(String person) {

        this._person = person;

    }

    // ------------------------------------------------------- Public Methods

    /**
     * This is a stub method that would be used for the Model to save
     * the information submitted to a persistent store. In this sample
     * application it is not used.
     */
    public void saveToPersistentStore() {
```

LISTING 3.5 Continued

```
        /*
         * This is a stub method that might be used to save the person's
         * name to a persistent store if this were a real application.
         *
         * The actual business operations that would exist within a Model
* component would depend upon the requirements of the application.
         */
    }
}
```

This is a very basic, simple Model component that is nothing more than a simple Java bean. The `saveToPersistentStore()` method is just a stub method that in a real application might store the person in a database of some kind.

Although this is a very basic example, it demonstrates a primary strength of the MVC framework. That is, the implementation details of Model components can be hidden from the rest of the Struts application.

If this Model component were changed to take the `person` property and store it in a database, the `Action` class might require no changes at all. The same could be true if `HelloModel` took the property and updated it through an EJB to a remote server or even if it sent it out through a Web service call.

Using Model components to hide the implementation details for interacting with remote systems is one of the keys to using Struts effectively.

Passing Data to the View Using Attributes: `Constants.java`

In the earlier section on the `Action` class (`HelloAction.java`), you saw how the `Action` class passed between itself and the View components using the `setAttribute()` and `getAttribute()` methods of the `request` object. Now let's look at this process in a bit more detail.

When you pass an object from the `ActionClass` to the View component (a JSP page) using the `request.setAttribute()`, you need to provide a name, or string identifier, that the JSP file can use to retrieve the object with. In Struts applications, a convention has been adopted for using a file named `Constants.java` to define these names. Listing 3.6 contains the `Constants.java` file for the HelloWorld! application.

LISTING 3.6 The Hello World! Application Constants file (Constants.java)

```
package ch03.hello;

/**
 * Constants to be used in the Hello World! Example
 * Chapter 03 of "Struts: Rapid Working Knowledge"
 *
 * @author Kevin Bedell
 */

public final class Constants {

   /**
     * The application scope attribute under which our user database
     * is stored.
     */
    public static final String HELLO_KEY = "ch03.hello";

}
```

For the HelloWorld! application, there is only a single bean passed between an `Action` class and a View component (JSP file).

Notice that the class and all `Strings` defined in it are defined as `public static final String` fields in the class. This is because they are used as constants and need never change.

The alternative to defining these values as constants is to enter them as text values in each file in which they are used (for example, in both `HelloAction.java` and `hello.jsp`). Typing in `Strings` as constants directly in files leads to errors when, inevitably, someone changes the value in one place and not the other. Then suddenly it looks to the JSP developer as if the bean has just disappeared!

Also, although the HelloWorld! example shows a bean being passed as an attribute on the request, there are times when it's better to pass the object by attaching it as an attribute to the session object using `session.setAttribute()`. Choosing either request or session scope for the form bean is fine; it just depends on the needs of your application.

Tying It All Together: The `struts-config.xml` File

As mentioned before, the Struts framework enables you to break an application down into components to simplify and speed development. The job of the `struts-config.xml` file is to let you specify how the components go together and identify when they should be used.

Listing 3.7 shows the `struts-config.xml` file for the HelloWorld application.

LISTING 3.7 The Struts Configuration File for HelloWorld! (`struts-config.xml`)

```
<?xml version="1.0" encoding="ISO-8859-1" ?>

<!DOCTYPE struts-config PUBLIC
          "-//Apache Software Foundation//DTD Struts Configuration 1.1//EN"
          "http://jakarta.apache.org/struts/dtds/struts-config_1_1.dtd">

<!--
     This is the Struts configuration file for the "Hello!" sample application
-->

<struts-config>

    <!-- ======== Form Bean Definitions =================================== -->
    <form-beans>
        <form-bean name="HelloForm" type="ch03.hello.HelloForm"/>
    </form-beans>

  <!-- ========== Action Mapping Definitions ============================== -->
  <action-mappings>
    <!-- Say Hello! -->
    <action    path      = "/HelloWorld"
               type      = "ch03.hello.HelloAction"
               name      = "HelloForm"
               scope     = "request"
               validate  = "true"
               input     = "/hello.jsp"
     >
        <forward name="SayHello" path="/hello.jsp"  />
    </action>
  </action-mappings>

  <!-- ========== Message Resources Definitions =========================== -->

  <message-resources parameter="ch03.hello.Application"/>

</struts-config>
```

This is a bare-bones configuration file with only a single `<form-bean>`, one `<action>`, and one `<message-resource>` entry. Other possible elements include `<plug-in>`, `<data-source>`, and `<global-forwards>`, among others. More detail on these elements is provided in Chapter 10, "The `struts-config.xml` File: Tying It All Together." For detailed information that is guaranteed to be correct for your version of Struts, refer to the Document Type Definition (DTD) file for your particular release of Struts. For Struts version 1.1, this DTD is located at `http://jakarta.apache.org/struts/dtds/struts-config_1_1.dtd`.

In real-world language, this configuration file says:

- There is only a single form bean defined for this application. It's referred to as `HelloForm` and is defined in the class `ch03.hello.HelloForm`.
- There is only a single `Action` defined for the application. It's invoked by requesting the path (or URI, to be specific) `/webappname/HelloWorld`. For example, if this application were deployed on the server myServer in the Web application archive `hello.war`, the `Action` would be invoked by requesting the path `http://myServer/hello/HelloWorld`.
- When the `Action` is invoked, it expects the `HelloForm` form bean to be passed to it. The form bean should be request scope and should validate the user's input prior to the `Action` class being invoked. If the validation fails, the user should be sent to the input page `/hello.jsp` to correct his entries.
- There is only a single `MessageResources` bundle associated with this application. The text messages to be stored in this `MessageResources` are located in the file `ch03/hello/Application.properties`, somewhere on the application classpath.

Conclusions

This chapter presented a complete, but basic, first Struts application. Its goal was to enable a programmer with a basic understanding of Java and JSP development to quickly come up to speed on how to build applications using Struts.

Specific information presented in the chapter included:

- The application requirements—these were basic and were designed to provide a little bit of functionality in each of the Model, View, and Controller components.
- How to analyze application requirements and break them down into components using the Model-View-Controller framework provided by Struts. A primary strength of Struts is the mental framework it provides, which enables developers to quickly break an application into components for development.

- View components and how they are built using JSP and Struts custom tags. Also, how the View components are tied to Struts form beans for processing and validating user input.
- How View components handle i18n and how presentation text is maintained by storing locale-specific text strings in property files, which are loaded into Struts `MessageProperties` objects.
- How user data entry can be maintained at two levels: Data entry validation is performed in the form bean and business logic validation is performed in the `Action` class.
- How `ActionError` objects store individual error messages and how `ActionErrors` objects store `ActionError` objects. Also, `ActionError` information is available to the Struts View components either directly or via the Struts `<html:errors>` custom tag.
- How `Action` classes work, including a detailed walk-through of a basic `Action` class.
- How Model components provide a powerful ability to hide implementation details and simplify interacting with remote systems. Also, how Controller components interact with Model components.
- How information is passed between the Controller and View components by using the `setAttribute()` and `getAttribute()` methods of the `request` or `session` objects. How the string constants used in this process are defined in a file called `Constants.java` by convention.
- How Struts applications are configured using the `struts-config.xml` file.

4 HTTP Protocol: Web Application Communications and Control

IN THIS CHAPTER

- HTTP Protocol and the Request/Response Cycle
- Control Information: HTTP Headers and HTTP Response Codes
- HTTP Cookies and Session/User Management
- Conclusions

This chapter provides a basic grounding in HTTP communications and the underlying technologies used for building applications in which the application is a browser.

Understanding the underlying protocol of Web applications is well worth the time spent learning about it. The HTTP protocol provides the basis for everything built on top of it (including browser communications, Web servers, servlet containers, servlets, and even Struts itself). Having a good basic understanding of HTTP is essential in helping you pick up the technology quickly and debugging issues when things go wrong.

In keeping with our series title, *Kick Start*, this chapter goes fast and covers a lot of ground. You'll acquire, in one chapter, a good, detailed working knowledge of the following topics:

- The basics of HTTP communications and how this protocol governs the request/response cycle in JSP and Struts
- How HTTP cookies work and their implications for user session management in JSP and Struts
- HTTP headers and HTTP response codes and how they are used in developing JSP and Struts applications

HTTP Protocol and the Request/Response Cycle

A *browser* is a program that communicates with remote servers (such as a Web server like Apache or a servlet engine like Tomcat) to access and retrieve information. These servers are located in remote locations and could be anywhere on the Internet. Yet

- Communications are fast.
- Communications are secure.
- The server always remembers who you are and keeps track of your information—even if 1000 other people around the world are hitting the same server at the same time!

Understanding the underlying architecture behind this and the details of how it works is key to building and debugging Web-based applications.

Browsers send and receive information using the Hypertext Transfer Protocol (or HTTP). At the core of HTTP is the idea of a request and a response. The browser issues a request when you type in a URL and press the Enter key. The server at the other end accepts the request and sends a response. Responses are made up of HTML, images, and control information. HTTP commands are generally readable English.

There is nothing mysterious or magic about HTTP. It simply provides a standard way for browsers to exchange information (HTML pages, images, and other control information) with Web servers. The easiest way to demonstrate this is to just try it. For example, Listing 4.1 contains a very simple HTML file.

LISTING 4.1 A Sample File for Testing the HTTP Protocol (`index.html`)

```
<html>
    <head>
        <title>Testing HTTP Protocol Communications</title>
    </head>
    <body>
        <p> This page is for testing HTTP Communications
    </body>
</html>
```

Given this simple file, Listing 4.2 demonstrates the HTTP communication that retrieves the file from a Web server.

NOTE

Note that for this listing (and all listings in this book) lines in **bold** are commands typed at the command line.

LISTING 4.2 Sample of HTTP Communications for Retrieving the `index.html` File

```
bash-2.05$ ./telnet -E localhost 8080
Trying 127.0.0.1...
Connected to localhost.
Escape character is 'off'.

GET /index.html HTTP/1.0

HTTP/1.1 200 OK
Content-Type: text/html
Content-Length: 186
Date: Thu, 30 May 2002 23:53:30 GMT
Server: Apache Tomcat/4.0.3 (HTTP/1.1 Connector)
Connection: close
Last-Modified: Thu, 30 May 2002 23:51:23 GMT
ETag: "186-1022802683343"

<html>
    <head>
        <title>Testing HTTP Protocol Communications</title>
    </head>
    <body>
        <p> This page is for testing HTTP Communications
    </body>
</html>
Connection closed by foreign host.
bash-2.05$
```

The HTTP `GET` command retrieves HTTP headers and the contents of the `index.html` file.

The `telnet` program established a TCP connection with a server at localhost (the machine I am typing on) on TCP port 8080, the port where my local installation of Tomcat was listening). After the connection was established, I typed the following HTTP command (terminated by two successive carriage returns):

```
GET /index.html HTTP/1.0
```

This `GET` request asked the server (identified as being Apache Tomcat/4.0.3) to find the file `/index.html` and send it to me in its response. I also specified that I wanted to communicate using HTTP version 1.0 (as opposed to the more recent—and more complex—HTTP version 1.1).

The server responded with the control information and the contents of the `index.html` file. Among other things, the control information included

- `HTTP/1.1 200 OK`
- `Server: Apache Tomcat/4.0.3 (HTTP/1.1 Connector)`
- `Last-Modified: Thu, 30 May 2002 23:51:23 GMT`

The control information included the fact that the request was processed correctly (the `HTTP/1.1 200 OK` response code), the server type, and the time the file was last modified.

USING TELNET FOR TCP COMMUNICATIONS TESTING

Why did I use the `telnet` utility in the previous example instead of using a browser?

The `telnet` utility simply opens a low-level TCP connection on a specified TCP port. It then enables you to enter HTTP commands directly from the command line. You get to actually see the low-level HTTP communications.

For example, the command

```
telnet -E localhost 8080
```

instructs the telnet utility to establish a TCP connection on TCP port 8080 and simply hold the connection open. (The `-E` option disables escape characters.)

This is a common way to test communications with a remote HTTP server, and will be used throughout the book when I want to demonstrate low-level HTTP communications.

Using the command-line version of `telnet` also provides an advantage in this situation over most GUI-based telnet utilities. This is because most GUI-based `telnet` utilities exit (and close their window!) when the TCP connection is closed by the remote host. By using the command-line utility, you can still see the results of the commands after the command is processed and the connection is closed.

If you're running these tests on a Windows-based computer, a good command-line `telnet` utility is the one included in Cygwin Tools (`http://www.cygwin.com/`). Cygwin Tools is free software released under the GNU General Public License (GPL).

The important thing here is to understand the request/response cycle is driven by the HTTP protocol. A request comes in to the server carrying with it information from (and about) the requester. The server processes the request and returns a response.

NOTE

This request/response cycle is also reflected in the JSP and Servlet specifications. By definition, a servlet has a `doGet()` method that's executed when an HTTP GET request is processed. (Similar `doPut()`, `doPost()`, and other methods exist as well.) This shows again how having an understanding of the underlying HTTP protocol can help you better understand the JSP/servlet technology that underlies Struts.

Control Information: HTTP Headers and HTTP Response Codes

When a browser issues a page request to a Web server, the server responds by sending back HTML and images for the browser to display. But, in addition to the HTML and images, control information in the form of HTTP headers and HTTP response codes are a big part of the HTTP conversation. This was demonstrated in the previous sections where each request had response code and control information included in the response.

HTTP Response Codes

HTTP response codes are how the Web server communicates the status of a request to the browser. All response codes are defined in the HTTP specifications (HTTP 1.1 codes are covered in RFC 2616). Categories of possible responses are

- Informational: Responses in the 100s provide information to the requesting client on the status of a request. These didn't exist before HTTP 1.1 and are not commonly used.
- Successful: Responses in the 200s indicate that the request was received, understood, and accepted by the server.
- Redirection: Responses in the 300s indicate the resource requested exists at a different location. For example, a request for the resource `/` may be redirected to the resource `/index.html`.
- Client Error: Responses in the 400s indicate an error of some sort on the part of the client. For example, the client might have requested a resource that doesn't exist or one that the client isn't authorized for.
- Server Error: Responses in the 500s indicate an error was encountered on the server while trying to fulfill the request. For example, a servlet or JSP page might have thrown an exception during processing.

As you saw for each of the examples earlier in this chapter, the first line of each response was *`HTTP/1.1 200 OK`*. This is the standard response when a request is processed correctly.

To demonstrate a different result, consider the JSP code in Listing 4.3.

LISTING 4.3 A Sample JSP File That Throws an Exception (`throwIt.jsp`)

```
<html>
  <head>
    <title>Throw an Exception!</title>
  </head>
  <body>
    <%
      boolean throwIt = true;

      if (throwIt) {
        throw new Exception();
      }
    %>
  </body>
</html>
```

This JSP file will compile correctly and throw an exception at run-time. Listing 4.4 shows what happens when this file is executed.

LISTING 4.4 Requesting the `throwIt.jsp` File and Seeing the `500 Internal Server Error` Response.

```
bash-2.05$ ./telnet -E localhost 8080
Trying 127.0.0.1...
Connected to localhost.
Escape character is 'off'.
GET /throwIt.jsp HTTP/1.0

HTTP/1.1 500 Internal Server Error
Connection: close
Set-Cookie: JSESSIONID=358F99EE5330C7B83BD2A73BE064ED0C;Path=/
<html><head><title>Apache Tomcat/4.0.3 - Error report</title>
[The rest of the output is not shown...]
```

In this listing you see an example of the dreaded `Error 500 Internal Server Error` that's so familiar to JSP developers! You can see here how the errors you deal with as a Struts/JSP developer are traceable directly back to the HTTP protocol.

Table 4.1 provides a listing of useful HTTP response codes.

TABLE 4.1 HTTP Response Code Categories and Sample Response Codes with Descriptions

Category	Response Code	Description
1*xx*	`100 Continue`	The Web server has received the initial part of the request correctly. Continue with the rest.
2*xx*	`200 OK`	The request has been received and processed correctly. The response follows.
3*xx*	`301 Moved`	The requested resource has moved. The new URI is provided so that the browser can issue a new request.
	`304 Not Modified`	The requested resource has not been modified. The page can safely be reloaded from cache. Commonly used when requesting images.
4*xx*	`401 Unauthorized`	The requested resource requires authorization. The user should resend the request with proper credentials.
	`403 Forbidden`	The resource is not available to the user, regardless of authentication.
	`404 Not Found`	The resource requested cannot be located on this server.
5*xx*	`500 Server Error`	An error occurred while the server attempted to fulfill the request.

All valid HTTP response codes are also defined as `public static final int` fields in `javax.servlet.http.HttpServletResponse`. For example, the `500 Server Error` code can be represented in code as `response.SC_INTERNAL_SERVER_ERROR`.

HTTP Request and Response Headers

HTTP headers are control information passed between a browser and a HTTP server. They provide information such as the type of the browser making the request (Internet Explorer, Mozilla, Netscape, and so on), the number of characters being sent, and the type of data that is contained in a response (for example `text/html` or `image/jpg`).

There are two general classes of HTTP headers: HTTP request headers and HTTP response headers. The difference between them being, of course, whether they are sent with the HTTP request or the HTTP response.

The most common HTTP headers are those defined by the HTTP protocol specification. They vary based on the version of HTTP that governs the conversation (usually HTTP 1.1, but occasionally still HTTP 1.0).

Sometimes special servers such as proxy or security servers will add additional HTTP headers for their own usage. It is not uncommon for application developers to add custom headers as well.

Cookies are a special type of a HTTP response header (the `Set-Cookie` header) and a HTTP request header (the `Cookie` header). Cookies are discussed in more detail in the next section.

Table 4.2 contains a listing of common HTTP request and response headers.

TABLE 4.2 Common HTTP Request and Response Headers

Header	Description
`Date`	The current date/time in GMT. The `setDateHeader()` method can be used to set this without worrying about formatting the date string.
`User-Agent`	Defines the browser type and version number.
`Set-Cookie`	Used by a server to set a cookie in the client browser.
`Cookie`	The header used by a browser to return a cookie to the server that set it.
`Host`	The hostname of the server that originated the request.
`Referrer`	The URL from which the browser that made the request was referred. Can be used to determine where traffic to a Web site came from.
`Server`	The type of server that sent the response. For example, `Apache Tomcat/4.0.3`.
`SoapAction`	Used in the SOAP protocol to tell a server which action to take to process the request.

To demonstrate how to work with HTTP headers, consider the JSP code in Listing 4.5.

LISTING 4.5 A Sample JSP File for Printing All HTTP Request Headers (`headerList.jsp`)

```
<html>
  <head>
    <title>List all HTTP Headers</title>
  </head>
  <body>
    <%
      java.util.Enumeration e = request.getHeaderNames();
      String requestHeaderName;
      String requestHeaderValue;

      for (int i = 0; e.hasMoreElements() ; i++ ) {

        requestHeaderName  = (String) e.nextElement();
```

LISTING 4.5 Continued

```
        requestHeaderValue = request.getHeader(requestHeaderName);

        out.print("HTTP Request Header #" + i + " is --->  " );
        out.print(requestHeaderName + ":  " + requestHeaderValue + " <br>\n" );
      }
    %>
  </body>
</html>
```

All this program does is return a listing containing all the HTTP request headers included in the request. Listing 4.6 shows what happens when this file is executed.

LISTING 4.6 Returning All the Headers in the HTTP Request

```
bash-2.05$ ./telnet -E localhost 8080
Trying 127.0.0.1...
Connected to localhost.
Escape character is 'off'.

GET /headerList.jsp HTTP/1.0
TestHeader: This is a test
YetAnotherHeader: Foo

HTTP/1.1 200 OK
Content-Type: text/html;charset=ISO-8859-1
Date: Sat, 29 Jun 2002 02:54:28 GMT
Server: Apache Tomcat/4.0.3 (HTTP/1.1 Connector)
Connection: close
Set-Cookie: JSESSIONID=9F0C62A7A7BEF9D4C1D2442EE3E94B21;Path=/

<html>
  <head>
    <title>List all HTTP Headers</title>
  </head>
  <body>
     HTTP Request Header #0 is --->  testheader:  This is a test <br>
     HTTP Request Header #1 is --->  yetanotherheader:  Foo <br>
  </body>
</html>

Connection closed by foreign host.
bash-2.05$
```

In this request, two HTTP headers are included. Their names and values are `TestHeader: This is a test` and `YetAnotherHeader: Foo`. As you can see, HTTP headers are simply name/value pairs that are part of the information passed between browsers and HTTP servers to allow control and coordination of the HTTP request and response cycle.

Browsers submit a number of HTTP request headers with every request. Listing 4.7 shows what is displayed in a browser when the `/headerList.jsp` file is requested.

LISTING 4.7 HTTP Request Headers Sent with a Browser Request

```
HTTP Request Header #0 is ---> connection: Keep-Alive
HTTP Request Header #1 is ---> user-agent: Mozilla/4.78   (WinNT; U)
HTTP Request Header #2 is ---> pragma: no-cache
HTTP Request Header #3 is ---> host: localhost:8080
HTTP Request Header #4 is --->
➥accept: image/gif, image/x-xbitmap, image/jpeg, image/pjpeg, image/png, */*
HTTP Request Header #5 is ---> accept-encoding: gzip
HTTP Request Header #6 is ---> accept-language: en
HTTP Request Header #7 is ---> accept-charset: iso-8859-1,*,utf-8
HTTP Request Header #8 is --->
➥cookie: JSESSIONID=3B3C644512905CD6448897A953AD8BD1
```

These are all the HTTP request headers that the browser sent with its request for the page.

NOTE

For more information on this topic, please refer to the HTTP 1.1 protocol specification (RFC 2616) located at `http://www.w3.org/Protocols/rfc2616/rfc2616.html`.

HTTP Cookies and Session/User Management

When the Web first came into use, it was governed by earlier versions of the HTTP protocol that provided no way to track user sessions between requests. Then Netscape published a "preliminary specification" defining how to track a "Persistent Client State" using what it called "a cookie, for no compelling reason."

The Internet being what it is, this preliminary specification was immediately adopted as a standard and it is still in wide use today. (A version of the original proposal was still viewable at the time of this writing at `http://wp.netscape.com/newsref/std/cookie_spec.html`.) When the IETF later published its cookie specification (RFC 2109) (`http://www.ietf.org/rfc/rfc2109.txt`), there were very few changes to Netscape's original proposal.

JSP/servlet containers, such as Tomcat, use cookies to track user sessions. The user session is associated with the HTTP request (as opposed to the response); this is because the servlet container uses the cookie provided by the request to track the session.

Because Struts is a framework built on JSP, it uses JSP/servlet session management to track session-scoped information, such as a user's shopping cart.

As an example, consider the simple JSP program in Listing 4.8.

LISTING 4.8 A Simple JSP Program Demonstrating User Session Management Driven by the HTTP Request and Cookies (`session.jsp`)

```
<html>
  <head>
    <title>Testing Session Management</title>
  </head>
  <body>
    <% out.print("Session ID = " + request.getSession().getId() );  %>
  </body>
</html>
```

Notice that the session is associated with the request object as opposed to the response object.

In Listing 4.9, requesting the `session.jsp` file shows how cookies are used to manage session information. (For illustration, this JSP file has been put into the JSP Web application named chapter04. The reason for this will be apparent in a moment.)

LISTING 4.9 A Sample HTTP Communication Demonstrating Session Management

```
bash-2.05$ ./telnet -E localhost 8080
Trying 127.0.0.1...
Connected to localhost.
Escape character is 'off'.

GET /chapter04/session.jsp HTTP/1.0

HTTP/1.1 200 OK
Content-Type: text/html;charset=ISO-8859-1
Date: Wed, 12 Jun 2002 00:39:49 GMT
Server: Apache Tomcat/4.0.3 (HTTP/1.1 Connector)
Connection: close
```

LISTING 4.9 Continued

```
Set-Cookie: JSESSIONID=AC75B22FD1D283D1CEF0136928110679;Path=/chapter04

<html>
  <head>
    <title>Testing Session Management</title>
  </head>
  <body>
    Session ID = AC75B22FD1D283D1CEF0136928110679
  </body>
</html>

Connection closed by foreign host.
bash-2.05$
```

Notice that the scope of the `JSESSIONID` cookie in this example is limited to the `/chapter04` Web application. (You can tell because the `Set-Cookie` HTTP response header specifies `PATH=/chapter04`, which means that the cookie will be sent back to the Web server only if more requests are made for files in the `/chapter04` Webapp.)

So, even if you have many Web applications (or Struts applications) deployed in a servlet container, session tracking is isolated between them. That is, even if a user has a valid session in one Struts application, his session is not valid in any other Struts applications deployed in the same server.

In Listing 4.10, you can see how submitting the request with a session ID allows the servlet container to match this request to an existing session. (Notice the session ID submitted is the same one that was received previously.) To demonstrate this, all that's needed is to request the same file again—this time sending the `JSESSIONID` cookie back with it.

LISTING 4.10 Associating a Request to an Existing User Session

```
bash-2.05$ ./telnet -E localhost 8080
Trying 127.0.0.1...
Connected to localhost.
Escape character is 'off'.

GET /chapter04/session.jsp HTTP/1.0
pragma: no-cache
Cookie: JSESSIONID=AC75B22FD1D283D1CEF0136928110679

HTTP/1.1 200 OK
```

LISTING 4.10 Continued

```
Content-Type: text/html;charset=ISO-8859-1
Date: Wed, 12 Jun 2002 01:43:21 GMT
Server: Apache Tomcat/4.0.3 (HTTP/1.1 Connector)
Connection: close

<html>
  <head>
    <title>Testing Session Management</title>
  </head>
  <body>
    Session ID = AC75B22FD1D283D1CEF0136928110679
  </body>
</html>

Connection closed by foreign host.
bash-2.05$
```

Notice that this time the session ID was submitted to the server using the `Cookie` HTTP request header. By submitting the session ID with the request, this request was able to be associated with its existing session. The server also didn't send another `Set-Cookie` HTTP response header in its response; it didn't need to because the `Cookie` HTTP request header submitted with the request indicates that there is already a session associated with the incoming request. (The `Pragma: no-cache` header tells the Web server that it should send the file even if the results from it haven't changed since last time it was requested.)

Conclusions

This chapter covered the fundamentals of the HTTP protocol and presented the concept that Struts applications (like all JSP and Web applications) are governed by the underlying HTTP protocol and its request/response cycle.

HTTP requests are made up of a request for a resource (for example, `GET /index.html`) and other control information in the form of HTTP request headers. After a server receives an HTTP request, the server processes it and sends a HTTP response. HTTP responses are made up of a response code (for example, `HTTP/1.1 200 OK`), control information in the form of HTTP response headers, and the actual resource requested.

Not all HTTP requests result in a resource being returned; the HTTP response code will indicate what the outcome of the request was. Response codes may indicate that the requested resource moved, doesn't exist, or that some client- or server-based error occurred while trying to fulfill the request.

The servlet container provides `request` and `response` objects that are used in Struts (and in JSP in general). These objects are programming representations of the underlying HTTP request and HTTP response.

HTTP cookies are a special case of a HTTP request and HTTP response headers. Sessions are managed by setting session IDs as HTTP cookies. User sessions in Struts (and in JSP in general) are isolated between Web applications in the same servlet container.

5 JSP, Taglibs, and JSTL: Extending Java onto the Page

IN THIS CHAPTER

- Servlets and JSP
- Object Scoping with JSP
- Hiding Business Logic Using Beans
- JSP Custom Tags
- Web Application Deployment
- JSTL: The Standard Tag Library
- JSP and J2EE: The Big Picture
- J2EE and Struts
- Conclusions

To understand how Struts processes Web pages, you should first have a good understanding of how the traditional Java Web services work. This is because Struts is built atop, rather than replacing, these traditional technologies. Specifically, Struts uses JavaServer Pages and the JSP tag library functionality.

By looking at how JSP and tags work, you'll be better prepared to leverage the additional power that Struts gives you, as well as adapt and extend Struts to new situations.

Servlets and JSP

As discussed in Chapter 4, "HTTP Protocol: Web Application Communications and Control," the HTTP protocol consists of a request being passed to a Web server, processed, and data returned in a stateless transaction. By using techniques such as session cookies, state can be maintained even though the HTTP protocol itself is stateless.

Servlets are the basic computational unit that a Java-based Web server uses to handle requests. Whereas a non-Java Web server such as Apache might use an external CGI program written in Perl or C, a Java-based Web server such as Tomcat uses Java classes that have been made available somewhere in the classpath to service incoming requests.

In a pure servlet implementation, the Web server has been told via a configuration file to associate certain URLs with servlets rather than with physical Web pages. When a request comes in that matches one of these URLs, the request is handed off to the appropriate method of the class (depending on whether the operation is a GET, POST, and so on), which is responsible for returning the content of the page.

Listing 5.1 shows a sample servlet. All HTTP-based servlets extend the HttpServlet class and should provide class-specific methods for the types of operations they're prepared to handle.

LISTING 5.1 BaseBallStatServlet.java

```
import javax.servlet.*;
import javax.servlet.http.*;

public class BaseBallStatServlet extends HttpServlet {
    protected void doGet(HttpServletRequest req, HttpServletResponse resp)
       throws java.io.IOException {
       resp.setContentType("text/html");
       java.io.PrintWriter html = resp.getWriter();

       String player = (String) req.getParameter("player");

       html.println("<HTML><HEAD><TITLE>MLB Player Stats</TITLE></HEAD>");
       html.println("<BODY>");

       if ((player == null) || (player.length() == 0)) {
           html.println("<H1>No Player Requested</H1>");
       } else {
           if (player.equals("Derek Lowe")) {
              html.println("<H1>Derek Lowe has an ERA of 1.76</H1>");
           } else {
              html.println("<H1>" + player + " has an ERA of 5.23</H1>");
           }
       }
       html.println("</BODY></HTML>");
    }
}
```

The main weakness of pure servlet programming is readily apparent from this example. Because all the content, even basic HTML formatting, must come from the servlet, you end up with a lot of simple print statements in the servlet whose only purpose is to get this content back to the client. In addition, even simple HTML formatting changes must be made in the Java source itself, meaning that non-Java staff can't work on the Web site design.

The Power of JSP

As an answer to these weaknesses, JavaServer Pages was developed. JSP lets the developer leverage all the power of Java that was present in servlets, but also create pages that look something like HTML.

A common mistake when first approaching JSP is to think of it as HTML with Java embedded inside of it. Although a JSP might seem to behave this way on the surface, it's really a Java servlet with HTML inside. To understand why this is the case, you need to look at how JSP services a request. For example, Listing 5.2 shows a very simple JSP page.

LISTING 5.2 `printloop.jsp`

```
<%
for (int i = 1; i < 10; i++) {
%>
This is loop #<%= i %><BR>
<%
}
%>
```

When a browser requests `printloop.jsp` from the JSP server, the source page is passed through a converter (in Tomcat, this converter is called *Jasper*), which turns the JSP into a Java source file that defines a single class, whose name is based on the name of the source file.

For example, Tomcat turns `printloop.jsp` into a file called `printloop$jsp.java`, whose contents are shown in Listing 5.3.

LISTING 5.3 `printloop$jsp.java`

```
package org.apache.jsp;

import javax.servlet.*;
import javax.servlet.http.*;
import javax.servlet.jsp.*;
import org.apache.jasper.runtime.*;


public class printloop$jsp extends HttpJspBase {


    static {
```

LISTING 5.3 Continued

```
    }
    public printloop$jsp( ) {
    }

    private static boolean _jspx_inited = false;

    public final void _jspx_init() throws org.apache.jasper.runtime.JspException {
    }

    public void _jspService(HttpServletRequest request,
                            HttpServletResponse  response)
        throws java.io.IOException, ServletException {

        JspFactory _jspxFactory = null;
        PageContext pageContext = null;
        HttpSession session = null;
        ServletContext application = null;
        ServletConfig config = null;
        JspWriter out = null;
        Object page = this;
        String  _value = null;
        try {

            if (_jspx_inited == false) {
                synchronized (this) {
                    if (_jspx_inited == false) {
                        _jspx_init();
                        _jspx_inited = true;
                    }
                }
            }
            _jspxFactory = JspFactory.getDefaultFactory();
            response.setContentType("text/html;charset=ISO-8859-1");
            pageContext = _jspxFactory.getPageContext(this, request, response,
                    "", true, 8192, true);

            application = pageContext.getServletContext();
            config = pageContext.getServletConfig();
            session = pageContext.getSession();
            out = pageContext.getOut();
```

LISTING 5.3 Continued

```
            // begin [file="/printloop.jsp";from=(0,2);to=(2,0)]

                for (int i = 1; i < 10; i++) {
            // end
            // HTML // begin [file="/printloop.jsp";from=(2,2);to=(3,14)]
                out.write("\r\nThis is loop #");

            // end
            // begin [file="/printloop.jsp";from=(3,17);to=(3,20)]
                out.print( i );
            // end
            // HTML // begin [file="/printloop.jsp";from=(3,22);to=(4,0)]
                out.write("<BR>\r\n");

            // end
            // begin [file="/printloop.jsp";from=(4,2);to=(6,0)]

                }
            // end
            // HTML // begin [file="/printloop.jsp";from=(6,2);to=(7,0)]
                out.write("\r\n");

            // end

        } catch (Throwable t) {
            if (out != null && out.getBufferSize() != 0)
                out.clearBuffer();
            if (pageContext != null) pageContext.handlePageException(t);
        } finally {
            if (_jspxFactory != null) _
                jspxFactory.releasePageContext(pageContext);
        }
    }
}
```

As you can see, all the HTML has been embedded inside calls to `out.write`, whereas the Java code is inserted untouched in the method. The method itself has access to the `HttpServletRequest` and `HttpServletResponse` objects, which are passed in to the method as the arguments `request` and `response`. This means that the Java code on the JSP page can gain access to these values by using the variables.

After the JSP file has been converted into Java, it's compiled and the `jspService` method of the class is called with the request and response objects. The class services the request exactly as a servlet would, and the resulting content is sent back to the client. The results from requesting this JSP page are shown in Listing 5.4.

LISTING 5.4 Results from Requesting `printloop.jsp`

```
This is loop #1
This is loop #2
This is loop #3
This is loop #4
This is loop #5
This is loop #6
This is loop #7
This is loop #8
This is loop #9
```

In addition to placing raw Java on the JSP page, there are also a number of tags that JSP makes available to make developing applications easier. You've already seen two of those tags: the `<% %>` tag, which escapes out to Java, and the `<%= %>` tag, which inserts a Java value into HTML.

Object Scoping with JSP

Another feature that JSP and servlets bring to the table is the idea of object persistence across HTTP requests. When a browser first connects to a server, a session is established that is uniquely connected to that client. This allows information to be available from one request to the next, making it seem to the user as if all the requests were part of one session.

HOW ARE SESSIONS TRACKED?

When a client makes a request to a JSP server, how does the server associate the client with a specific session? The answer is, it depends.

If the client browser has enabled session cookies (that is, cookies that are kept only as long as the browser is running and are lost on shutdown), they are used to track the session. On first contact, a new session cookie is generated and sent to the client. Each subsequent request will include the cookie, allowing the server to make the match.

Some users, out of paranoia or ignorance, have disabled session cookies. This requires the server to adopt a different strategy—URL rewriting. Under this scheme, every form and `HREF` are rewritten before being sent to the client so that a unique session token is included. For example, the `HREF` `foo.jsp` might be rewritten as `foo.jsp?sessionid=24234235`.

Obviously, this is a much less aesthetic approach and is used by the server only as a last resort.

There are several ways that a developer can gain access to these persistent objects. For example, the session object is available by calling the `getSession()` method on an `HttpRequest` object. Listings 5.5 and 5.6 show examples of two JSP pages; the first page sets a value, and the second retrieves it later in the session.

LISTING 5.5 `setvalue.jsp`

```
<% request.getSession().setAttribute("myage", new Integer(39)); %>
<H2>Value Set</H2>
```

LISTING 5.6 `getvalue.jsp`

```
<H2> Age = <%= request.getSession().getAttribute("myage") %> </H2>
```

As expected, after loading the first page, you get this in your browser:

```
Value Set
```

Then, when you load `getvalue.jsp`, it displays

```
Age = 39
```

The first page gets a reference to the session object from the request, and then uses the `setAttribute` call to establish a persistent value. The second page uses the `getAttribute` call to retrieve the previously stored value.

Scopes Other than Session Scoping

Although session-scoped objects are by far the most frequently used, three other types of scoping are available.

A page-scoped object is available only on the specific JSP page on which it is referenced. You can think of it as a local variable of the `jspRequest()` method for the Java class created from the JSP source.

A request-scoped object is available during the life of the current request/reply cycle. It is somewhat like a page-scoped object, but would be available (for example) if one JSP page used a redirect to send the browser to another JSP page.

Finally, an application-scoped object is available to any request in the current Web application. These objects are most frequently used to store information that's required globally. For example, information that's being cached by the application for fast access would be a good candidate to be application-scoped.

Accessing Scoped Objects from JSP

Although you've already seen how you can access a session-scoped object from the `request` parameter, this is more often used from Java code that's called from a JSP page. On a JSP page itself, it is preferable to use a JSP tag: the `useBean` tag. Listings 5.7 and 5.8 provide an example of this tag, as well as demonstrate how each of the scopes behaves.

LISTING 5.7 `page1.jsp`

```
<jsp:useBean id="pagevar" scope="page" class="java.lang.StringBuffer"/>
<jsp:useBean id="requestvar" scope="request" class="java.lang.StringBuffer"/>
<jsp:useBean id="sessionvar" scope="session" class="java.lang.StringBuffer"/>
<jsp:useBean id="appvar" scope="application" class="java.lang.StringBuffer"/>

<% pagevar.append("page1");
   requestvar.append("page1");
   sessionvar.append("page1");
   appvar.append("page1");
%>
<jsp:forward page="page2.jsp"/>
```

LISTING 5.8 `page2.jsp`

```
<jsp:useBean id="pagevar" scope="page" class="java.lang.StringBuffer"/>
<jsp:useBean id="requestvar" scope="request" class="java.lang.StringBuffer"/>
<jsp:useBean id="sessionvar" scope="session" class="java.lang.StringBuffer"/>
<jsp:useBean id="appvar" scope="application" class="java.lang.StringBuffer"/>

<% pagevar.append("page2");
   requestvar.append("page2");
   sessionvar.append("page2");
   appvar.append("page2");
%>

page = <%= pagevar.toString() %><BR>
request = <%= requestvar.toString() %><BR>
session = <%= sessionvar.toString() %><BR>
appvar = <%= appvar.toString() %><BR>
```

If you request page1.jsp, you'll get the requests shown here:

```
page = page2
request = page1page2
session = page1page2
appvar = page1page2
```

As you can see, the request, session, and application versions of the StringBuffer are the same on both page1 and page2 (page1 does a forward, too). But because the page scope works only for a physical JSP page, page1 and page2 are each given a new copy of the StringBuffer for pagevar, and only page2 is printed as its value.

If you then load page2.jsp explicitly, you'll see the following:

```
page = page2
request = page2
session = page1page2page2
appvar = page1page2page2
```

Because this is a different request, the page and request values are new, but the session and application values carry over from the last request. Finally, if a different user were to request page2, he would see

```
page = page2
request = page2
session = page2
appvar = page1page2page2 page2
```

These are different sessions, but the value associated with the application still remains.

Hiding Business Logic Using Beans

One of the first good principles of software design using JSP (and a core principle of Struts) is that you should keep business logic off the JSP page itself at all costs. This is for several reasons:

- It limits reuse of the business logic.
- It clutters up the JSP source code.
- It exposes critical code to potential abuse or neglect by HTML and design staff.

It helps to think of the JSP page as the presentation layer of the application. It is responsible for the user interface but should leave the actual computation and other business-related actions for a lower level.

The way that JSP allows this is through the use of beans. Beans are simply Java classes that follow a few basic conventions. These are

- Each attribute of the bean that will be exposed publicly should have at least a method called `getX()`. For example, an attribute called `height` should have a method called `getHeight()`.
- If the bean will allow the attribute to be modified, it needs to provide a method called `setX()`.
- The `getX()` method should return the same type value that the `setX()` method takes as an argument.
- If a value is Boolean, it uses the accessor `isX()` rather than `getX()`.

JSP supports an introspection mechanism on beans that allows form values to be automatically populated into beans from a JSP page by using the `jsp:setProperty` tag. Listings 5.9, 5.10, and 5.11 show a sample application that shows how all this ties together.

LISTING 5.9 `Animal.java`

```
package demo;

public class Animal {
    String commonName = null;
    String speciesName = null;
    float adultHeight = 0;
    float adultWeight = 0;
    int topSpeed = 0;
    String description;

    public String getCommonName() {
       return this.commonName;
    }

    public void setCommonName(String commonName) {
       this.commonName = commonName;
    }

    public String getSpeciesName() {
       return this.speciesName;
    }
```

LISTING 5.9 Continued

```
    public void setSpeciesName(String speciesName) {
        this.speciesName = speciesName;
    }

    public float getAdultHeight() {
        return this.adultHeight;
    }

    public void setAdultHeight(float adultHeight) {
        this.adultHeight = adultHeight;
    }

    public float getAdultWeight() {
        return this.adultWeight;
    }

    public void setAdultWeight(float adultWeight) {
        this.adultWeight = adultWeight;
    }

    public int getTopSpeed() {
        return this.topSpeed;
    }

    public void setTopSpeed(int topSpeed) {
        this.topSpeed = topSpeed;
    }

    public String getDescription() {
        return this.description;
    }

    public void setDescription(String description) {
        this.description = description;
    }
}
```

This is a simple bean that implements a few properties of animal. Three types of properties are defined here: `String` properties such as species name; `float` properties such as height and weight; and an `integer` property, the top speed of the animal.

Now you can create a form to enter the values you want to assign to an animal using the JSP page shown in Listing 5.10.

LISTING 5.10 animalinput.jsp

```
<!DOCTYPE HTML PUBLIC "-//IETF//DTD HTML//EN">
<html> <head>
<title>Input an Animal</title>
</head>

<body>
<h1>Input an Animal</h1>
<FORM action="animaldisplay.jsp" method="POST">
Common Name: <INPUT TYPE="text" name="commonName"><BR>
Species Name: <INPUT TYPE="text" name="speciesName"><BR>
Adult Height: <INPUT TYPE="text" name="adultHeight"><BR>
Adult Weight: <INPUT TYPE="text" name="adultWeight"><BR>
Top Speed: <INPUT TYPE="text" name="topSpeed"><BR>
Description:<BR> <TEXTAREA rows="5" cols="50"  name="description">
</TEXTAREA><BR>
<INPUT TYPE="SUBMIT">
</FORM>

</body> </html>
```

This page is actually straight HTML, defining a standard form that takes the various properties of an animal. This page, after it's filled out, is shown in Figure 5.1. When the submit button is clicked, the values are sent to a second page, shown in Listing 5.11.

LISTING 5.11 animaldisplay.jsp

```
<!DOCTYPE HTML PUBLIC "-//IETF//DTD HTML//EN">
<html> <head>
<title>Display an Animal</title>
</head>

<body>
<h1>Display an Animal</h1>
<jsp:useBean id="animal" scope="request" class="demo.Animal"/>
<jsp:setProperty name="animal" property="*"/>
<H2><jsp:getProperty name="animal" property="commonName"/><H2>
Species Name: <jsp:getProperty name="animal" property="speciesName"/><BR>
```

LISTING 5.11 Continued

```
Adult Weight: <jsp:getProperty name="animal" property="adultWeight"/> Kg
(<%= animal.getAdultWeight() * 2.2 %> Lbs)<BR>
Adult Height: <jsp:getProperty name="animal" property="adultHeight"/> m
(<%= animal.getAdultHeight() * 3.28 %> ft)<BR>
Top Speed: <jsp:getProperty name="animal" property="topSpeed"/> kph
(<%= animal.getTopSpeed() * 0.621 %> mph)<BR>
Description:<BR>
<jsp:getProperty name="animal" property="description"/>

</body> </html>
```

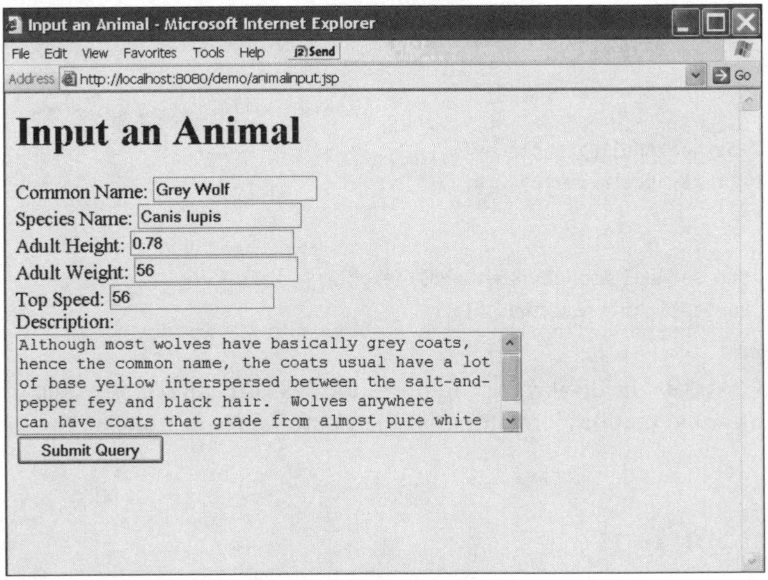

FIGURE 5.1 Pointing your browser at `animalinput.jsp`.

This page is where all the interesting action occurs. First, the code uses `jsp:useBean` to create an instance of the `Animal` class, and associates it with the ID (which is to say, the local JSP variable name) `animal`.

The `jsp:setProperty` tag is a very powerful tool. When used as in the previous example, it looks at all the values available on the form that was just submitted, and then uses introspection to determine whether any of the property names match up with bean property names in the object specified by the `name` argument.

The result of this is that the newly created animal bean is populated with the values from the previous page. Type conversions of the object varieties (String to int, String to float) are handled automatically by the code. However, if the type conversion fails (if, for example, a float is typed into a field that is mapped into an int bean property), an exception is thrown—something that your code should handle gracefully.

Note that the display code uses both the jsp:getProperty tag and the raw getX() calls to the object itself. You need to use the raw calls to compute the English unit equivalents of the metric values. An alternative is to provide a read-only get method in the class, such as the one shown in Listing 5.12.

LISTING 5.12 Providing English Units in the Class

```
public float getAdultWeight() {
   return this.adultWeight;
}

public float getAdultWeightInLbs() {
   return this.adultWeight * 2.2;
}

public void setAdultWeight(float adultWeight) {
   this.adultWeight = adultWeight;
```

Figure 5.2 shows the display page in operation. As you can see, it would look prettier if you did some number formatting on the float values to truncate the long decimal results.

JSP Custom Tags

As you develop your JSP application, you might find common functionalities that you repeatedly have to code in Java on the JSP page. For example, you might need to present metric values in English units, as in the previous example. JSP enables you to extend the JSP syntax by adding new custom tag libraries to JSP.

There are two pieces to a JSP tag library (taglib). The first is a Java class that actually handles the JSP. The second is a tag library descriptor file (TLD) that lets JSP know about the new tags.

To begin, you need to define a Java class that extends BodyTagSupport. This class provides all the helper functions and default methods needed to implement the BodyTag. Listing 5.13 shows an implementation of a meters-to-feet tag.

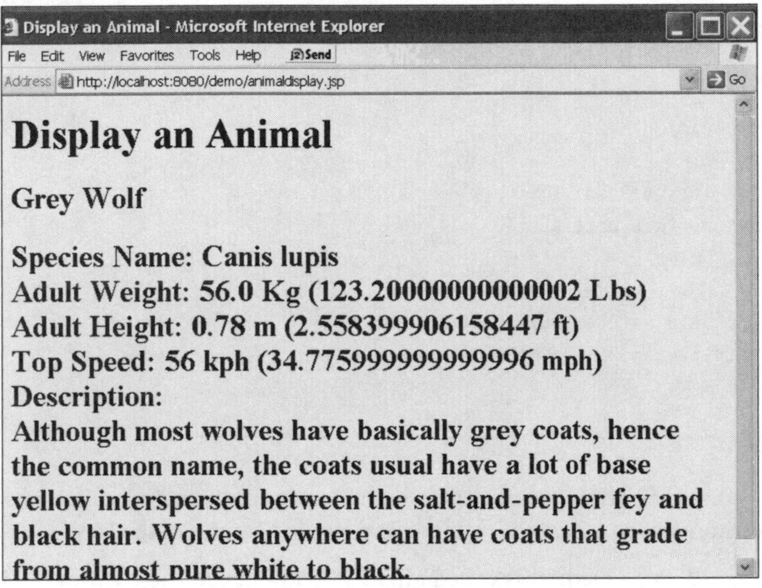

FIGURE 5.2 Submitting the values to `animaldisplay.jsp`.

LISTING 5.13 `MetersToFeet.java`

```
package taglib.metric;

import javax.servlet.jsp.tagext.BodyTagSupport;
import javax.servlet.jsp.tagext.BodyContent;
import javax.servlet.jsp.PageContext;
import javax.servlet.http.HttpServletResponse;
import java.text.DecimalFormat;

public class MetersToFeet extends BodyTagSupport {
    public int doAfterBody() {
       BodyContent body = getBodyContent();
       try {
           float meters = Float.valueOf(body.getString()).floatValue();
           DecimalFormat df = new DecimalFormat();
           df.setMaximumFractionDigits(precision);
           body.getEnclosingWriter().println(df.format(meters * 3.28));
       } catch (Exception ex) {
           ex.printStackTrace();
       }
       return EVAL_PAGE;
```

LISTING 5.13 Continued

```
    }

    int precision = 2;

    public int getPrecision () {
       return this.precision;
    }

    public void setPrecision (int precision) {
       this.precision = precision;
    }
}
```

As you can see, all this class does is to define one bean property called `precision`, and overrides the `doAfterBody()` method provided by the base class.

The `doAfterBody()` method is called after the body inside the custom tag is encountered. In this case, all it does is to covert the `String` into a `float`, format it to the specified number of decimal places (two if no argument is given in the tag), get a handle on the stream to write to, and send out the converted number.

After the class is written, you must inform JSP that the new tag is available. This is done via a TLD file. The TLD for the metric taglib is shown in Listing 5.14.

LISTING 5.14 `metric.tld`

```
<?xml version="1.0" encoding="UTF-8"?>
<!DOCTYPE taglib PUBLIC "-//Sun Microsystems, Inc.//DTD JSP Tag Library 1.1//EN"
          "http://java.sun.com/j2ee/dtds/web-jsptaglibrary_1_1.dtd">
<taglib>
<tlibversion>1.0</tlibversion>
<jspversion>1.1</jspversion>
<shortname>metric</shortname>
<tag>
<name>m2f</name>
<tagclass>taglib.metric.MetersToFeet</tagclass>
<bodycontent>JSP</bodycontent>
<attribute>
   <name>precision</name>
   <required>false</required>
</attribute>
</tag>
</taglib>
```

This simple TLD defines the `metric` taglib, which has a single tag called `m2f` (meters to feet). `m2f` is mapped to the class you just created and defined to have one attribute: the precision. Just as in a set property, any attributes of a tag are mapped to the accessor methods of the class.

With the TLD file placed in the `WEB-INF` subdirectory of your application, you can write a JSP file that uses it (see Listing 5.15).

LISTING 5.15 `tagtest.jsp`

```
<%@ taglib uri="/WEB-INF/metric.tld" prefix="metric" %>
<!DOCTYPE HTML PUBLIC "-//IETF//DTD HTML//EN">
<html> <head>
<title>Testing Metric Tags</title>
</head>

<body>
<h1>Testing Metric Tags</h1>
30 meters is <metric:m2f>30</metric:m2f> feet<BR>
37.98345 meters is about
<metric:m2f precision="4">37.98345</metric:m2f>feet<BR>

</body> </html>
```

After loading the new taglib using the `<%@ taglib` directive, you can use the new tag by simply putting `<metric:m2f` in your JSP. This example shows versions using both a specific precision and the default. Figure 5.3 shows the results.

Web Application Deployment

In the previous section, I mentioned the `WEB-INF` subdirectory. This is just one of several required components of a working JSP application. In this section, you'll learn what JSP expects to see and where it expects to see it.

Figure 5.4 shows a typical directory structure in JSP. At the top level is a directory, typically called `webapps`, which is the parent directory to all the applications installed on the JSP server. Beneath it are a number of subdirectories, each of which corresponds to a specific application. In this figure, only one subdirectory (`app2`) has been fully expanded; the others have been shaded out for space.

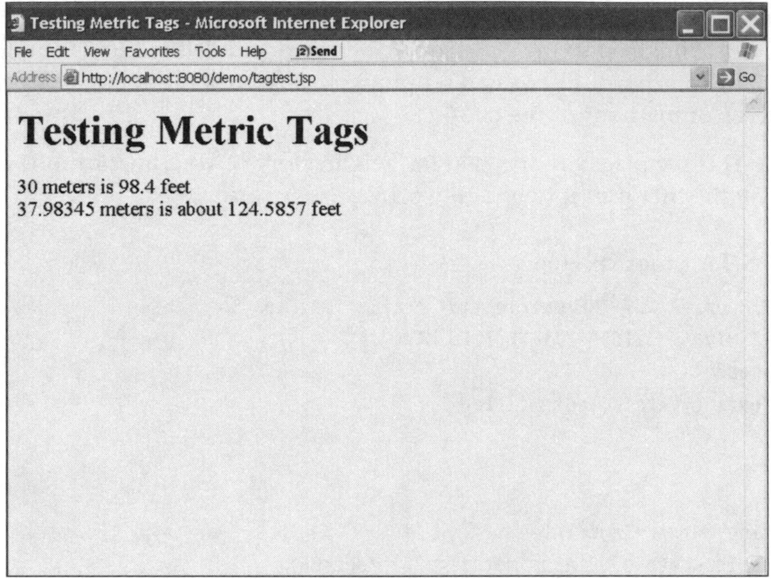

FIGURE 5.3 Pointing your browser at `tagtest.jsp`.

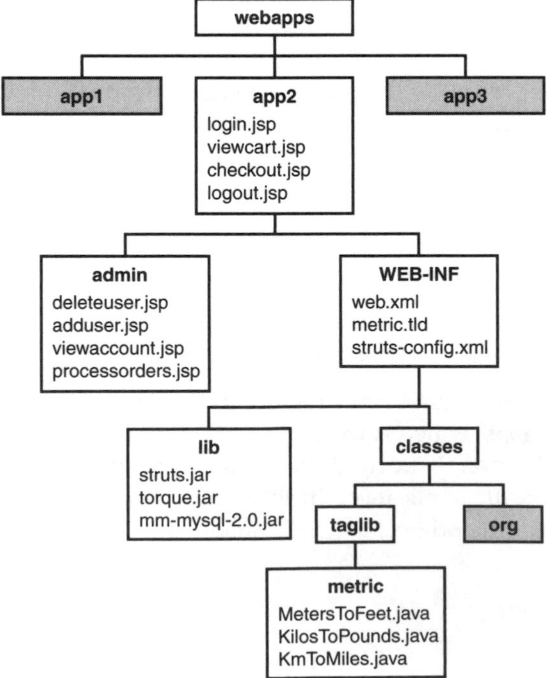

FIGURE 5.4 A typical JSP deployment structure.

Under the app2 directory, you find the root of your JSP files. On a server, you would access them as http://*servername*/app2/login.jsp, to use the login JSP as an example. From this directory, you can create other JSP subdirectories (such as admin, shown in this example). You also have a special directory called WEB-INF. The WEB-INF directory contains one very important file: web.xml. This is the file that configures the application and is used by the JSP server when initializing the application. Listing 5.16 shows the contents on a simple web.xml file.

LISTING 5.16 web.xml

```
<?xml version="1.0" encoding="UTF-8"?>
<!DOCTYPE web-app PUBLIC "-//Sun Microsystems, Inc.//DTD Web Application 2.2//EN"
                          "http://java.sun.com/j2ee/dtds/web-app_2_2.dtd">
<web-app>
  <welcome-file-list>
    <welcome-file>Index.jsp</welcome-file>
  </welcome-file-list>
</web-app>
```

All this web.xml does is define a welcome file, which is a file that can serve as the index file for a directory if no filename is specified. Even if all the web.xml file has is a start and end web-app tag, it must be in WEB-INF because it tells the JSP server to create a Web application instance when it starts.

Also in WEB-INF, you might find TLD files or other initialization files such as the Struts XML definition file.

Beneath WEB-INF are two critical directories: classes and lib. The classes directory is the root of a classpath that's used by the container for your Web application. This is normally where all the classes you've created for your application go.

The lib subdirectory holds JAR files. Any JAR file placed in this directory will become available as if the JAR file was on the classpath explicitly. The difference between lib and classes is that JAR files in classes won't be looked at, and .class files in lib won't be used.

In addition to application-specific lib and classes directories, there is usually a serverwide pair of directories that do the same thing, but for all applications. These directories are a useful place to put libraries that all applications will want to make use of, or to store a property file that you want to be independent of an application.

WAR Files

To make it easier to transport applications to new servers, JSP servers understand how to unpack a WAR file. A WAR (Web application resource) file is just a JAR file but with a different extension. Inside a WAR file, you'll find the entire contents of an application, relative to the application subdirectory. For example, if you did a listing of a WAR file build from the app2 application shown in the diagram, you'd see Listing 5.17.

LISTING 5.17 A Typical WAR File

```
WEB-INF/web.xml
WEB-INF/struts.xml
WEB-INF/lib/torque.jar
WEB-INF/lib/struts.jar
WEB-INF/lib/mm-mysql-2.0.jar
WEB-INF/classes/taglib/metric/MetersToFeet.jsp
WEB-INF/classes/taglib/metric/KilosToPounds.jsp
WEB-INF/classes/taglib/metric/KmToMiles.jsp
login.jsp
logout.jsp
viewcart.jsp
checkout.jsp
admin/deleteuser.jsp
admin/adduser.jsp
admin/viewaccount.jsp
admin/processorders.jsp
```

As you can see, the name of the application itself is left out; it is determined from the name of the WAR file. To deploy a WAR file, just place it in the webapps subdirectory and restart your JSP server. The server will automatically unpack the WAR file and deploy the application.

A WAR FILE GOTCHA

WAR files are great, but there's one gotcha to remember. Most JSP servers won't unpack a new WAR file over an old application directory. That means if you deploy shop.war (which will create a new subdirectory called shop), and later upload a new copy of shop.war and place it in the webapps directory, it won't replace the old version. You must stop the server, delete the old shop subdirectory (using rm -r shop under Linux, for example), and then restart the server so that it can unpack the application freshly.

JSTL: The Standard Tag Library

As developers have created more and more custom tag libraries, they discovered a need to come up with a standard library of the most commonly used ones. This led to the Java Standard Tag Library standard (JSTL).

JSTL can be broken up into a number of large sections. Each one will be briefly summarized in the following sections.

General Purpose Actions

The general purpose tags are `c.out`, which writes a value to the JSP stream; `c.set`, which sets a scoped variable; `c.remove`, which removes a scoped variable; and `c.catch`, which is used to catch exceptions inside its body.

Conditional Actions

The conditional action tags implement control flow. `c:if` is a straightforward conditional evaluation, whereas `c:choose` in combination with the `c:when` and `c:otherwise` tags implements a flow similar to the `switch` statement.

Iterator Actions

The other half of flow control, these tags define the looping constructs for JSTL. The `c:forEach` tag will loop either over a collection of objects or for a certain number of times. The `c:forTokens` tag uses a delimiter character to break a string into pieces, and then iterates over the pieces.

URL-Related Actions

These actions relate to Web pages. The `c:import` tag causes another Web page to be inserted at this point in the JSP document. Using `c:url`, a relative URL will be correctly rewritten as an absolute one. Finally, `c:redirect` causes a redirect to another page. All these actions can use a `c:param` tag inside them to pass a parameter to the new page.

Internationalization Actions

Using these tags, Web content can be internationalized. Using `fmt:setLocale`, the locale of the page can be altered. The `fmt:setBundle` and `fmt:bundle` tags let multiple message resource bundles be used on a page. After a bundle is available, the `fmt:message` tag is used to look up the specific message. Finally, the `fmt:requestEncoding` tag enables the developer to change the character encoding used on the page.

Formatting Actions

This set of tags handles common formatting requirements. The `fmt:timeZone` and `fmt:setTimeZone` tags are used to establish the correct time zone, which is used by `fmt:formatDate` and `fmt:parseDate`. The `fmt:formatNumber` and `fmt:parseNumber` tags supply similar functions for numbers.

SQL Actions

By using these tags, actions can be taken against a database. After using `sql:setDataSource` to gain access to a database, the `sql:query` and `sql:update` tags can be used to read and write from it. If transaction control is needed, it's available from the `sql:transaction` tag.

XML Actions

The final set of standard tags is used to work with XML files. The `x:parse` tag parses an XML file. After the file is parsed, the `x:out` tag will send XML data to the JspWriter, whereas `x:set` can be used to set variables to XML values.

The XML tags also include a set of control tags (`x:if`, `x:choose`, `x:when`, `x:otherwise`, and `x:forEach`) that work similarly to the control flow tags, but for XML data.

Finally, the `x:transform` tag can be used to transform an XML document to HTML using an XSLT stylesheet.

Scripting Language

In addition to all the new tags, JSTL also introduces an entire scripting language intended to allow the same degree of functionality as is currently available using Java scriptlets but in the normalized form of tags. Some developers consider the scripting language to be the most powerful piece of the emerging JSTL standard.

These descriptions are meant to serve only as a basic introduction to what JSLT offers. They can be explored through the online specifications available at `java.sun.com`.

JSP and J2EE: The Big Picture

The phrase *J2EE* is bandied about a lot these days. It's worth understanding just what J2EE is, and how JSP (and Struts) fits into it.

J2EE (The Java 2 Enterprise Edition) can be thought of very narrowly or as a code word for a much larger body of technologies. As strictly defined by Sun, J2EE encompasses a bundle of Java technologies:

- JavaServer Pages (JSP)
- Java Servlets
- Enterprise Java Beans (EJB)
- The Java Naming and Directory Interface (JNDI)

- The Java Transaction API (JTA)
- The Java Database Connectivity API (JDBC)
- Java Management Extension (JMX)
- J2EE/CORBA Interface
- J2EE Connector Architecture
- Java Mail
- Java Messaging Service (JMS)

Used together, these tools enable developers to create applications that are distributable across multiple tiers and are highly abstractable.

That said, there's a time and place for all of the above, and not necessarily all on the same projects. Just because you have a tool in your toolbelt doesn't mean you need to use it on every project.

THE RIGHT TOOL FOR THE RIGHT JOB

As an example, I have a friend who is working on a real-time application in which several subcomponents of a device need to communicate with each other over a private ethernet. A design decision was made early on to use CORBA for the various subdevices to communicate, which meant that each device had to implement a full TCP/IP stack. As a result, they were unable to achieve the cycle time they required because they kept hitting performance issues in the networking. My first question when I heard about this was, "Why didn't you just use raw ethernet packets to send the data around?" The answer was that someone had decided early on that CORBA was the "politically correct" technology to use, and mandated it.

In the same way, just because the platform you are deploying to supports J2EE, it doesn't mean you need to take advantage of every piece. Most applications will use JDBC because most applications talk to databases. You'll probably be using JSP (especially in light of the fact that you're reading a book about Struts). But do you really need to deploy with EJB? Does this application need to be three-tiered, or can it be implemented two-tier? Many of these tools can greatly complicate a project if they're used when inappropriate.

So, in the broadest sense, any platform that includes all the pieces of the J2EE spec can be thought of as a J2EE platform. These include all the major Java application servers, such as WebLogic Server and WebSphere. But many people mistake other features offered by these platforms, such as integration with MQueue, as being part of the J2EE spec. They are not, and should not be assumed to be part of a platform just because the platform is J2EE compliant.

J2EE and Struts

So, how does J2EE fit into the Struts picture? Apart from the fact that a Struts-based application will always be runnable on a J2EE platform because it contains all of the request components, there's a bigger picture.

Assume for the moment that you're on a project large and complex enough to require technologies like EJB. Struts provides a natural front end to an EJB application.

EJB applications divide things into the business logic, which lives on the EJB server, and the stubs, which are used by applications to gain access to the backend code.

In a Struts-fronted EJB application, the model piece of the MVC pattern would be EJB client objects. The Struts standard already coerces developers into dividing their application into the presentation side and the business logic side. That means the model can integrate directly into the EJB beans without having to worry about the JSP page or control flow logic having been written to require access to business logic objects because Struts does not allow it (or at least strongly discourages it). You'll see how this works in Chapter 18, "Using Struts with Enterprise JavaBeans."

Conclusions

JSP represents an attempt to turn servlets inside out, by making it easy to generate the HTML portion of a Web page without having to worry about placing it inside print statements.

The JSP page is turned into a Java class, which acts as a servlet. Each request is associated with a session, which represents a given user, and is tracked using cookies or URL rewriting.

Objects can be persistent on several levels, from page and request through session, and even to the entire application or server.

JSTL provides a large library of common tags, as well as a scripting language that enables developers to use tags instead of Java scriptlets for many programmatic functionalities on Web pages. Developers can also develop their own tag libraries.

J2EE represents a bundle of Java standards that allow multitier complex enterprise applications to be created. Struts can serve as a natural front end to a J2EE/EJB application.

6 The Sample Application: A Financial Portfolio

IN THIS CHAPTER

- Requirements: Covering Your Rear End
- Starting with the Wireframes
- Developing Use Cases
- Data Sources and Storage
- Choosing Technologies
- Conclusions

It's always useful to have a concrete example to follow along with when you're learning a new technology. Rather than seeing abstract code fragments floating in limbo, you'll learn Struts in detail by watching the construction of a complete Web application.

This application also will serve as a jumping-off point for later chapters, which will demonstrate how to incorporate various technologies such as DynaBeans and Web Services into a Struts application.

The application that will be developed in this book is a stock portfolio manager. You've probably seen more than a few of these because most portal sites such as Yahoo! offer one as a way to make their site "sticky."

This chapter will walk through the requirements, use cases, database schema, and technology selections involved in developing the application. In the next chapter, the application itself will begin to emerge.

Requirements: Covering Your Rear End

If you've ever done a serious software project, you should understand that requirements-gathering is crucial to success. If you don't know what your customer wants, it's hard to deliver it. Short of developing psychic skills, your best bet is a solid functional requirements document (FRD) up front.

Of course, requirements-gathering is like anything else in software development. It's possible to become so bogged down trying to capture every nuance of the site that you never actually get around to coding it.

The analogy I use is this: Imagine that you're trying to get a rocket ship to Mars. I offer you two choices:

- Make one extremely well-calculated rocket burn at the launch pad, designed to deliver the ship into Mars orbit
- Make a reasonably accurate initial burn, and then do a series of mid-course corrections in flight

Now, the first approach is probably a little more fuel-efficient, but it requires an inhuman degree of precision in the original calculations. The second approach gets the ship off the pad much faster, but at the cost of a little more fuel (in the case of software, possible refactoring during development).

The punch line, of course, is that the first approach won't work at all if the customer suddenly moves Mars somewhere else. And moving Mars, or in this case changing requirements during development, is a fact of life.

So, with that in mind, the requirements-gathering shown here is a middle road between the search for total truth and jumping right in without understanding anything.

Starting with the Wireframes

Most Web-based projects start with wireframes—nonfunctional HTML documents that show the layout, design, and flow of the site. They serve two purposes: to illustrate the site functionality at an early stage of requirements-gathering, and as templates for the JSP developers as they begin to build the site.

The Main Page

The site you'll be looking at, Stock Tracker, starts with a main page (shown in Figure 6.1).

The top of the page has a common banner that's used throughout the site. In a second-generation site, this banner might have buttons or links that would take a visitor to various parts of the site, but in this sample app, it's static.

In the left-side column, the top section has a login form and a link to an account creation page. Beneath that is a market update section that will be automatically updated by a secondary program. At the bottom, a list of hot technology stocks is listed along with current market quotes.

In the right-side section, a number of news stories are shown. These stories will be updated by site staffers and are static HTML documents.

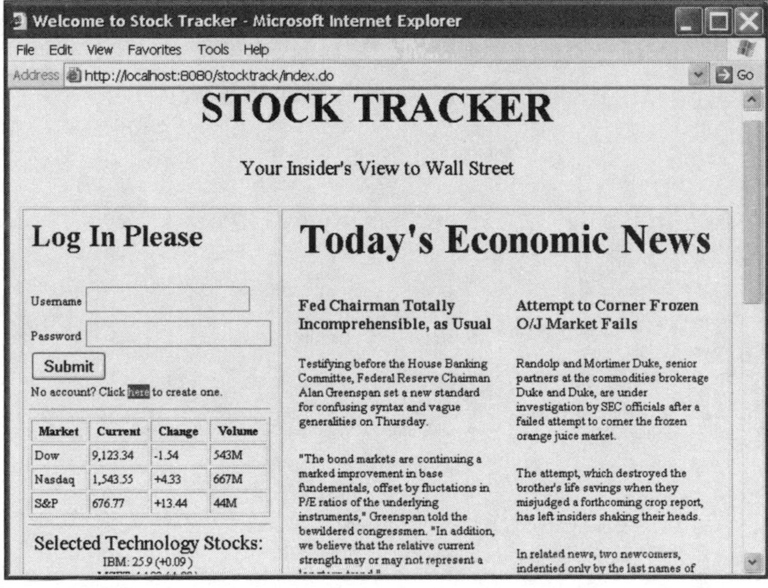

FIGURE 6.1 The main page of the Stock Tracker Web site.

The Create Account Page

If the user wants to create a new account, he clicks on the link in the left section, which brings him to the page shown in Figure 6.2.

The left side of the page remains as before, which means that the visitor could still choose to log in at this point instead of creating a new account. The right side has been replaced with a form (which could stand to be prettied up in the finished application).

This form, which also includes work phone and extension (they're cut off in the screen capture), is used to create a new user account. At this point, the visitor is taken around to the main page again, but with new contents in the upper left. This view (seen in Figure 6.3) is the same as would be seen by a user who entered a correct username and password at the login screen in Figure 6.1.

The main page for a logged-in user replaces the login form with an area displaying a mini-view of his or her portfolio. Because Mr. Gecko is new to the site, nothing is displayed in this area. Clicking on the portfolio tracking link brings him to the transaction entry page.

Transaction Entry

This page (shown in Figure 6.4) enables a user to enter a purchase or sale of stock. After submitting the form, the user is taken back to the main page, which now displays the new stock entry (see Figure 6.5).

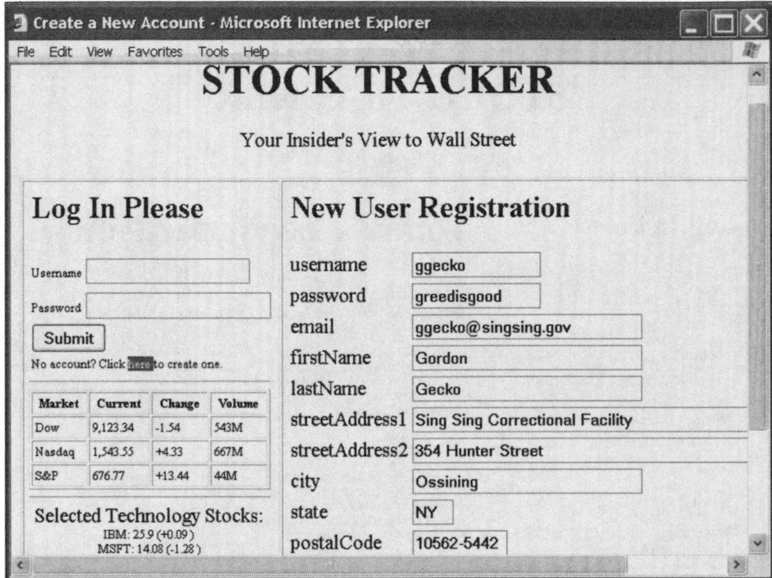

FIGURE 6.2 The create account page.

FIGURE 6.3 The main page with a logged-in user page.

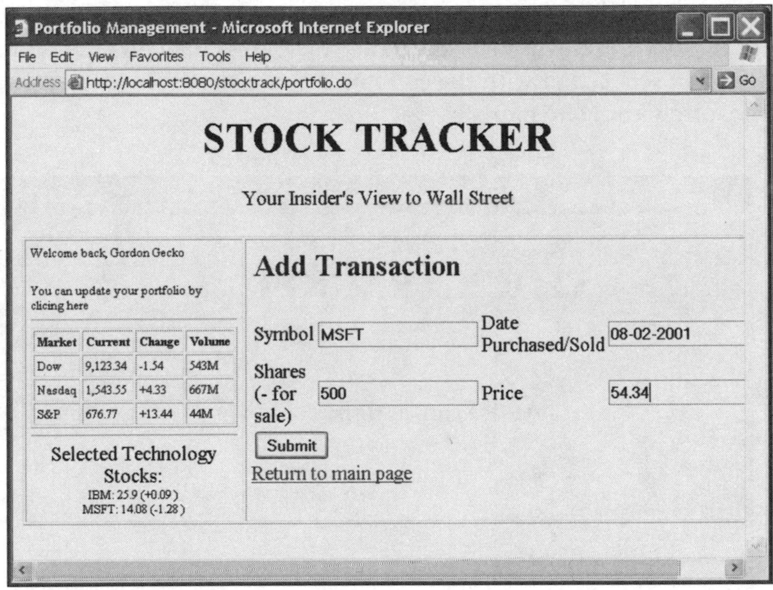

FIGURE 6.4 The transaction entry screen.

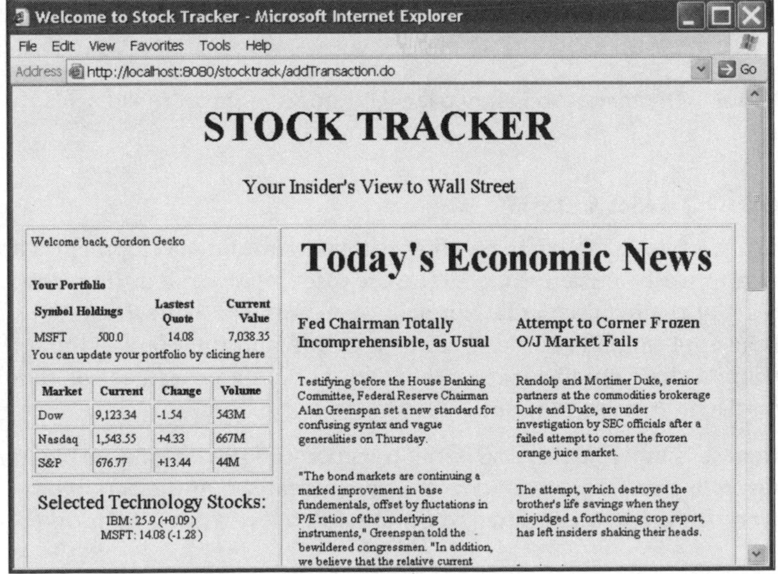

FIGURE 6.5 The main page showing stocks in the mini-view.

As you can see, the mini-view now shows the total holdings along with the latest quote for the stock. If the user clicks on the portfolio update link, he is taken back to the transaction screen, but with the current portfolio shown in greater detail underneath the form (see Figure 6.6).

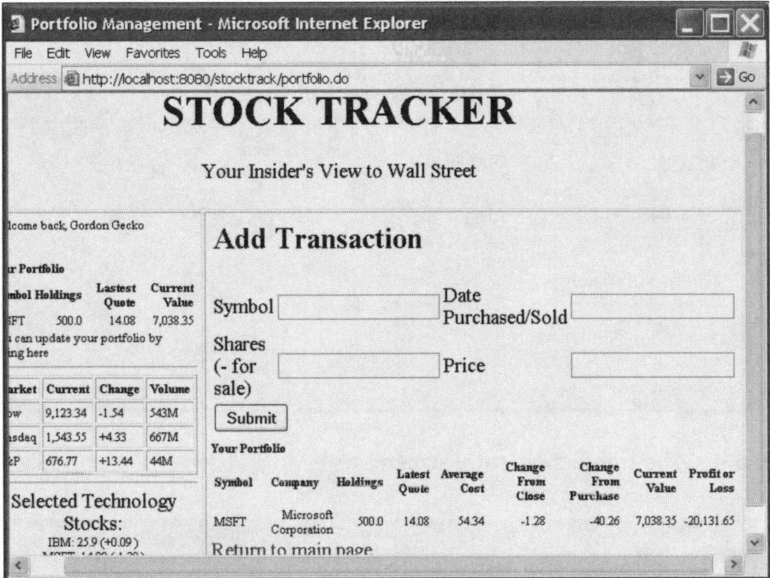

FIGURE 6.6 The transaction entry page with stocks in the portfolio.

Developing Use Cases

After the wireframes are complete, the customer and the development team usually sits down to work up the use cases. The use cases represent a drilling down into the particulars of the requirements. Normally, use cases start with the initial state at which the application is encountered by a visitor, and then proceed to follow every possible path that could be taken, asking what could go wrong (error conditions) and what actions must be taken.

This exercise is especially critical with Struts because the list of possible jumping points from a given page represents the possible targets of the action bean. But, as with everything, it's not required to get absolutely everything right on the first pass.

Use Case: Initial Page

When a visitor requests the index page of the site, she is presented with the main site page. The market quotes are contained in a separate file, which is updated by a `cron` job. The technology stock quotes are looked up in real-time during the page creation. The news stories on the right are created manually by the staff and exist in separate files.

The possible transitions from this page are

- By filling in a username and password, which brings the user back to the same page, but as a logged-in user
- By clicking on the create account link, which brings the user to the Create Account page

The possible error conditions on this page are

- The username or password is incorrect, in which case an error message will be displayed above the login form.

Use Case: Account Creation Page

From the account creation page, the visitor can establish a new account. The possible transitions from this page are

- By filling in a username and password, which brings the user to the main page, but as a logged-in user
- By filling in the create account form, which causes the account to be created in the database, and logs in the visitor as the newly created user, returning her to the main page

The possible error conditions on this page are

- The username or password is incorrect, in which case an error message will be displayed above the login form.
- Any of the mandatory fields is blank (only street address 2 and work extension are optional). Missing fields are flagged with an error message.
- The username is already in use. This causes an error message to be printed above the form.
- The e-mail address does not contain an `@`, which is flagged as an error on the field.

- The state is not a proper two-letter state abbreviation, which is flagged as an error on the field.
- The postal code is not a five- or nine-digit number, possibly with a dash, which is flagged as an error on the field.
- The home or work phones are not 10-digit numbers, possibly with parentheses, dashes, or spaces, which is flagged as an error on the field.
- An error occurs during the database write operation, which causes the visitor to be sent to a general error page.

Use Case: Logged-In User on Main Page

After the user has logged in, either by creating a new account or by using the login form successfully, the main page replaces the login form with the mini-view of the portfolio. If there are no stocks in the portfolio, the visitor is given a link to the add transaction page. If there are stocks in the portfolio, a mini-view is presented with the same link underneath the view.

The possible transitions from this page are

- By clicking the add transaction link, which takes the visitor to the add transaction page

Use Case: Add Transaction Page

At the add transaction page, the visitor is offered a form with which to add a stock transaction to her portfolio. Beneath that, a full display of their current portfolio is shown, listing the following items:

- Symbol—The stock symbol of the company.
- Company Name—The full name of the company.
- Holdings—Number of shares held in aggregate the total of all stock purchases minus all stock sales).
- Latest Quote—Last quote for that stock.
- Average Cost—Computed as follows: Iterate over the stock purchases and sales. For each purchase, use the following formula where AC is the current average cost, initialized at 0; NS is the number of shares, which also starts at 0; SC is the per share price of the new shares; and SI is the number of shares being added:

  ((AC * NS) + (SC * SI)) / (NS + SI) = AC

  NS + SI = NS

For stock sales, AC is not changed, but NS is decremented by the shares sold.

For example, in the case in which 500 shares of IBM are bought at 10, 250 are sold, and then another 250 are bought at 20, the calculation would be

((0 * 0) + (10 * 500)) / (0 + 500) = 10

0 + 500 = 500

500 - 250 = 250

((10 * 250) + (20 * 250)) / (250 + 250) = 15

250 + 250 = 500

- Change From Close—Per-share price change since the last market close, or the word CLOSE if the market is currently closed.
- Change From Purchase—Per share price change since the stock was purchased.
- Current Value—Current holdings times current quote.
- Profit or Loss—Change from Purchase times holdings.

As you can see from this, it is important to gather crucial details of business logic as early as possible. Asking a question such as, "How do you compute the average cost of a share?" can save a developer from going up the wrong path later.

The possible transitions from this page are

- By filling in a stock transaction, which brings the visitor back to the main page after adding the stock transaction
- By clicking on the return to main page link, which brings the user back to the main page with no change in the portfolio
- By clicking on the update portfolio link on the mini-view, which brings the user back to this page

The possible error conditions on this page are

- Any of the fields is blank. Missing fields are flagged with an error message.
- The stock symbol is not found in the database, which is flagged as an error on the field.
- The date is not in a valid date format or is after today's date, which is flagged as an error on the field.
- The price or quantity is not a number, which is flagged as an error on the field.
- A database error occurs while saving the transaction, which causes the visitor to be taken to the general errors page.

Data Sources and Storage

The next question that you, as a developer, need to consider is where the data from the application is coming from and where it will be stored. This application is particularly complex because there will be data coming from outside sources (stock quotes), data entered by the user (transactions and account information), and data entered by the staff (news stories).

Because historical as well as current stock information will be needed (eventually, for example, it would be good to be able to display charts of stock prices over time), the stock quotes will be stored in the database and updated hourly. In the finished application, a separate program would run, getting the quotes and writing them into the database. For this example, the quotes will be made up randomly and stored for future use.

A quick pass over the requirements can pull out all the objects that will be needed to make the application run:

- A user object that stores the account information
- A stock object that stores permanent information about each stock
- A stock price object that stores a stock quote at a given moment for a stock
- A transaction object that stores a user's purchase or sale of a stock

CHOOSING PRIMARY KEYS

It might be tempting to use the stock symbol as the primary key for the stock table. After all, there's a one-to-one relationship between stock symbols and stocks. However, a general rule of thumb in database schema design is to avoid that kind of direct mapping in favor of sequential ID numbers.

There are several good reasons for this. For one, most databases can do a join against a number much faster than they can against a string. In addition, stock symbols do change on occasion, and if you were using the symbol as a key, you'd have to update it wherever it was being used as a foreign key. By using a sequence number instead, you would have to update the value in only one database row.

This object list can be turned into an entity relation diagram (ERD), as shown in Figure 6.7.

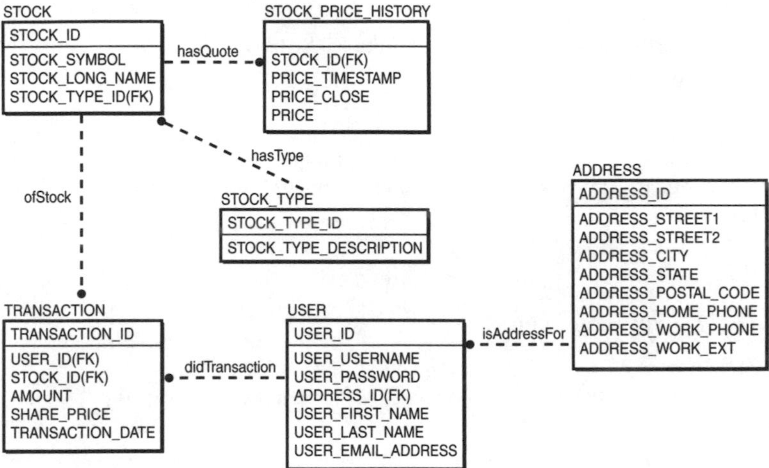

FIGURE 6.7 The ERD for the Stock Tracker application.

Choosing Technologies

After the ERD is complete, you can create your database schema from it. At this point, you need to begin making a list of the technologies that you'll use to develop the application.

This application would be a good candidate for Struts for several reasons. For one, it has some flows between different parts of the site that must be controlled to ensure correct authentication and access control. In addition, there are some forms with moderately complex validations that must be run, and Struts offers easy form validation, as you'll see.

Having chosen Struts, you have a wide choice of platforms to run it on. You probably don't have tens of thousands of dollars to spend to try out a sample application, so the Jakarta Tomcat platform is a good choice because it's both free and reliable.

Similar factors might lead you to choose the MySQL database for the data storage portion of the application. One of the nice features of applications written using JDBC is that it's easy to move them between databases, so you could move to Oracle or another commercial database product if your needs grow larger.

Torque

By using the Torque object-modeling tool, you can make it even easier to move between databases. Torque is a wonderful new tool from the Jakarta team that automatically creates a set of Java objects that map one-to-one against database tables, including foreign key relationships. It's worth taking a brief moment to see how Torque works.

The heart of Torque is the `project-schema.xml` file. This file describes, in vendor-neutral terms, the structure of your database. Listing 6.1 shows the `project-schema.xml` file for this application.

NOTE

As with all other source code in this book, you can find this file on the companion CD with this book.

LISTING 6.1 `project-schema.xml`

```
<?xml version="1.0" encoding="ISO-8859-1" standalone="no" ?>
<!DOCTYPE database SYSTEM "file:/torque/schema/database.dtd">

<!-- ==================================================================== -->
<!--                                                                      -->
<!-- STOCKTRACK  T O R Q U E  S C H E M A                             -->
<!--                                                                      -->
<!-- ==================================================================== -->

<!--
  Note: You must now specify a database name.
-->

<database name="stocktrack"
  defaultIdMethod="native">

  <table name="STOCK">
    <column name="STOCK_ID" primaryKey="true" required="true"
                            autoIncrement="true" type="INTEGER"/>
    <column name="STOCK_SYMBOL" required="true" type="VARCHAR" size="10"/>
    <column name="STOCK_LONG_NAME" required="true" type="VARCHAR" size="30"/>
    <column name="STOCK_TYPE_ID" required="true" type="CHAR" size="1"/>
    <foreign-key foreignTable="STOCK_TYPE">
      <reference local="STOCK_TYPE_ID" foreign="STOCK_TYPE_ID"/>
    </foreign-key>
  </table>
  <table name="STOCK_TYPE" idMethod="none">
    <column name="STOCK_TYPE_ID" primaryKey="true"
            required="true" type="CHAR" size="1"/>
    <column name="STOCK_TYPE_DESCRIPTION" required="true"
            type="VARCHAR" size="50"/>
  </table>
```

LISTING 6.1 Continued

```
<table name="STOCK_PRICE_HISTORY"  idMethod="none">
   <column name="STOCK_ID" required="true" type="INTEGER"/>
   <column name="PRICE_TIMESTAMP" required="true" type="BIGINT"/>
   <column name="PRICE_CLOSE" type="CHAR" size="1"/>
   <column name="PRICE" required="true" type="FLOAT"/>
   <foreign-key foreignTable="STOCK">
      <reference local="STOCK_ID" foreign="STOCK_ID"/>
   </foreign-key>
</table>
<table name="USER">
  <column name="USER_ID" primaryKey="true" required="true"
          autoIncrement="true" type="INTEGER"/>
  <column name="USER_USERNAME" required="true" type="CHAR" size="15"/>
  <column name="USER_PASSWORD" required="true" type="CHAR" size="15"/>
  <column name="ADDRESS_ID" required="false" type="INTEGER"/>
  <column name="USER_FIRST_NAME" required="true" type="VARCHAR" size="30"/>
  <column name="USER_LAST_NAME" required="true" type="VARCHAR" size="30"/>
  <column name="USER_EMAIL_ADDRESS" required="false" type="VARCHAR" size="30"/>
  <foreign-key foreignTable="ADDRESS">
      <reference local="ADDRESS_ID" foreign="ADDRESS_ID"/>
  </foreign-key>
</table>

<table name="ADDRESS">
  <column name="ADDRESS_ID" primaryKey="true" required="true"
          autoIncrement="true" type="INTEGER"/>
  <column name="ADDRESS_STREET1" required="true" type="VARCHAR" size="60"/>
  <column name="ADDRESS_STREET2" required="false" type="VARCHAR" size="60"/>
  <column name="ADDRESS_CITY" required="true" type="VARCHAR" size="30"/>
  <column name="ADDRESS_STATE" required="false" type="VARCHAR" size="2"/>
  <column name="ADDRESS_POSTAL_CODE" required="false" type="VARCHAR" size="10"/>
  <column name="ADDRESS_HOME_PHONE" required="false" type="VARCHAR" size="15"/>
  <column name="ADDRESS_WORK_PHONE" required="false" type="VARCHAR" size="15"/>
  <column name="ADDRESS_WORK_EXT" required="false" type="VARCHAR" size="10"/>
</table>
<table name="TRANSACTION">
  <column name="TRANSACTION_ID" primaryKey="true" required="true"
          autoIncrement="true" type="INTEGER"/>
  <column name="USER_ID" type="INTEGER" required="true"/>
  <column name="STOCK_ID" type="INTEGER" required="true"/>
  <column name="AMOUNT" type="FLOAT" required="true"/>
```

LISTING 6.1 Continued

```
    <column name="SHARE_PRICE" type="FLOAT" required="true"/>
    <column name="TRANSACTION_DATE" type="BIGINT" required="true"/>
    <foreign-key foreignTable="USER">
      <reference local="USER_ID" foreign="USER_ID"/>
    </foreign-key>
    <foreign-key foreignTable="STOCK">
      <reference local="STOCK_ID" foreign="STOCK_ID"/>
    </foreign-key>
  </table>
</database>
```

Much of this file can be recognized as a direct XML representation of an SQL schema. There are a few features, however, that are important to note.

First, notice the `defaultIdMethod` and `idMethod` parameters on the database and tables, respectively. The `defaultIdMethod` is used to set how Torque handles auto-incrementing columns. If set to `native`, Torque tries to use the native auto-increment feature of the database it is run against. If set to `idbroker`, Torque will use its own ID generation mechanism. In this case, using MySQL's auto-incrementing columns is fine.

If you have a table without a primary key (for example, a cross-referencing table), Torque will be confused unless you specify that the table has no ID by using `idMethod=none` on the table itself.

After you've set up the XML file and a property file that tells Torque which database and connection pooling scheme to use, you use Ant to have Torque automatically use both the SQL files to create the database and the Java files to map classes to tables. For example, Listing 6.2 shows the `project-schema.sql` file that results from the XML file shown in Listing 6.1.

LISTING 6.2 `project-schema.sql`

```
# -----------------------------------------------------------------------
# STOCK
# -----------------------------------------------------------------------
drop table if exists STOCK;

CREATE TABLE STOCK
(
    STOCK_ID INTEGER NOT NULL AUTO_INCREMENT,
    STOCK_SYMBOL VARCHAR (10) NOT NULL,
```

LISTING 6.2 Continued

```
    STOCK_LONG_NAME VARCHAR (30) NOT NULL,
    STOCK_TYPE_ID CHAR (1) NOT NULL,
    PRIMARY KEY(STOCK_ID),
    FOREIGN KEY (STOCK_TYPE_ID) REFERENCES STOCK_TYPE (STOCK_TYPE_ID)
);

# -----------------------------------------------------------------------
# STOCK_TYPE
# -----------------------------------------------------------------------
drop table if exists STOCK_TYPE;

CREATE TABLE STOCK_TYPE
(
    STOCK_TYPE_ID CHAR (1) NOT NULL,
    STOCK_TYPE_DESCRIPTION VARCHAR (50) NOT NULL,
    PRIMARY KEY(STOCK_TYPE_ID)
);

# -----------------------------------------------------------------------
# STOCK_PRICE_HISTORY
# -----------------------------------------------------------------------
drop table if exists STOCK_PRICE_HISTORY;

CREATE TABLE STOCK_PRICE_HISTORY
(
    STOCK_ID INTEGER NOT NULL,
    PRICE_TIMESTAMP BIGINT NOT NULL,
    PRICE_CLOSE CHAR (1),
    PRICE FLOAT NOT NULL,
    FOREIGN KEY (STOCK_ID) REFERENCES STOCK (STOCK_ID)
);

# -----------------------------------------------------------------------
# USER
# -----------------------------------------------------------------------
drop table if exists USER;

CREATE TABLE USER
(
    USER_ID INTEGER NOT NULL AUTO_INCREMENT,
    USER_USERNAME CHAR (15) NOT NULL,
```

LISTING 6.2 Continued

```
    USER_PASSWORD CHAR (15) NOT NULL,
    ADDRESS_ID INTEGER,
    USER_FIRST_NAME VARCHAR (30) NOT NULL,
    USER_LAST_NAME VARCHAR (30) NOT NULL,
    USER_EMAIL_ADDRESS VARCHAR (30),
    PRIMARY KEY(USER_ID),
    FOREIGN KEY (ADDRESS_ID) REFERENCES ADDRESS (ADDRESS_ID)
);

# -------------------------------------------------------------------------
# ADDRESS
# -------------------------------------------------------------------------
drop table if exists ADDRESS;

CREATE TABLE ADDRESS
(
    ADDRESS_ID INTEGER NOT NULL AUTO_INCREMENT,
    ADDRESS_STREET1 VARCHAR (60) NOT NULL,
    ADDRESS_STREET2 VARCHAR (60),
    ADDRESS_CITY VARCHAR (30) NOT NULL,
    ADDRESS_STATE VARCHAR (2),
    ADDRESS_POSTAL_CODE VARCHAR (10),
    ADDRESS_HOME_PHONE VARCHAR (15),
    ADDRESS_WORK_PHONE VARCHAR (15),
    ADDRESS_WORK_EXT VARCHAR (10),
    PRIMARY KEY(ADDRESS_ID)
);

# -------------------------------------------------------------------------
# TRANSACTION
# -------------------------------------------------------------------------
drop table if exists TRANSACTION;

CREATE TABLE TRANSACTION
(
    TRANSACTION_ID INTEGER NOT NULL AUTO_INCREMENT,
    USER_ID INTEGER NOT NULL,
    STOCK_ID INTEGER NOT NULL,
    AMOUNT FLOAT NOT NULL,
    SHARE_PRICE FLOAT NOT NULL,
    TRANSACTION_DATE BIGINT NOT NULL,
```

LISTING 6.2 Continued

```
    PRIMARY KEY(TRANSACTION_ID),
    FOREIGN KEY (USER_ID) REFERENCES USER (USER_ID),
    FOREIGN KEY (STOCK_ID) REFERENCES STOCK (STOCK_ID)
);
```

The Java classes created follow a strict naming convention. For example, for the table `STOCK`, Torque will create `BaseStock`, `BaseStockPeer`, `Stock`, and `StockPeer`. `BaseStock` and `BaseStockPeer` are automatically re-created each time Ant is run, and should never be edited by the developer. `Stock` and `StockPeer` are created only the first time Ant is run; they can then be edited and extended.

Here's a code snippet that shows how Torque is used to talk to the database:

```
Criteria crit = new Criteria();
crit.add(StockPeer.STOCK_SYMBOL, "IBM");
List l = StockPeer.doSelect(crit);
Stock stock = (Stock) l.get(0);
System.out.println("Full name of IBM is " + stock.getLongName());
```

Notice that among other things, Torque has automatically created static variables on the `StockPeer` class (actually, in the `BaseStockPeer` class that `StockPeer` inherits from) that correspond to each of the columns, and getters and setters on the `Stock` class for each column.

Here's a snippet that shows how to create a new database record:

```
Stock stock = new Stock();
stock.setSymbol("IBM");
stock.setLongName("International Business Machines, Inc.");
stock.setTypeId("Y"); //NYSE
stock.save();
```

As you can see, Torque eliminates most of the pain that used to be associated with persisting Java objects to the database.

Conclusions

Successful projects are built from thorough requirements. Requirements-gathering for a Web site usually starts with a set of wireframes, which are then pored over by the customer and development team to develop use cases. These use cases document the business logic, site flow, validations and error conditions.

In this case, an FRD and use cases were presented for a stock tracking application. This application requires attention to both site flow concerns and the detailed business logic involved in stock transactions.

After the requirements are complete, an ERD can be developed, which in turn can be used to generate a schema. By using Torque, the schema, represented in XML, can directly create both the SQL source file and a full set of object-mapped classes for all the tables in the schema.

7

View Components: What the End User Sees

IN THIS CHAPTER

- The `ActionForm`
- JSP Files: The Alpha and the Omega
- The Perils of Automatic Type Conversion
- The `html:errors` Tag
- Internationalization
- Conclusions

When you look at Struts in relationship to the MVC pattern, the view component is probably the easiest one to map directly from MVC to Struts entities.

In Struts, the view is implemented by the JSP pages themselves and the `ActionForm`s that interact with them. They are also the easiest part to understand conceptually because to some extent they work like traditional servlets or pure JSP user interfaces.

This chapter discusses the view in isolation from the rest of Struts. As a result, certain details (for example, how an action name in a form tag is mapped to an `ActionForm` and what happens after a form is validated) have been put off until the next chapter.

The `ActionForm`

The JSP pages and `ActionForm` beans work hand-in-hand in Struts because the JSP submits the user input to the bean, and the bean returns validation errors to the JSP.

To understand how they work together, take a look at one `ActionForm` and the JSP page it relates to. Listing 7.1 shows the `NewUserForm` bean, which is the `ActionForm` for the create account screen of the application.

NOTE

This file is available on the companion CD with this book.

LISTING 7.1 NewUserForm.java

```
package stocktrack.struts.form;

import javax.servlet.http.*;
import org.apache.struts.action.ActionMapping;
import org.apache.struts.action.ActionErrors;
import org.apache.struts.action.ActionError;
import org.apache.struts.action.ActionForm;
import stocktrack.struts.form.BaseForm;

/**
 * stocktrack.struts.form.NewUserForm class.
 * this class used by Struts Framework to store data from newUserForm
 *
 * struts-config declaration:
 * <form-bean name="newUserForm"
 *         type="stocktrack.struts.form.NewUserForm" />
 *
 * @see org.apache.struts.action.ActionForm org.apache.struts.action.ActionForm
 * Generated by StrutsWizard.
 */

public class NewUserForm extends BaseForm {
  public void reset(ActionMapping mapping, HttpServletRequest request) {
    username = "";
    password = "";
    firstName = "";
    lastName = "";
    streetAddress1 = "";
    streetAddress2 = "";
    city = "";
    state = "";
    postalCode = "";
    homePhone = "";
    workPhone = "";
    workExt = "";
    alert = "";
  }
  public ActionErrors validate(ActionMapping mapping, HttpServletRequest request) {
    ActionErrors errors = new ActionErrors();
    if (this.isBlankString(username)) {
        errors.add("username", new ActionError("stocktrack.newuser.required"));
    }
```

LISTING 7.1 Continued

```
  if (this.isBlankString(password)) {
      errors.add("password", new ActionError("stocktrack.newuser.required"));
  }
  if (this.isBlankString(email)) {
      errors.add("email", new ActionError("stocktrack.newuser.required"));
  } else {
      if (email.indexOf("@") == -1) {
      errors.add("email", new ActionError("stocktrack.newuser.invalid.email"));
      }
  }
  if (this.isBlankString(firstName)) {
      errors.add("firstName", new ActionError("stocktrack.newuser.required"));
  }
  if (this.isBlankString(lastName)) {
      errors.add("lastName", new ActionError("stocktrack.newuser.required"));
  }
  if (this.isBlankString(streetAddress1)) {
      errors.add("streetAddress1",
                  new ActionError("stocktrack.newuser.required"));
  }
  if (this.isBlankString(city)) {
      errors.add("city", new ActionError("stocktrack.newuser.required"));
 }
  if (this.isBlankString(state)) {
      errors.add("state", new ActionError("stocktrack.newuser.required"));
 } else {
    if (!this.isValidState(state)) {
      errors.add("state", new ActionError("stocktrack.newuser.invalid.state"));
    }
 }
  if (this.isBlankString(postalCode)) {
      errors.add("postalCode", new ActionError("stocktrack.newuser.required"));
  } else {
    if (!this.isValidPostalCode(postalCode)) {
        errors.add("postalCode",
                    new ActionError("stocktrack.newuser.invalid.postalCode"));
    }
  }
  if (this.isBlankString(homePhone)) {
      errors.add("homePhone", new ActionError("stocktrack.newuser.required"));
  } else {
```

LISTING 7.1 Continued

```
        if (!this.isValidPhone(homePhone)) {
          errors.add("homePhone",
                     new ActionError("stocktrack.newuser.invalid.phone"));
        }
    }
    if (this.isBlankString(workPhone)) {
        errors.add("workPhone", new ActionError("stocktrack.newuser.required"));
    } else {
        if (!this.isValidPhone(workPhone)) {
          errors.add("workPhone",
                     new ActionError("stocktrack.newuser.invalid.phone"));
        }
    }
    return errors;
  }
  private String username;
  private String password;
  private String email;
  private String firstName;
  private String lastName;
  private String streetAddress1;
  private String streetAddress2;
  private String city;
  private String state;
  private String postalCode;
  private String homePhone;
  private String workPhone;
  private String workExt;
  private String alert;

  public String getUsername() {
    return username;
  }
  public void setUsername(String username) {
    this.username = username;
  }
  public String getPassword() {
    return password;
  }
  public void setPassword(String password) {
    this.password = password;
```

LISTING 7.1 Continued

```
  }
  public String getEmail() {
    return email;
  }
  public void setEmail(String email) {
    this.email = email;
  }
  public String getFirstName() {
    return firstName;
  }
  public void setFirstName(String firstName) {
    this.firstName = firstName;
  }
  public String getLastName() {
    return lastName;
  }
  public void setLastName(String lastName) {
    this.lastName = lastName;
  }
  public String getStreetAddress1() {
    return streetAddress1;
  }
  public void setStreetAddress1(String streetAddress1) {
    this.streetAddress1 = streetAddress1;
  }
  public String getStreetAddress2() {
    return streetAddress2;
  }
  public void setStreetAddress2(String streetAddress2) {
    this.streetAddress2 = streetAddress2;
  }
  public String getCity() {
    return city;
  }
  public void setCity(String city) {
    this.city = city;
  }
  public String getState() {
    return state;
  }
```

LISTING 7.1 Continued

```
  public void setState(String state) {
    this.state = state;
  }
  public String getPostalCode() {
    return postalCode;
  }
  public void setPostalCode(String postalCode) {
    this.postalCode = postalCode;
  }
  public String getHomePhone() {
    return homePhone;
  }
  public void setHomePhone(String homePhone) {
    this.homePhone = homePhone;
  }
  public String getWorkPhone() {
    return workPhone;
  }
  public void setWorkPhone(String workPhone) {
    this.workPhone = workPhone;
  }
  public String getWorkExt() {
    return workExt;
  }
  public void setWorkExt(String workExt) {
    this.workExt = workExt;
  }
}
```

This `ActionForm` bean (and most of the other Struts-related files in the application) were generated using the excellent Struts Wizard for JBuilder, which automatically generates `ActionForms`, `Actions`, and JSP files for Struts.

The bottom of the file can be ignored for the most part. It contains the get and set methods for the bean properties, just as in any other JavaBean. The two interesting methods of the class are `reset()` and `validate()`.

The `reset()` method is called when a form is initialized before being used by Struts. It's responsible for clearing all the bean properties back to their initial state values. This method can also be used to provide a default value for a property.

The validate() method is the real heart of an ActionForm. It looks at all the user input to the form, and makes sure that it is consistent with the data that the application requires.

You might notice that this bean does not directly extend ActionForm, but instead extends BaseForm. BaseForm is a class that extends ActionForm and provides a number of useful helper functions for validation, such as isValidPostalCode. Listing 7.2 shows the source for BaseForm.

LISTING 7.2 BaseForm.java

```
package stocktrack.struts.form;

import org.apache.struts.action.ActionForm;
import org.apache.regexp.*;
import java.util.Vector;

/**
 * <p>Title: Stock Tracking Application</p>
 * <p>Description: Example application from the book:
➥Struts - Rapid Working Knowledge</p>
 * <p>Copyright: Copyright (c) 2002</p>
 * <p>Company: </p>
 * @author James Turner and Kevin Bedell
 * @version 1.0
 */

public class BaseForm extends ActionForm {
  protected boolean  isBlankString(String str) {
      if (str == null) return true;
      return (str.length() == 0);
  }

  protected boolean isValidPostalCode(String str) {
  try {
      RE postal = new RE("\\d\\d\\d\\d\\d(\\-\\d\\d\\d\\d)?");
      return (postal.match(str));
  } catch (Exception ex) {
      ex.printStackTrace();
      return false;
  }
  }
```

LISTING 7.2 Continued

```
protected boolean isDouble(String str) {
  try {
      Double.parseDouble(str);
      return true;
  } catch (Exception ex) {
      return false;
    }
  }

  protected boolean isValidPhone(String str) {
  try {
      RE phone = new RE("\\(?\\d\\d\\d\\)? *\\-? *\\d\\d\\d *\\-? *\\d\\d\\d\\d");
      return (phone.match(str));
  } catch (Exception ex) {
      ex.printStackTrace();
      return false;
  }
  }

  protected String states[] = {"AL","AK","AS","AZ","AR","CA","CO","CT","DE",
                               "DC","FM","FL","GA","GU","HI","ID","IL","IN",
                               "IA","KS","KY","LA","ME","MH","MD","MA","MI",
                               "MN","MS","MO","MT","NE","NV","NH","NJ","NM",
                               "NY","NC","ND","MP","OH","OK","OR","PW","PA",
                               "PR","RI","SC","SD","TN","TX","UT","VT","VI",
                               "VA","WA","WV","WI","WY"};

  protected boolean isValidState(String str) {
    for (int i = 0; i < states.length; i++) {
      if (states[i].equalsIgnoreCase(str)) return true;
    }
    return false;
  }
}
```

The `validate()` method is passed two arguments: the `ActionMapping` for the action (which will be discussed in the next chapter) and the `HttpServletRequest`. In most cases, the `validate()` method needs neither of these values, but must take them to match the signature. The method returns an `ActionErrors` object, which is a collection of all the `ActionError` objects created during validation.

In this class, the method first instantiates an ActionErrors object, storing it in errors. The method proceeds to validate each property in turn. If the property doesn't validate (because of an empty required field, for example), the code creates a new ActionError object and uses the add() method on errors to associate the error with a field.

The add() method takes two arguments. The first argument should match the property name of the field as used in the form. For example, if the bean supplies the get method getUsername(), the property name that should be used on the form and as the first argument to ActionError.add should be username. This is the standard JavaBean/JSP convention.

The second argument passed to add() is an ActionError. This class is really just an error message to be passed back to the form, but it is designed so that the error messages come from the application property file instead of a fixed string. This enables nondevelopers to maintain the text of the errors messages, and also automatically makes the error messages "internationalizable" because the application property file can be customized to different locales.

Listing 7.3 shows the portion of ApplicationResources.properties that holds the error messages for this form.

LISTING 7.3 A Portion of ApplicationResources.properties

```
stocktrack.newuser.required=REQUIRED FIELD
stocktrack.newuser.invalid.phone=(NNN) NNN-NNNN
stocktrack.newuser.invalid.state=No such state
stocktrack.newuser.invalid.postalCode=NNNNN or NNNNN-NNNN
stocktrack.newuser.duplicate.user=The username you requested is already in use,
➥please try another one
```

After all the validations have been run, the validate() method returns the ActionErrors object. If it contains no errors, the controller runs the Action associated with the form. If there were validation errors, control is returned to the JSP, which is responsible for displaying the error messages.

VALIDATING BUSINESS LOGIC

Sometimes there are validations that need to run on a form, but require business logic to determine whether the field or form is valid. For example, in the create account processing, the code must determine whether the username is already in use, because it must be unique.

To be consistent with the MVC design pattern, however, you should never place business logic in an ActionForm because the ActionForm is part of the view. Views are not supposed to contain any actual knowledge of the back end. This information lives in the model.

In Struts, the Action provides the interface between the View and the Model. As you'll see in Chapter 8, "The Controller: Directing the Action," there are ways to do validations inside the Action as well as in the ActionForm.

JSP Files: The Alpha and the Omega

I call the JSP files the alpha and omega because every Struts transaction begins and ends on a JSP page. They represent the outermost layer of the view, controlling the formatting of information as it is presented to the user and (through JavaScript and other client-side scripting) providing the first level of validation to input from the user.

JSP files under Struts look much the same as normal JSP files, except that the Struts taglibs are used to provide quick access to common Struts functionality and to reduce the number of raw Java scriptlets used on the page.

JAVA SCRIPTLETS VERSUS TAGS

There's a certain amount of programmatic dogma floating around the software industry right now. The basic premise is that raw Java should never appear on a JSP page.

The primary argument is that Java confuses nonprogrammers who have to maintain the pages, and that by using tags, you avoid the risk of having stray keystrokes contaminate the logic.

In theory, I agree that whenever you can conveniently use a tag instead of a Java scriptlet, you should. However, the keyword here is *conveniently*. I've seen two or three lines of compact Java replaced with dozens of lines of tags because of someone's zeal to keep a JSP file Java-clean.

As a rule of thumb, if using tags will make a JSP file significantly longer and if the functionality needed will not be repeated enough to consider writing a custom tag, don't reject using some Java.

The JSP page fits hand and glove with the `ActionForm`; any properties that must be populated in the form bean must have corresponding form fields on the JSP, and the JSP page must be able to display any errors that occur during processing.

Again, the best perspective on how this works can be achieved by looking at a JSP file. In this case, we'll examine `newUser.jsp` (see Listing 7.4).

LISTING 7.4 `newUser.jsp`

```
<%@ taglib uri="/WEB-INF/struts-html.tld" prefix="html"%>
<%@ taglib uri="/WEB-INF/struts-logic.tld" prefix="logic"%>
<%@ taglib uri="/WEB-INF/struts-bean.tld" prefix="bean"%>
<%@ taglib uri="/WEB-INF/struts-template.tld" prefix="tmp"%>
<%@ taglib uri="/WEB-INF/stock.tld" prefix="stock"%>
<tmp:insert template="header.jsp">
<tmp:put name="title">Create a New Account</tmp:put>
</tmp:insert>
<table width="100%" BORDER="1" CELLPADDING="5"><TR>
```

LISTING 7.4 Continued

```
<TD WIDTH="250" VALIGN="TOP" HALIGN="LEFT">
<tmp:insert template="minibar.jsp"/>
</TD><TD VALIGN="TOP">
<html:errors property="org.apache.struts.action.GLOBAL_ERROR"/>
<table>
  <html:form action="/newUser.do">
  <tr>
    <td colspan="2">
      <h2>New User Registration</h2>
    </td>
  </tr>
  <tr>
    <td>username</td><td>
    <html:text property="username" maxlength="15" size="15"/>
    </td><td><html:errors property="username"/></td>
  </tr>
  <tr>
    <td>password</td><td>
     <html:text property="password"  maxlength="15" size="15"/></td>
    <td><html:errors property="password"/></td>
  </tr>
  <tr>
    <td>email</td><td>
     <html:text property="email"  maxlength="30" size="30"/></td>
    <td><html:errors property="email"/></td>
  </tr>
  <tr>
    <td>firstName</td><td>
     <html:text property="firstName" maxlength="30" size="30"/></td>
    <td><html:errors property="firstName"/></td>
  </tr>
  <tr>
    <td>lastName</td><td>
     <html:text property="lastName" maxlength="30" size="30"/></td>
    <td><html:errors property="lastName"/></td>
  </tr>
  <tr>
    <td>streetAddress1</td><td>
     <html:text property="streetAddress1" maxlength="60" size="60"/></td>
    <td><html:errors property="streetAddress1"/></td>
  </tr>
```

LISTING 7.4 Continued

```
  <tr>
    <td>streetAddress2</td><td>
      <html:text property="streetAddress2" maxlength="60" size="60"/></td>
    <td><html:errors property="streetAddress2"/></td>
  </tr>
  <tr>
    <td>city</td><td><html:text property="city" maxlength="30" size="30"/></td>
    <td><html:errors property="city"/></td>
  </tr>
  <tr>
    <td>state</td><td><html:text property="state" maxlength="2" size="2"/></td>
    <td><html:errors property="state"/></td>
  </tr>
  <tr>
    <td>postalCode</td><td>
      <html:text property="postalCode" maxlength="10" size="10"/></td>
    <td><html:errors property="postalCode"/></td>
  </tr>
  <tr>
    <td>homePhone</td><td>
      <html:text property="homePhone" maxlength="13" size="13"/></td>
    <td><html:errors property="homePhone"/></td>
  </tr>
  <tr>
    <td>workPhone</td><td>
      <html:text property="workPhone" maxlength="13"size="13"/></td>
    <td><html:errors property="workPhone"/></td>
  </tr>
  <tr>
    <td>workExt</td><td>
      <html:text property="workExt" maxlength="10" size="10"/></td>
    <td><html:errors property="workExt"/></td>
  </tr>
  <tr>
    <td colspan="2"><html:submit property="ok"/></td>
  </tr>
  </html:form>
</table>
</TD></TR></TABLE>
</body>
</html>
```

In many ways, this page is very similar to a normal HTML form that would be submitted to a CGI or servlet. As with most things, however, the devil is in the details.

To begin with, the JSP page immediately loads the taglibs for Struts, as well as a custom taglib called `stock`, which is used to generate stock quotes for the Web app.

After the tablibs are loaded, the page uses the template tags `insert` and `put` to request a copy of the standard page header (shown in Listing 7.5).

LISTING 7.5 `header.jsp`

```
<%@ taglib uri="/WEB-INF/struts-template.tld" prefix="tmp"%>
<html>
<head>
<title>
<tmp:get name="title"/>
</title>
</head>
<body>
<table width="100%">
<tr><td align="CENTER"><H1>STOCK TRACKER</H1></td></tr>
<tr><td align="CENTER">Your Insider's View to Wall Street</td></tr>
</table><P>
```

All the header does is write out a `TITLE` tag with a title string handed in to the template using the `put` tag and read using the `get` tag. It also puts a banner across the top of the Web page.

Next, `newUser.jsp` sets up a two-column table and again uses `insert` to place the contents of `minibar.jsp` (Listing 7.6) in the left-side column.

LISTING 7.6 `minibar.jsp`

```
<%@ taglib uri="/WEB-INF/struts-html.tld" prefix="html"%>
<%@ taglib uri="/WEB-INF/struts-logic.tld" prefix="logic"%>
<%@ taglib uri="/WEB-INF/struts-bean.tld" prefix="bean"%>
<%@ taglib uri="/WEB-INF/struts-template.tld" prefix="tmp"%>
<%@ taglib uri="/WEB-INF/stock.tld" prefix="stock"%>
<logic:present name="validatedUser" scope="session">
<font size="-2">Welcome back,
     <bean:write name="validatedUser" property="userFirstName"/>
<bean:write name="validatedUser" property="userLastName"/></FONT><P/>
<logic:notEmpty name="validatedUser" property="holdings" scope="session">
<font size="-2"><B>Your Portfolio</B></font>
```

LISTING 7.6 Continued

```
<TABLE WIDTH="100%"><TR><TH><font size="-2">Symbol</font></TH>
<TH align="right"><font size="-2">Holdings</font></TH>
<TH align="right"><font size="-2">Latest Quote</font></TH>
<TH align="right"><font size="-2">Current Value</font></TH></TR>
<logic:iterate id="holding" name="validatedUser" property="holdings">
<TR><TD><font size="-2">
     <bean:write name="holding" property="stock.stockSymbol"/></font></TD>
<TD align="right"><font size="-2">
     <bean:write name="holding" property="numShares"/></font></TD>
<TD align="right"><font size="-2"><stock:lastquote holding="holding"/></font></TD>
<TD align="right"><font size="-2">
     <stock:lastquote holding="holding" multiply="yes"/></font></TD></TR>
</logic:iterate>
</TABLE>
<font size="-2">You can update your portfolio by clicking
<html:link href="addTransaction.do">here</html:link></font>
</logic:notEmpty>
<logic:empty name="validatedUser" property="holdings" scope="session">
<font size="-2">You can track your portfolio by clicking
<html:link href="portfolio.do">here</html:link></font>
</logic:empty>
</logic:present>
<logic:notPresent name="validatedUser" scope="session">
<table>
  <html:form action="/login.do">
  <tr>
    <td colspan="2">
      <h2>Login Please</h2>
    </td>
  </tr>
  <logic:equal name="RESULT" scope="request" value="INVALID">
  <tr><td colspan="2">Invalid User Name or Password</td></tr>
  </logic:equal>
  <tr><TD COLSPAN="2"><html:errors property="username"/></TR>
    <TR><td><FONT SIZE="-2">Username</FONT></td>
        <td><html:text property="username"/></td></tr>
  <tr><td><html:errors property="password"/></td></tr>
    <tr><td><FONT SIZE="-2">Password</FONT></td>
        <td><html:password property="password"/></td></td>
  </tr>
  <tr>
```

LISTING 7.6 Continued

```
    <td colspan="2"><html:submit property="ok"/></td>
  </tr>
  </html:form>
  <tr><td colspan="2">
    <FONT SIZE="-2">No account?  Click
       <html:link page="/newaccount.do">here</html:link>
        to create one.</FONT></td></tr>
</table>
</logic:notPresent>
<CENTER>
<HR>
<tmp:insert template="marketupdate.jsp"/>
</CENTER>
<HR>
Selected Technology Stocks:<BR>
<FONT SIZE="-2">IBM: <stock:lastquote symbol="IBM"/>
                (<stock:dfc symbol="IBM"/>)<BR>
MSFT: <stock:lastquote symbol="MSFT"/> (<stock:dfc symbol="MSFT"/>)<BR>
</FONT>
```

The minibar is a much more complex piece of JSP/Struts. First, it checks to see whether the `validatedUser` property has been placed on the session (this is done after a successful login). If the property is there (checked using the `logic:present` tag), the JSP generates a greeting with the first and last names of the user using the `bean:write` tag to look inside the `validatedUser` bean. Next, it checks whether the user has any stocks in the portfolio using the `logic:notEmpty` tag, which displays its body only if the argument is not null or an empty collection.

The `logic:iterate` tag loops over the stocks in the holdings, and then uses some custom tags from the stock taglib to display various attributes and quotes for each stock.

If there is no current portfolio, the user is given a link to start entering one. If no one is logged in, a login form is presented instead. This form submits values to the `LoginForm`, shown in Listing 7.7.

LISTING 7.7 `LoginForm.java`

```
package stocktrack.struts.form;


import javax.servlet.http.*;
import org.apache.struts.action.ActionMapping;
import org.apache.struts.action.ActionErrors;
```

LISTING 7.7 Continued

```
import org.apache.struts.action.ActionError;
import org.apache.struts.action.ActionForm;
import stocktrack.struts.form.BaseForm;

/**
 * stocktrack.struts.form.LoginForm class.
 * this class used by Struts Framework to store data from loginForm
 *
 * struts-config declaration:
 * <form-bean name="loginForm"
 *         type="stocktrack.struts.form.LoginForm" />
 *
 * @see org.apache.struts.action.ActionForm org.apache.struts.action.ActionForm
 * Generated by StrutsWizard.
 */

public class LoginForm extends BaseForm {
  public void reset(ActionMapping mapping, HttpServletRequest request) {
    username = "";
    password = "";
  }

  public ActionErrors validate(ActionMapping mapping, HttpServletRequest request) {
    ActionErrors errors = new ActionErrors();
    if (this.isBlankString(username)) {
     errors.add("username", new ActionError("stocktrack.login.username.required"));
    }
    if (this.isBlankString(password)) {
     errors.add("password", new ActionError("stocktrack.login.password.required"));
    }
  return errors;
  }

  private String username;
  private String password;
  public String getUsername() {
    return username;
  }
  public void setUsername(String username) {
    this.username = username;
  }
```

LISTING 7.7 Continued

```
  public String getPassword() {
    return password;
  }
  public void setPassword(String password) {
    this.password = password;
  }
}
```

This form provides two validations for missing username or password. If the login fails, that is handled in the Action.

Returning to the main newUser page (Listing 7.4), you can see how the form fields, properties, and errors all tie together. At the top of the page, an `html:errors` tag looks for what are called global errors. *Global errors* are errors not associated with validations of a specific field, and are typically created in the `Action`. In this case, the `Action` will check to make sure that there is no user already with the requested username, and return a global error if there is.

Each field consists of an `html:text` tag for the property, followed by an `html:errors` tag asking for errors for that property. Using the `html:text` tag rather than a plain `INPUT` tag is important because the `html:text` tag automatically places the last value from a submit into the field if the form fails validation. Essentially, it does the opposite of a `jsp:setProperty`: It takes bean values and plops them into the form fields.

The Perils of Automatic Type Conversion

One of JSP's features is that it will automatically convert text fields from forms into a number of common data types (including `floats` and `ints`) during form submission. However, you shouldn't use this feature with Struts.

The reason is that if you use this feature, any nonnumeric value placed in this field will cause it to stick a zero in the field.

You could check to make sure that the values were nonzero in your validator (assuming that zero isn't a valid value). But, even then, when you returned to the form with the error, the field would have put in zero as the last value submitted, rather than what the user typed.

For example, if you had a field called height that was defined in your `ActionForm` as an `int`, and you typed the words **`too tall`** in the field, the property would be set to zero. If you returned to the form, the field would now have `0` in it.

So, how should you do it? By making all the properties of the form `Strings`, and doing the conversions using `NumberFormat` (or `DateFormat` and so on) after the form is submitted. This might mean that you end up with two sets of get and set methods for the same property. Listing 7.8 shows the `ActionForm` that handles form submissions from the portfolio page.

LISTING 7.8 `AddTransactionForm.java`

```
package stocktrack.struts.form;

import javax.servlet.http.*;
import org.apache.struts.action.ActionMapping;
import org.apache.struts.action.ActionErrors;
import org.apache.struts.action.ActionError;
import org.apache.struts.action.ActionForm;
import stocktrack.torque.Stock;
import java.text.SimpleDateFormat;
import stocktrack.struts.form.BaseForm;

/**
 * stocktrack.struts.form.AddTransactionForm class.
 * this class used by Struts Framework to store data from addTransactionForm
 *
 * struts-config declaration:
 * <form-bean name="addTransactionForm"
 *        type="stocktrack.struts.form.AddTransactionForm" />
 *
 * @see org.apache.struts.action.ActionForm org.apache.struts.action.ActionForm
 * Generated by StrutsWizard.
 */

public class AddTransactionForm extends BaseForm {
  public void reset(ActionMapping mapping, HttpServletRequest request) {
    symbol = "";
    date = "";
    shares = "";
    price = "";
  }

  private static SimpleDateFormat df = new SimpleDateFormat("MM-dd-yyyy");
```

LISTING 7.8 Continued

```
public ActionErrors validate(ActionMapping mapping, HttpServletRequest request) {
  ActionErrors errors = new ActionErrors();

  if (this.isBlankString(symbol)) {
    errors.add("symbol", new ActionError("addtransaction.required"));
}
  if (this.isBlankString(price)) {
    errors.add("price", new ActionError("addtransaction.required"));
} else {
  if (!this.isDouble(price)) {
    errors.add("price", new ActionError("addtransaction.invalid.price"));
  }
}
  if (this.isBlankString(shares)) {
    errors.add("shares", new ActionError("addtransaction.required"));
} else {
  if (!this.isDouble(shares)) {
    errors.add("shares", new ActionError("addtransaction.invalid.shares"));
  }
}
  try {
    if (df.parse(date) == null) {
      errors.add("symbol", new ActionError("addtransaction.invalid.date"));
    } else {
      dateAsLong = df.parse(date).getTime();
    }
  } catch (Exception ex) {
      ex.printStackTrace();
      errors.add("symbol", new ActionError("addtransaction.invalid.date"));
  }

  return errors;
}

private String symbol;
private String date;
private String shares;
private long dateAsLong;
private String price;
```

LISTING 7.8 Continued

```
  public long getDateAsLong() {
      return dateAsLong;
  }

  public String getSymbol() {
    return symbol;
  }
  public void setSymbol(String symbol) {
    this.symbol = symbol;
  }
  public String getDate() {
    return date;
  }
  public void setDate(String date) {
    this.date = date;
  }
  public String getShares() {
    return shares;
  }

  public double getSharesAsDouble() {
    return Double.parseDouble(this.shares);
  }

  public void setShares(String shares) {
    this.shares = shares;
  }
  public String getPrice() {
    return price;
  }
  public double getPriceAsDouble() {
    return Double.parseDouble(price);
  }
  public void setPrice(String price) {
    this.price = price;
  }
}
```

This `ActionForm` shows two different ways you can handle this issue. The stock price and number of shares properties have get and set methods for the `String` version of the value, but also have a get method that returns the `String` converted into a `double`.

The transaction date property has a parallel `long` property that stores the date as a `long`. But instead of doing the conversion on-the-fly when requested, the date is converted at the same time as it is being validated and is stored for future use.

The `html:errors` Tag

The `html:errors` tag can be used in two different ways. If used without a `property` attribute, it will display all the errors for the form. When used with the attribute, it displays only the errors for that specific property. There are two special values you can put into your `ApplicationResources.properties` file to control how these errors are displayed:

```
errors.header=<FONT COLOR="#ff0000">

errors.footer=</BR></FONT>
```

The value of `errors.header` is placed just before the error; the `footer` is placed just after the error. The ones shown here put the error in red.

Internationalization

You've already seen how the error messages returned from a form validation can be internationalized. The same can be done with the contents of a JSP file.

The `bean:message` tag looks for a value in the specified message bundle (your friend `ApplicationResources.properties` by default) and sends it to the browser, and can even take up to five parameterized arguments. Listing 7.9 shows `minibar.jsp` rewritten to support international text.

LISTING 7.9 `minibar.jsp` Rewritten

```
<%@ taglib uri="/WEB-INF/struts-html.tld" prefix="html"%>
<%@ taglib uri="/WEB-INF/struts-logic.tld" prefix="logic"%>
<%@ taglib uri="/WEB-INF/struts-bean.tld" prefix="bean"%>
<%@ taglib uri="/WEB-INF/struts-template.tld" prefix="tmp"%>
<%@ taglib uri="/WEB-INF/stock.tld" prefix="stock"%>
<logic:present name="validatedUser" scope="session">
<font size="-2">
<bean:message key="stocktrack.minibar.welcomeback"/>
<bean:write name="validatedUser" property="userFirstName"/>
<bean:write name="validatedUser" property="userLastName"/>
</FONT><P/>
<logic:notEmpty name="validatedUser" property="holdings" scope="session">
<font size="-2"><B><bean:message key="stocktrack.minibar.yourport"/></B></font>
```

LISTING 7.9 Continued

```
<TABLE WIDTH="100%"><TR><TH><font size="-2">
     <bean:message key="stocktrack.minibar.symbol"/></font></TH>
<TH align="right"><font size="-2">
      <bean:message key="stocktrack.minibar.holdings"/></font></TH>
<TH align="right"><font size="-2">
      <bean:message key="stocktrack.minibar.latestquote"/></font></TH>
<TH align="right"><font size="-2">
      <bean:message key="stocktrack.minibar.currentvalue"/></font></TH></TR>
<logic:iterate id="holding" name="validatedUser" property="holdings">
<TR><TD><font size="-2">
       <bean:write name="holding" property="stock.stockSymbol"/></font></TD>
<TD align="right"><font size="-2">
       <bean:write name="holding" property="numShares"/></font></TD>
<TD align="right"><font size="-2">
       <stock:lastquote holding="holding"/></font></TD>
<TD align="right"><font size="-2">
       <stock:lastquote holding="holding" multiply="yes"/></font></TD></TR>
</logic:iterate>
</TABLE>
<font size="-2">
<bean:message key="stocktrack.minibar.updatemessage"/>
<html:link href="addTransaction.do"/><bean:message key="stocktrack.minibar.here"/>
</html:link>
</font>
</logic:notEmpty>
<logic:empty name="validatedUser" property="holdings" scope="session">
<font size="-2">
<bean:message key="stocktrack.minibar.updatemessage"/>
<html:link href="addTransaction.do"/><bean:message key="stocktrack.minibar.here"/>
</html:link>
</font>
</logic:empty>
</logic:present>
<logic:notPresent name="validatedUser" scope="session">
<table>
  <html:form action="/login.do">
  <tr>
    <td colspan="2">
      <h2><bean:message key="stocktrack.minibar.loginplease"/></h2>
    </td>
  </tr>
```

LISTING 7.9 Continued

```
  <tr><td colspan="2">
     <html:errors property="org.apache.struts.action.GLOBAL_ERROR"/>
  </td></tr>
  <tr><TD COLSPAN="2"><html:errors property="username"/></TR>
    <TR><td><FONT SIZE="-2">
      <bean:message key="stocktrack.minibar.username"/></FONT>
    </td><td><html:text property="username"/></td></tr>
  <tr><td><html:errors property="password"/></td></tr>
    <tr><td><FONT SIZE="-2">
       <bean:message key="stocktrack.minibar.password"/></FONT>
    </td><td><html:password property="password"/></td></td>
  </tr>
  <tr>
    <td colspan="2"><html:submit property="ok"/></td>
  </tr>
  </html:form>
  <tr><td colspan="2">
  <FONT SIZE="-2">
  <bean:message key="stocktrack.minibar.noaccount1"/>
   <html:link href="/newaccount.do"/>
      <bean:message key="stocktrack.minibar.here"/></html:link>
  <bean:message key="stocktrack.minibar.noaccount2"/>
</FONT></td></tr>
</table>
</logic:notPresent>
<CENTER>
<HR>
<tmp:insert template="marketupdate.jsp"/>
</CENTER>
<HR>
<bean:message key="stocktrack.minibar.techstocks"/>:<BR>
<FONT SIZE="-2">IBM: <stock:lastquote symbol="IBM"/>
               (<stock:dfc symbol="IBM"/>)<BR>
MSFT: <stock:lastquote symbol="MSFT"/> (<stock:dfc symbol="MSFT"/>)<BR>
</FONT>
```

The additions to the resource bundle to support these new messages are

```
stocktrack.minibar.welcomeback=Welcome back,
stocktrack.minibar.yourport=Your Portfolio
stocktrack.minibar.symbol=Symbol
```

```
stocktrack.minibar.holdings=Holdings
stocktrack.minibar.latestquote=Lastest Quote
stocktrack.minibar.currentvalue=Current Value
stocktrack.minibar.updatemessage=You can update your portfolio by clicking
stocktrack.minibar.loginplease=Log In Please
stocktrack.minibar.username=Username
stocktrack.minibar.password=Password
stocktrack.minibar.noaccount1=No account?  Click
stocktrack.minibar.here=here
stocktrack.minibar.noaccount2=to create one.
stocktrack.minibar.techstocks=Selected Technology Stocks
```

Conclusions

The ActionForm and JSP page perform the duties of the view under Struts. The ActionForm is responsible for validation of the input from forms, and is handed off to the Action for actual processing with the model.

The ActionForm should contain no business logic, and should treat all of the input fields as Strings. The ActionErrors and ActionError classes are used to return validation errors from the ActionForm. If no errors are found, control passes to the Action.

The JSP page uses the html:text (and other) tags to tie the form to the ActionForm. It also can use the html:errors tag to display validation errors. The bean:message tag allows JSP pages to be internationalized.

8 The Controller: Directing the Action

IN THIS CHAPTER

Getting data back and forth to the user is great, but at some point your code has to actually act on that data and figure out what to do next. This is the job of the Controller.

In Struts, the Controller is implemented in two pieces: the `Action` classes and Struts itself. The `Action` receives user input, coordinates access to remote systems or data stores, implements business logic, and decides what View component should be displayed to the user next. Struts, which is configured with the `struts-config.xml` file, takes care of actually dispatching to that next page.

In this chapter, you'll see how to use the controller to handle control flow and set error conditions related to business logic. You'll also see how to combine data from two forms into a single final action.

The `Action` Class

The `Action` can be very simple or very complicated. For example, when a user clicks on the create new account button, control is passed to `NewAccountAction` (shown in Listing 8.1).

LISTING 8.1 NewAccountAction.java

```
package stocktrack.struts.action;

import java.io.IOException;
import javax.servlet.ServletException;
import javax.servlet.http.*;
import org.apache.struts.action.ActionMapping;
import org.apache.struts.action.ActionForward;
import org.apache.struts.action.ActionForm;
import org.apache.struts.action.Action;

/**
 * stocktrack.struts.action.IndexAction class.
 * this class used by Struts Framework process the
 * stocktrack.struts.form.BlankForm form.
 * - method invoked by HTTP request is perform(....)
 * - form name is blankForm
 * - input page is /home.jsp
 * - scope name is request
 * - path for this action is /newaccount
 *
 * struts-config declaration:
 * <action name="blankForm"
 *         path="/newaccount"
 *         type="stocktrack.struts.action.NewAccountAction"
 *         input="/home.jsp"
 *         scope="request"
 *         validate="true" >
 *            <!-- yours forwards -->
 * </action>
 *
 * @see org.apache.struts.action.Action org.apache.struts.action.Action
 * Generated by StrutsWizard.
 */

public class NewAccountAction extends org.apache.struts.action.Action {
  public ActionForward perform(ActionMapping mapping, ActionForm form,
                               HttpServletRequest request,
                               HttpServletResponse response)
                        throws IOException, ServletException {
    return mapping.findForward("newUser");
  }
}
```

As you can see, all the `perform()` method of this class does is to immediately tell Struts to go to the page identified by the tag `newUser` in the configuration file.

NEVER USE REFERENCES TO JSP FILES

One of the strengths of Struts is that filenames are referenced in only one place: the `struts-config.xml` file. Everywhere else, pages are referenced by logical names that are mapped to the actual JSP. One big advantage of this is that if a file is renamed or moved to a different directory, only one file must be changed.

So, given this imperative, how do you do a simple page-to-page link? You've just seen the solution. You create a blank form (which can be reused for all the interpage transitions), and a small `Action` that simply dispatches to the page you want to go to.

Then, instead of saying `<html:link HREF="page.jsp/">`, you say `<html:link HREF="page.do"/>`. If you've configured Struts to associate `page` with the blank form and new `Action` you've created, you'll be delivered to the page.

Another benefit of this approach is that if you decide in the future that you want to restrict access to this page, you've already got an `Action` set up to check the permissions.

If you don't need the full power of an `Action`, Struts will also enable you to map a `.do` URI directly to a JSP page by using the `forward=` directive in an `action` tag inside the `struts-config.xml` file.

This type of ultra-simple `Action` is the exception, however. Most `Action` classes do a significant piece of work. For example, Listing 8.2 shows the `Action` that implements new user creation.

LISTING 8.2 `NewUserAction.java`

```
package stocktrack.struts.action;

import java.io.IOException;
import javax.servlet.ServletException;
import javax.servlet.http.*;
import org.apache.struts.action.ActionMapping;
import org.apache.struts.action.ActionForward;
import org.apache.struts.action.ActionForm;
import org.apache.struts.action.ActionErrors;
import org.apache.struts.action.ActionError;
import org.apache.struts.action.Action;
import stocktrack.torque.*;
import stocktrack.struts.form.NewUserForm;

/**
 * stocktrack.struts.action.NewUserAction class.
 * this class used by Struts Framework process the
```

LISTING 8.2 Continued

```
 * stocktrack.struts.form.NewUserForm form.
 * - method invoked by HTTP request is perform(....)
 * - form name is newUserForm
 * - input page is newUser.jsp
 * - scope name is request
 * - path for this action is /newuser
 *
 * struts-config declaration:
 * <action name="newUserForm"
 *         path="/newuser"
 *         type="stocktrack.struts.action.NewUserAction"
 *         input="newUser.jsp"
 *         scope="request"
 *         validate="true" >
 *            <!-- yours forwards -->
 * </action>
 *
 * @see org.apache.struts.action.Action org.apache.struts.action.Action
 * Generated by StrutsWizard.
 */

public class NewUserAction extends org.apache.struts.action.Action {
  public ActionForward perform(ActionMapping mapping, ActionForm form,
                               HttpServletRequest request,
                               HttpServletResponse response)
                               throws IOException, ServletException {
      NewUserForm uf = (NewUserForm) form;
      try {
        User u = UserPeer.findUserByUsername(uf.getUsername());
        if (u != null) {
          ActionErrors errors = new ActionErrors();
          errors.add(ActionErrors.GLOBAL_ERROR,
                     new ActionError("stocktrack.newuser.duplicate.user"));
          this.saveErrors(request, errors);
          return mapping.getInputForward();
        }
        u = new User();
        u.setUserEmailAddress(uf.getEmail());
        u.setUserFirstName(uf.getFirstName());
        u.setUserLastName(uf.getLastName());
        u.setUserPassword(uf.getPassword());
```

LISTING 8.2 Continued

```
        u.setUserUsername(uf.getUsername());
        Address a = new Address();
        a.setAddressStreet1(uf.getStreetAddress1());
        a.setAddressStreet2(uf.getStreetAddress2());
        a.setAddressCity(uf.getCity());
        a.setAddressState(uf.getState());
        a.setAddressPostalCode(uf.getPostalCode());
        a.setAddressWorkPhone(uf.getWorkPhone());
        a.setAddressWorkExt(uf.getWorkExt());
        a.setAddressHomePhone(uf.getHomePhone());
        a.save();
        u.setAddress(a);
        u.save();
        request.getSession().setAttribute(stocktrack.Constants.
➥VALIDATED_USER, u);
        return mapping.findForward("home");
      }
      catch (Exception ex) {
        ex.printStackTrace();
        return mapping.findForward("error");
      }
  }
}
```

The first thing most `Actions` do in their `perform()` method is to cast the generic `ActionForm` argument to the actual class of the form that is being submitted to it. This allows the method to gain access to the properties of the form.

Because you don't want the user to create an account if someone is already using that username, the next thing the method does is to call the model for the user to ask whether there is already such an account.

If there is, the method creates a new `ActionErrors` and `ActionError`, just as an `ActionForm` `validate()` method would. Because you're no longer in the `validate()` method, you need to use the `saveErrors` call to add the errors, so that the view will see them correctly when it redisplays the form. Finally, the code must redirect back to the form. Because a single `Action` could be used by several forms, the `getInputForward` call makes sure that control is returned to the form that actually did the submit.

Assuming that there's no username conflict, the model is used to create a `User` and `Address`. If things go well, the `Action` then returns an `ActionForward` that causes the Controller to return to the home page. If an exception is thrown for some reason, such as a database error, the Controller is directed to go to a general error page.

Accessing the Session and Other Form Beans

Sometimes, you need to get a handle on the `Session` during `Action` processing. Fortunately, it's easy to get at. All you need to do is to use `request.getSession()`. After you have a handle on the session, you can use `getAttribute` and `setAttribute` to gain access to session properties.

In more complex applications, you'll commonly have several pages of input awaiting processing. For example, you could decide that the user creation page is too long and should be broken down into two pages. To do this, you would begin by dividing the JSP form into two pieces, as shown in Listings 8.3 and 8.4.

LISTING 8.3 `newUserName.jsp`

```
<%@ taglib uri="/WEB-INF/struts-html.tld" prefix="html"%>
<%@ taglib uri="/WEB-INF/struts-logic.tld" prefix="logic"%>
<%@ taglib uri="/WEB-INF/struts-bean.tld" prefix="bean"%>
<%@ taglib uri="/WEB-INF/struts-template.tld" prefix="tmp"%>
<%@ taglib uri="/WEB-INF/stock.tld" prefix="stock"%>
<tmp:insert template="header.jsp">
<tmp:put name="title">Create a New Account</tmp:put>
</tmp:insert>
<table width="100%" BORDER="1" CELLPADDING="5">
    <TR><TD WIDTH="250" VALIGN="TOP" HALIGN="LEFT">
<tmp:insert template="minibar.jsp"/>
</TD><TD VALIGN="TOP">
        <html:errors property="org.apache.struts.action.GLOBAL_ERROR"/>
<table>
  <html:form action="/newUserName.do">
  <tr>
    <td colspan="2">
      <h2>New User Registration (Part 1)</h2>
    </td>
  </tr>
  <tr>
    <td>username</td>
    <td><html:text property="username" maxlength="15" size="15"/>
    </td><td><html:errors property="username"/></td>
  </tr>
  <tr>
    <td>password</td>
    <td><html:text property="password"  maxlength="15" size="15"/></td>
    <td><html:errors property="password"/></td>
  </tr>
```

LISTING 8.3 Continued

```
  <tr>
    <td>email</td><td><html:text property="email"  maxlength="30" size="30"/></td>
    <td><html:errors property="email"/></td>
  </tr>
  <tr>
    <td>firstName</td>
    <td><html:text property="firstName" maxlength="30" size="30"/></td>
    <td><html:errors property="firstName"/></td>
  </tr>
  <tr>
    <td>lastName</td>
    <td><html:text property="lastName" maxlength="30" size="30"/></td>
    <td><html:errors property="lastName"/></td>
  </tr>
  <tr>
    <td colspan="2"><html:submit property="ok"/></td>
  </tr>
  </html:form>
</table>
</TD></TR></TABLE>
</body>
</html>
```

LISTING 8.4 newUserAddress.jsp

```
<%@ taglib uri="/WEB-INF/struts-html.tld" prefix="html"%>
<%@ taglib uri="/WEB-INF/struts-logic.tld" prefix="logic"%>
<%@ taglib uri="/WEB-INF/struts-bean.tld" prefix="bean"%>
<%@ taglib uri="/WEB-INF/struts-template.tld" prefix="tmp"%>
<%@ taglib uri="/WEB-INF/stock.tld" prefix="stock"%>
<tmp:insert template="header.jsp">
<tmp:put name="title">Create a New Account</tmp:put>
</tmp:insert>
<table width="100%" BORDER="1" CELLPADDING="5"><TR>
    <TD WIDTH="250" VALIGN="TOP" HALIGN="LEFT">
<tmp:insert template="minibar.jsp"/>
</TD><TD VALIGN="TOP">
   <html:errors property="org.apache.struts.action.GLOBAL_ERROR"/>
<table>
  <html:form action="/newUserAddress.do">
```

LISTING 8.4 Continued

```
<tr>
  <td colspan="2">
    <h2>New User Registration (Part 2)</h2>
  </td>
</tr>
<tr>
  <td>streetAddress1</td><td><html:text property="streetAddress1"
                                  maxlength="60" size="60"/></td>
  <td><html:errors property="streetAddress1"/></td>
</tr>
<tr>
  <td>streetAddress2</td><td><html:text property="streetAddress2"
                                  maxlength="60" size="60"/></td>
  <td><html:errors property="streetAddress2"/></td>
</tr>
<tr>
  <td>city</td><td><html:text property="city" maxlength="30" size="30"/></td>
  <td><html:errors property="city"/></td>
</tr>
<tr>
  <td>state</td><td><html:text property="state" maxlength="2" size="2"/></td>
  <td><html:errors property="state"/></td>
</tr>
<tr>
  <td>postalCode</td><td><html:text property="postalCode"
                              maxlength="10" size="10"/></td>
  <td><html:errors property="postalCode"/></td>
</tr>
<tr>
  <td>homePhone</td><td><html:text property="homePhone"
                             maxlength="13" size="13"/></td>
  <td><html:errors property="homePhone"/></td>
</tr>
<tr>
  <td>workPhone</td><td><html:text property="workPhone"
                             maxlength="13"size="13"/></td>
  <td><html:errors property="workPhone"/></td>
</tr>
<tr>
  <td>workExt</td><td><html:text property="workExt"
                           maxlength="10" size="10"/></td>
```

LISTING 8.4 Continued

```
    <td><html:errors property="workExt"/></td>
  </tr>
  <tr>
    <td colspan="2"><html:submit property="ok"/></td>
  </tr>
  </html:form>
</table>
</TD></TR></TABLE>
</body>
</html>
```

These are essentially the same as before, only broken into two pieces. The actions of the forms have also been changed to `newUserName.do` and `newUserAddress.do`.

Next, the `ActionForms` must also be broken in half (Listings 8.5 and 8.6).

LISTING 8.5 `NewUserNameForm.java`

```
package stocktrack.struts.form;

import javax.servlet.http.*;
import org.apache.struts.action.ActionMapping;
import org.apache.struts.action.ActionErrors;
import org.apache.struts.action.ActionError;
import org.apache.struts.action.ActionForm;
import stocktrack.struts.form.BaseForm;

/**
 * stocktrack.struts.form.NewUserNameForm class.
 * this class used by Struts Framework to store data from newUserForm
 *
 * struts-config declaration:
 * <form-bean name="newUserNameForm"
 *         type="stocktrack.struts.form.NewUserNameForm" />
 *
 * @see org.apache.struts.action.ActionForm org.apache.struts.action.ActionForm
 * Generated by StrutsWizard.
 */

public class NewUserNameForm extends BaseForm {
  public void reset(ActionMapping mapping, HttpServletRequest request) {
    username = "";
```

LISTING 8.5 Continued

```
    password = "";
    firstName = "";
    lastName = "";
  }
  public ActionErrors validate(ActionMapping mapping, HttpServletRequest request) {
    ActionErrors errors = new ActionErrors();
    if (this.isBlankString(username)) {
        errors.add("username", new ActionError("stocktrack.newuser.required"));
    }
    if (this.isBlankString(password)) {
        errors.add("password", new ActionError("stocktrack.newuser.required"));
    }
    if (this.isBlankString(email)) {
        errors.add("email", new ActionError("stocktrack.newuser.required"));
    } else {
        if (email.indexOf("@") == -1) {
        errors.add("email", new ActionError("stocktrack.newuser.invalid.email"));
        }
    }
    if (this.isBlankString(firstName)) {
        errors.add("firstName", new ActionError("stocktrack.newuser.required"));
    }
    if (this.isBlankString(lastName)) {
        errors.add("lastName", new ActionError("stocktrack.newuser.required"));
    }
    return errors;
  }
  private String username;
  private String password;
  private String email;
  private String firstName;
  private String lastName;

  public String getUsername() {
    return username;
  }
  public void setUsername(String username) {
    this.username = username;
  }
  public String getPassword() {
    return password;
  }
```

LISTING 8.5 Continued

```
  public void setPassword(String password) {
    this.password = password;
  }
  public String getEmail() {
    return email;
  }
  public void setEmail(String email) {
    this.email = email;
  }
  public String getFirstName() {
    return firstName;
  }
  public void setFirstName(String firstName) {
    this.firstName = firstName;
  }
  public String getLastName() {
    return lastName;
  }
  public void setLastName(String lastName) {
    this.lastName = lastName;
  }
}
```

LISTING 8.6 NewUserAddressForm.java

```
package stocktrack.struts.form;

import javax.servlet.http.*;
import org.apache.struts.action.ActionMapping;
import org.apache.struts.action.ActionErrors;
import org.apache.struts.action.ActionError;
import org.apache.struts.action.ActionForm;
import stocktrack.struts.form.BaseForm;

/**
 * stocktrack.struts.form.NewUserAddressForm class.
 * this class used by Struts Framework to store data from newUserAddressForm
 *
 * struts-config declaration:
 * <form-bean name="newUserAddressForm"
 *        type="stocktrack.struts.form.NewUserAddressForm" />
 *
```

LISTING 8.6 Continued

```
 * @see org.apache.struts.action.ActionForm org.apache.struts.action.ActionForm
 * Generated by StrutsWizard.
 */

public class NewUserAddressForm extends BaseForm {
  public void reset(ActionMapping mapping, HttpServletRequest request) {
    streetAddress1 = "";
    streetAddress2 = "";
    city = "";
    state = "";
    postalCode = "";
    homePhone = "";
    workPhone = "";
    workExt = "";
  }
  public ActionErrors validate(ActionMapping mapping, HttpServletRequest request) {
    ActionErrors errors = new ActionErrors();
    if (this.isBlankString(streetAddress1)) {
        errors.add("streetAddress1",
                   new ActionError("stocktrack.newuser.required"));
    }
    if (this.isBlankString(city)) {
        errors.add("city", new ActionError("stocktrack.newuser.required"));
   }
    if (this.isBlankString(state)) {
        errors.add("state", new ActionError("stocktrack.newuser.required"));
   } else {
      if (!this.isValidState(state)) {
        errors.add("state", new ActionError("stocktrack.newuser.invalid.state"));
      }
   }
    if (this.isBlankString(postalCode)) {
        errors.add("postalCode", new ActionError("stocktrack.newuser.required"));
    } else {
      if (!this.isValidPostalCode(postalCode)) {
          errors.add("postalCode",
                     new ActionError("stocktrack.newuser.invalid.postalCode"));
      }
    }
    if (this.isBlankString(homePhone)) {
        errors.add("homePhone", new ActionError("stocktrack.newuser.required"));
```

LISTING 8.6 Continued

```
    } else {
        if (!this.isValidPhone(homePhone)) {
          errors.add("homePhone",
                      new ActionError("stocktrack.newuser.invalid.phone"));
        }
    }
    if (this.isBlankString(workPhone)) {
        errors.add("workPhone", new ActionError("stocktrack.newuser.required"));
    } else {
        if (!this.isValidPhone(workPhone)) {
          errors.add("workPhone",
                       new ActionError("stocktrack.newuser.invalid.phone"));
        }
    }
    return errors;
  }
  private String streetAddress1;
  private String streetAddress2;
  private String city;
  private String state;
  private String postalCode;
  private String homePhone;
  private String workPhone;
  private String workExt;
  public String getStreetAddress1() {
    return streetAddress1;
  }
  public void setStreetAddress1(String streetAddress1) {
    this.streetAddress1 = streetAddress1;
  }
  public String getStreetAddress2() {
    return streetAddress2;
  }
  public void setStreetAddress2(String streetAddress2) {
    this.streetAddress2 = streetAddress2;
  }
  public String getCity() {
    return city;
  }
  public void setCity(String city) {
    this.city = city;
  }
```

LISTING 8.6 Continued

```
  public String getState() {
    return state;
  }
  public void setState(String state) {
    this.state = state;
  }
  public String getPostalCode() {
    return postalCode;
  }
  public void setPostalCode(String postalCode) {
    this.postalCode = postalCode;
  }
  public String getHomePhone() {
    return homePhone;
  }
  public void setHomePhone(String homePhone) {
    this.homePhone = homePhone;
  }
  public String getWorkPhone() {
    return workPhone;
  }
  public void setWorkPhone(String workPhone) {
    this.workPhone = workPhone;
  }
  public String getWorkExt() {
    return workExt;
  }
  public void setWorkExt(String workExt) {
    this.workExt = workExt;
  }
}
```

Again, you've simply split the form beans in half, and made sure that the validations validate only for the properties of the form in question.

AN ALTERNATIVE TO SPLITTING THE FORM BEAN

One of the interesting things about co-authoring a book is that sometimes the authors have two different approaches to the same problem. For example, my (James) initial impulse when breaking the form in two was to split the `ActionForm` bean as well.

Kevin, on the other hand, says he would have used a single ActionForm, had the validate() method check for a property called action that was set by a hidden form field in the JSP, and choose which set of fields to validate based on the value of this property. He points out that the advantage of this approach is that you can easily move fields from one form to another by just changing the validate code, and that it lets the validate code for the second form have easy access to the data from the first form (if, for example, a validation on the second page is dependent on a value set on the first).

And thus are the differences in style that make life interesting...

Finally, the interesting part of the exercise. The Action classes also are broken in two, as shown in Listings 8.7 and 8.8.

LISTING 8.7 NewUserNameAction.java

```
package stocktrack.struts.action;

import java.io.IOException;
import javax.servlet.ServletException;
import javax.servlet.http.*;
import org.apache.struts.action.ActionMapping;
import org.apache.struts.action.ActionForward;
import org.apache.struts.action.ActionForm;
import org.apache.struts.action.ActionErrors;
import org.apache.struts.action.ActionError;
import org.apache.struts.action.Action;
import stocktrack.torque.*;
import stocktrack.struts.form.NewUserNameForm;

/**
 * stocktrack.struts.action.NewUserNameAction class.
 * this class used by Struts Framework process the
 * stocktrack.struts.form.NewUserForm form.
 * - method invoked by HTTP request is perform(....)
 * - form name is newUserNameForm
 * - input page is newUserName.jsp
 * - scope name is request
 * - path for this action is /newusername
 *
 * struts-config declaration:
 * <action name="newUserNameForm"
 *         path="/newusername"
 *         type="stocktrack.struts.action.NewUserNameAction"
 *         input="newUserName.jsp"
```

LISTING 8.7 Continued

```
 *         scope="session"
 *         validate="true" >
 *            <!-- yours forwards -->
 * </action>
 *
 * @see org.apache.struts.action.Action org.apache.struts.action.Action
 * Generated by StrutsWizard.
 */

public class NewUserNameAction extends org.apache.struts.action.Action {
  public ActionForward perform(ActionMapping mapping, ActionForm form,
                               HttpServletRequest request,
                               HttpServletResponse response)
           throws IOException, ServletException {
       return mapping.findForward("newUserAddress");
  }
}
```

The first Action, which handles input from the name form, simply passes control on to the second screen, which has the address fields. Because the form is of scope "session", the form and the data it holds will be held as a session property until they're explicitly removed or the session terminates. This means that it will be available to the Action that handles the address form submission, allowing the data to be merged into a single record.

LISTING 8.8 NewUserAddressAction.java

```
package stocktrack.struts.action;

import java.io.IOException;
import javax.servlet.ServletException;
import javax.servlet.http.*;
import org.apache.struts.action.ActionMapping;
import org.apache.struts.action.ActionForward;
import org.apache.struts.action.ActionForm;
import org.apache.struts.action.ActionErrors;
import org.apache.struts.action.ActionError;
import org.apache.struts.action.Action;
import stocktrack.torque.*;
import stocktrack.struts.form.NewUserNameForm;
import stocktrack.struts.form.NewUserAddressForm;
```

LISTING 8.8 Continued

```
/**
 * stocktrack.struts.action.NewUserAddressAction class.
 * this class used by Struts Framework process the
 * stocktrack.struts.form.NewUserForm form.
 * - method invoked by HTTP request is perform(....)
 * - form name is newUserAddressForm
 * - input page is newUserAddress.jsp
 * - scope name is request
 * - path for this action is /newusername
 *
 * struts-config declaration:
 * <action name="newUserAddressForm"
 *         path="/newuseraddress"
 *         type="stocktrack.struts.action.NewUserAddressAction"
 *         input="newUserAddress.jsp"
 *         scope="session"
 *         validate="true" >
 *            <!-- yours forwards -->
 * </action>
 *
 * @see org.apache.struts.action.Action org.apache.struts.action.Action
 * Generated by StrutsWizard.
 */

public class NewUserAddressAction extends org.apache.struts.action.Action {
  public ActionForward perform(ActionMapping mapping,
                               ActionForm form,
                               HttpServletRequest request,
                               HttpServletResponse response)
                  throws IOException, ServletException {
      NewUserAddressForm uf = (NewUserAddressForm) form;
      NewUserNameForm nf =
        (NewUserNameForm) request.getSession().getAttribute("newUserNameForm");
      if (nf == null) return mapping.findForward("newUserName");
      try {
        User u = UserPeer.findUserByUsername(nf.getUsername());
        if (u != null) {
          ActionErrors errors = new ActionErrors();
          errors.add(ActionErrors.GLOBAL_ERROR,
                     new ActionError("stocktrack.newuser.duplicate.user"));
```

LISTING 8.8 Continued

```
          this.saveErrors(request, errors);
          return mapping.findForward("newUserName");
        }
        u = new User();
        u.setUserEmailAddress(nf.getEmail());
        u.setUserFirstName(nf.getFirstName());
        u.setUserLastName(nf.getLastName());
        u.setUserPassword(nf.getPassword());
        u.setUserUsername(nf.getUsername());
        Address a = new Address();
        a.setAddressStreet1(uf.getStreetAddress1());
        a.setAddressStreet2(uf.getStreetAddress2());
        a.setAddressCity(uf.getCity());
        a.setAddressState(uf.getState());
        a.setAddressPostalCode(uf.getPostalCode());
        a.setAddressWorkPhone(uf.getWorkPhone());
        a.setAddressWorkExt(uf.getWorkExt());
        a.setAddressHomePhone(uf.getHomePhone());
        a.save();
        u.setAddress(a);
        u.save();
        request.getSession().setAttribute(stocktrack.Constants.VALIDATED_USER, u);
        request.getSession().setAttribute("newUserNameForm", null);
        request.getSession().setAttribute("newUserAddressForm", null);
        return mapping.findForward("home");
      }
      catch (Exception ex) {
        ex.printStackTrace();
        return mapping.findForward("error");
      }
  }
}
```

The `Action` for the address form is much meatier. First, it checks to make sure that there has been a name form filled out. The name form was defined in `struts-config.xml` to have session scope, which means that it was stored in the `session` object as an attribute. The attribute `name` is the name of the form as defined in the Struts configuration.

In other words, unlike your previous forms, which kept the `ActionForm` around only long enough to get it back to the JSP form if there was a validation error (or to the

Action if it was valid), you'll now keep the contents of the form around as a session property until it is explicitly removed.

You need to check whether the property is there because someone could conceivably type the URL for the second form into the browser (or bookmark it), which will cause problems when the code looks for those form values. If the property isn't there, the Controller is told to send the user over to the first page of the form.

Next, the check for duplicate users is made. Because the browser just came from the address form but the username is on the name form, the controller must redirect flow back to the name form. For that reason, an explicit `findForward` is used rather than a `getInputForward`.

The only other difference between the remainder of this code and the original `Action` class is that this class needs to take input from two different `ActionForms` to populate the model. Also, after the form successfully submits, the session properties for the two forms are set to null so that none of the data will appear the next time the forms are used. (Alternatively, you could call the `reset` methods on both forms, which would also clear the data out.)

Figures 8.1 and 8.2 show this new pair of forms in operation. From the user's perspective, the only difference is that there are now two forms instead of a single one.

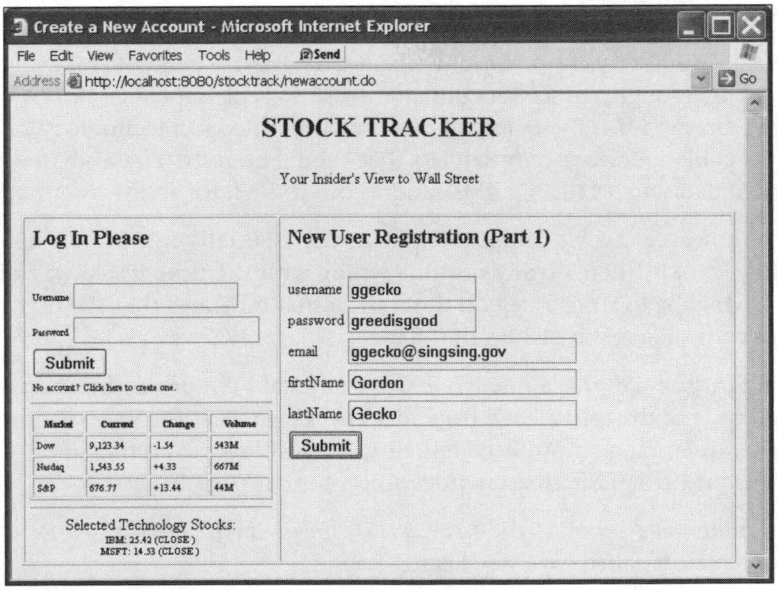

FIGURE 8.1 Submitting data to `newUserName.jsp`.

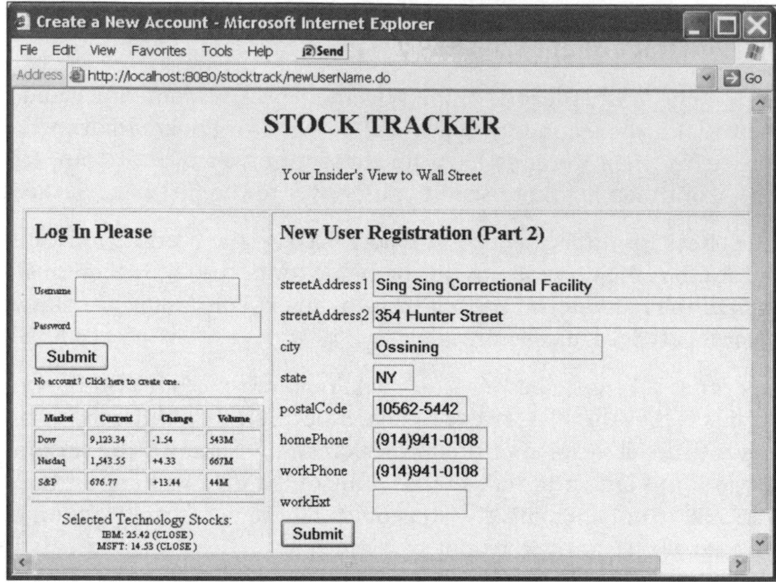

FIGURE 8.2 The second part of creating a user, `newUserAddress.jsp`.

User Validation and Struts

There are several ways to perform user validation and access control using Struts. One way is through the servlet container itself. Recent implementations of JSP servers (Tomcat 4.0.1, for example) offer an authentication technology called Realms. Realms enables you to specify servlets that should be restricted, and attach to a variety of datasources (JDBC, XML, and so on) to look up access information.

Realms, however, is a bit complicated to set up, especially in a sample application like this. Frankly, there's really nothing wrong with the time-tested way of doing things, which is to store a flag on the session that indicates that the user has logged in, and control access based on that flag.

In fact, Struts makes this approach easier. In model I JSP processing, you need to include code at the top of each page that checks whether the user is allowed to view the page. In Struts, you can decouple this business logic from the view by putting the check in the `Action` that provides access to that page.

For example, take a look at the `Action` class for the action that provides access to the portfolio maintenance page (see Listing 8.9).

LISTING 8.9 PortfolioAction.java

```
package stocktrack.struts.action;

import java.io.IOException;
import javax.servlet.ServletException;
import javax.servlet.http.*;
import org.apache.struts.action.ActionMapping;
import org.apache.struts.action.ActionForward;
import org.apache.struts.action.ActionForm;
import org.apache.struts.action.Action;

/**
 * stocktrack.struts.action.IndexAction class.
 * this class used by Struts Framework process the
 * stocktrack.struts.form.BlankForm form.
 * - method invoked by HTTP request is perform(....)
 * - form name is blankForm
 * - input page is /inde1x.jsp
 * - scope name is request
 * - path for this action is /index
 *
 * struts-config declaration:
 * <action name="blankForm"
 *         path="/index"
 *         type="stocktrack.struts.action.IndexAction"
 *         input="/index.jsp"
 *         scope="request"
 *         validate="true" >
 *            <!-- yours forwards -->
 * </action>
 *
 * @see org.apache.struts.action.Action org.apache.struts.action.Action
 * Generated by StrutsWizard.
 */

public class PortfolioAction extends org.apache.struts.action.Action {
  public ActionForward perform(ActionMapping mapping,
                               ActionForm form,
                               HttpServletRequest request,
                               HttpServletResponse response)
     throws IOException, ServletException {
```

LISTING 8.9 Continued

```
    if (request.getSession().getAttribute(stocktrack.Constants.VALIDATED_USER)
                                                                   == null) {
      return mapping.findForward("home");
    }
    return mapping.findForward("portfolio");
  }
}
```

Because the `Action` checks whether the user is logged in before returning the mapping to the portfolio, there's no way that a user can gain access to the portfolio page until he logs in. Even if he bookmarks the page, it will run this `Action` first. That's because the user never actually sees the real URL of the JSP file, only the *`action`*`.do` Struts `Action` name.

Transferring Control Inside and Outside the Application

Under normal circumstances, the last thing an `Action` does is return an `ActionForward`. This is used by the Controller to determine the next page to display. But the `Action` doesn't actually know where that is because the Controller has final responsibility for determining the forward. The same `Action` can be used by several different Struts actions, with different forward paths for the same returned forward mappings.

In fact, you can even forward to another `Action` without going to an intermediate JSP file. If the path in the `struts-config.xml` for the requested forward matches the URI pattern used for `Actions` (usually that it ends in `.do`), and Struts will immediate transfer control to the `Action` (run the validation on the `FormAction` and pass control to the `Action` if it succeeds).

One place that the Controller can't send you is outside the current application. That's because the forwards that you define in the Struts configuration file have to be relative to the current application.

So, if you want an `Action` to send the user off your site, you have to do it the good old-fashioned way. That is to say, by doing a `response.sendRedirect` in the `Action`. If you do this, you return null instead of an `ActionForward`.

In fact, you can actually process the entire response in the `Action` (in other words, treat it exactly like a traditional servlet) by using the `response`. So, your `Action` can generate an HTTP error, send a GIF file, anything you want. Just remember to return that null instead of an `ActionForward`.

Conclusions

The `Action` is responsible for integrating the View with the business logic. It also decides where to pass control to by returning an `ActionForward`, or by processing the request itself and returning null.

You can store multiple `ActionForms` on the session, and then have one `Action` process them all, using `getAttribute` to retrieve them all by their form name.

Struts also offers an opportunity to do access control on pages without requiring the pages themselves to have access control code in them. This is done by placing the access control in the `Action` classes that are used to forward to the restricted pages. Because Struts doesn't reveal the underlying JSP files that it displays, the user will have no way of knowing how to get to them without going through the `Action`.

9

Model Components: Modeling the Business

IN THIS CHAPTER

- Well-Designed Models
- Further Isolation Techniques
- Conclusions

The model is the least tightly defined piece of the Struts MVC architecture, and for good reason. Models, by definition, are used to control access to the tangled world of business logic—all the stuff that isn't display or control flow, but comprises the actual mechanisms of what happens underneath.

Because of this, the model can be composed of just about anything at all. For example, it may be made up of any or all of the following:

- A JDOM parser talking to an XML file
- A JNDI implementation communicating with an LDAP server
- An EJB stub communicating to an EJB server
- A SOAP client communicating with a remote Web service

As far as Struts is concerned, it's the job of the `Action` to perform whatever communications are required with the model. So, in one sense, this could be a very short chapter: "Write your models and hook them up to the `Action`."

You don't get off quite that easily, however. Before moving on, there are a few words to be said about designing models using best practices. This chapter will attempt to illustrate a few of them.

Well-Designed Models

To begin with, the Action should be as insulated as possible from the actual implementation of the model. This can be done by using abstraction. For example, if the model uses JNDI to look up a username and password in an LDAP server, you shouldn't put JNDI-specific code in the Action.

Instead, the Action should communicate through an interface (or at least a well-defined API) to the model, and the model should do all the work of setting up and making the JNDI call. That means if you want to change the model later to have it use JDBC to talk to Oracle, for example, only the model code would change; the Action could remain untouched.

To illustrate this, take a look at Stock.java (see Listing 9.1), which implements the model for stocks through Torque.

LISTING 9.1 Stock.java

```
package stocktrack.torque;


import org.apache.torque.om.Persistent;
import java.util.Date;
import java.util.GregorianCalendar;
import stocktrack.torque.StockPriceHistory;
import java.util.Random;
import java.util.List;
import org.apache.torque.util.Criteria;
import org.apache.log4j.Category;

/**
 * The skeleton for this class was autogenerated by Torque on:
 *
 * [Wed Jul 03 23:37:59 EDT 2002]
 *
 * You should add additional methods to this class to meet the
 * application requirements.  This class will only be generated as
 * long as it does not already exist in the output directory.
 */
public  class Stock
    extends stocktrack.torque.BaseStock
    implements Persistent
{

  static Category cat = Category.getInstance(Stock.class);
```

LISTING 9.1 Continued

```
// Always make sure this is an actual date the
// market would be open (not Sat or Sun).
private Date firstRecordedDay =
       new GregorianCalendar(2002,0,1,9,0,0).getTime();

public static Stock findStockBySymbol(String symbol) {
  try {
    Criteria c = new Criteria();
    c.add(StockPeer.STOCK_SYMBOL, symbol);
    List l = StockPeer.doSelect(c);
    if ((l == null) || (l.size() == 0)) return null;
    return (Stock)l.get(0);
  } catch (Exception ex) {
    cat.error("findStockBySymbol", ex);
  }
  return null;
}


public StockPriceHistory getLastQuote() throws Exception {
  return StockPriceHistory.getLastQuoteForId(this.getStockId());
}

public StockPriceHistory getLastClose() throws Exception {
  return StockPriceHistory.getLastCloseForId(this.getStockId());
}


public StockPriceHistory getLatestQuote() throws Exception{
  Random r = new Random();
    Date today = new Date();
    StockPriceHistory sph = this.getLastQuote();
    Date lastRecordedPrice = null;
    double lastPrice = 0;
    if (sph == null) {
      cat.debug("No prior quote found");
      lastRecordedPrice = firstRecordedDay;
      lastPrice = (r.nextInt(20)+10) + r.nextFloat();
      sph = new StockPriceHistory();
      sph.setPrice(lastPrice);
      sph.setPriceTimestamp(lastRecordedPrice.getTime());
```

LISTING 9.1 Continued

```
          sph.setStock(this);
          sph.setPriceClose("N");
          sph.save();
        } else {
          lastRecordedPrice =  new Date(sph.getPriceTimestamp());
          lastPrice = sph.getPrice();
        }
        GregorianCalendar current = new GregorianCalendar();
        GregorianCalendar last = new GregorianCalendar();
        last.setTime(lastRecordedPrice);
        last.add(GregorianCalendar.HOUR, 1);
        while (current.after(last)) {
           //Markets close at 4 PM
          if (last.get(GregorianCalendar.HOUR_OF_DAY) > 16) {
              //Reset to 9AM the next morning
              last.set(GregorianCalendar.HOUR_OF_DAY, 9);
              //Move it forward 1 day
              last.add(GregorianCalendar.DATE, 1);
          }
          if ((last.get(GregorianCalendar.DAY_OF_WEEK) ==
              GregorianCalendar.SATURDAY)) {
            //Move it forward to Monday
            last.add(GregorianCalendar.DATE, 2);
          }
          if (!current.after(last)) break;
          lastPrice = lastPrice + (r.nextFloat() - 0.50);
          if (lastPrice < 10) lastPrice += 1;
          if (lastPrice > 40) lastPrice -= 1;

         sph = new StockPriceHistory();
         sph.setStock(this);
         sph.setNew(true);
         sph.setPrice(lastPrice);
         sph.setPriceTimestamp(last.getTime().getTime());
        if (last.get(GregorianCalendar.HOUR_OF_DAY) == 16) {
          sph.setPriceClose("Y");
         } else {
          sph.setPriceClose("N");
         }
        sph.save();
        last.add(GregorianCalendar.HOUR, 1);
```

LISTING 9.1 Continued

```
    }
    return sph;
  }
}
```

There are two important things to note in this file. First, all the Torque-specific details of the model implementation have been coded here, leaving the `Action` pure. For example, if the `Action` needs access to a stock by looking up the symbol name, it calls `Stock.findStockBySymbol` rather than setting up a Torque Criteria and doing the SQL search in the `Action`. So if, at a later date, you were to switch from Torque to another object-modeling tool or replace this entirely with an EJB implementation, the only thing you'd have to do is make sure that you continued to respect the `findStockBySymbol` API.

The `getLatestQuote` code illustrates another important value of placing all your business logic in the model. At the moment, the stock quotes are being created out of thin air by a random number generator. Hopefully, this will not be the case in the finished application. However, by isolating this fact from the `Action`, it doesn't care where the quotes are coming from, only that they are available. So, at a later date, the correct code could be put in, and the rest of the application would continue unaware of the change.

If the symbol is not available at all or if an exception is thrown during the lookup, `null` is returned. There's an active debate in the Java community whether these types of errors should return null or throw an explicit exception that must be caught by the calling code. I tend to prefer to reserve throwing an exception for an actual error condition or a case in which returning `null` would be semantically meaningful.

Further Isolation Techniques

The one problem with this approach is that you would have to physically replace the `Stock` class with a new one when you changed the implementation. You can get around this by using an intermediate model, which is configurable. As an exercise, here's the `Stock` class rewritten to be configurable.

To begin, you need to define an interface that the new class will use to talk to all of the possible implementation-level classes. This interface, `StockInterface`, is shown in Listing 9.2.

LISTING 9.2 StockInterface.java

```
package stocktrack;
import stocktrack.torque.StockPriceHistory;

/**
 * <p>Title: Stock Tracking Application</p>
 * <p>Description: Example application from the book:
 * Struts - Rapid Working Knowledge</p>
 * <p>Copyright: Copyright (c) 2002</p>
 * <p>Company: </p>
 * @author James Turner and Kevin Bedell
 * @version 1.0
 */

public interface StockInterface {
  public StockInterface findStockBySymbol(String symbol);
  public String getLongName();
  public String getStockSymbol();
  public String getType();
  public StockPriceHistory getLatestQuote() throws Exception;
  public StockPriceHistory getLastQuote() throws Exception;
  public StockPriceHistory getLastClose() throws Exception;
}
```

This interface defines the common methods that any provider of stock quotes would need to offer. With this in place, you next create the `Stock` class itself (see Listing 9.3).

LISTING 9.3 The Stock Interface (`Stock.java`)

```
package stocktrack;
import stocktrack.StockInterface;
import java.lang.Class;
import java.lang.reflect.Method;
import stocktrack.torque.StockPriceHistory;
import stocktrack.StocktrackObjectFactory;
import javax.naming.InitialContext;

public class Stock {
  private StockInterface stock = null;
```

LISTING 9.3 Continued

```
  static String factoryName;
  static Class factoryClass;

static {
  try {
    factoryName  = (String) new InitialContext().
➥lookup("java:comp/env/stocktrack.ObjectFactory");
    factoryClass  = Class.forName(factoryName);
  } catch (Exception ex) {ex.printStackTrace(); }
}
  public Stock() {
    try {

    stock = ((StocktrackObjectFactory)
             factoryClass.newInstance()).getStockObject();
    } catch (Exception ex) {
      ex.printStackTrace();
    }
  }

  public static Stock findStockBySymbol(String symbol) {
    try {
      Stock st = new Stock();
      StockInterface stock = st.stock.findStockBySymbol(symbol);
      if (stock == null) return null;
      st.stock = stock;
      return st;
    } catch (Exception ex) {
      ex.printStackTrace();
      return null;
    }
  }

  public StockInterface getUnderlyingStock() {
    return this.stock;
  }

  public String getStockLongName() {
      return stock.getLongName();
  }
```

LISTING 9.3 Continued

```
  public String getStockSymbol() {
    return stock.getStockSymbol();
  }

  public String getype() {
    return stock.getType();
  }

  public StockPriceHistory getLatestQuote() throws Exception {
    return stock.getLatestQuote();
  }

  public StockPriceHistory getLastQuote() throws Exception {
    return stock.getLastQuote();
  }

  public StockPriceHistory getLastClose() throws Exception {
    return stock.getLastClose();
  }

}
```

There are a couple of interesting things going on in this file, so it's worth going over carefully. First, this class is really just a wrapper on the implementation-specific class, so the first thing it defines is a class property called `stock`, which is used to hold the implementation object. By declaring it of type `StockInterface`, `stock` can hold any class that implements the interface.

Next, the code uses JNDI to look up an environment variable declared in the Web application deployment descriptor (`web.xml`). This variable holds the name of the object factory that is used to create the various implementation-specific objects used by the application. You'll see how this works in a little bit.

The constructor for the class uses the object factory to instantiate an object for this class, and then places it in the wrapper's `stock` property.

The remaining methods implement `StockInterface`. In most of the cases, they merely call the same or similar method of the implementation class. However, because a static method can't be put in an interface, the `findStockBySymbol()` method (which is a static method) needs to create a temporary copy of the implementation class in order to pass the call on.

A few changes must be made to the Torque version of `Stock.java`, such as adding a nonstatic version of `findStockBySymbol()`, but it pretty much remains the same.

The object factory interface definition is shown in Listing 9.4.

LISTING 9.4 `StocktrackObjectFactory.java`

```
package stocktrack;
import stocktrack.StockInterface;

/**
 * <p>Title: Stock Tracking Application</p>
 * <p>Description: Example application from the book:
 * Struts - Rapid Working Knowledge</p>
 * <p>Copyright: Copyright (c) 2002</p>
 * <p>Company: </p>
 * @author James Turner and Kevin Bedell
 * @version 1.0
 */

public interface StocktrackObjectFactory {
  public StockInterface getStockObject();
  public UserInterface getUserObject();
  public TransactionInterface getTransactionObject();
  public AddressInterface getAddressObject();
  public StockPriceHistoryInterface getStockPriceHistoryObject();
}
```

The actual implementation factory for the Torque version of the code is shown in Listing 9.5.

LISTING 9.5 `TorqueObjectFactory.java`

```
package stocktrack;
import stocktrack.StockInterface;
import stocktrack.StocktrackObjectFactory;
import stocktrack.torque.*;

/**
 * <p>Title: Stock Tracking Application</p>
 * <p>Description: Example application from the book:
 * Struts - Rapid Working Knowledge</p>
 * <p>Copyright: Copyright (c) 2002</p>
 * <p>Company: </p>
```

LISTING 9.5 Continued

```
 * @author James Turner and Kevin Bedell
 * @version 1.0
 */

public class TorqueObjectFactory implements StocktrackObjectFactory {
  public StockInterface getStockObject() {
    return (StockInterface) new stocktrack.torque.Stock();
  }

  public UserInterface getUserObject()
   return (UserInterface) new stocktrack.torque.User();
  }

  public TransactionInterface getTransactionObject()
   return (TransactionInterface) new stocktrack.torque.Transaction ();
  }

  public AddressInterface getAddressObject()
   return (AddressInterface) new stocktrack.torque.Address();
  }

  public StockPriceHistoryInterface getStockPriceHistoryObject()
   return (StockPriceHistoryInterface) new stocktrack.torque.StockPriceHistory();
  }

}
```

Finally, you need to add an entry into the `web.xml` file for this application (see Listing 9.6).

LISTING 9.6 Entry in `web.xml`

```
<env-entry>
 <env-entry-name>stocktrack.ObjectFactory</env-entry-name>
 <env-entry-value>stocktrack.TorqueObjectFactory</env-entry-value>
 <env-entry-type>java.lang.String</env-entry-type>
</env-entry>
```

With all the pieces in place, you can follow the new flow. For example, consider this code fragment from `AddTransactionAction.java`:

```
Stock stock = Stock.findStockBySymbol(af.getSymbol());
```

When `Stock.findStockBySymbol` is called (`stocktrack.Stock` now, not `stocktrack.torque.Stock`), the `findStockBySymbol()` method (which is static) first creates an instance of itself. By doing this, it causes the object factory (as configured by the `web.xml` file) to create the appropriate implementation class, after which the constructor stores it inside the newly created wrapper.

Then, the next thing that `findStockBySymbol` does is to call the `findStockBySymbol()` method on the implementation class (`stocktrack.torque.Stock` in this case), and if it returns a stock, replace the temporary stock held in the wrapper with the one returned.

Now consider what happens if you decide to re-implement everything using EJB. You'd create a new set of implementation classes (perhaps calling them things like `stocktrack.ejb.StockHome`), which complies with `StockInterface`. Next, you'd create a `stocktrack.EJBObjectFactory` that returns the appropriate implementation classes for each wrapper class.

Finally, you'd edit `web.xml` to change the factory name to be `stocktrack.EJBObjectFactory`, and you'd be done. You'd have changed the underlying model without changing the rest of your code at all. That's one of the real powers of the MVC pattern, when it's used correctly.

Conclusions

One of the primary strengths of the MVC architecture is the flexibility surrounding model components. The architecture enables you to hide the implementation details of how the model class actually accesses its information.

The model is the piece of the MVC pattern that is least tightly controlled by Struts, specifically because it's Struts' job to shield the Web application from it.

You should follow through with this idea by keeping all your implementation-specific business logic out of the Struts components. For example, you should never be doing raw JDBC calls in an `Action`.

You can achieve even greater independence from the implementation by abstracting your business logic through some kind of object factory, which would enable you to refactor your application to another data source or remote application server with minimal code rewrite in the view and controller.

10

The `struts-config.xml` File: Tying All the Pieces Together

IN THIS CHAPTER

- The `struts-config` DTD
- The Configuration File in Context
- Conclusions

So far, you've seen the View (the `ActionForm`), the Model, and part of the Controller (the `Action`). But the `Action` is really only half of the controller. Although the `Action` returns a forwarding request, the actual destination of the forward is defined in the `struts-config.xml` file (which will also be referred to in this chapter simply as *the config file*.

This file is responsible for telling Struts what forms are available, what actions are available, and also allows a number of plug-in models to be added to the base Struts package.

In this chapter, you'll learn what elements go into this file, what options they take, and how the config file brings together all the elements you've seen so far.

The `struts-config` DTD

A good first look at the file can be gotten by looking at the DTD for the XML (see Listing 10.1). The full file (for Struts version 1.1) can be found on the Jakarta Web site at

`http://jakarta.apache.org/struts/dtds/struts-config_1_1.dtd`

LISTING 10.1 A Portion of the struts-config.xml DTD

```
<!ELEMENT struts-config (data-sources?, form-beans?,
                         global-exceptions?, global-forwards?,
                         action-mappings?, controller?,
                         message-resources*, plug-in*)>
```

One reason that it's important to take a look at the DTD is that the parameters in the config file (like most XML files) are order-dependent, so it's crucial to put the subelements in the correct order. Now we'll consider each element in turn.

READING DTDS

If you haven't been exposed to XML DTDs before, they can look a little confusing. They are similar to BNF descriptions, which you might have run into, but DTDs have their own unique quirks.

There are essentially two types of items in a DTD: `ELEMENT`s and `ATTLIST`s. An `ELEMENT` is used to describe the overall syntax of an XML (what its name is, what tags can be contained inside it), whereas the `ATTLIST` values define the attributes that the tag can have.

The format of `ELEMENT` is

```
<!ELEMENT tag-name (subtags)>
```

The *`subtags`* are references to other `ELEMENT` entries. If a *`subtag`* is following by a `?`, it means one or zero of these tags can be placed inside the parent tag. If an `*` follows the name, it means zero or more can be used. If no symbol follows the name, it means exactly one of these *`subtags`* must be placed inside the parent tag. Also, the ordering of the tags is important; the tags must occur in the order in which they are shown in the list.

Attributes, on the other hand, can occur in any order. Attributes are defined by `ATTLIST`, which has four arguments: the tag name, the attribute name, the type of the attribute, and a default value.

The tag name matches the attribute to the `ELEMENT` tag that defined the tag. The attribute name is the name that is used on the left side of an attribute assignment in the XML. The type specifies the type of data that can be placed on the right side of the assignment. The default value can have either a value specified directly in the DTD, or the string `"#IMPLIED"`, which means that the value is not required. The string `"#REQUIRED"` means that the XML based on this DTD must supply that attribute in all cases.

Data Sources

The `data-sources` element is defined in Listing 10.2. It defines the preconfigured JDBC data sources that are made available to your application.

LISTING 10.2 The data-sources Element

```
<!ELEMENT data-sources (data-source*)>
<!ELEMENT data-source (set-property*)>
<!ATTLIST data-source     id             ID               #IMPLIED>
<!ATTLIST data-source     className      %ClassName;      #IMPLIED>
<!ATTLIST data-source     key            %AttributeName;
                           "org.apache.struts.action.DATA_SOURCE">
<!ATTLIST data-source     type           %ClassName;      #IMPLIED>
```

The individual data-source tags inside the surrounding data-sources tag can be used to configure database connections (specifically, JDBC 2.0 DataSource objects).

The first real attribute, className, can be left off (in which case it defaults to the regular Struts DataSource configuration bean class, org.apache.struts.config.Config). This class is used to configure the data source, so it should handle all the properties used to instantiate a DataSource of the type being requested. In other words, it should handle all the properties specified in the set-property clauses of the tag.

The second argument, key, is a handle that the application can use to get the configured DataSource. If there is an application module prefix, it will be appended to this key. The default, if nothing is specified, is org.apache.struts.action.DATA_SOURCE. For example, the StockTrack application would use the servlet context attribute org.apache.struts.action.DATA_SOURCE/stocktrack.

The last argument, type, specifies the class name of the DataSource, which must implement javax.sql.DataSource. This DataSource is configured using the configuration bean class in order to instantiate an instance of the DataSource.

All these values can and will be left off in most normal cases.

Contained in the data-source tag is a series of set-property tags that are used to configure the DataSource. The DTD fragment for set-property (which is also used by some of the other tags in the DTD) is shown in Listing 10.3.

LISTING 10.3 The set-property Tag DTD

```
<!ELEMENT set-property   EMPTY>
<!ATTLIST set-property   id             ID               #IMPLIED>
<!ATTLIST set-property   property       %PropName;       #REQUIRED>
<!ATTLIST set-property   value          CDATA            #REQUIRED>
```

As you can see, the set-property tag consists of a property name and a value to assign to the property.

If you look at an actual data-sources clause taken from the copy of the config file supplied with Struts, it will probably help make sense of what you've just read. For that, see Listing 10.4.

LISTING 10.4 A Sample data-sources Clause

```
<data-sources>
  <data-source>
    <set-property
      property="autoCommit"
      value="false"/>
    <set-property
      property="description"
      value="Example Data Source Configuration"/>
    <set-property
      property="driverClass"
      value="org.postgresql.Driver"/>
    <set-property
      property="maxCount"
      value="4"/>
    <set-property
      property="minCount"
      value="2"/>
    <set-property
      property="password"
      value="mypassword"/>
    <set-property
      property="url"
      value="jdbc:postgresql://localhost/mydatabase"/>
    <set-property
      property="user"
      value="myusername"/>
  </data-source>
</data-sources>
```

An important thing to note is that the class for the database driver itself is not configured using either of the classes in the data-source tag attributes, but is instead supplied as an argument using the set-property tag.

To gain access to the data source from an action, you use the following snippet of code:

```
ds = servlet.getServletContext().getAttribute("org.apache.struts.action.DATA_
➥SOURCE/stocktrack");
```

Form Beans

The form-beans and form-bean tags are used to tell Struts what ActionForm classes are associated with what unique identifier. It is also used to initialize DynaForms (see Chapter 17, "DynaForms and the Validator").

Listing 10.5 shows the applicable piece of the DTD for these tags.

LISTING 10.5 form-bean DTD

```
<!ELEMENT form-beans (form-bean*)>
<!ATTLIST form-beans     id             ID              #IMPLIED>
<!ATTLIST form-beans     type           %ClassName;     #IMPLIED>

<!ELEMENT form-bean (icon?, display-name?, description?,
                     set-property*, form-property*)>
<!ATTLIST form-bean      id             ID              #IMPLIED>
<!ATTLIST form-bean      className      %ClassName;     #IMPLIED>
<!ATTLIST form-bean      dynamic        %Boolean;       #IMPLIED>
<!ATTLIST form-bean      name           %BeanName;      #REQUIRED>
<!ATTLIST form-bean      type           %ClassName;     #REQUIRED>

<!ELEMENT form-property  (set-property*)>
<!ATTLIST form-property  className      %ClassName;     #IMPLIED>
<!ATTLIST form-property  initial        CDATA           #IMPLIED>
<!ATTLIST form-property  name           %PropName;      #REQUIRED>
<!ATTLIST form-property  type           %ClassName;     #REQUIRED>

<!ELEMENT icon           (small-icon?, large-icon?)>
<!ATTLIST icon           id             ID              #IMPLIED>
```

The form-beans tag is simply a wrapper around the list of defined form beans. The type attribute has been deprecated.

Each form-bean tag defines a single form. The className attribute can be used to define a configuration bean for this form, similar to the way one can be defined for data sources. You should rarely be required to use this.

The dynamic attribute has been deprecated.

The name attribute is the unique identifier used to access the form, and also to associate a form with an action later in the file. Importantly, if a form has session or application scoping, you can use this name to get a handle to the form using getAttribute().

The type should be set to a valid ActionForm class. This is the class that will be instantiated for the form.

The icon, display-name, and description subtags are used to define a graphical icon, short name, and descriptive information for this form, respectively, but only for use by graphical IDE tools that may be used with Struts itself.

If the type extends (or is) org.apache.struts.action.DynaActionForm, the form-property tags are also inspected by Struts. Each form-property tag defines an initial value, a name, and a type (java.lang.String, for example) for each property of the form. DynaForms are discussed in more detail in Chapter 17.

Listing 10.6 shows the form-beans clause of the StockTrack application.

LISTING 10.6 The form-beans Clause

```
<form-beans type="org.apache.struts.action.ActionFormBean">
    <form-bean name="blankForm" type="stocktrack.struts.form.BlankForm" />
    <form-bean name="loginForm" type="stocktrack.struts.form.LoginForm" />
    <form-bean name="newUserNameForm"
               type="stocktrack.struts.form.NewUserNameForm" />
    <form-bean name="newUserAddressForm"
               type="org.apache.struts.validator.DynaValidatorForm">
      <form-property name="streetAddress1" type="java.lang.String"/>
      <form-property name="streetAddress2" type="java.lang.String"/>
      <form-property name="city" type="java.lang.String"/>
      <form-property name="state" type="java.lang.String"/>
      <form-property name="postalCode" type="java.lang.String"/>
      <form-property name="homePhone" type="java.lang.String"/>
      <form-property name="workPhone" type="java.lang.String"/>
      <form-property name="workExt" type="java.lang.String"/>
      <form-property name="bankRouting" type="java.lang.String"/>
    </form-bean>
    <form-bean name="addTransactionForm" type=
     "stocktrack.struts.form.AddTransactionForm" />
</form-beans>
```

Global Exceptions

Using the global-exceptions tag, you can define handlers for exceptions that might occur during processing of Web pages. The global-exceptions clause is defined by the DTD fragment shown in Listing 10.7.

LISTING 10.7 The global-exceptions Portion of the DTD

```
<!ELEMENT exception (icon?, display-name?, description?, set-property*)>
<!ATTLIST exception      id            ID               #IMPLIED>
<!ATTLIST exception      bundle        %AttributeName;  #IMPLIED>
<!ATTLIST exception      className     %ClassName;      #IMPLIED>
<!ATTLIST exception      handler       %ClassName;      #IMPLIED>
<!ATTLIST exception      key           CDATA            #REQUIRED>
<!ATTLIST exception      path          %RequestPath;    #IMPLIED>
<!ATTLIST exception      scope         CDATA            #IMPLIED>
<!ATTLIST exception      type          %ClassName;      #REQUIRED>
```

The `bundle` attribute specifies the name of the resource bundle that will hold the message resources for this exception.

`handler` is the class that's called when this exception occurs. It defaults to and must extend `org.apache.struts.action.ExceptionHandler`.

The `key` attribute is used to specify the template for the error message that will be generated, which is looked up in the message resource bundle.

When the exception occurs, control is redirected to the (module-relative) URL specified in the `path` attribute.

The `scope` attribute tells Struts whether to store the `ActionErrors` created by handling the exception in session or request scope.

Finally, the `type` attribute names the exception that is to be intercepted by this handler.

Listing 10.8 shows an example of a global exception handler.

LISTING 10.8 A global-exceptions Clause

```
<global-exceptions>
   <exception key="database.error" path="/errors/generalErrors.jsp"
              scope="request" type="javax.sql.SQLException"/>
</global-exceptions>
```

With this exception in place, if a SQL exception were thrown during processing, the default resource bundle (`ApplicationResources.properties`) would be used to find the `database.error` template, a new `ActionError` would be created using the template and placed on the request's attributes, and control would be handed over to the general errors page.

Global Forwards

Global forwards are used to define forwarding paths that are available to all actions defined in the configuration. For example, if a number of actions might pass control to a login screen, you can define that forward here rather than individually in each action. The DTD is shown in Listing 10.9.

LISTING 10.9 The global-mappings DTD

```
<!ELEMENT global-forwards (forward*)>
<!ATTLIST global-forwards id             ID               #IMPLIED>
<!ATTLIST global-forwards type           %ClassName;      #IMPLIED>

<!ELEMENT forward (icon?, display-name?, description?, set-property*)>
<!ATTLIST forward        id              ID               #IMPLIED>
<!ATTLIST forward        className       %ClassName;      #IMPLIED>
<!ATTLIST forward        contextRelative %Boolean;        #IMPLIED>
<!ATTLIST forward        name            CDATA            #REQUIRED>
<!ATTLIST forward        path            %RequestPath;    #REQUIRED>
<!ATTLIST forward        redirect        %Boolean;        #IMPLIED>
```

The `contextRelative` tag (which defaults to false) tells Struts whether the `path` should be considered relative to the module of a modular application (if false) or to the entire Web application (if true).

`name` is the unique identifier used in the `findForward()` method inside an `Action` to return the path.

If `redirect` is true, control will be transferred to the page with a redirect rather than a forward, meaning that a new request is created.

Although you can specify `set-property` tags inside the `global-forward` tag, the base class has no useful properties to set. However, you if extend the class and specify your new class in the `className` attribute, you can pass in bean values using `set-property`.

Listing 10.10 shows global forwards in use.

LISTING 10.10 Global Forwards

```
<global-forwards>
    <forward name="home" path="/home.jsp" />
</global-forwards>
```

Action Mappings

The `action` tag is where Struts ties forms, actions, and forwards together. They are bundled together under the `action-mappings` DTD shown in Listing 10.11.

LISTING 10.11 The action-mappings DTD

```
<!ELEMENT action-mappings (action*)>
<!ATTLIST action-mappings id              ID              #IMPLIED>
<!ATTLIST action-mappings type            %ClassName;     #IMPLIED>

<!ELEMENT action (icon?, display-name?, description?,
                  set-property*, exception*, forward*)>
<!ATTLIST action          id              ID              #IMPLIED>
<!ATTLIST action          attribute       %BeanName;      #IMPLIED>
<!ATTLIST action          className       %ClassName;     #IMPLIED>
<!ATTLIST action          forward         %RequestPath;   #IMPLIED>
<!ATTLIST action          include         %RequestPath;   #IMPLIED>
<!ATTLIST action          input           %RequestPath;   #IMPLIED>
<!ATTLIST action          name            %BeanName;      #IMPLIED>
<!ATTLIST action          parameter       CDATA           #IMPLIED>
<!ATTLIST action          path            %RequestPath;   #REQUIRED>
<!ATTLIST action          prefix          CDATA           #IMPLIED>
<!ATTLIST action          roles           CDATA           #IMPLIED>
<!ATTLIST action          scope           %RequestScope;  #IMPLIED>
<!ATTLIST action          suffix          CDATA           #IMPLIED>
<!ATTLIST action          type            %ClassName;     #IMPLIED>
<!ATTLIST action          unknown         %Boolean;       #IMPLIED>
<!ATTLIST action          validate        %Boolean;       #IMPLIED>
```

Starting at the top, the `attribute` attribute enables you to specify a different unique ID to store the `ActionForm` under the request or session scope; otherwise, the `name` is used.

The `forward` and `include` attributes can be used to directly pass on control to a new path rather than processing the action directly.

The `input` attribute allows the action to redirect back to the form that was used to enter the form values by specifying its path.

The `parameter` attribute can be used to pass a single parameter to the action, but you're probably better off using the more general `set-property` tag and defining specify bean properties for the class.

The path attribute is used to match up the request with the action—it should be the path of the action without any suffixes. For example, if you specified action="/foo/bar.do" in a form, it would match up with an action whose path is /foo/bar.

The prefix attribute enables you to specify a prefix that is added to the bean property names of the action form before matching them to the request parameter names. Similarly, the suffix attribute adds a suffix at the end of the property names.

By specifying a comma-separated list of security role names in the roles attribute, you can restrict access to this mapping to certain classes of users.

The value of scope determines whether the form is kept around for the length of the request or the entire session.

You specify the class of the Action that will process this action with the type attribute.

If you want an action that can be used to process action requests that would not otherwise find a match, set unknown to true. Only one action per configuration can have this set.

Finally, if validate (which defaults true) is false, the validate method of the ActionForm will not be called.

Because the ActionForm (and even the Action itself) are optional, there are a large number of different varieties of this tag. A few are shown in Listing 10.12.

LISTING 10.12 The Action Tag

```
<action-mappings>
      <action path="/index" forward="home.jsp"/>

      <action path="/newaccount"
              type="stocktrack.struts.action.NewAccountAction"
              name="blankForm" scope="request" input="/home.jsp">
          <forward name="newUser" path="/newUserName.jsp" />
      </action>

      <action path="/login" type="stocktrack.struts.action.LoginAction"
              name="loginForm" scope="request" input="/home.jsp" />

      <action path="/newUserName"
              type="stocktrack.struts.action.NewUserNameAction"
              name="newUserNameForm" scope="session" input="/newUserName.jsp">
          <forward name="newUserAddress" path="/newUserAddress.jsp" />
      </action>
```

Note that local uses of the forward, exception, and set-property tags are allowed inside an action; they pertain only to the action being defined. The set-property tag can be very useful to pass in information to an action. For example, if a single action class is being used to process several different forms, you can use a set-property tag to tell the action which form is being processed.

The Controller

The controller tag (whose DTD is shown in Listing 10.13) is probably the least-used tag in Struts. You probably won't use it unless you really enjoy messing with the innards of the implementation.

LISTING 10.13 The Controller DTD

```
<!ELEMENT controller     (set-property*)>
<!ATTLIST controller     id             ID              #IMPLIED>
<!ATTLIST controller     bufferSize     %Integer;       #IMPLIED>
<!ATTLIST controller     className      %ClassName;     #IMPLIED>
<!ATTLIST controller     contentType    CDATA           #IMPLIED>
<!ATTLIST controller     debug          %Integer;       #IMPLIED>
<!ATTLIST controller     forwardPattern CDATA           #IMPLIED>
<!ATTLIST controller     inputForward   %Boolean;       #IMPLIED>
<!ATTLIST controller     locale         %Boolean;       #IMPLIED>
<!ATTLIST controller     maxFileSize    CDATA           #IMPLIED>
<!ATTLIST controller     multipartClass %ClassName;     #IMPLIED>
<!ATTLIST controller     nocache        %Boolean;       #IMPLIED>
<!ATTLIST controller     pagePattern    CDATA           #IMPLIED>
<!ATTLIST controller     processorClass %ClassName;     #IMPLIED>
<!ATTLIST controller     tempDir        CDATA           #IMPLIED>
```

By setting bufferSize, you can change the size of the input buffer used when processing file uploads. The maxFileSize attribute defines the largest file that can be uploaded, and can include a K, M, or G afterward to specify kilobytes, megabytes, and so on. The multipartClass value can be set to a fully qualified class name, which is used to handle file uploads. tempDir is the temporary directory to be used when uploading files.

If you will be typically delivering pages other than HTML, the contentType attribute enables you to define a different default content type (such as "text/xml").

You can enable debugging by setting debug to a value greater than 0.

You can alter how an application-specific path is mapped into a context-relative URL by using the forwardPattern. The value $A is expended to the application prefix (/stocktrack, for example) and $P is expanded into the path requested. The default is AP.

If you set `inputForward` to true, the `input` parameters of `action` tags are treated as forwards rather than paths. That means they are looked up against the locally and globally defined `forward` tags rather than being used as raw URIs.

If the `locale` attribute set to true, it tells Struts to store a locale in the user's session if one isn't already there.

By setting `nocache` to true, a request to disable content caching will be sent to the client browser with each HTTP response.

The `pagePattern` setting tells Struts how to relate pages to the underlying URL, in much the same way that the `forwardPattern` does.

Finally, the `processorClass` enables you to replace the default Struts request processor with one of your own, should you want to change basic functionality of Struts.

Listing 10.14 shows a few of these values being configured.

LISTING 10.14 Some Controller Values Being Set

```
<controller nocache="true" contentType="image/jpg"/>
```

Message Resources

The `message-resources` tag (whose DTD in Listing 10.15) enables you to configure message resource bundles for use with your application.

LISTING 10.15 The `message-resources` DTD

```
<!ELEMENT message-resources (set-property*)>
<!ATTLIST message-resources id          ID              #IMPLIED>
<!ATTLIST message-resources className   %ClassName;     #IMPLIED>
<!ATTLIST message-resources factory     %ClassName;     #IMPLIED>
<!ATTLIST message-resources key         %AttributeName;
                                        "org.apache.struts.action.MESSAGE">
<!ATTLIST message-resources null        %Boolean;       #IMPLIED>
<!ATTLIST message-resources parameter   CDATA           #REQUIRED>
```

The `factory` attribute enables you to specify where the message resource will get its data. By default, it is configured to use property files.

When the application goes looking for the resource bundle in the servlet context, it will use the `key` as the lookup, similar to how `DataSources` are stored. By default, the StockTrack application would store its message bundle in `org.apache.struts.action.MESSAGE/stocktrack`.

The null attribute enables you to specify what to do if no match is found in the bundle for a given message key. If set to true, it will return null; if set to false, it will return a message with the bad key.

The parameter is handed to the factory when the bundle is created. For property-file-based factories, this is the path to the property file. Listing 10.16 shows an example of a message-resources tag in use.

LISTING 10.16 Using the message-resources Tag

```
<message-resources
  key="com.stocktrack.STOCKTICKER_MESSAGES"
  parameter="com.stocktrack.StocktickerMessages"/>
```

This enables you to get a handle on the resource bundle stored in the StocktickerMessages.properties file by using the servlet context attribute called com.stocktrack.STOCKTICKER_MESSAGES/stocktrack.

Plug-ins

The final element of the DTD is the plug-in tag, which allows additional functionality to be dynamically loaded into the Struts framework. Listing 10.17 shows the DTD for the tag.

LISTING 10.17 The plug-in DTD

```
<!ELEMENT plug-in          (set-property*)>
<!ATTLIST plug-in          id          ID             #IMPLIED>
<!ATTLIST plug-in          className   %ClassName;    #REQUIRED>
```

In the case of this tag, the only things you need to do are to specify the className, which specifies the class that loads the plug-in, and to use the set-property tag to pass in any required arguments to the plug-in. Listing 10.18 shows how you can use this tag to load the Struts Validator plug-in, which is discussed in Chapter 17.

LISTING 10.18 Using the Validator Plug-in

```
<plug-in className="org.apache.struts.validator.ValidatorPlugIn">
  <set-property property="pathnames"
                   value="/WEB-INF/validator-rules.xml,
                          /WEB-INF/validation.xml"/>
</plug-in>
```

Accessing and Altering the Configuration Dynamically

The struts-config.xml file is what Struts uses to load its initial configuration. After Struts is up and running, you can gain access to the in-memory version of this data using this snippet:

```
ApplicationConfig ap =
                  (ApplicationConfig) request.getAttribute(Action.APPLICATION_KEY);
```

From the ApplicationConfig object, you can gain access to all the various parts of the Struts configuration, using accessors such as findConfigs and findForwardConfig. You can also add and remove values from the configuration. For example, Listing 10.19 shows how you could configure a new Action on the fly.

LISTING 10.19 Adding an Action from Java

```
ApplicationConfig ap =
                  (ApplicationConfig) request.getAttribute(Action.APPLICATION_KEY);
ActionConfig ac = new ActionConfig();
ac.setInput("/bankruptcy.jsp");
ac.setPath("/goBankrupt");
ac.setName("bankruptcyForm");
ac.setType("stocktrack.struts.action.BankruptcyAction");
ap.addActionConfig(ac);
```

Clearly, this functionality is not intended for everyday use, although it can be useful for Actions and ActionForms to be able to introspect their ApplicationConfig.

You can also access the Struts configuration information using the bean:struts tag. For more information on this tag, see Chapter 13, "Struts Bean Tags: Storing and Passing Data."

The Configuration File in Context

Now that you've seen the format of the configuration file, it's worth talking about how the file interrelates all the other elements of Struts.

For example, you can begin by looking at it from the perspective of the JSP page. When a page uses an <html:form> tag with an action attribute, the attribute is looked up in the configuration file to discover the corresponding <action> tag. This tag in turn defines the form class, which allows the JSP page to make use of the <html:text> and other form input tags, and the action class, which is used to process the results after validation.

In addition, the action might need to communicate with a database, which could have been configured using a data source directive in the configuration file. When the action finishes processing, it uses an `ActionForward` to pass control to a new JSP page (or `Action`), which is configured using local and global forward tags in the configuration file.

Centralizing all the relationships between forms, actions, and JSP pages in one file makes it easy to change functionality or move a file without impacting a large number of source files. For example, if you decide to move all the error pages into a common `errors` subdirectory, you need to change the URI in only one location—where the forward was defined in the configuration file.

Conclusions

The `struts-config.xml` file offers a myriad of configuration options, most of which will never be used by a developer working on simple Struts applications. However, the large degree of configuration—from being able to change the way paths are created, to changing out the entire controller itself—means that there is just about nothing that a Struts developer can't do if he or she is willing to take the time.

Also, the configuration file is the common point that brings together the Actions, Forms, and JSP pages. In a well-designed Struts application, the JSP page doesn't know anything about the `Action` or `Form` classes that support it. The `Action` doesn't know what a given forwarding request actually translates to in terms of a URI, and the `Form` may be reused by one or more `Actions` and JSP pages. The configuration file is where all these elements are conjoined and interrelated.

For mundane day-to-day operations with `struts-config.xml`, your best bet is to get your hands on one of the new GUI-based tools for Struts maintenance. In my opinion, the EasyStruts plug-in for JBuilder and Eclipse, by Emmanuel Boudrant, is one of the best out there. It will automatically create forms, actions, and JSP forms, and maintain the `struts-config` file for you.

The Struts Console is a standalone tool written by James Holmes, and is available at `http://www.jamesholmes.com/struts/console/`.

XDoclet (which is becoming popular for EJB and WebApp development) now also has support for creating the `struts-config` file.

11

How the Struts Tag Libraries Work: The View from Inside

IN THIS CHAPTER

- Review of JSP Tag Libraries
- Understanding How Struts Tags Work: The `<bean:page>` Tag
- Comparison to the Java Standard Tag Library
- Conclusions

The Struts tag libraries are a big part of the Struts framework. They simplify development of the View components (JSP pages) and tie the Views into the rest of the framework.

As a result, you'll find yourself spending a lot of time building and debugging JSP pages filled with Struts tags. This is actually a good thing because doing so is much easier than writing and debugging regular JSP files—especially if you have a good understanding of exactly how the tags work.

The reason for this chapter is that sometimes it helps to resolve a problem or bug if you're comfortable reading the source code for the tags. In addition, by reading a bit of the source code and understanding the ways in which Struts stores and handles data and beans in the tags, you'll come up to speed much faster on Struts as a whole.

In this chapter, you'll learn the ins and outs of how the Struts tags work. You'll start with a quick review of the development of JSP custom tags in general, take a speedy journey through one of the actual Struts tags just to be able to say you've been there, and finish by reading a comparison of how the Struts tag libraries compare to the Java standard tag libraries.

After you complete the material in this chapter, take some time to look through the source code for the Struts tags that you use. Doing so will give you a deeper understanding of how they work and help you resolve problems faster.

Review of JSP Tag Libraries

The Struts tag libraries are nothing more than a specialized set of JSP custom tags. JSP custom tags are a fundamental part of JSP development in general. Some of the advantages of using tag libraries are

- They enable you to extend and customize JSP functionality
- They provide a way to avoid using Java scriptlets in your programs by enabling you to embed Java code inside a custom tag
- They make it easier for non-Java coders to maintain JSP files because understanding how to use a tag is easier than understanding scriptlets

JSP custom tags are created by writing Java code that implements the `Tag` or `BodyTag` interface (defined in the package `javax.servlet.jsp.tagext`).

JSP custom tag development involves three basic steps:

- **Define the tag syntax**—For example, a tag that prints a customer's name given the customer number might have this syntax: `<customer:getName id="idNum" />`. This example identifies the tag library prefix (`customer`), the tag name (`getName`), and an attribute (`id`).
- **Create the tag library descriptor (TLD) file**—The TLD file contains information about the overall tag library (the `customer` tag library, in this case) as well as providing the details for each tag in the library.
- **Write the actual code that implements the tag**—This will be one or more classes that provide handler methods for processing start tags, end tags, tag attributes, and so on.

NOTE

For a good, basic introduction to JSP custom tag development, you can refer to Sams Publishing's *JavaServer Pages 2.0 Unleashed* (ISBN: 0-672-32438-5).

In addition, Sun Microsystems has published a short tutorial at `http://java.sun.com/products/jsp/tutorial/TagLibrariesTOC.html`.

Understanding How Struts Tags Work: The `<bean:page>` Tag

It's important to know about JSP custom tag development in general, but what you really need to know is how Struts tags in particular work. The Struts tag libraries were developed using a series of common techniques. Understanding these can help you both develop code and debug problems faster.

The sample tag that we'll use is the <bean:page> tag. It was chosen because it's not particularly long or complex, and it illustrates some of the basic ideas behind how *all* Struts tags work.

Only a single tag is presented here. This is done specifically so that if you want more information you'll look into the source code directly on your own. I recommend that you begin by looking at the source code for tags you're actually using. All the source code for Struts can be downloaded from the Struts Web site (http://jakarta.apache.org/struts).

The <bean:page> Tag Java Code

The first stop in our tag deconstruction project is the actual tag Java file. All Struts tags are located in subpackages of org.apache.struts.taglib. For example, the bean tags are located in org.apache.struts.taglib.bean. Listing 11.1 is the Java file for this tag.

LISTING 11.1 org.apache.struts.taglib.bean.PageTag.java

```
/*
 * $Header: /home/cvspublic/jakarta-struts/src/share/org/apache/struts/taglib
➥/bean/PageTag.java,v 1.6 2001/04/23 22:52:20 craigmcc Exp $
 * $Revision: 1.6 $
 * $Date: 2001/04/23 22:52:20 $
 *
 * ====================================================================
 *
 * The Apache Software License, Version 1.1
 *
 * Copyright (c) 1999-2001 The Apache Software Foundation.  All rights
 * reserved.
 *
 * Redistribution and use in source and binary forms, with or without
 * modification, are permitted provided that the following conditions
 * are met:
 *
 * 1. Redistributions of source code must retain the above copyright
 *    notice, this list of conditions and the following disclaimer.
 *
 * 2. Redistributions in binary form must reproduce the above copyright
 *    notice, this list of conditions and the following disclaimer in
 *    the documentation and/or other materials provided with the
 *    distribution.
 *
```

LISTING 11.1 Continued

```
 * 3. The end-user documentation included with the redistribution, if
 *    any, must include the following acknowlegement:
 *       "This product includes software developed by the
 *        Apache Software Foundation (http://www.apache.org/)."
 *    Alternately, this acknowlegement may appear in the software itself,
 *    if and wherever such third-party acknowlegements normally appear.
 *
 * 4. The names "The Jakarta Project", "Struts", and "Apache Software
 *    Foundation" must not be used to endorse or promote products derived
 *    from this software without prior written permission. For written
 *    permission, please contact apache@apache.org.
 *
 * 5. Products derived from this software may not be called "Apache"
 *    nor may "Apache" appear in their names without prior written
 *    permission of the Apache Group.
 *
 * THIS SOFTWARE IS PROVIDED "AS IS" AND ANY EXPRESSED OR IMPLIED
 * WARRANTIES, INCLUDING, BUT NOT LIMITED TO, THE IMPLIED WARRANTIES
 * OF MERCHANTABILITY AND FITNESS FOR A PARTICULAR PURPOSE ARE
 * DISCLAIMED.  IN NO EVENT SHALL THE APACHE SOFTWARE FOUNDATION OR
 * ITS CONTRIBUTORS BE LIABLE FOR ANY DIRECT, INDIRECT, INCIDENTAL,
 * SPECIAL, EXEMPLARY, OR CONSEQUENTIAL DAMAGES (INCLUDING, BUT NOT
 * LIMITED TO, PROCUREMENT OF SUBSTITUTE GOODS OR SERVICES; LOSS OF
 * USE, DATA, OR PROFITS; OR BUSINESS INTERRUPTION) HOWEVER CAUSED AND
 * ON ANY THEORY OF LIABILITY, WHETHER IN CONTRACT, STRICT LIABILITY,
 * OR TORT (INCLUDING NEGLIGENCE OR OTHERWISE) ARISING IN ANY WAY OUT
 * OF THE USE OF THIS SOFTWARE, EVEN IF ADVISED OF THE POSSIBILITY OF
 * SUCH DAMAGE.
 * ====================================================================
 *
 * This software consists of voluntary contributions made by many
 * individuals on behalf of the Apache Software Foundation.  For more
 * information on the Apache Software Foundation, please see
 * <http://www.apache.org/>.
 *
 */


package org.apache.struts.taglib.bean;
```

LISTING 11.1 Continued

```
import java.io.IOException;
import javax.servlet.jsp.JspException;
import javax.servlet.jsp.PageContext;
import javax.servlet.jsp.tagext.TagSupport;
import org.apache.struts.util.MessageResources;
import org.apache.struts.util.RequestUtils;


/**
 * Define a scripting variable that exposes the requested page context
 * item as a scripting variable and a page scope bean.
 *
 * @author Craig R. McClanahan
 * @version $Revision: 1.6 $ $Date: 2001/04/23 22:52:20 $
 */

public class PageTag extends TagSupport {


    // ----------------------------------------------------------- Properties


    /**
     * The name of the scripting variable that will be exposed as a page
     * scope attribute.
     */
    protected String id = null;

    public String getId() {
        return (this.id);
    }

    public void setId(String id) {
        this.id = id;
    }


    /**
     * The message resources for this package.
     */
```

LISTING 11.1 Continued

```
    protected static MessageResources messages =
        MessageResources.getMessageResources
        ("org.apache.struts.taglib.bean.LocalStrings");


    /**
     * The name of the page context property to be retrieved.
     */
    protected String property = null;

    public String getProperty() {
        return (this.property);
    }

    public void setProperty(String property) {
        this.property = property;
    }


    // ------------------------------------------------------- Public Methods


    /**
     * Retrieve the required configuration object and expose it as a
     * scripting variable.
     *
     * @exception JspException if a JSP exception has occurred
     */
    public int doStartTag() throws JspException {

        // Retrieve the requested object to be exposed
        Object object = null;
        if ("application".equalsIgnoreCase(property))
            object = pageContext.getServletContext();
        else if ("config".equalsIgnoreCase(property))
            object = pageContext.getServletConfig();
        else if ("request".equalsIgnoreCase(property))
            object = pageContext.getRequest();
        else if ("response".equalsIgnoreCase(property))
            object = pageContext.getResponse();
```

LISTING 11.1 Continued

```
        else if ("session".equalsIgnoreCase(property))
            object = pageContext.getSession();
        else {
            JspException e = new JspException
                (messages.getMessage("page.selector", property));
            RequestUtils.saveException(pageContext, e);
            throw e;
        }

        // Expose this value as a scripting variable
        pageContext.setAttribute(id, object);
        return (SKIP_BODY);

    }


    /**
     * Release all allocated resources.
     */
    public void release() {

        super.release();
        id = null;
        property = null;

    }

}
```

Here are the important things to understand from this listing:

- **The license at the top of the file**—This is the standard Apache Software License. Item 1 in the license indicates that the code can't be redistributed with without including the license—so, here it is!
- **The properties section**—Nearly all Struts tags use properties as a way to store information. This is how the different tag handler methods (`doStartTag()`, `doEndTag()`, and so on) that are present share data with each other.

- **The MessageResources file for this particular taglib package**—All tags in the org.apache.struts.taglib.bean package share the same MessageResources file. This is generally used for defining error messages employed by the tag. Changing or localizing error text is done by modifying these properties files or by creating your own.
- **Expose the results as pageAttributes**—Notice these lines:

  ```
  // Expose this value as a scripting variable
          pageContext.setAttribute(id, object);
  ```

  This is how virtually all Struts tags work. They manipulate data and then pass results into the main JSP page by attaching objects (usually Strings or beans) to the PageContext. This makes them visible only while this page is being built.
- **The org.apache.struts.utilities classes**—For example, this tag uses the RequestUtils utility class. Getting to know these classes will help you understand a great deal more about how all the Struts tag libraries work.

After you've examined a few of these tags, they'll all begin to look the same and you can figure them out quickly. When you get to that point, you'll find debugging Struts JSP files will go much quicker.

Now might be a good time to go to your computer and look through the source code of one or two more tags. Start by looking at tags you're familiar with.

The Struts Bean Taglib Descriptor File (struts-bean.tld)

The next stop on this whirlwind tour of the <bean:page> tag is the taglib descriptor files. The TLD files are located directly in the WEB-INF directory of your Web application. The structure and syntax of these files are defined by the Java Servlet specification.

The struts-bean.tld file is a bit long, but the section that defines <bean:page> is pretty short. It is as follows:

```
<tag>
<name>page</name>
<tagclass>org.apache.struts.taglib.bean.PageTag</tagclass>
<teiclass>org.apache.struts.taglib.bean.PageTei</teiclass>
<bodycontent>empty</bodycontent>
<attribute>
<name>id</name>
<required>true</required>
<rtexprvalue>true</rtexprvalue>
```

```
</attribute>
<attribute>
<name>property</name>
<required>true</required>
<rtexprvalue>true</rtexprvalue>
</attribute>
</tag>
```

The important information here is the following:

- The name of the Java file used for this tag is `org.apache.struts.taglib.bean.PageTag.java`
- The line `<bodycontent>empty</bodycontent>` means that no content can be specified in the body of the tag. That is, you should always specify it as `<bean:page ... />` and never as `<bean:page . . . >I'm the body!</bean:page>`.
- Only two attributes can be specified with this tag: `id` and `property`. Both are required.

That's it for the TLD file. There's not much there, but it can be useful if you're unsure which attributes are required.

One thing to watch out for is to make sure that your TLD files are from the same version as your Struts classes. Because the Struts classes are usually stored in the `struts.jar` file and the TLD files are stored with your Web application, it's possible for them to get out of synch. Each time you upgrade the `struts.jar` file you're working with, you should watch out for changes that might have occurred in the TLD files. The most common mistake is specifying a tag attribute that is in the current release of Struts and then finding that you have an old TLD file from before that attribute came into existence. If this happens, an error will be thrown to tell you that the attribute isn't valid. Be especially careful when copying TLD files from old projects—the TLD files might be out of date.

Using the `<bean:page>` Tag: Tying It All Together

Now that you've looked over the Java file and the TLD file entry for `<bean:page>`, it's time to review how the tag is used.

According to the Struts user guide, the purpose of the `<bean:page>` tag is to "Expose a specified item from the page context as a bean." The documentation goes on to say that this tag is used to "Retrieve the value of the specified item from the page context for this page, and define it as a scripting variable, and a page scope attribute accessible to the remainder of the current page."

This is pretty easy to see from the source file. Remember the following lines:

```
public int doStartTag() throws JspException {

        // Retrieve the requested object to be exposed
        Object object = null;
        if ("application".equalsIgnoreCase(property))
            object = pageContext.getServletContext();
        else if ("config".equalsIgnoreCase(property))
            object = pageContext.getServletConfig();
        else if ("request".equalsIgnoreCase(property))
            object = pageContext.getRequest();
        else if ("response".equalsIgnoreCase(property))
            object = pageContext.getResponse();
        else if ("session".equalsIgnoreCase(property))
            object = pageContext.getSession();
        else {
            JspException e = new JspException
                (messages.getMessage("page.selector", property));
            RequestUtils.saveException(pageContext, e);
            throw e;
        }

        // Expose this value as a scripting variable
        pageContext.setAttribute(id, object);
        return (SKIP_BODY);
```

As you can see, the tag accepts the `property` attribute that's passed into it, stores the appropriate page context item in the `object`, and then sets the result on to the page context as a scripting variable with the `id` attribute.

So, it's clear that both the `property` and `id` attributes are required and that the tag syntax must be

```
<bean:page id="nameToStoreItUnder" property="session" />
```

After you understand how the tags work, it's easy to quickly put them to use and debug your code if you make a mistake.

Comparison to the Java Standard Tag Library

As this book was being written, a lot of work was being done on other tag libraries and changes were being made to the way JSP fundamentally works. The Struts tag libraries are really just one of a number of ongoing efforts, although they are among the best developed and are currently in widespread use. The Struts tag libraries are

- Available today on a wide variety of platforms
- Tightly integrated with Struts MVC architecture
- Supported by a broad user base
- Easy to learn and easy to use

However, it's important that you keep your eye on a number of other efforts. The most visible of these are based on work currently being done to extend JSP itself by including in it a number of standard tag libraries. These efforts are referred to as the *Java standard tag libraries* or *JSTL* (sometimes referred to as the *JSP tag libraries* or *JSPTL*). The JSTL specification is covered by JSR-52 (Java Specification Request 52) and can be reviewed on the site of the Java Community Process (`http://www.jcp.org/jsr/detail/52.jsp`).

JSTL itself is a moving target right now, but it will be adopted rapidly because of the significant value it adds by speeding the development and maintenance of your code. Here's a very high-level description of JSTL features:

- **Container hosted**—For a servlet container (such as Tomcat) to be considered JSP 1.2 compliant, it must support JSTL. That means the JSTL tag libraries will work on any servlet container that meets this requirement.
- **Expression language**—In addition to providing JSP custom tags, JSTL also requires a container to provide a basic expression language (EL) that enables the developer to define Boolean and other expressions without having to use Java scriptlets.
- **Multiple tag libraries**—The JSTL specification actually defines multiple tag libraries. This is similar to the way Struts has multiple tag libraries (for example, the bean and HTML libraries). The four initial JSTL libraries are the core, xml, sql, and i18n libraries.

There is some overlap between Struts and JSTL. Over time, the two will likely come closer together and some Struts tags probably will be deprecated as JSTL matures and is more widely supported. It is also very likely that Struts will influence future directions of JSTL to some extent. Many of the people involved in developing JSTL specifications are also involved in the Struts or other Apache/Jakarta projects.

In summary, if your servlet container supports JSP 1.2 and JSTL, it's possible that some functionality for which you would otherwise require Struts might be available directly within the JSTL provided by your container. Whether or not you use Struts or JSTL will depend on your application, your expected migration path, and the timing of your project. The trade-off you'll have to make will be based on your desire for Java standards-compliance versus your desire to leverage Struts and its MVC architecture and tag library.

Until JSP 2.0 becomes final and widely supported, I recommend using Struts where appropriate. Doing so should enhance portability while allowing JSTL to mature.

NOTE

For more information on the JSP standard tag library, read Sams Publishing's *JSTL: JSP Standard Tag Library Kick Start* by Jeff Heaton (ISBN: 0672324505).

Conclusions

In this chapter, you looked behind the curtain at the inner workings of the Struts tag libraries. You found that not only is understanding the inner workings of the tag libraries not difficult, it also gives you valuable insight into how the rest of Struts works.

I highly recommend that, after completing this chapter, you take some time to review other Struts tags directly in the Struts source code itself. Be sure to review the Java source code, the TLD file entries for the tag, and the tag usage as defined in the Struts documentation.

It is important that you learn how to figure out what a tag is doing if you have trouble using it. That knowledge will enable you to code and debug faster, and make maintaining your pages easier.

The Struts tags are a set of well-developed JSP custom tags that were developed by the authors of Struts to make the job of the JSP developer easier. Another set of tag libraries with this same goal is the Java standard tag library (JSTL). JSTL is governed by JSR-052 and provides multiple tag libraries, is hosted with the container itself, and provides a basic expression language.

12

Struts HTML Tags: Page Construction and Form Processing

IN THIS CHAPTER

- Struts Tags, JSP Custom Tags, and Java Scriptlets: What's the Right Balance?
- Using Struts HTML Tags to Render Basic HTML Elements
- The Basics of Form Processing
- Check Boxes and Radio Buttons
- Drop Downs and Select/Option Lists
- Input Validation and `<html:errors>`
- Uploading a File Using `<html:file>`
- Conclusions

This chapter is the first in a series of chapters examining the Struts tags. This first chapter examines the HTML custom tags. These tags are used in JSP files for generating HTML elements, coordinating form processing, and, in general, linking the JSP pages (View components) into the rest of the Struts framework.

This chapter is focused on *how to use* the HTML tags. It isn't meant to be a reference for these tags. If you want a listing of every valid option for these tags, consult the Struts Web site or the documentation that came with the version of Struts you downloaded. (This documentation is located by default at `/struts-documentation/index.html` on the server where you installed Struts.)

However, if you want to know how to build Web pages using these tags, you've come to the right place. We wrote this chapter by first developing sample applications using the tags, and then providing screen shots and sample code for you to reuse. We felt this was the fastest way to get you up to speed.

A final note before we dive in. Many of the options relating to the Struts HTML tags have to do with specifying attributes that are simply passed through unchanged by Struts into the resulting HTML file that's sent to the client browser. For example, virtually every Struts HTML tag has an `onclick` attribute (and other similar `on`*`This`* or `on`*`That`* attributes) that enables you to specify a JavaScript event handler to be executed for that particular event type. We don't cover these attributes, nor other attributes that specifically relates to HTML and not Struts.

NOTE

For more information, please refer to another Sams title, such as *Sams Teach Yourself Web Publishing with HTML and XHTML in 21 Days* or *Sams Teach Yourself HTML and XHTML in 24 Hours*.

All the files referred to in this chapter are available in the `StrutsTaglib.war` Web application available on the companion CD-ROM. The sample applications for this chapter are pulled together and made accessible from a single JSP page in the StrutsTaglib Web application. This JSP page, shown in Figure 12.1, is located at the URL `http://localhost:8080/StrutsTaglibs/html.jsp`, assuming that you're using a default Tomcat installation.

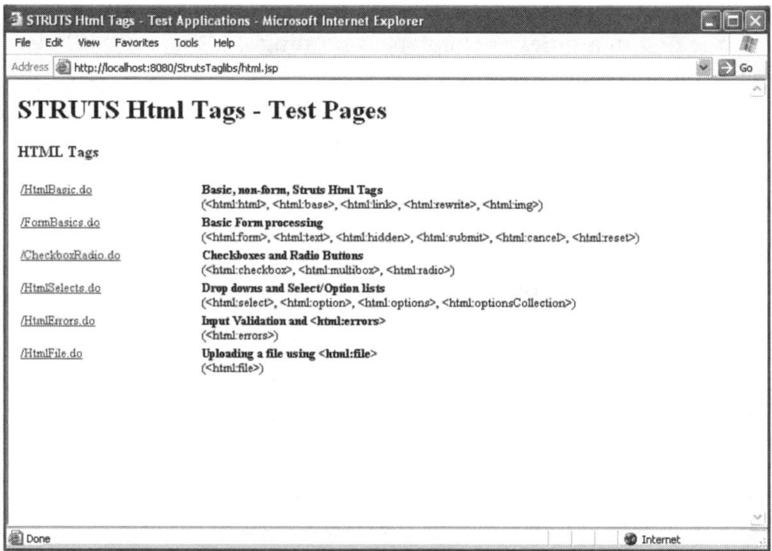

FIGURE 12.1 The sample applications for Chapter 12.

Struts Tags, JSP Custom Tags, and Java Scriptlets: What's the Right Balance?

It's probably appropriate to mention up front that you can use Struts without using any of the Struts custom tags. If you want to, you can develop straight JSP files and still use the MVC architecture, `Action` classes, and most of the rest of the framework. We don't recommend it, but it's possible.

It's common to wonder whether you can use Struts tags and completely avoid the use of any Java scripting. This, too, is possible, but it requires a great deal of effort.

The scripting capability of JSP and Struts is very limited if you don't use Java scriptlets. You can develop JSP custom tags that hide the scripting, but sometimes doing so is overkill.

This changed a great deal with the latest versions of JSP and the introduction of JSTL. It'll be improved even more when the upcoming specifications for Java ServerFaces are released and application servers provide support for it.

NOTE

For more information about Java Server Faces, please refer to its specification, which is located at `http://jcp.org/jsr/detail/127.jsp`.

For now, we recommend that you do your best to eliminate Java scriptlets, but advise you not to take a hard line against them. What you'll likely find is that on every project there are a few places where Java scriptlets can save you a lot of time. Just don't overuse them or you'll run into the maintenance problems that caused people to try to avoid their use to begin with.

Using Struts HTML Tags to Render Basic HTML Elements

This section provides information about the following tags:

- `<html:html>`—Render an HTML `<html>` element
- `<html:base>`—Render an HTML `<base>` element
- `<html:link>`—Render an HTML Anchor tag `<a>` element
- `<html:rewrite>`—Render only the URI portion of a `<html:link>` tag
- `<html:img>`—Render an HTML `<img>` element

If you point your browser to the URL

`http://myAppServer/StrutsTaglibs/html.jsp`

you'll bring up the main page linking to all the sample code for the Struts tag chapters. This section uses the HTML Basics page at `/StrutsTaglibs/HtmlBasic.do`. The rendered page is shown in Figure 12.2.

As you can see from the figure, this page has no forms or Submit buttons. Listing 12.1 is the JSP file that creates this page.

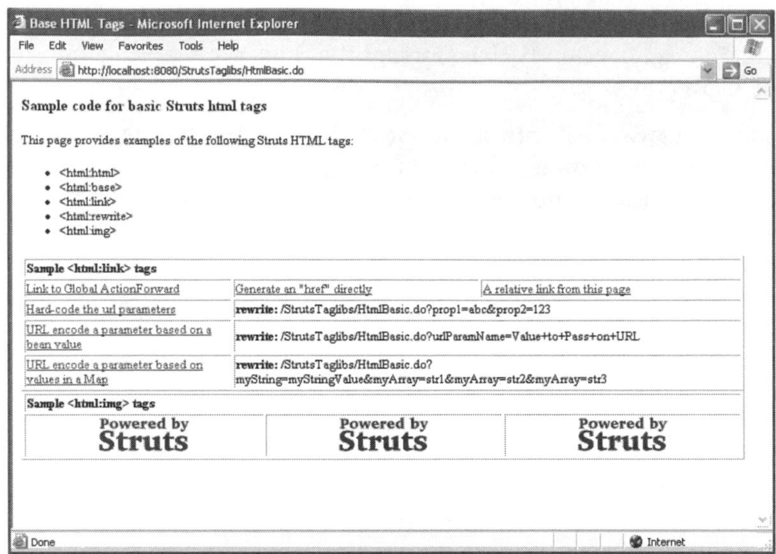

FIGURE 12.2 The HTML Basics page at `/StrutsTaglibs/HtmlBasic.do`.

LISTING 12.1 JSP File Demonstrating Usage of Struts HTML Tags That Generate Basic HTML Tags (Not `FORM`-Related) (`HtmlBasic.jsp`)

```
<%@ page language="java"%>
<%@ taglib uri="/WEB-INF/struts-html.tld" prefix="html" %>
<html:html>
<head>
<title>Base HTML Tags</title>
<html:base/>
</head>
<body bgcolor="white">

<h3>Sample code for basic Struts html tags</h3>

<p>This page provides examples of the following Struts HTML tags:<br>
<ul>
<li>&lt;html:html&gt;</li>
<li>&lt;html:base&gt;</li>
<li>&lt;html:link&gt;</li>
<li>&lt;html:rewrite&gt;</li>
<li>&lt;html:img&gt;</li>
</ul>
```

LISTING 12.1 Continued

```
<table border="1" width="100%">
  <tr>
    <th colspan="3" align="left">
      Sample &lt;html:link&gt; tags
    </th>
  </tr>

  <%--
  The following section contains three <html:link> tags. Each
  demonstrates a different way of creating an anchor tag (<a href=...>).
  --%>
  <tr>
    <td align="left">
      <%-- Create link from a Global Forward in the struts-config.xml --%>
      <html:link forward="index">
        Link to Global ActionForward
      </html:link>
    </td>
    <td align="left">
      <%-- Create link by specifying a full URL --%>
      <html:link href="http://jakarta.apache.org/struts/index.html">
        Generate an "href" directly
      </html:link>
    </td>
    <td align="left">
      <%-- Create the link as a relative link from this page --%>
      <html:link page="/HtmlBasic.do">
        A relative link from this page
      </html:link>
    </td>
  </tr>

  <%--
  The <html:link> and <html:rewrite> tags a very similar. The only difference
  is that <html:rewrite> creates the URI without prepending the
  "http://hostname:port/" part.
  --%>
  <tr>
    <%-- Create link and hard-code request parameters --%>
    <td colspan="1" align="left">
      <html:link page="/HtmlBasic.do?prop1=abc&amp;prop2=123">
```

LISTING 12.1 Continued

```
        Hard-code the url parameters
      </html:link>
    </td>
    <%-- Create the same rewrite string for the above link. --%>
    <td colspan="2" align="left">
      <b>rewrite: </b>
      <html:rewrite page="/HtmlBasic.do?prop1=abc&amp;prop2=123" />
    </td>
  </tr>

<%
   /*
    * Create a String object to store as a bean in
    * the page context and embed in this link
    */
  String beanName = "Value to Pass on URL";
  pageContext.setAttribute("pageAttribute1", beanName);
%>

  <tr>
    <%-- Create link with request parameters from a bean --%>
    <td colspan="1" align="left">
      <%-- For this version of the <html:link> tag:                      --%>
      <%--   paramID  = the name of the url parameter                     --%>
      <%--   paraName = the "attribute" for the bean holding the value --%>
      <html:link page="/HtmlBasic.do"
              paramId="urlParamName" paramName="pageAttribute1">
      URL encode a parameter based on a bean value
      </html:link>
    </td>
    <%-- Create the same rewrite string for the above link. --%>
    <td colspan="2" align="left">
      <b>rewrite: </b>
      <html:rewrite page="/HtmlBasic.do"
              paramId="urlParamName" paramName="pageAttribute1" />
    </td>
  </tr>

<%
   /*
    * Store values in a Map (HashMap in this case)
```

LISTING 12.1 Continued

```
    * and construct the URL based on the Map
    */
  java.util.HashMap myMap =  new java.util.HashMap();
  myMap.put("myString", new String("myStringValue") );
  myMap.put("myArray",  new String[] { "str1", "str2", "str3" });
  pageContext.setAttribute("map", myMap);
%>
 <tr>
    <%-- Create a link with request parameters from a Map --%>
    <td colspan="1" align="left">
      <%-- For this version of the <html:link> tag:  --%>
      <%--   map  = a map with name/value pairs to pass on the url --%>
      <html:link page="/HtmlBasic.do" name="map">
      URL encode a parameter based on values in a Map
      </html:link>
    </td>
    <%-- Create the same rewrite string for the above link. --%>
    <td colspan="2" align="left">
      <b>rewrite: </b>
      <html:rewrite page="/HtmlBasic.do" name="map"/>
    </td>
  </tr>

</table>

<table border="1" width="100%">
  <tr>
    <th colspan="3" align="left">
      Sample &lt;html:img&gt; tags
    </th>
  </tr>

  <tr>
    <%-- Create a default <img> tag --%>
    <td align="center">
      <html:img page="/struts-power.gif" />
    </td>

    <%-- Create an <img> tag with request parameters from a bean --%>
    <td align="center">
      <%-- Note "src" requires using full relative path --%>
```

LISTING 12.1 Continued

```
      <html:img src="/StrutsTaglibs/struts-power.gif"
                     paramId="urlParamName" paramName="pageAttribute1" />
    </td>

    <%-- Create an <img> tag with request parameters from a map --%>
    <td align="center">
      <html:img page="/struts-power.gif" name="map" />
    </td>
  </tr>
</table>

</html:html>
```

The following sections outline the functionality related to the tags demonstrated in the preceding listing.

The `<html:html>` Tag

The `<html:html>` tag simply generates the `<html>` HTML element at the beginning of the file. In our case, this is a very basic tag.

If this application were written to provide locale-specific text, the tag could have been written as

```
<html:html locale="true">
```

Using the `local="true"` option causes this page to set its `locale` value based on the `Accept-Language` header submitted by the client browser (if a locale was not already set).

The `<html:base>` Tag

The `<html:base>` tag generates an HTML `<base>` element in the `<head>` section of the document. The `<base>` HTML element is used to assist the client browser in correctly forming relative URL paths if they're present in the HTML page.

In this case, our `<html:base/>` tag rendered the following HTML:

```
<base href="http://localhost:8080/StrutsTaglibs/HtmlBasic.jsp">
```

For more information about this tag, please refer to an appropriate HTML reference guide.

The `<html:link>` and `<html:rewrite>` Tags

The `<html:link>` tag is the tag used to generate anchor tags, or hyperlinks. It's a very useful tag that you'll use a great deal if you need to build your application either to

- Pass parameters on the URL (as opposed to submitting them all from forms)
- Maintain session state with users who have cookies turned off

Because it's very likely that one conditions of these is true, you should plan to create hyperlinks using the `<html:link>` tag rather than by directly creating hyperlinks without it.

The `<html:rewrite>` is very similar to the `<html:link>` tag. The only difference between them is that the `<html:rewrite>` tag creates only the URI portion of the hyperlink.

The URI portion of a Web address is that part that comes after the protocol, host, and port are specified for the request. The URI simply defines the resource being requested. For example, given the URL `http://localhost:8080/StrutsTaglibs/HtmlBasic.do`, the URI part is `/StrutsTaglibs/HtmlBasic.do`.

For example, the `<html:rewrite>` tag can be useful if you need to pass the URI of a resource into a JavaScript function.

URL ENCODING VERSUS FORM POSTING

There are two ways that parameters get passed from a user request in the client browser into your application running on the server: posting them via a form or encoding them in the request URL.

URL encoding refers to literally embedding name/value pairs directly into the URL that the client browser requests. For example, the client browser may issue an HTTP `GET` command for the resource `/myApp/myFile.jsp?var1=abc&var2=def`.

In this situation, the server passes the request parameters `var1` and `var2` to the application with the values `abc` and `def`, respectively.

In URL encoding, parameters are visible in the URL address section of the client's browser. It's also possible that a user might manually change parameters in the request and then refresh the browser to reexecute a request—this could potentially pose a security threat.

In form posting, parameters are posted to the server using the HTTP `POST` method. This has the security advantage of not making the parameters visible in the URL.

That being said, there are good reasons to use URL encoding. Sometimes building hyperlinks with parameters embedded in them is a good way to pass information into a page when it doesn't make sense to use a form. Also, if a user has cookies disabled, you might not be able to store Session IDs or other information in a cookie on the user's browser.

The <html:link> tag provides convenience and a great deal of flexibility if it makes sense for your application to URL encode request parameters. It also automatically handles URL encoding of Session IDs to ensure that you can maintain session state with users who have cookies turned off in their browser.

The following sections describe the various ways our sample application uses the <html:link> tag.

Create Link from a Global Forward in the struts-config.xml

First, define a global forward in the struts-config.xml file similar to:

```
<global-forwards>
    <forward  name="index"  path="/index.jsp"/>
  </global-forwards>
```

Next, create the <html:link> tag in the JSP file:

```
<html:link forward="index">
  Link to Global ActionForward
</html:link>
```

The HTML generated is

```
<a href="/StrutsTaglibs/index.jsp">Link to Global ActionForward</a>
```

Be careful that you only use <forward>s that are defined as <global-forwards>. If you reference a <forward> defined down in the <action> section of your struts-config.xml file, you'll throw an exception similar to the following:

```
Cannot create rewrite URL: Java.net.MalformedURLException:
➥Cannot retrieve ActionForward
```

Create Link by Specifying a Full URL

This is the best way to generate hyperlinks to sites outside your application. Simply use the href attribute of the <html:link> tag in a way similar to the following:

```
<html:link href="http://jakarta.apache.org/struts/index.html">
  Generate an "href" directly
</html:link>
```

The HTML generated is

```
<a href="http://jakarta.apache.org/struts/index.html">
➥Generate an "href" directly</a>
```

This is the only `<html:link>` tag that isn't rewritten to URL encode the user's Session ID if the user has cookies turned off.

Create the Link as a Relative Link from the Current Page

This is the method to use if you're linking to another page within your application and you don't need to URL encode any request parameters into the request. Just create an `<html:link>` tag similar to the following:

```
<html:link page="/HtmlBasic.do">
  A relative link from this page
</html:link>
```

The HTML generated is

```
<a href="/StrutsTaglibs/HtmlBasic.do">A relative link from this page</a>
```

Hard-Code Request Parameters on the URL or URI

This section covers both `<html:link>` and `<html:rewrite>`.

This is the method to use if you need to create a URL or URI containing request parameters and the request parameters will *never vary.*

When you code the tag, simply add the request parameters to the end of the attribute specifying the page, similar to the following:

```
<html:link page="/HtmlBasic.do?prop1=abc&amp;prop2=123">
  Hard-code the url parameters
</html:link>
<%-- or --%>
rewrite: <html:rewrite page="/HtmlBasic.do?prop1=abc&amp;prop2=123" />
```

The HTML generated is

```
<a href="/StrutsTaglibs/HtmlBasic.do?prop1=abc&amp;prop2=123">
➥Hard-code the url parameters</a>

rewrite: /StrutsTaglibs/HtmlBasic.do?prop1=abc&amp;prop2=123
```

Encode a Single Request Variable on the URL or URI

This section covers both `<html:link>` and `<html:rewrite>`.

Use this approach if you have a single request parameter that you need to encode, and that value is (or can be) stored in a bean accessible to the page.

First, here's an example of how to save a value so that you can access it using this tag. The basic approach is to save it as an attribute on the page context. (This approach is used throughout Struts itself as a method to save and pass data around.)

```
<%
   /*
    * Create a String object to store as a bean in
    * the page context and embed in this link
    */
  String beanName = "Value to Pass on URL";
  pageContext.setAttribute("pageAttribute1", beanName);
%>
```

Now the value is stored in the page context, ready to be passed to the tags like so:

```
<%-- For this version of the <html:link> tag:                   --%>
<%--   paramID  = the name of the url parameter                 --%>
<%--   paraName = the "attribute" for the bean holding the value --%>
<html:link page="/HtmlBasic.do"
           paramId="urlParamName" paramName="pageAttribute1">
URL encode a parameter based on a bean value
</html:link>

<%-- Create the same rewrite string for the above link. --%>
rewrite: <html:rewrite page="/HtmlBasic.do"
              paramId="urlParamName" paramName="pageAttribute1" />
```

The HTML generated is

```
<a href="/StrutsTaglibs/HtmlBasic.do?urlParamName=Value+to+Pass+on+URL">
    ➥URL encode a parameter based on a bean value</a>

rewrite: /StrutsTaglibs/HtmlBasic.do?urlParamName=Value+to+Pass+on+URL
```

Encode a Multiple Request Variables on the URL or URI

This section covers both `<html:link>` and `<html:rewrite>`.

Use this approach if you have multiple request parameters that you need to encode.

To pass multiple values to the tags, you must use a map. Several classes in the `java.util` package meet this criterion. Here's an example using `java.util.HashMap`:

```
<%
   /*
    * Store values in a Map (HashMap in this case)
    * and construct the URL based on the Map
    */
  java.util.HashMap myMap =  new java.util.HashMap();
  myMap.put("myString", new String("myStringValue") );
  myMap.put("myArray",  new String[] { "str1", "str2", "str3" });
  pageContext.setAttribute("map", myMap);
%>
```

Note that one of the values stored in the `HashMap` is itself an array containing multiple values. Now everything is stored in the page context, ready to be passed to the tags like so:

```
<%-- For this version of the <html:link> tag:              --%>
<%-- map = a map with name/value pairs to pass on the url --%>
<html:link page="/HtmlBasic.do" name="map">
  URL encode a parameter based on values in a Map
</html:link>
<%-- Create the same rewrite string for the above link. --%>
rewrite:  <html:rewrite page="/HtmlBasic.do" name="map"/>
```

The HTML generated is

```
<a href="/StrutsTaglibs/HtmlBasic.do?myString=myStringValue&amp;
         ➥myArray=str1&amp;myArray=str2&amp;myArray=str3">
         ➥URL encode a parameter based on values in a Map</a>

rewrite: /StrutsTaglibs/HtmlBasic.do?myString=myStringValue&amp;
         ➥myArray=str1&amp;myArray=str2&amp;myArray=str3
```

The `<html:img>` Tag

The `<html:img>` tag is used to embed images in HTML pages. Generally it's a simple, straightforward tag that simply links an image to the page. If needed, however, it can also pass request parameters along with its request. This might, for example, allow the images to be generated dynamically based on the passed parameters.

There are three examples of this tag's use in the sample application.

Generate a Basic <img> Tag Linking to an Image

This example simply generates a standard <img> tag:

```
<html:img page="/struts-power.gif" />
```

The HTML generated is

```
<img src="/StrutsTaglibs/struts-power.gif">
```

Generate an <img> Containing a Single Request Parameter

This example generates an <img> tag with a single request parameter. The parameter is created based on the stored bean from the corresponding <html:link> section earlier:

```
<%-- Note "src" requires using full relative path --%>
<html:img src="/StrutsTaglibs/struts-power.gif"
          paramId="urlParamName" paramName="pageAttribute1" />
```

The HTML generated is

```
<img src="/StrutsTaglibs/struts-power.gif?urlParamName=Value+to+Pass+on+URL">
```

Generate an <img> Containing a Multiple Request Parameters

This example generates an <img> tag with a multiple request parameters. The parameters are created based on the stored HashMap from the corresponding <html:link> section earlier:

```
<html:img page="/struts-power.gif" name="map" />
```

The HTML generated is

```
<img src="/StrutsTaglibs/struts-power.gif?
     ➥myString=myStringValue&myArray=str1&myArray=str2&myArray=str3">
```

The Basics of Form Processing

This section provides information on the following tags:

- <html:form>—Render an HTML <form> element
- <html:text>—Place a text box INPUT element on a form
- <html:hidden>—Place a INPUT type=hidden element on a form
- <html:submit>—Place a Submit INPUT element on a form

- `<html:cancel>`—Place a Cancel `INPUT` element on a form
- `<html:reset>`—Place a Reset `INPUT` element on a form

If you point your browser to the URL

`http://myAppServer/StrutsTaglibs/html.jsp`

you'll bring up the main page that links to all the sample code for the Struts tag chapters. This section uses the Form Basics page at `http://localhost:8080/StrutsTaglibs/FormBasics.do`. The rendered page is shown in Figure 12.3.

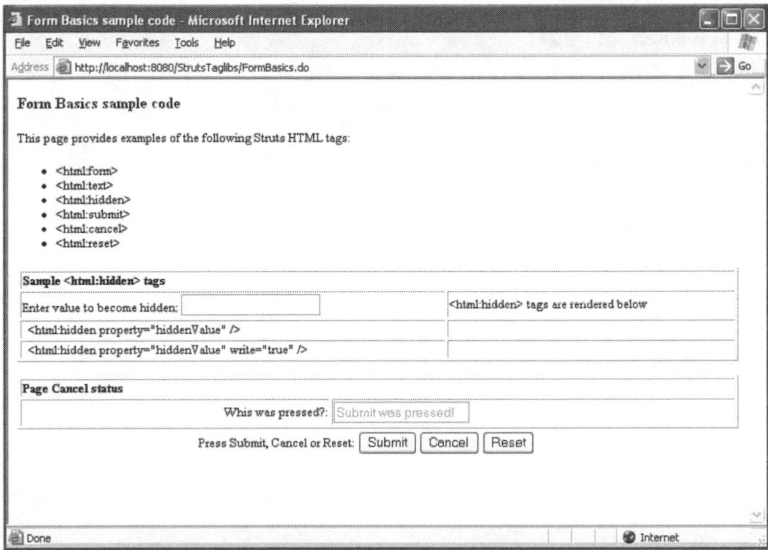

FIGURE 12.3 The Form Basics page at `/StrutsTaglibs/FormBasics.do`.

As you can see, Figure 12.3 contains a very basic form along with some hidden variables and Submit, Cancel, and Reset buttons. Listing 12.2 is the JSP file that creates this page.

LISTING 12.2 JSP File Demonstrating the Basic Struts HTML Tags for Form Processing (`FormBasics.jsp`)

```
<%@ page language="java" %>
<%@ taglib uri="/WEB-INF/struts-html.tld" prefix="html" %>
<html:html>
<head>
<title>Form Basics sample code</title>
```

LISTING 12.2 Continued

```
</head>
<body bgcolor="white">

<h3>Form Basics sample code</h3>

<p>This page provides examples of the following Struts HTML tags:<br>
<ul>
<li>&lt;html:form&gt;</li>
<li>&lt;html:text&gt;</li>
<li>&lt;html:hidden&gt;</li>
<li>&lt;html:submit&gt;</li>
<li>&lt;html:cancel&gt;</li>
<li>&lt;html:reset&gt;</li>
</ul>

<html:form action="FormBasics.do">

<table border="1" width="100%">

  <tr>
    <th colspan="3" align="left">
      Sample &lt;html:hidden&gt; tags
    </th>
  </tr>

  <tr>
    <td align="left" >
      Enter value to become hidden: <html:text property="hiddenValue"/>
    </td>
    <td align="left" >
      &lt;html:hidden&gt; tags are rendered below
    </td>
  </tr>

  <tr>
    <td align="left" >
        &lt;html:hidden property="hiddenValue" /&gt;
    </td>
    <td align="left" >
        <html:hidden property="hiddenValue" />
```

LISTING 12.2 Continued

```
    </td>
  </tr>

  <tr>
    <td align="left" >
        &lt;html:hidden property="hiddenValue" write="true" /&gt;
    </td>
    <td align="left" >
        <html:hidden property="hiddenValue" write="true" />
    </td>
  </tr>
</table>
<br>

<table border="1" width="100%">

  <tr>
    <th colspan="3" align="left">
      Page Cancel status
    </th>
  </tr>

  <tr>
    <td align="right">
      Which was pressed?:
    </td>
    <td align="left">
      <html:text property="status" disabled="true" />
    </td>
  </tr>
</table>

<table border="0" width="100%">

  <tr>
    <td align="right">
      Press Submit, Cancel or Reset:
    </td>
    <td align="left">
      <html:submit>Submit</html:submit>
      <html:cancel>Cancel</html:cancel>
```

LISTING 12.2 Continued

```
      <html:reset>Reset</html:reset>
    </td>
  </tr>

</table>

</html:form>

</body>
</html:html>
```

The following sections outline the functionality related to the tags demonstrated in this listing.

Form Basics: The `<html:form>` Tag

Form processing is at the heart of most Web-based applications. In Struts, every form processed requires an `<html:form>` at its beginning and an `</html:form>` tag at its end.

For example, in the sample code, here's the `<html:form>` tag we used:

```
<html:form action="FormBasics.do">
```

This generates the HTML `<form>` tag:

```
<form name="FormBasicsForm" method="POST"
                            action="/StrutsTaglibs/FormBasics.do">
```

This is the most basic type of `<html:form>` tag. It simply specifies which `<action>` section of the `struts-config.xml` is used to determine how the form will be processed. Here's the corresponding `struts-config.xml` entry for this `<html:form>` tag:

```
<!-- Form Basics example code  -->
    <action     path="/FormBasics"
                type="ch12.FormBasicsAction"
                name="FormBasicsForm"
                scope="session"
                validate="false"
    >
      <forward name="default" path="/FormBasics.jsp"/>
    </action>
```

Because only the action attribute of the <html:form> tag is specified in this example, Struts takes defaults for the form processing from this <action> entry.

If you need to override these defaults and change how your form processes, you can do so by directly specifying new values for the type, name, and/or scope attributes in the <html:form> tag. For example, we could specify a different form bean using the following example:

```
<html:form action="FormBasics.do" name="ch12.diffBean" type="ch12.diffBean">
```

This line enables you to override the struts-config.xml entry and lets you specify the form bean directly in the <html:form> tag itself.

The <html:text> Tag

This tag creates an input text field. It's one of the most-used Struts tags.

There are two examples of the <html:text> tag in this example. The examples are similar in that they both map a text field directly to a property in the form bean. Here's one of the examples:

```
<html:text property="hiddenValue"/>
```

In this example, hiddenValue is mapped to the "hiddenValue" property of the form bean. When the form is posted, the value in this text field is used to populate the "hiddenValue" property of the form bean. In addition, when the page is created, the value of this form bean property becomes the initial value for the field.

Using the <html:text> tag with Struts DynaForms is covered in Chapter 17.

The <html:cancel> Tag

The <html:cancel> tag generates a form Cancel button.

Processing the <html:cancel> tag requires both placing the tag in the JSP file, and coding business logic in the Action class to capture the cancel event when it occurs. This is because it's in the Action class that a cancel event most likely must be processed.

When a user cancel event is detected, it's possible that the user has previously clicked submit and then grown tired of waiting for a response. (Okay, I know: Users *never* do that!) If this is the case, you might appreciate a chance to clean things up rather than leaving things in an unpredictable state. Here's how you do it.

First, place the <html:cancel> tag on the form. In our example, this is simply coded as

```
<html:cancel>Cancel</html:cancel>
```

This places a Cancel button on the form and generates the following HTML in the page:

```
<input type="submit" name="org.apache.struts.taglib.html.CANCEL"
                     value="Cancel">
```

You need to place code in the `Action` class to detect the cancel when it occurs. Listing 12.3 is the `Action` class for this example.

LISTING 12.3 The `Action` Class for the FormBasics Example; This Demonstrates Handling a Cancel Event (`FormBasicsAction.java`)

```
package ch12;

import javax.servlet.http.HttpServletRequest;
import javax.servlet.http.HttpServletResponse;
import org.apache.struts.action.Action;
import org.apache.struts.action.ActionForm;
import org.apache.struts.action.ActionForward;
import org.apache.struts.action.ActionMapping;

/**
 * Action class to demonstrate handling an <html:cancel> tag
 *
 * @author Kevin Bedell & James Turner
 * @version 1.0
 */

public class FormBasicsAction extends Action {

    /**
     * Do Nothing except forward the request
     *
     * @param mapping The ActionMapping from this struts-config.xml entry
     * @param actionForm The ActionForm to process, if any
     * @param request The JSP request object
     * @param response The JSP response object
     *
     * @exception Exception if business logic throws an exception
     */
    public ActionForward execute(ActionMapping mapping,
                                 ActionForm form,
                                 HttpServletRequest request,
                                 HttpServletResponse response)
```

LISTING 12.3 Continued

```
        throws Exception {

        FormBasicsForm fbf = (FormBasicsForm) form;

        if (isCancelled(request)) {

            /*
             * If request was cancelled, we would clean up any processing
             * that was unfinished and release any resources we may
             * have locked.
             */

            // Set status to reflect that cancel WAS pressed!
            fbf.setStatus("Cancel was pressed!");

            return (mapping.findForward("default"));
        }  else {

            // Set status to reflect that cancel WAS NOT pressed!
            fbf.setStatus("Submit was pressed!");

            return (mapping.findForward("default"));
        }
    }
}
```

As you can see, the way to detect a cancel is by using the `isCancelled(request)` method. If this method returns true, you perform any required clean up. You can also forward the page to a particular JSP (View component), as the code demonstrates.

The `<html:reset>` Tag

This tag generates a form Reset button.

This example places a Reset button on the form. The Struts tag in our example is

```
<html:reset>Reset</html:reset>
```

The HTML generated is

```
<input type="reset" name="reset" value="Reset">
```

This is a basic, no-frills tag and virtually all the attributes for it are simply to pass through HTML attributes.

The <html:submit> Tag

This tag generates a form Submit button.

This example places a Submit button on the form. The Struts tag in our example is

```
<html:submit>Submit</html:submit>
```

The HTML generated is

```
<input type="submit" name="submit" value="Submit">
```

As with the <html:reset> button, this is a basic, no-frills tag and virtually all the attributes for it are simply to pass through HTML attributes.

The <html:hidden> Tag

This tag generates a hidden input element in a form.

Hidden values are commonly used to store information on a form that the user doesn't need to see. The values are hidden from the user, but they become visible if the user chooses to view source on the page. Hidden values are sometimes used to store state information in the client browser without using cookies.

This sample application demonstrates two versions of this tag. Both versions create an HTML <input type="hidden" > tag. The second also echoes the value of the hidden property to allow it to be displayed in the page.

Here's the first version:

```
<html:hidden property="hiddenValue" />
```

The HTML created is

```
<input type="hidden" name="hiddenValue" value="propValue">
```

The second version adds the write=true attribute:

```
<html:hidden property="hiddenValue" write="true" />
```

The HTML created is

```
<input type="hidden" name="hiddenValue" value="propValue">propValue
```

As you can see, the second version simply echoes the value of the hidden variable. This can be useful if you need to display a value from your form bean and don't want the user to be able to change it.

Check Boxes and Radio Buttons

This section provides information on the following tags:

- `<html:checkbox>`—Render an HTML `<form>` element
- `<html:multibox>`—Place a text box `INPUT` element on a form
- `<html:radio>`—Place a Cancel `INPUT` element on a form

If you point your browser to the URL

```
http://myAppServer/StrutsTaglibs/html.jsp
```

you'll bring up the main page that links to all the sample code for the Struts tag chapters. This section uses the Checkboxes and Radio Buttons page at `/StrutsTaglibs/CheckboxRadio.do`. The page rendered is shown in Figure 12.4.

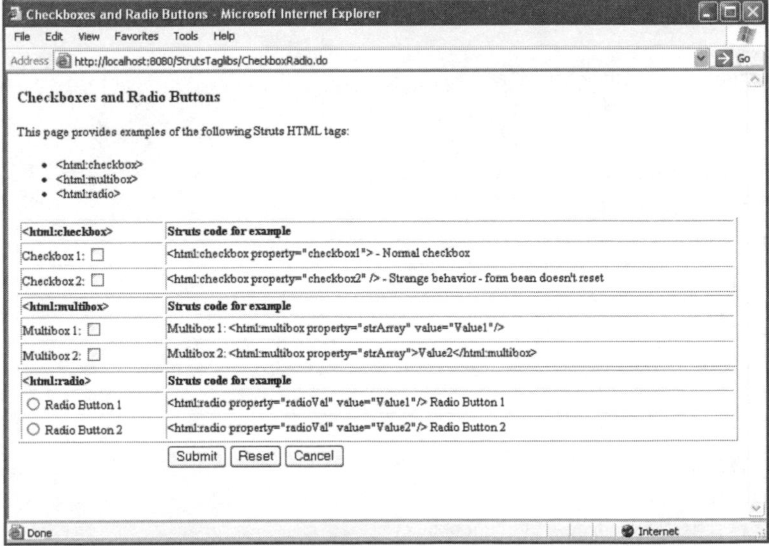

FIGURE 12.4 The Checkboxes and Radio Buttons page at `/StrutsTaglibs/CheckboxRadio.do`.

This page contains two <html:checkbox> tags, two <html:multibox> tags, and two <html:radio> tags. Listing 12.4 is the JSP file that creates this page.

LISTING 12.4 JSP File Demonstrating the Use of <html:checkbox>, <html:multibox>, and <html:radio> Tags (CheckboxRadio.jsp)

```
<%@ page language="java" %>
<%@ taglib uri="/WEB-INF/struts-html.tld" prefix="html" %>
<%@ taglib uri="/WEB-INF/struts-bean.tld" prefix="bean" %>
<html:html>
<head>
<title>Checkboxes and Radio Buttons</title>
</head>
<body bgcolor="white">

<h3>Checkboxes and Radio Buttons</h3>

<p>This page provides examples of the following Struts HTML tags:<br>
<ul>
<li>&lt;html:checkbox&gt;</li>
<li>&lt;html:multibox&gt;</li>
<li>&lt;html:radio&gt;</li>
</ul>

<html:form action="CheckboxRadio.do">

<table border="1" width="100%">

  <tr>
    <th align="left" width="20%">
    &lt;html:checkbox&gt;
    </th>
    <th align="left" width="80%">
    Struts code for example
    </th>
  </tr>

  <tr>
    <td align="left">
      Checkbox 1:
      <html:checkbox property="checkbox1"/>
    </td>
```

LISTING 12.4 Continued

```
    <td align="left">
        &lt;html:checkbox property="checkbox1"&gt;
        - Normal checkbox
    </td>
  </tr>

  <tr>
    <td align="left">
      Checkbox 2:
      <html:checkbox property="checkbox2" />
    </td>
    <td align="left">
        &lt;html:checkbox property="checkbox2" /&gt;
        - Strange behavior - form bean doesn't reset
    </td>
  </tr>

</table>

<table border="1" width="100%">

  <tr>
    <th align="left" width="20%">
      &lt;html:multibox&gt;
    </th>
    <th align="left" width="80%">
      Struts code for example
    </th>
  </tr>

  <tr>
    <td align="left" width="20%">
      Multibox 1:
      <html:multibox property="strArray" value="Value1"/>
    </td>
    <td align="left" width="80%">
      Multibox 1:
      &lt;html:multibox property="strArray" value="Value1"/&gt;
    </td>
  </tr>
```

LISTING 12.4 Continued

```
  <tr>
    <td align="left" width="20%">
      Multibox 2:
      <html:multibox property="strArray">Value2</html:multibox>
    </td>
    <td align="left" width="80%">
      Multibox 2:
      &lt;html:multibox property="strArray"&gt;Value2&lt;/html:multibox&gt;
    </td>
  </tr>

</table>

<table border="1" width="100%">

  <tr>
    <th align="left" width="20%">
    &lt;html:radio&gt;
    </th>
    <th align="left" width="80%">
    Struts code for example
    </th>
  </tr>

  <tr>
    <td align="left" width="20%">
      <html:radio property="radioVal" value="Value1"/>
      Radio Button 1
    </td>
    <td align="left" width="80%">
      &lt;html:radio property="radioVal" value="Value1"/&gt;
      Radio Button 1
    </td>
  </tr>

  <tr>
    <td align="left" width="20%">
      <html:radio property="radioVal" value="Value2"/>
      Radio Button 2
    </td>
    <td align="left" width="80%">
```

LISTING 12.4 Continued

```
      &lt;html:radio property="radioVal" value="Value2"/&gt;
      Radio Button 2
    </td>
  </tr>

</table>

<table border="0" width="100%">

  <tr>
    <td align="left" width="20%"> </td>
    <td align="left">
      <html:submit>Submit</html:submit>
      <html:reset>Reset</html:reset>
      <html:cancel>Cancel</html:cancel>
    </td>
  </tr>

</table>

</html:form>

</body>
</html:html>
```

For this example, reviewing the form bean is valuable to help demonstrate how these three types of elements are managed. Listing 12.5 is the form bean that goes with this JSP file (`CheckboxRadioForm.java`).

LISTING 12.5 Form Bean That Corresponds with `CheckboxRadio.jsp` (`CheckboxRadioForm.java`)

```
package ch12;

import javax.servlet.http.HttpServletRequest;
import org.apache.struts.action.ActionForm;
import org.apache.struts.action.ActionMapping;

/**
 * <p>Title: HtmlCheckboxForm.java </p>
 * <p>Description:  Form Bean for the &lt;html:checkbox&gt; example</p>
 * <p>Copyright: Copyright (c) 2002</p>
```

LISTING 12.5 Continued

```
 * @author Kevin Bedell & James Turner
 * @version 1.0
 *
 */
public class CheckboxRadioForm extends ActionForm {

  // Default bean constructor
  public CheckboxRadioForm() { }

  // For <html:checkbox> sample code
  private boolean checkbox1;
  public boolean getCheckbox1() { return this.checkbox1; }
  public void setCheckbox1(boolean checkbox1) { this.checkbox1 = checkbox1;}

  // For <html:checkbox> sample code
  private boolean checkbox2;
  public boolean getCheckbox2() { return this.checkbox2; }
  public void setCheckbox2(boolean checkbox2) { this.checkbox2 = checkbox2;}

  // For <html:multibox> sample code
  private String strArray[] = new String[0];
  public String[] getStrArray() { return (this.strArray); }
  public void setStrArray(String strArray[]) { this.strArray = strArray;}

  // For <html:radio> sample code
  private String radioVal = "";
  public String getRadioVal() { return (this.radioVal); }
  public void setRadioVal(String radioVal) { this.radioVal = radioVal;}

  public void reset(ActionMapping mapping, HttpServletRequest request) {

    this.setCheckbox1(false);
//    Note: With checkbox2 never reset here, it won't ever appear "unset"
//    this.setCheckbox2(false);

    this.strArray = new String[0];
    this.radioVal = "";
  }
}
```

The properties and methods in this class are discussed in the following sections.

The <html:checkbox> Tag

The <html:checkbox> tag generates a standalone check box tied to a specific property in a form bean. It should be used when you have a property that can be represented as being either chosen or not chosen (that is, its status is true or false).

The sample code contains two <html:checkbox> elements. They're mapped, appropriately, to the checkbox1 and checkbox2 properties in the CheckboxRadioForm form bean.

The Struts tags for both elements in this sample are of the following format:

```
<html:checkbox property="checkbox1"/>
```

The only difference between them is the value of the property they map to. They both render similar HTML <input> tags:

```
<input type="checkbox" name="checkbox2" value="on">
```

The first thing to notice is that the underlying properties in the form bean behind the <html:checkbox> tag are boolean. This is the only tag that requires its underlying property to be boolean.

This example doesn't specify a default value for the check boxes, which causes them to take their initial value from the property they're associated with. If you want to, you can override this behavior as follows:

- value="true"—When the box is checked and the form is submitted, set the boolean value to true.
- value="false"—When the box is checked and the form is submitted, set the boolean value to false.

Notice that this could be misleading. For example, specifying the attribute to value="false" causes the boolean to be set to true if the box is submitted unchecked.

The string "true" can also be specified as "on" or "yes". Similarly, the value "false" can be set to "off" or "no".

By looking at the form bean, you can see an additional difference in how the two properties are handled during the reset() method. Here's the code:

```
this.setCheckbox1(false);
//    Note: With checkbox2 never reset here, it won't ever appear "unset"
//    this.setCheckbox2(false);
```

Notice that the `reset()` method doesn't reset the value of `checkbox2`. This was done to demonstrate a common gotcha: forgetting to reset a check box value. Because the field isn't reset, after the underlying `boolean` is set to `true`, the form always initializes as checked. If you uncheck the check box and submit again, it again returns as checked. In other words, the check box value is never reset.

The `<html:multibox>` Tag

The `<html:multibox>` tag renders an HTML `<input type="checkbox" >` tag similar to `<html:checkbox>`. The difference is in the underlying interactions with the form bean.

The `<html:multibox>` tag expects its underlying property value to be an array, as opposed to an individual property. Use this tag if you have a number of check boxes and want to manage them all in a single array in the form bean, rather than creating individual form bean properties for each check box.

Here's how to use this tag:

- First, define an array in the form bean to hold the values submitted by the check boxes on the form.
- Second, add `<html:multibox>` elements to your form and map each one to the underlying array in the form bean using the `property="arrayName"` attribute.
- For each of the `<html:multibox>` elements, specify the value to be stored in the array if that element is checked when the form is submitted. This value can be specified in one of two ways: either by using the `value="`*`valueToSubmit`*`"` attribute, or by nesting the value between opening and closing `<html:multibox>` tags. For example, you can use either

  ```
  <html:multibox property="strArray" value="Value1"/>
  ```

  or

  ```
  <html:multibox property="strArray">Value2</html:multibox>
  ```

When the form is submitted, the array is populated with the values from each of the multiboxes that's checked. If an `<html:multibox>` element is unchecked, the array simply won't contain its value.

This provides more flexibility than the simpler `<html:checkbox>` elements in that they allow you to store more than just `true` or `false` `boolean` values. In addition, the form beans end up being much simpler if you have more than just a few check box elements.

A potentially more important benefit is that the number of <html:multibox> elements on a page can be dynamic. That is, you have to add a boolean property to the form bean for each <html:checkbox> element on the form, but any number of <html:multibox> elements can be posted to the same array as long as they have different values.

The <html:radio> Tag

The <html:radio> tag renders an HTML <input type="radio"> tag.

Struts <html:radio> tags are used in groups all having the property attribute. For example, here are the two <html:radio> tags included in the sample application:

```
<html:radio property="radioVal" value="Value1"/>

<html:radio property="radioVal" value="Value2"/>
```

These tags differ only in that they have different value attributes. Here are the HTML tags that they render:

```
<input type="radio" name="radioVal" value="Value1">

<input type="radio" name="radioVal" value="Value2">
```

Because these two elements share the same name attribute, only one of them can be selected at a time. When the form is submitted, the value of whichever element is selected is posted to the form bean property specified in the <html:radio> tag. If neither element is selected, an empty string is stored in the form bean property.

Drop Downs and Select/Option Lists

This section provides information on the following tags:

- <html:select>—Render an HTML <select> drop-down or multi-select element
- <html:option>—Define an individual <option> element within a <select> element
- <html:options>—Define one or more <option> elements within a <select> element
- <html:optionsCollection>—Define one or more <option> elements within a <select> element based on a collection

If you point your browser to the URL

```
http://myAppServer/StrutsTaglibs/html.jsp
```

you'll bring up the main page that links to all the sample code for the Struts tag chapters. This section uses the Select and Option Tags page at `/StrutsTaglibs/HtmlSelects.do`. The rendered page is shown in Figure 12.5.

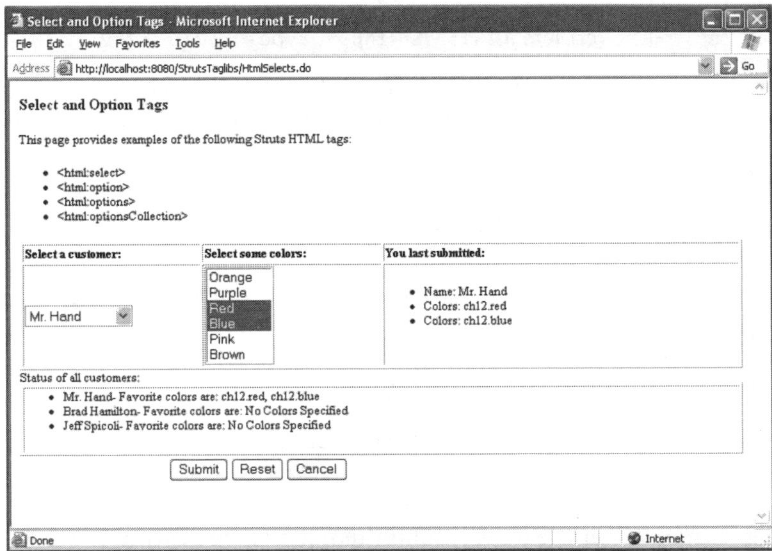

FIGURE 12.5 The Select and Option Tags page at `/StrutsTaglibs/HtmlSelects.do`.

Listing 12.6 is the JSP file that creates this page.

LISTING 12.6 JSP File Demonstrating the Use of `<html:select>`, `<html:option>`, `<html:options>`, and `<html:optionsCollection>` Tags (`HtmlSelects.jsp`)

```
<%@ page language="java" import="ch12.*, java.util.*" %>
<%@ taglib uri="/WEB-INF/struts-html.tld" prefix="html" %>
<%@ taglib uri="/WEB-INF/struts-bean.tld" prefix="bean" %>
<%@ taglib uri="/WEB-INF/struts-logic.tld" prefix="logic" %>
<html:html>
<head>
<title>Select and Option Tags</title>
</head>
<body bgcolor="white">

<h3>Select and Option Tags</h3>
```

LISTING 12.6 Continued

```
<p>This page provides examples of the following Struts HTML tags:<br>
<ul>
<li>&lt;html:select&gt;</li>
<li>&lt;html:option&gt;</li>
<li>&lt;html:options&gt;</li>
<li>&lt;html:optionsCollection&gt;</li>
</ul>
<html:form action="HtmlSelects.do">

<table border="1" width="100%">

  <tr>

    <%
      Vector colorCollection = new Vector();
      colorCollection.add(
         new org.apache.struts.util.LabelValueBean("Pink", "ch12.pink"));
      colorCollection.add(
         new org.apache.struts.util.LabelValueBean("Brown", "ch12.brown"));
      pageContext.setAttribute("colorCollection", colorCollection);
    %>

    <th align="left" width="25%" >Select a customer: </th>

    <th align="left" width="25%" >Select some colors: </th>

    <th align="left" width="50%" >You last submitted: </th>

  </tr>

  <tr>

    <td align="left" width="25%" >
      <html:select property="custId">
        <html:optionsCollection property="customers"
                                label="name"
                                value="custId" />
      </html:select>
    </td>
```

LISTING 12.6 Continued

```
    <td align="left" width="25%" >
      <html:select property="colors" size="6" multiple="true" >

        <%-- Specify some options using the basic version of the tag --%>
        <html:option value="ch12.orange">Orange</html:option>
        <html:option value="ch12.purple" value="Purple" />

        <%-- Specify some by referring to a properties file --%>
        <html:option value="ch12.red"   bundle="ch12.Colors" key="ch12.red"/>
        <html:option value="ch12.blue"  bundle="ch12.Colors" key="ch12.blue"/>

        <%-- Specify some from our collection of LabelValueBean's --%>
        <html:options collection="colorCollection"
                      property="value"
                      labelProperty="label" />

      </html:select>
    </td>

    <td align="left" width="50%" >
        <ul>
          <li>Name: <bean:write name="HtmlSelectsForm" property="cust.name" />
          <logic:iterate id="element" name="HtmlSelectsForm"
          ➥property="cust.favColors">
          <li>Colors: <bean:write name="element" />
          </logic:iterate>
        </ul>
    </td>

  </tr>

</table>

<table border="1" width="100%">

  Status of all customers:<br>

    <td align="left">
        <ul>
          <logic:iterate id="c" name="HtmlSelectsForm" property="customers">
            <li><bean:write name="c" />
```

LISTING 12.6 Continued

```
        </logic:iterate>
      </ul>
    </td>

</table>

<table border="0" width="100%">
  <tr>
    <td align="left" width="20%"> </td>
    <td align="left">
      <html:submit>Submit</html:submit>
      <html:reset>Reset</html:reset>
      <html:cancel>Cancel</html:cancel>
    </td>
  </tr>

</table>

</html:form>
</html:html>
```

For this example, it's valuable to review the form bean to help demonstrate how these three types of elements are managed. Listing 12.7 is the form bean that goes with this JSP file (`HtmlSelectsForm.java`).

LISTING 12.7 Form Bean That Corresponds with `HtmlSelects.jsp` (`HtmlSelectsForm.java`)

```
package ch12;

import javax.servlet.http.HttpServletRequest;
import javax.servlet.http.HttpServletResponse;
import org.apache.struts.action.Action;
import org.apache.struts.action.ActionError;
import org.apache.struts.action.ActionErrors;
import org.apache.struts.action.ActionForm;
import org.apache.struts.action.ActionForward;
import org.apache.struts.action.ActionMapping;

/**
 * @author Kevin Bedell & James Turner
```

LISTING 12.7 Continued

```
 * @version 1.0
 *
 */
public class HtmlSelectsForm extends ActionForm {

  private CustomerBean customers[];
  public CustomerBean [] getCustomers() { return this.customers; }
  public void setCustomers(CustomerBean [] customers) {
    this.customers = customers;
  }

  private CustomerBean cust = new CustomerBean();
  public CustomerBean getCust() { return cust; }
  public void setCust(CustomerBean cust) { this.cust = cust; }

  private int custId;
  public int getCustId() { return this.custId; }
  public void setCustId(int custId) { this.custId = custId; }

  private String colors[];
  public String [] getColors() { return this.colors; }
  public void setColors(String [] colors) { this.colors = colors; }

  // Default bean constructor
  public HtmlSelectsForm() {

    customers = new CustomerBean[3];

    for (int i=0; i<3 ; i++ ) {
      customers[i] =  new CustomerBean();
      customers[i].setCustId(i);
    }

    customers[0].setName("Mr. Hand");
    customers[1].setName("Brad Hamilton");
    customers[2].setName("Jeff Spicoli");
  }

  public void reset(ActionMapping mapping, HttpServletRequest request) {
```

LISTING 12.7 Continued

```
    this.cust = new CustomerBean();
    this.colors = new String[0];
    this.custId = -1;
  }

  public ActionErrors validate(ActionMapping mapping,
                               HttpServletRequest request) {

      ActionErrors errors = new ActionErrors();

      // if custId is -1, then no customer was chosen yet.

      if (custId == -1) {
        return errors;
      }

      /*
       * No real validation done. Just set values based on input.
       */

      this.customers[this.custId].setFavColors(this.colors);
      this.cust = this.customers[this.custId];

      return errors;
  }
}
```

The properties and methods in this class are discussed in the following sections.

The `<html:select>` Tag

The `<html:select>` tag renders an HTML `<select>` tag. These tags are used for both drop-down lists and multiselect or scrolling lists. Figure 12.5 shows examples of both these elements.

The basic format of this tag is

```
<html:select property="custId">
  [1 or more <html:option>, <html:options>, <html:optionCollections> tags]
</html:select>
```

That is, all the option elements can be mixed in a single <html:select> tag.

A drop-down list is rendered if the size attribute is set to 1 (or is omitted) and the multiple attribute isn't set to true (or is omitted). Otherwise, a multiselect list is rendered.

The property attribute defines the property in the form bean that this element is tied to. When the page is rendered, the value of this property becomes the initial value and is shown as selected.

If the multiple attribute is omitted, only a single value is submitted from the <select> element when the form is submitted. In that case, the property in the form bean must be a simple property (that is, not an array). If the multiple attribute is set to true, the underlying property must be an array because more than one value could be submitted.

By default, the property attribute specifies a property of the default form bean specified for this <html:form> element. It's possible to override this behavior by using the name attribute to specify the name of another bean.

The <html:option> Tag

The <html:option> tag renders an HTML <option> tag. It's the basic Struts tag for rendering a single <option> tag inside a <select> element.

This tag represents a possible value for the enclosing <select> element. If the value of the <select> element matches the value of the <option> tag, this <option> is shown as highlighted.

The display value of the <html:option> tag is taken from one of two places:

- The value enclosed by <html:option> and </html:option> tags
- A value in a properties file (resource bundle) as specified by the key, locale, and bundle attributes of the <html:option> tag

To specify a display value using a resource bundle, you should first define a <message-resources> element in the struts-config.xml file.

For example, consider the list of colors in the sample program. Here are the <option> tags that specify the first four elements in the list:

```
<%-- Specify some options using the basic version of the tag --%>
<html:option value="ch12.orange">Orange</html:option>
<html:option value="ch12.purple">Purple</html:option>
```

```
<%-- Specify some by referring to a properties file --%>
<html:option value="ch12.red"   bundle="ch12.Colors" key="ch12.red"/>
<html:option value="ch12.blue"  bundle="ch12.Colors" key="ch12.blue"/>
```

As you can see, `<option>` tags can be mixed and used in multiple forms. The Orange and Purple options have their values specified directly in the tag. The Red and Blue options are defined in the message resource bundle defined as `ch12.Colors`.

The resource bundle is defined by this line in the `struts-config.xml` file:

```
<message-resources parameter="ch12.Colors" key="ch12.Colors" />
```

The `parameter` attribute identifies the properties as being in the `ch12.Colors.properties` file. Here are the contents of that file:

```
ch12.red=Red
ch12.blue=Blue
```

If you wanted to provide locale-specific `<option>` values, you could simply provide properties files for each locale that you must support.

The `<html:options>` Tag

The `<html:options>` tag is very flexible and enables you to generate HTML `<option>` elements in a number of ways. For a complete description, please refer to the Struts documentation. This section presents only some of the ways the tag can be used.

No matter how the HTML `<option>` elements are used, the basic idea is they're generated from a collection (or array) of values. The differences in the attributes you specify determine where the collection is fetched from and where the labels and values for each element come from.

The `<html:options>` tag works differently depending on whether the `collection` attribute is specified. In general,

- If the `collection` attribute is specified, the bean referred to *is itself the collection.*
- If the collection attribute is not specified, the bean referred to *contains a property holding the collection.*

Here are some examples to help clarify this concept. First, here's an example in which the `collection` attribute is specified:

```
<html:options collection="coll" property="value" labelProperty="label" />
```

In English, this means, "The options are stored in a bean named `coll`. This bean itself is a collection that holds individual option elements. The `value` property of each element holds the value to be submitted if this option is selected. The `label` property of each element holds the value of the label to show each user on the list."

Second, here's an example in which the collection attribute *isn't* specified:

```
<html:options property="values" labelProperty="labels" />
```

In English, this means, "A form bean property named `values` holds the collection of option values. A form bean property named `labels` holds the collection of option labels to display to the user."

Finally, here's an example in which the labels and values are stored in collections in different beans:

```
<html:options name="valueBean" property="values"
              labelName="labelsBean"  labelProperty="labels" />
```

In English, this means, "The values are stored in a bean named `valueBean` in a property named `values`, which is a collection holding the value elements. The labels are stored in a bean named `labelsBean` in a property named `labels`, which is a collection holding the label elements."

There are many combinations of these attributes. As you can see, the flexibility of this tag is extreme!

Given this background, let's interpret the `<html:options>` tag used in the sample program:

```
<%-- Specify some from our collection of LabelValueBean's --%>
<html:options collection="colorCollection"
              property="value"
              labelProperty="label" />
```

In English, this means, "The values are stored in a bean named `colorCollection`, which itself is a collection. Each element of the collection has a property named `value` containing the value and a property named `label` containing the label to display to the user."

The need for a bean with properties named `value` and `label` came up so often in Struts that a Struts utility class based on this was added to the framework. The class is named `org.apache.struts.utility.LabelValueBean` and its use is demonstrated in this sample program.

The following is the code in which the `colorCollection` is initialized. It demonstrates the use of the Struts `LabelValueBean` utility class.

```
<%
  Vector colorCollection = new Vector();
  colorCollection.add(
     new org.apache.struts.util.LabelValueBean("Pink", "ch12.pink"));
  colorCollection.add(
     new org.apache.struts.util.LabelValueBean("Brown", "ch12.brown"));
  pageContext.setAttribute("colorCollection", colorCollection);
%>
```

The preceding code takes advantage of the constructor that takes `label` and `value` properties and returns the initialized object.

The `<html:optionsCollection>` Tag

The `<html:optionsCollection>` is very similar to the `<html:options>` tag. The approach you should take depends on the specifics of the classes and data you're working with.

In the sample application, the list of user options in the drop-down box is displayed using the following tag:

```
<html:select property="custId">
    <html:optionsCollection property="customers"
                            label="name"
                            value="custId" />
</html:select>
```

The form bean contains an array of objects in the property `customers` that we want the labels and values to come from. For each object in the array, the `<option>` label comes from the `name` property and the `value` comes from the `custId` property.

The `<html:optionsCollection>` tag is designed to work well with the `LabelValueBean` described in the previous section. If the label and value properties in each element of the collection are literally named `label` and `value`, these attributes can be omitted!

That means if the sample application used `LabelValueBean` objects instead of the custom bean that was used, this section could have been written as

```
<html:select property="custId">
        <html:optionsCollection property="customers" />
</html:select>
```

Whether you should use the Struts `<html:options>` or `<html:optionsCollection>` tag for a particular application depends on exactly how your application is written and the nature of the objects you're using to store your labels and values.

Input Validation and <html:errors>

This section provides information on the following tag:

- <html:errors>—Output error text to the user

If you point your browser to the URL

```
http://myAppServer/StrutsTaglibs/html.jsp
```

you'll bring up the main page that links to all the sample code for the Struts tag chapters. This section uses <html:errors> Sample Code page at /StrutsTaglibs/HtmlErrors.do.

This page is shown in two different stages. The first stage, shown in Figure 12.6, shows the page as it appears when no validation errors have occurred.

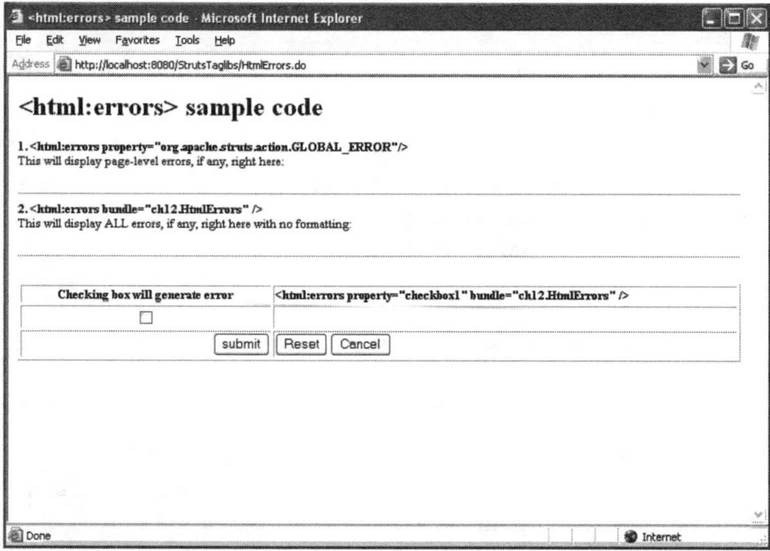

FIGURE 12.6 The <html:errors> Sample Code page with no errors shown at /StrutsTaglibs/HtmlErrors.do.

Figure 12.7 displays the same file with errors showing. Simply checking the check box element and submitting the form generates these errors. Two types of errors are shown: a global error that's shown at the form level, and a field-level error shown for just the check box element itself.

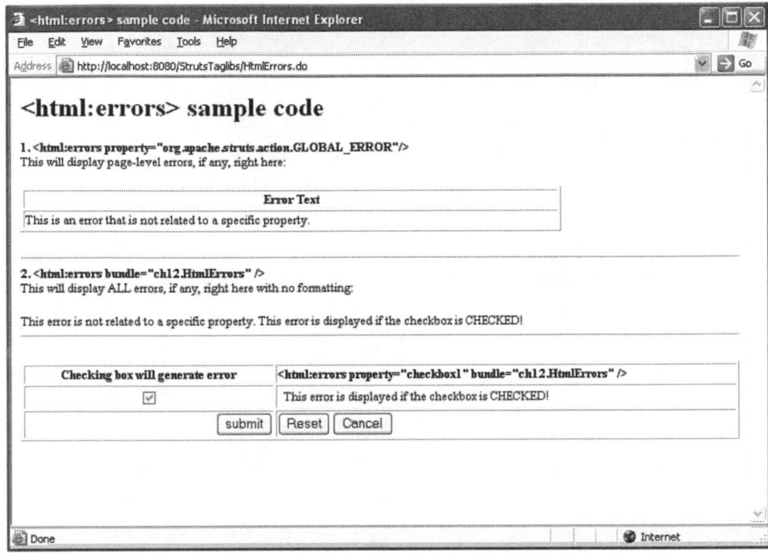

FIGURE 12.7 The <html:errors> Sample Code page with global and field-level errors shown at /StrutsTaglibs/HtmlErrors.do.

Listing 12.8 is the JSP file that creates this page.

LISTING 12.8 JSP File Demonstrating Use of the <html:errors> Tag for Both Global and Form-Level Errors (HtmlErrors.jsp)

```
<%@ page language="java" %>
<%@ page import="org.apache.struts.action.*" %>
<%@ taglib uri="/WEB-INF/struts-html.tld" prefix="html" %>
<html:html>
<head>
<title>&lt;html:errors&gt; sample code</title>
</head>
<body bgcolor="white">

<h1>&lt;html:errors&gt; sample code</h1>
<b>1. &lt;html:errors property="org.apache.struts.action.GLOBAL_ERROR"/&gt;</b>
<br>This will display page-level errors, if any, right here:<p>
<html:errors property="org.apache.struts.action.GLOBAL_ERROR"/>
<hr>
<b>2. &lt;html:errors bundle="ch12.HtmlErrors" /&gt;</b>
<br>This will display ALL errors, if any, right here with no formatting:<p>
<html:errors bundle="ch12.HtmlErrors" />
```

LISTING 12.8 Continued

```
<hr><br>
<html:form action="HtmlErrors.do">

<table border="1" width="100%">

  <tr>
    <th align="center" width="35%">
      Checking box will generate error
    </th>
    <th align="left" width="65%">
     &lt;html:errors property="checkbox1" bundle="ch12.HtmlErrors" /&gt;
    </th>
  </tr>

  <tr>
    <td align="center">
      <html:checkbox property="checkbox1"/>
    </td>
    <td align="left">
        <html:errors property="checkbox1" bundle="ch12.HtmlErrors" />
     </td>
  </tr>

  <tr>
    <td align="right">
      <html:submit>submit</html:submit>
    </td>
    <td align="left">
      <html:reset>Reset</html:reset>
      <html:cancel>Cancel</html:cancel>
    </td>
  </tr>

</table>

</html:form>

</body>
</html:html>
```

Reviewing the form bean for this example is valuable to help demonstrate how the error tags are handled during form validation. Listing 12.9 is the form bean that goes with this JSP file (HtmlErrorsForm.java).

LISTING 12.9 Form Bean That Corresponds with HtmlErrors.jsp (HtmlErrorsForm.java)

```
package ch12;

import javax.servlet.http.HttpServletRequest;
import javax.servlet.http.HttpServletResponse;
import org.apache.struts.action.Action;
import org.apache.struts.action.ActionError;
import org.apache.struts.action.ActionErrors;
import org.apache.struts.action.ActionForm;
import org.apache.struts.action.ActionForward;
import org.apache.struts.action.ActionMapping;

/**
 * <p>Title: HtmlErrorsForm.java </p>
 * <p>Description:  Form Bean for the &lt;html:errors&gt; example</p>
 * <p>Copyright: Copyright (c) 2002</p>
 * @author Kevin Bedell & James Turner
 * @version 1.0
 *
 */
public class HtmlErrorsForm extends ActionForm {

  // Default bean constructor
  public HtmlErrorsForm() { }

  private boolean checkbox1;
  public boolean getCheckbox1() { return this.checkbox1; }
  public void setCheckbox1(boolean checkbox1) { this.checkbox1 = checkbox1; }

  // -------------------------------------------------------- Public Methods

    /**
     * Reset all properties to their default values.
     *
     * @param mapping The mapping used to select this instance
     * @param request The servlet request we are processing
     */
```

LISTING 12.9 Continued

```
    public void reset(ActionMapping mapping, HttpServletRequest request) {
        this.setCheckbox1(false);
    }

    /**
     * Validate the properties posted in this request. If validation errors are
     * found, return an <code>ActionErrors</code> object containing the errors.
     * If no validation errors occur, return <code>null</code> or an empty
     * <code>ActionErrors</code> object.
     *
     * @param mapping The current mapping (from struts-config.xml)
     * @param request The servlet request object
     * @return ActionErrors The ActionErrors object containing the errors.
     */
    public ActionErrors validate(ActionMapping mapping,
                                 HttpServletRequest request) {

        ActionErrors errors = new ActionErrors();

        /*
         * If the checkbox is checked, display error messages
         */
        if ( this.getCheckbox1() ) {

            // First, a GLOBAL_ERROR message for the entire page.
            errors.add(ActionErrors.GLOBAL_ERROR,
                       new ActionError("ch12.global.error") );
            // Also, display a specific error for this parameter
            errors.add("checkbox1", new ActionError("ch12.checkbox.error"));
        }

        return errors;
    }
}
```

Processing logic for this form bean is described in the following sections.

The `<html:errors>` Tag

The `<html:errors>` tag provides a method for managing the placement and formatting of text relating to errors encountered in form processing.

The <html:errors> tag, as part of the overall error processing framework that comes with Struts, provides a great deal of flexibility in how you process errors. The following are among its features:

- Error text can be localized to the language of the user, based on the locale of the user's browser.
- Error text messages can be taken from the primary ApplicationResources for the application or they can be defined in their own .properties file.
- Errors can be identified as global, or relating to the form as a whole; they can also be mapped to a specific field on a form.
- Error text can be parameterized using any information available to the form bean or Action class.

How Error Processing Works

To begin with, the <html:errors> tag only displays information if there are errors to display. If there are no errors to display, nothing is printed. So, to use this tag, you place it on your form where you want the errors to display and it does nothing until errors occur.

For example, there's an <html:errors> tag in the sample application that's used to display an error message depending on the status of the HTML check box element, checkbox1. Here's the JSP code for the check box with the <html:errors> tag as well:

```
<tr>
  <td align="center">
    <html:checkbox property="checkbox1"/>
  </td>
  <td align="left">
      <html:errors property="checkbox1" bundle="ch12.HtmlErrors" />
   </td>
</tr>
```

As you can see, both the <html:checkbox> and <html:errors> tags specify checkbox1 as the property they're tied to. For this example, an error condition is considered to have occurred if the check box is checked (this is enforced in the form bean, which is reviewed shortly).

Reviewing Figure 12.5, you can see the check box isn't checked and the error text isn't displayed. However, in Figure 12.6, the check box is checked and the error message is displayed.

The error messages are created in either the `validate` method of the form bean or in the `Action` class. In our sample application, they're created in the form bean using the following code:

```
ActionErrors errors = new ActionErrors();

/*
 * If the checkbox is checked, display error messages
 */
if ( this.getCheckbox1() ) {

     // First, a GLOBAL_ERROR message for the entire page.
    errors.add(ActionErrors.GLOBAL_ERROR,
                   new ActionError("ch12.global.error") );
    // Also, display a specific error for this parameter
    errors.add("checkbox1", new ActionError("ch12.checkbox.error"));
}
```

The same `ActionErrors` object created here is passed back to the View component (the `.jsp` file) in a bean identified by the string constant `Action.ERROR_KEY`. This bean is stored on in the request scope.

The `<html:errors>` tag operates by first seeing whether this bean is available while the JSP file is being processed. If the bean is available, it's assumed that there are valid errors to display.

Specifying the Resource Bundle for the Error Text and Localizing the Text
Notice that the `<html:errors>` tag for `checkbox1` specifies the attribute `bundle="ch12.HtmlErrors`. This directs the tag to take the error text from the `message-resource` named as `ch12.HtmlErrors`. The `message-resource` must be configured in the `struts-config.xml` file. The configuration for our example is

```
<message-resources parameter="ch12.HtmlErrors" key="ch12.HtmlErrors" />
```

This tells us that the resource bundle being defined is in a file named `HtmlErrors.properties`, which is stored in the `ch12` package somewhere on the `Classpath`.

The actual file from which these properties are loaded depends on the `Locale` of the user. They are the normal rules specified by the i18n features of the Java class `java.util.ResourceBundle`. For more information, please see the Javadoc for the class `java.util.ResourceBundle` or the Sun tutorial on i18n at `http://java.sun.com/docs/books/tutorial/i18n/index.html`.

Specifying Global Versus Field-Specific Error Messages

If no `property` attribute is specified in the `<html:errors>` tag, all the available error messages are printed. To print an individual error message, specify the error you want to print using the `property` attribute.

The `ActionErrors.Global` property is available to identify error messages that are global in nature; that is, messages that aren't tied to an individual property.

The sample application uses the following code in the form bean to add an `ActionErrors.Global` error:

```
errors.add(ActionErrors.GLOBAL_ERROR, new ActionError("ch12.global.error"));
```

The JSP file then uses the following code to print only the `ActionErrors.Global` errors:

```
<html:errors property="org.apache.struts.action.GLOBAL_ERROR"/>
```

The string `"org.apache.struts.action.GLOBAL_ERROR"` is the actual value of the alias, `ActionErrors.Global`.

To print an error associated with an individual field, you simply specify the property name associated with the field both when you create the `ActionError` in the form bean and you create the `<html:errors>` tag in the JSP file.

Customizing Error Messages Using Parameters

Although the sample application doesn't demonstrate it, it's also possible to customize error messages using parameters. This is done when you create the `ActionError` entry in the form bean or `Action` class—no modifications are required to the `<html:errors>` tag in the JSP file.

First, here's an error message and an `ActionError` being constructed with no parameter:

- Specify the error message in the properties file:

  ```
  msg.without.parameter=Your entry is a BAD ENTRY!
  ```

- Create the `ActionError` with no parameter:

  ```
  errors.add("field1", new ActionError("msg.without.paramter"));
  ```

Now, here's an error message and an `ActionError` being constructed with a parameter:

- Specify the error message in the properties file:

  ```
  msg.with.parameter={0} is a BAD ENTRY!
  ```

- Create the ActionError with no parameter:

```
errors.add("field1", new ActionError("msg.with.paramter", field1));
```

The second example passes the value of field1 as a parameter to customize the error message when it's displayed.

You can add additional parameters by using placeholders such as {1}, {2}, and so on, and then adding them as additional parameters to the ActionError constructor.

Uploading a File Using <html:file>

This section provides information on the following tag:

- <html:file>—Render an HTML <input type=file> element to support file uploading from forms

If you point your browser to the URL

http://myAppServer/StrutsTaglibs/html.jsp

you'll bring up the main page that links to all the sample codes for the Struts tag chapters. This section uses the <html:file> Sample Code page at /StrutsTaglibs/HtmlFile.do.

The input form page for this application is very basic and is presented in Figure 12.8.

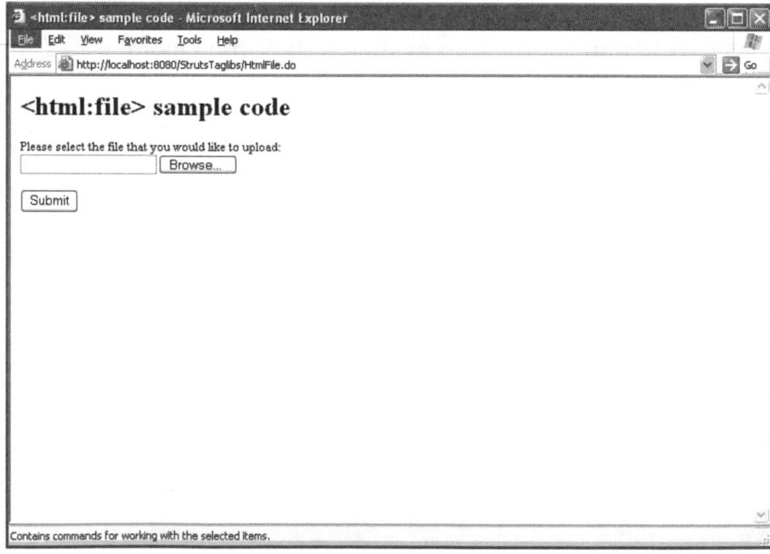

FIGURE 12.8 The <html:file> Sample Code page showing a file upload form at /StrutsTaglibs/HtmlFile.do.

Listing 12.10 is the JSP file that creates this page.

LISTING 12.10 JSP File Demonstrating Use of the <html:file> Tag for Uploading a File (HtmlFile.jsp)

```
<%@ page language="java" %>
<%@ page import="org.apache.struts.action.*" %>
<%@ taglib uri="/WEB-INF/struts-html.tld" prefix="html" %>
<%@ taglib uri="/WEB-INF/struts-bean.tld" prefix="bean" %>
<%@ taglib uri="/WEB-INF/struts-logic.tld" prefix="logic" %>
<html:html>
<head>
<title>&lt;html:file&gt; sample code</title>
</head>
<body bgcolor="white">

<h1>&lt;html:file&gt; sample code</h1>
<!--
        The most important part is to declare your form's enctype
        to be "multipart/form-data", and to have an html:file
        element that maps to your ActionForm's FormFile property
-->
<html:form action="HtmlFile.do" enctype="multipart/form-data">

        Please select the file that you would like to upload:<br />
        <html:file property="file" /><br /><br />

        <html:submit />

</html:form>

<p>
<logic:notEmpty name="HtmlFileForm" property="fname" >
    The file just uploaded was:<p>
    <ul>
      <li>Name = <bean:write name="HtmlFileForm" property="fname" />
      <li>Size = <bean:write name="HtmlFileForm" property="size" />
   </ul>
</logic:notEmpty>

</body>
</html:html>
```

Reviewing the form bean for this example is valuable to help demonstrate how the `<html:file>` tag is handled during form processing. Listing 12.11 is the form bean that goes with this JSP file (`HtmlFileForm.java`).

LISTING 12.11 Form Bean That Corresponds with `HtmlFile.jsp` (`HtmlFileForm.java`)

```
package ch12;

import org.apache.struts.action.ActionForm;
import org.apache.struts.upload.FormFile;
import org.apache.struts.upload.MultipartRequestHandler;

import javax.servlet.http.HttpServletRequest;
import org.apache.struts.action.ActionMapping;

/**
 * <p>Title: HtmlFileForm.java </p>
 * <p>Description:  Form Bean for the &lt;html:file&gt; example</p>
 * <p>Copyright: Copyright (c) 2002</p>
 * @author Kevin Bedell & James Turner
 * @version 1.0
 *
 */
public class HtmlFileForm extends ActionForm
{

    // Default bean constructor
    public HtmlFileForm() { }

    /**
     * The file that the user has uploaded
     */
    private FormFile file;
    public FormFile getFile() { return this.file; }
    public void setFile(FormFile file) { this.file = file; }

    /**
     * The name of the file - only for displaying results
     */
    private String fname;
    public String getFname() { return this.fname; }
    public void setFname(String fname) { this.fname = fname; }
```

LISTING 12.11 Continued

```
    /**
     * The size of the file - only for displaying results
     */
    private String size;
    public String getSize() { return this.size; }
    public void setSize(String size) { this.size = size; }

}
```

The processing logic for this form bean is described in the following sections.

For the `<html:file>` tag, the processing in the `Action` class is also important. Listing 12.12 is the `Action` class for this example (`HtmlFileAction.java`).

LISTING 12.12 `Action` Class That Corresponds with `HtmlFile.jsp` (`HtmlFileAction.java`)

```
package ch12;

import java.io.InputStream;
import java.io.IOException;
import java.io.OutputStream;
import java.io.FileOutputStream;
import java.io.ByteArrayOutputStream;
import java.io.FileNotFoundException;

import javax.servlet.http.HttpServletRequest;
import javax.servlet.http.HttpServletResponse;

import org.apache.struts.action.Action;
import org.apache.struts.action.ActionForm;
import org.apache.struts.action.ActionMapping;
import org.apache.struts.action.ActionForward;
import org.apache.struts.action.ForwardingActionForward;
import org.apache.struts.upload.FormFile;
import org.apache.struts.util.MessageResources;

import org.apache.commons.logging.Log;
import org.apache.commons.logging.LogFactory;

/**
 * Action class to demonstrate handling a <html:file> tag
```

LISTING 12.12 Continued

```
 *
 * @author Kevin Bedell & James Turner
 * @version 1.0
 */
public class HtmlFileAction extends Action
{

    public ActionForward execute(ActionMapping mapping,
                                 ActionForm form,
                                 HttpServletRequest request,
                                 HttpServletResponse response)
    throws Exception {

        MessageResources messages = getResources(request);
        String dir = messages.getMessage("save.dir");

        HtmlFileForm hff = (HtmlFileForm) form;

        // org.apache.struts.upload.FormFile contains the uploaded file
        FormFile file = hff.getFile();

        // If no file was uploaded (e.g. first form load), then display View
        if (file == null ) {
                return mapping.findForward("default");
        }

        // Get the name and file size
        String fname       = file.getFileName();
        String size        = Integer.toString(file.getFileSize()) + " bytes";

        InputStream  streamIn  = file.getInputStream();
        OutputStream streamOut = new FileOutputStream(dir + fname);

        int bytesRead = 0;
        byte[] buffer = new byte[8192];
        while ((bytesRead = streamIn.read(buffer, 0, 8192)) != -1) {
            streamOut.write(buffer, 0, bytesRead);
        }

        streamOut.close();
        streamIn.close();
```

LISTING 12.12 Continued

```
        // Populate the form bean with the results for display in the View
        hff.setFname(fname);
        hff.setSize(size);

        // Clean up our toys when done playing
        file.destroy();

       // Forward to default display
        return mapping.findForward("default");
    }
}
```

The important points from this `Action` class are covered in the following sections.

The `<html:file>` Tag

The `<html:file>` tag provides a method for building applications in which uploading files is a requirement. This tag provides a great deal of flexibility in terms of the file uploading process, naming and storing of files, and so on.

The biggest advantage this tag provides is how much it simplifies handling the uploading of files after you understand the material in this section.

In addition to the example we defined here, additional attributes are available for this tag that can limit the size of the file upload that's accepted (the `maxlength` attribute) and that indicate to the client browser the content types you can accept (the `accept` attribute).

Using the `<html:file>` Tag in the JSP File

Using the `<html:file>` tag in a JSP file is straightforward. Here's the code from our sample application:

```
<html:form action="HtmlFile.do" enctype="multipart/form-data">

        Please select the file that you would like to upload:<br />
        <html:file property="file" /><br /><br />
        <html:submit />
</html:form>
```

Two pieces of information in this short listing are important. They are the following:

- The encoding type on the `<html:form>` tag must be set to `enctype="multipart/form-data"`.
- The `<html:file>` tag itself must specify the property file of the form bean that the file is to be stored in. The code that supports this in the form bean is discussed in the next section.

Specifying a Private `FormFile` Property in the Form Bean

To support the tag we specified in our JSP file, `<html:file property="file" />`, there must be a property named `file` in the form bean. This property must be of type `org.apache.struts.upload.FormFile`. This is taken care of in our form bean by the following two code snippets:

```
import org.apache.struts.upload.FormFile;
```

and

```
/**
 * The file that the user has uploaded
 */
private FormFile file;
public FormFile getFile() { return this.file; }
public void setFile(FormFile file) { this.file = file; }
```

These lines in the form bean are all we need to support file uploading.

Processing the File Upload in the `Action` Class

A file is actually uploaded as a multipart request and is a bit more complex than a normal HTTP form posting. Fortunately, the Struts framework takes care of the hard parts for you. To handle actually uploading and saving the file, we use the following code snippet:

```
// Get the name and file size
String fname       = file.getFileName();
String size        = Integer.toString(file.getFileSize()) + " bytes";

InputStream  streamIn  = file.getInputStream();
OutputStream streamOut = new FileOutputStream(dir + fname);

int bytesRead = 0;
byte[] buffer = new byte[8192];
while ((bytesRead = streamIn.read(buffer, 0, 8192)) != -1) {
```

```
    streamOut.write(buffer, 0, bytesRead);
}

streamOut.close();
streamIn.close();
```

At a high level, this code simply defines an `InputStream` for reading the file contents as they're uploaded and an `OutputStream` to write the uploaded data to the file system. The code then loops, reading in data and writing it to a file, until there's no more data to read in (that is, the file upload is complete).

Conclusions

The Struts HTML library provides functionality in Struts for generating HTML elements, coordinating form processing, and, in general, linking the JSP pages (View components) into the rest of the Struts framework.

This chapter isn't meant to be a reference for these tags. If you want a listing of every valid option for these please refer to the Struts Web site or to the documentation that came with the version of Struts you're using.

It's possible to minimize the use of embedded Java scriptlets in your JSP pages by using the Struts HTML tags (and other Struts tags in general). Although it might be possible to completely eliminate Java scriptlets from your pages using a combination of Struts tags and JSP custom tags, we don't advise doing so. This can add to development time and make tasks harder than they need to be, without always adding a great deal of value for the effort. We recommend using Struts tags to minimize the use of scriptlets, but we recognize that at times using scriptlets is the best solution.

This chapter provided sample code and instructions for using a large number of the Struts HTML tags. Our intent is for you to cut, paste, and reuse the code samples we provided in your own applications.

13

Struts Bean Tags: Storing and Passing Data

IN THIS CHAPTER

- Using Struts Bean Tags That Access Aspects of the Servlet Context
- Using Struts Bean Tags That Access Java Resources
- Using Struts Bean Tags That Access Bean Properties
- Conclusions

The tags in the Struts Bean library are used to directly interact with Java classes and resources. They deal with aspects of the servlet context, the request, the application resources, and the user-defined classes.

As in the previous chapter, all the files referred to in this chapter are available in the StrutsTaglib Web application. The main JSP page for this chapter, shown in Figure 13.1, is located at the URL `http://myAppServer/StrutsTaglibs/bean.jsp`.

Using Struts Bean Tags That Access Aspects of the Servlet Context

This section provides information about the following tags:

- `<bean:cookie>`—Accesses a previously written cookie
- `<bean:header>`—Accesses information in the request header
- `<bean:parameter>`—Accesses a form parameter
- `<bean:page>`—Accesses information stored in a page, request, session, or application object

If you point your browser to the URL

`http://myAppServer/StrutsTaglibs/bean.jsp`

you'll bring up the main page linking to all the sample code for the Struts tag chapters. This section uses the Bean Servlet page at `/StrutsTaglibs/BeanServlet.do`. The rendered page is shown in Figure 13.2. See the Note on page 269, for details.

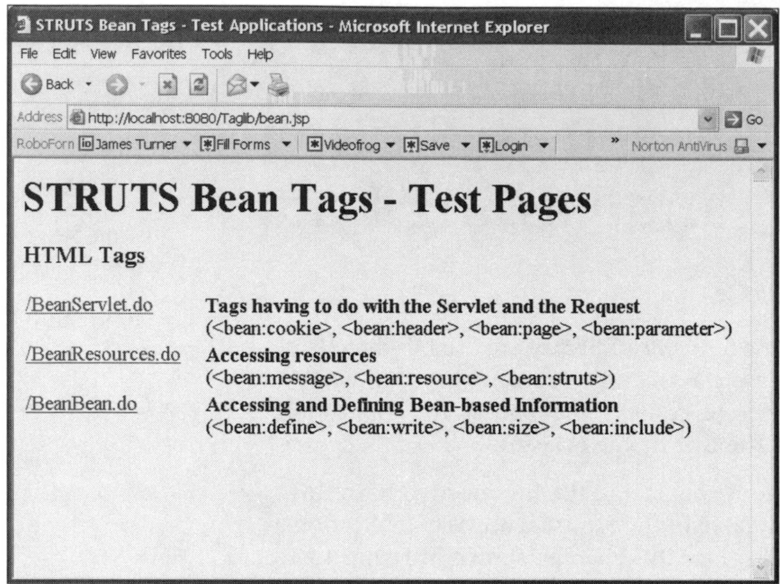

FIGURE 13.1 The sample application.

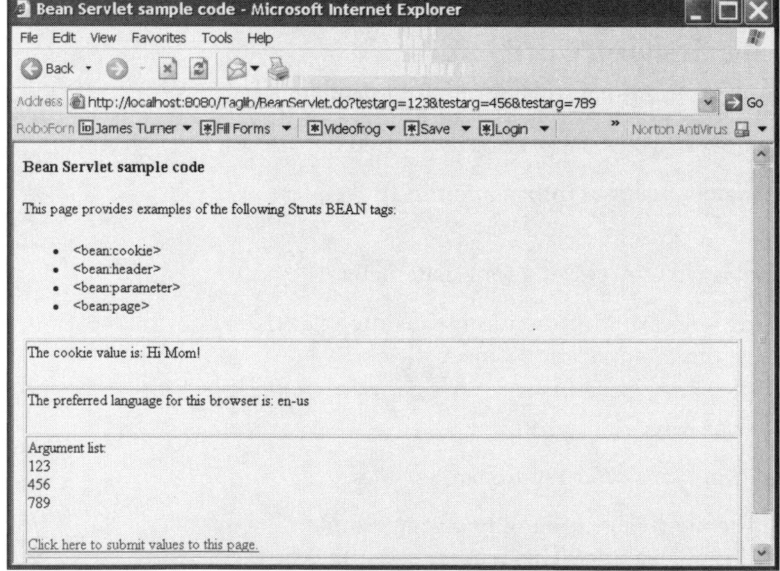

FIGURE 13.2 The Bean Servlet page.

This page demonstrates a typical use of each of the tags. The source is shown in Listing 13.1.

LISTING 13.1 JSP File Demonstrating Use of Struts Bean Tags Accessing Aspects of the Servlet (`BeanServlet.jsp`)

```
<%@ page language="java" %>
<%@ taglib uri="/WEB-INF/struts-bean.tld" prefix="bean" %>
<%@ taglib uri="/WEB-INF/struts-html.tld" prefix="html" %>
<%@ page import="javax.servlet.http.Cookie" %>
<html:html>
<head>
<title>Bean Servlet sample code</title>
</head>
<body bgcolor="white">

<h3>Bean Servlet sample code</h3>

<p>This page provides examples of the following Struts BEAN tags:<br>
<ul>
<li>&lt;bean:cookie&gt;</li>
<li>&lt;bean:header&gt;</li>
<li>&lt;bean:parameter&gt;</li>
<li>&lt;bean:page&gt;</li>
</ul>

<table border="1" width="100%">
  <%--
  The following section contains creating and displaying a cookie.
  --%>
  <tr>
    <td align="left">

     <bean:cookie id="cookie" name="/tags/cookiedemo" value="firsttime"/>
     <%
       if (cookie.getValue().equals("firsttime")) {
         Cookie c = new Cookie("/tags/cookiedemo", "Hi Mom!");
         c.setComment("A test cookie");
         c.setMaxAge(3600); //60 seconds times 60 minutes
         response.addCookie(c);
      }
     %>
```

LISTING 13.1 Continued

```
     The cookie value is: <bean:write name="cookie" property="value"/><P>

   </td>
 </tr>
 <%--
 The following section gets a value from the request header.
 --%>
 <tr>
   <td align="left">
     <bean:header id="lang" name="Accept-Language"/>

     The preferred language for this browser is: <bean:write name="lang"/><P>

   </td>
 </tr>
 <%--
 The following section looks at some parameters passed in.
 --%>
 <tr>
   <td align="left">
    <bean:parameter id="arg" multiple="yes" name="testarg" value="noarg"/>

   Argument list:<BR>
   <% for (int i = 0; i < arg.length; i++) {
      out.write(arg[i] + "<BR>");
    }
    %>
    <P>
    <html:link page="/BeanServlet.do?testarg=123&testarg=456&testarg=789">
    Click here to submit values to this page.</html:link>
   </td>
 </tr>
 <%--
 The following section finds a value from the session.
 --%>
 <tr>
   <td align="left">
     <bean:page id="this_session" property="session"/>
     Session Created = <bean:write name="this_session"
                        property="creationTime"/>
   </td>
 </tr>
```

LISTING 13.1 Continued

```
</table>
</body>
</html:html>
```

The following sections outline functionality related to the tags demonstrated in this listing.

The `<bean:cookie>` Tag

The `<bean:cookie>` tag retrieves a cookie or cookies sent to the server from the browser. The `id` attribute is the name of the page context variable in which to store the result. The `name` attribute specifies the name of the cookie to match against. The `value` attribute enables you to give a value to be returned if no cookie is found. Note that this is a little more complicated than it sounds because the tag will actually create and return a fake cookie.

One attribute that's not shown, `multiple`, enables you to retrieve all the cookies that match a name, not just the default one that would be chosen by the server as the correct value. If you specify a nonblank value for this attribute, the `id` variable will be handed an array of type `Cookie` rather than a single `Cookie`. For a similar example, see the `<bean:parameter>` tag later in the chapter.

The example shows an attempt to read the `/tags/cookiedemo` cookie. If it isn't found, the default value of `"firsttime"` is placed into a dummy cookie. Later, if that value is found in the cookie, a new cookie with different values is placed on the response, with a one-hour timeout.

The `<bean:header>` Tag

If you need to retrieve one of the values transmitted to the server from the client in the HTTP request header, you can use the `<bean:header>` tag. The syntax is identical to the `<bean:cookie>` tag, with the exception that the values returned are strings or arrays of strings (in the case of the `multiple` attribute) as opposed to the pseudo-cookie objects returned by `<bean:cookie>`.

In the example, the client's language preference is extracted and printed.

The `<bean:parameter>` Tag

The `<bean:parameter>` tag enables you to explicitly get a parameter passed into this page (either by a form submit or by arguments in the URL). Again, the syntax is identical to the previous two tags, except that the `name` attribute now refers to a parameter name, rather than to a cookie or HTTP header value.

In this example, you see how the `multiple` attribute works.

The `<bean:page>` Tag

Sometimes you need to gain access to the request, session, response, Struts config, or application data. That's the purpose of the `<bean:page>` tag. You specify the variable you want to hold the object using the `id` attribute, and which object you want it to hold (which must be one of the strings `"request"`, `"session"`, `"config"`, `"response"`, or `"application"`).

This example uses the session object to find out when the session was created. You should consult the appropriate Javadoc for the object you're interested in to find out what properties are available.

Using Struts Bean Tags That Access Java Resources

This section provides information about the following tags:

- `<bean:message>`—Displays an internationalized message
- `<bean:resource>`—Loads a Web application resource as a bean
- `<bean:struts>`—Accesses the internal configuration of Struts
- `<bean:include>`—Gets the response from a Web application request

This section uses the Bean Resources page at `/StrutsTaglibs/BeanResources.do`. The rendered page is shown in Figure 13.3.

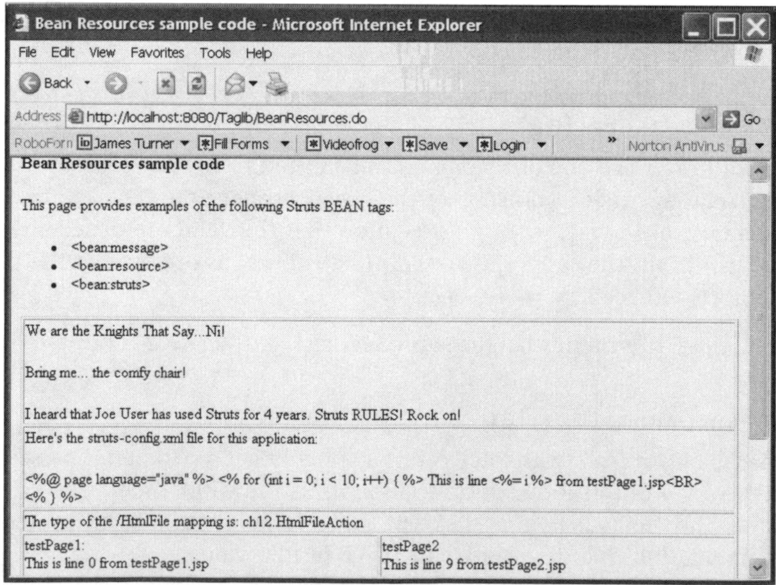

FIGURE 13.3 The Bean Resources page.

This page demonstrates a typical use of each of the tags. The source is shown in Listing 13.2.

LISTING 13.2 JSP File Demonstrating Use of Struts Bean Tags Accessing Java Resources (BeanResources.jsp)

```
<%@ page language="java" %>
<%@ taglib uri="/WEB-INF/struts-html.tld" prefix="html" %>
<%@ taglib uri="/WEB-INF/struts-bean.tld" prefix="bean" %>
<%@ page import="ch13.RandomQuote" %>
<%@ page import="java.util.PropertyResourceBundle" %>
<%@ page import="org.apache.struts.action.Action" %>
<%@ page import="org.apache.struts.util.MessageResources" %>
<html:html>
<head>
<title>Bean Resources sample code</title>
</head>
<body bgcolor="white">

<h3>Bean Resources sample code</h3>

<p>This page provides examples of the following Struts BEAN tags:<br>
<ul>
<li>&lt;bean:message&gt;</li>
<li>&lt;bean:resource&gt;</li>
<li>&lt;bean:struts&gt;</li>
</ul>

<table border="1" width="100%">
  <%--
  The following section contains code getting messages.
  --%>
  <tr>
    <td align="left" colspan="2">
     <% RandomQuote rq = new RandomQuote();
     request.setAttribute("rq", rq);
     MessageResources python =
        MessageResources.getMessageResources("ch13.pythonquotes");
     MessageResources normal =
        MessageResources.getMessageResources("ch13.ApplicationResources");

     session.getServletContext().setAttribute("ch13.pythonquotes", python);
     session.getServletContext().setAttribute(Action.MESSAGES_KEY, normal);
```

LISTING 13.2 Continued

```
%>
     <bean:message bundle="ch13.pythonquotes" key="ni"/><P>
     <bean:message bundle="ch13.pythonquotes" name="rq"
                   property="randomQuoteName"/><P>
     <bean:message key="application.uses.struts" arg0="Joe User" arg1="4"/>
    </td>
  </tr>
  <%--
  The following section shows how to use web resources.
  --%>
  <tr>
    <td align="left" colspan="2">
Here's the struts-config.xml file for this application:<P>
<bean:resource id="resource" name="/testPage1.jsp"/>
<bean:write name="resource"/>
</td>
</tr>
  </tr>
  <%--
  The following section shows how to get a Struts configuration object.
  --%>
  <tr>
    <td align="left" colspan="2">
The type of the /HtmlFile mapping is:
<bean:struts id="map" mapping="/HtmlFile"/>
<bean:write name="map" property="type"/>
</td>
  </tr>
  <%--
  The following section shows how to get an application web response.
  --%>
  <tr>
    <td align="left">
testPage1:<BR>
<bean:include id="tp1" page="/testPage1.jsp"/>
<bean:write name="tp1" filter="false"/><P>
</td><td align="left">
testPage2<BR>
<bean:include id="tp2" forward="testpage2"/>
<bean:write name="tp2" filter="false"/><P>
</td>
```

LISTING 13.2 Continued

```
</tr>
</table>
</body>
</html:html>
```

The <bean:message> Tag

The `<bean:message>` tag is probably the second-most used tag in the Bean taglib after `<bean:write>`. It is also relatively simple in nature. You provide a message key by using either the `key` attribute or the `name` (and possibly `property`) attribute. The corresponding string is retrieved from the locale-specific message resource and displayed. If the `bundle` attribute is used, it specifies the `MessageResource` bundle that is available under that name on the servlet's context. The `arg[0-4]` attributes are used to insert values into the message where the corresponding placeholders (`{0}`, `{1}`, and so on) are located. You also can specify a particular `locale` using the attribute of that name, and the `scope` of the bean to find using the `name` attribute.

The examples show how to retrieve a message from an explicit bundle, from an explicit bundle using `name` and `property`, and from the default bundle with arguments.

The `RandomQuote` class simply returns a random key from the Monty Python quote file. The source is shown in Listing 13.3, the Python message file is shown in Listing 13.4, and the default message file is shown in Listing 13.5.

LISTING 13.3 Java Class That Returns a Random Quote Key (`RandomQuote.java`)

```
package ch13;
import java.util.Random;

public class RandomQuote {
  String quoteStrings[] = {"ni", "lake", "chair"};

  public String getRandomQuoteName() {
    Random r = new Random();
    int i = r.nextInt(quoteStrings.length);
    return quoteStrings[i];
  }
}
```

LISTING 13.4 Monty Python Quote File (`pythonquotes.properties`)

```
#Silly Monty Python Quotes
ni=We are the Knights That Say...Ni!

lake=Listen, strange women lyin' in ponds distributin' swords is no basis for \
a system of government! Supreme executive power derives from a mandate from \
the masses, not from some farcical aquatic ceremony!

chair=Bring me... the comfy chair!
```

LISTING 13.5 Default Quote File (`ApplicationResources.properties`)

```
# Slightly less silly message... but still pretty darn silly.

application.totally.lost=I'm sorry, I have no idea how you got here, you \
shouldn't even be seeing this page.  In fact, I'll have to kill you now.

application.on.486=You dare run an application as great as this on a 486?!!

application.uses.struts=I heard that {0} has used Struts for {1} years. \
Struts RULES! Rock on!
```

The `<bean:resource>` Tag

If you ever need to have the contents of a Web resource (which is to say, a file inside the current Web application) available in a local variable, you can use the `<bean:resource>` tag. It takes two required attributes: `id` (which is the name of the variable) and `name` (which is the application-relative path to the file). If you supply any value for the optional `input` attribute, the `id` variable is given an `InputStream` pointing at the file rather than a `String` containing its contents.

In the example, the tag is used to retrieve the `struts-config.xml` file and display it. A more typical case might be to retrieve the contents of an XML file so that it can be handed off to a parser for processing.

The `<bean:struts>` Tag

In the unlikely event that you want to dive into your Struts configuration from JSP, the `<bean:struts>` tag enables you to gain access to values from the `struts-config.xml` file. As usual, `id` is the variable to hold the results. You have your choice of three attributes to use: `formBean`, `forward`, or `mapping`. You must choose one and only one of these, and set it to the name of a form bean, global forward, or action mapping (the path), respectively. The object returned is described in the Javadoc for Struts (respectively, `ActionFormBean`, `ActionForward`, or `ActionMapping`).

The sample JSP file gets the `/HtmlFile` mapping and displays the type of the `Action` defined for it.

The `<bean:include>` Tag

The `<bean:include>` tag operates along the same lines as the `<jsp:include>` tag, except that the data from the Web request is returned in a local variable rather than being displayed on the page. The variable is specified with the `id` attribute. You give exactly one of `forward`, `page`, or `href` to specify the page to retrieve based on a global `ActionForward`, an application-relative page URI, or an absolute URL, respectively.

The sample Web page uses a `page` and `forward` version of the tag to retrieve two local JSP files. You should note that unlike the `<bean:resource>` tag, this tag gets the contents by making a request to the server, which means that the JSP is executed rather than being returned verbatim. Again, a good use of this tag might be to get XML content on a foreign server for local processing.

Using Struts Bean Tags That Access Bean Properties

This section provides information on the following tags:

- `<bean:define>`—Defines a local variable based on a property
- `<bean:write>`—Displays a value from a bean
- `<bean:size>`—Gets the length of a map or collection

This section uses the Bean Bean page at `/StrutsTaglibs/BeanBean.do`. The rendered page is shown in Figure 13.4.

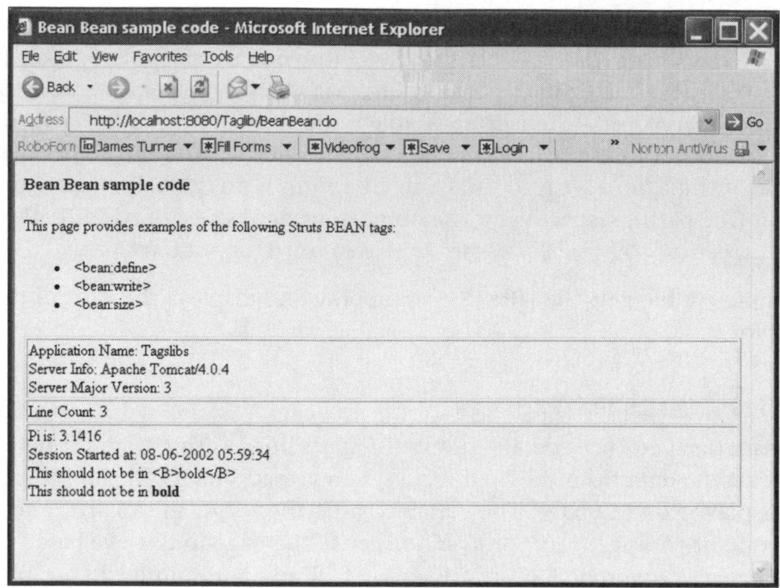

FIGURE 13.4 The Bean Bean page.

This page demonstrates a typical use of each of the tags. The source is shown in Listing 13.6.

LISTING 13.6 JSP File Demonstrating Use of Struts Bean Tags Accessing Bean Properties (`BeanBean.jsp`)

```
<%@ page language="java" %>
<%@ taglib uri="/WEB-INF/struts-html.tld" prefix="html" %>
<%@ taglib uri="/WEB-INF/struts-bean.tld" prefix="bean" %>
<%@ page import="java.util.HashMap" %>
<%@ page import="java.util.GregorianCalendar" %>
<%@ page import="java.util.Calendar" %>
<html:html>
<head>
<title>Bean Bean sample code</title>
</head>
<body bgcolor="white">

<h3>Bean Bean sample code</h3>

<p>This page provides examples of the following Struts BEAN tags:<br>
<ul>
```

LISTING 13.6 Continued

```
<li>&lt;bean:define&gt;</li>
<li>&lt;bean:write&gt;</li>
<li>&lt;bean:size&gt;</li>
</ul>

<table border="1" width="100%">
  <%--
  The following section contains code defining variables.
  --%>
  <tr>
    <td align="left" colspan="2">
    <bean:define id="name" value="Tagslibs"/>
    Application Name: <bean:write name="name"/><BR>
     <% request.setAttribute("session", session); %>
     <bean:define id="context" name="session" property="servletContext"/>
     Server Info: <bean:write name="context" property="serverInfo"/><BR>
     <bean:define id="context_copy" name="context"
                  type="javax.servlet.ServletContext"/>
     Server Major Version:
              <bean:write name="context_copy" property="minorVersion"/>
</td>
</tr>
<%--
The following section contains code getting the size of a collection.
--%>
  <tr>
<% HashMap lines = new HashMap();
    lines.put("1", "Line 1");
    lines.put("2", "Line 2");
    lines.put("3", "Line 3");
    request.setAttribute("lines", lines);
    %>
    <td align="left" colspan="2">
    <bean:size id="length" name="lines"/>
    Line Count: <bean:write name="length"/>
</td>
</tr>
<%--
The following section contains code showing how to write bean values.
--%>
  <tr>
```

LISTING 13.6 Continued

```
<%
     request.setAttribute("floatval", Float.valueOf("3.14159"));
     Calendar gc = GregorianCalendar.getInstance();
     gc.setTime(new java.util.Date(session.getCreationTime()));
     request.setAttribute("now", gc);
     String boldStart = "<B>";
     String boldEnd = "</B>";
     request.setAttribute("bs", boldStart);
     request.setAttribute("be", boldEnd);


    %>
    <td align="left" colspan="2">
    Pi is: <bean:write format="#.####" name="floatval"/><BR>
    Session Started at: <bean:write format="MM-dd-yyyy hh:mm:ss"
                                    name="now" property="time"/><BR>
    This should not be in <bean:write name="bs"/>bold
                          <bean:write name="be"/><BR>
    This should be in <bean:write name="bs" filter="false"/>bold
                      <bean:write name="be" filter="false"/><BR>

</td>
</tr>
</table>
</body>
</html:html>
```

The `<bean:define>` Tag

If you need to define a new bean in a given scope, you can do so using the `<bean:define>` tag. This tag can work in three ways. First, it can create a new attribute set to a string value. Second, it can create a new attribute set to an old attribute's value. Finally, it can create a new attribute from a property of an old attribute.

Again, `id` is used to tell Struts what the name of the new attribute will be. If you set `value` equal to a string, the value will be that string. If you set `name` equal to an existing bean name, the value will be the value of that bean. If you use both `name` and `property`, the value will be that property of that bean. You can use `scope` to specify the scope of the bean that is used as the source (defaults to page context), and `toScope` to specify the scope of the new bean. If you're setting one bean directly to another or to a property of that bean, you can use the `type` attribute to tell Struts what the type of the value being set is.

BEAN SCOPE AND STRUTS TAGS

Information can be stored in any number of places in a Web application. Data might be stored in page scope, request scope, session scope, or application score.

Most Struts tags that look up a bean value by name enable you to specify a scope (usually by employing the `scope` attribute). If you don't specify a value for the attribute, different tags behave in different ways. Some tags default to a particular scope (request, for example). Other tags start at page scope and "work their way up" to application scope using the first value that's found.

Some tags simply use `null` as the value if a value is not specified; others throw an exception.

The Struts taglib documentation is pretty good about letting you know how a given tag will behave, and you can never go wrong explicitly specifying the scope in the tags.

The example shows three variants: setting a bean to a property of another bean, setting a bean to a string, and setting a bean to another bean.

The `<bean:size>` Tag

The `<bean:size>` tag enables you to set a variable to the size of a map, collection, or array. You can use `name`, `name` combined with `property`, or `collection` (which should be a run-time expression that returns an array, collection, or map).

As usual, `id` holds the value and `scope` enables you to specify the scope of the bean named by the `name` attribute.

The example shows a simple example of getting the size of a `HashMap`.

The `<bean:write>` Tag

In my experience, this is the most commonly used tag in the entire Struts taglib package. Its purpose is to display a bean or bean property, and possibly format it.

The simplest use cases merely specify `name` or `name` and `property`. In those cases, the value is written to the output stream using default formatting for numbers, dates, and other non-string values. The `scope` attribute, as always, specifies where to look for the bean.

If you want to specify formatting, you can do it in one of two different ways. You can use the `format` attribute and an appropriate format string for the type (`###.###` for a number, for example). Alternatively, you can use the `formatKey` attribute to specify a key into a resource bundle, which is used to retrieve the formatting string. If you want to use a bundle other than the default, the `bundle` attribute allows that. The `locale` value enables you to define the locale that will be used both for finding a bundle and for locale-specific formatting.

If the bean isn't found, an exception is thrown. However, if you set `ignore` to true, the `<bean:write>` will simply be ignored instead.

Finally, the value sent to the output stream is normally enclosed in quotation marks so that the HTML instructions won't be processed. If you want the output to be sent raw, set `filter` to false.

The examples show printing a float in a bean with formatting, printing a date that is a property of a bean with formatting, and displaying HTML directives both with and without filtering.

Conclusions

The Struts Bean library is a mixed bag of tags—some more useful than others. In general, the tags expose some internal aspect of the application to the JSP page.

As in previous chapters, the definitive documentation for these tags can be found in the Struts user guide and, in some cases, the Javadoc. However, especially in the case of less commonly used tags such as `<bean:resource>`, you might find this documentation less than helpful due to its sparseness. Hopefully, the examples given here help to shed some light on exactly what the tags do.

14

Struts Logic Tags: Conditional Presentation Logic

IN THIS CHAPTER

- Using Struts Logic Tags That Perform Conditional Display Based on a Value
- Using Struts Logic Tags That Match Substrings
- Using the Struts Logic Tags for Iteration
- Using the Struts Logic Tags to Test for Absence or Presence of Values
- Using the Struts Logic Tags to Transfer Control
- Conclusions

Sometimes you need to control whether something is displayed on the JSP page. In traditional JSP, you must break out into a scriptlet to do this, wrapping HTML in an `if` (or perhaps a `for` loop to iterate).

The `struts:logic` taglib provides a tag-based alternative to scriptlets that can handle many common conditional cases. However, some of these tags can be a bit tricky to use. You might still find that you must break out into Java to handle some of the more complex requirements of your application. When JSTL is fully integrated into JSP, you'll finally be able to do almost everything without needing to do this.

You can find all the files used here in the StrutsTaglib Web application. The main JSP page for this chapter, shown in Figure 14.1, is located at the URL `http://myAppServer/StrutsTaglibs/logic.jsp`.

NOTE

In all URLs in the chapter, replace `myAppServer` with the hostname and port that you've configured your JSP server to run on. For Tomcat, this is usually localhost:8080.

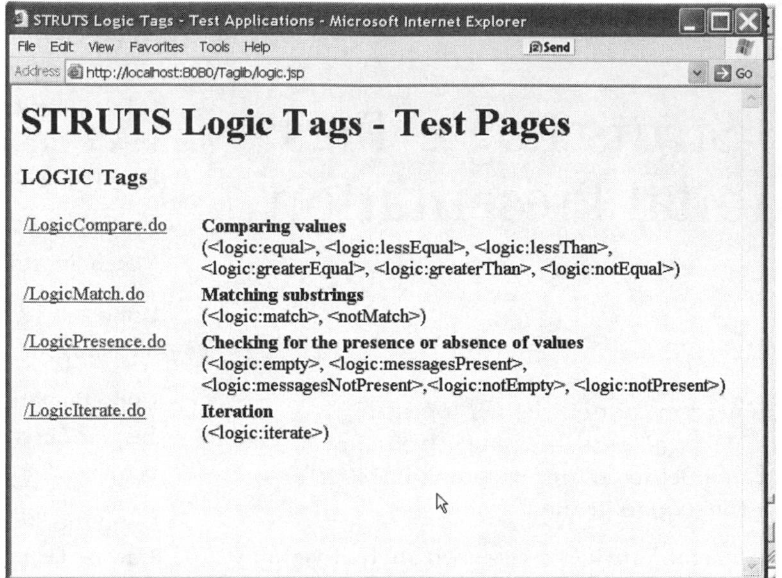

FIGURE 14.1 The sample applications for Chapter 14.

Using Struts Logic Tags That Perform Conditional Display Based on a Value

This section provides information about the following tags:

- `<logic:equal>`—Evaluates its contents if the variable is equal to a value
- `<logic:greaterEqual>`—Evaluates its contents if the variable is greater than or equal to a value
- `<logic:greaterThan>`—Evaluates its contents if the variable is greater than a value
- `<logic:lessEqual>`—Evaluates its contents if the variable is less than or equal to a value
- `<logic:lessThan>`—Evaluates its contents if the variable is less than a value
- `<logic:notEqual>`—Evaluates its contents if the variable is not equal to a value

If you point your browser to the URL

```
http://myAppServer/StrutsTaglibs/logic.jsp
```

you bring up the main page that links to all the sample code for the Struts tag chapters. This section uses the Logic Servlet page at `/StrutsTaglibs/LogicCompare.do`. The rendered page is shown in Figure 14.2.

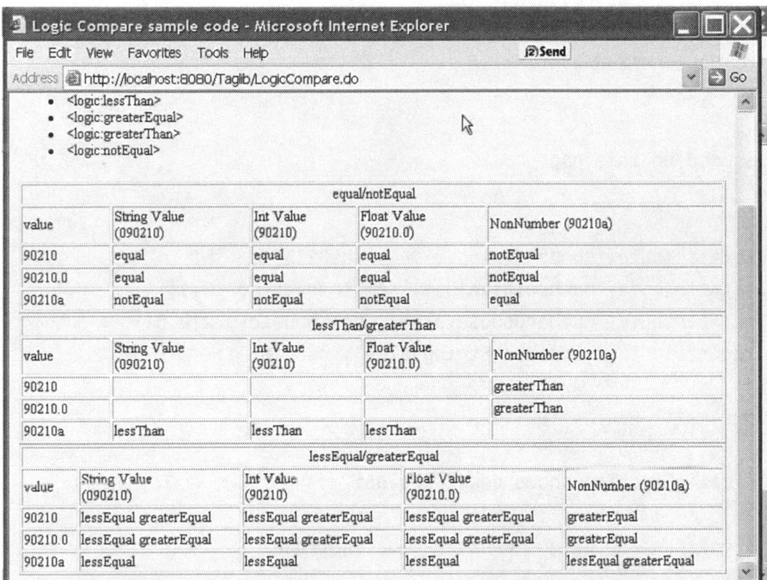

equal/notEqual				
value	String Value (090210)	Int Value (90210)	Float Value (90210.0)	NonNumber (90210a)
90210	equal	equal	equal	notEqual
90210.0	equal	equal	equal	notEqual
90210a	notEqual	notEqual	notEqual	equal

lessThan/greaterThan				
value	String Value (090210)	Int Value (90210)	Float Value (90210.0)	NonNumber (90210a)
90210				greaterThan
90210.0				greaterThan
90210a	lessThan	lessThan	lessThan	

lessEqual/greaterEqual				
value	String Value (090210)	Int Value (90210)	Float Value (90210.0)	NonNumber (90210a)
90210	lessEqual greaterEqual	lessEqual greaterEqual	lessEqual greaterEqual	greaterEqual
90210.0	lessEqual greaterEqual	lessEqual greaterEqual	lessEqual greaterEqual	greaterEqual
90210a	lessEqual	lessEqual	lessEqual	lessEqual greaterEqual

FIGURE 14.2 Logic Compare page at `/StrutsTaglibs/LogicCompare.do`.

This page demonstrates a typical use of each of the tags. The source is shown in Listing 14.1.

LISTING 14.1 JSP File Demonstrating Use of Struts Logic Tags That Compare Values and Conditionally Display (`LogicCompare.jsp`)

```
<%@ page language="java" %>
<%@ taglib uri="/WEB-INF/struts-html.tld" prefix="html" %>
<%@ taglib uri="/WEB-INF/struts-bean.tld" prefix="bean" %>
<%@ taglib uri="/WEB-INF/struts-logic.tld" prefix="logic" %>
<html:html>
<head>
<title>Logic Compare sample code</title>
</head>
<body bgcolor="white">
<h3>Logic Compare sample code</h3>
```

LISTING 14.1 Continued

```
<p>This page provides examples of the following Struts LOGIC tags:<br>
<ul>
  <li>&lt;logic:equal&gt;</li>
  <li>&lt;logic:lessEqual&gt;</li>
  <li>&lt;logic:lessThan&gt;</li>
  <li>&lt;logic:greaterEqual&gt;</li>
  <li>&lt;logic:greaterThan&gt;</li>
  <li>&lt;logic:notEqual&gt;</li>
</ul>
<%--
Variables used on this page
--%>
<%
request.setAttribute("numberStringValue", "090210");
request.setAttribute("numberIntValue", new Integer(90210));
request.setAttribute("numberDoubleValue", new Double(90210.0));
request.setAttribute("nonnumberStringValue", "90210a");
%>
<table border="1" width="100%">
  <%--
  The following section shows equal and not equal.
  --%>
  <tr><td colspan="5" align="center">equal/notEqual
  </td>
</TR>
<tr>
  <td align="left" >value
  </td>
  <td>
    String Value<BR>(090210)
  </td>
  <td>
    Int Value<BR>(90210)
  </td>
  <td>
    Float Value<BR>(90210.0)
  </td>
  <td>
    NonNumber (90210a)
  </td>
</tr>
<tr>
```

LISTING 14.1 Continued

```
  <td>
    90210
  </td>
  <td>
    <logic:equal name="numberStringValue"  value="90210" scope="request">
    equal
    </logic:equal>
    <logic:notEqual name="numberStringValue"  value="90210" scope="request">
    notEqual
    </logic:notEqual>
  </td>
  <td>
    <logic:equal name="numberIntValue"  value="90210" scope="request">
    equal
    </logic:equal>
    <logic:notEqual name="numberIntValue"  value="90210" scope="request">
    notEqual</logic:notEqual>

  </td>
  <td>
    <logic:equal name="numberDoubleValue"  value="90210" scope="request">
    equal
    </logic:equal>
    <logic:notEqual name="numberDoubleValue"  value="90210" scope="request">
    notEqual
    </logic:notEqual>
  </td>
  <td>
    <logic:equal name="nonnumberStringValue"  value="90210" scope="request">
    equal
    </logic:equal>
    <logic:notEqual name="nonnumberStringValue"  value="90210" scope="request">
    notEqual
    </logic:notEqual>
  </td>
</tr>
<tr>
  <td>
    90210.0
  </td>
  <td>
    <logic:equal name="numberStringValue"  value="90210.0" scope="request">
```

LISTING 14.1 Continued

```
    equal
    </logic:equal>
    <logic:notEqual name="numberStringValue"  value="90210.0" scope="request">
    notEqual
    </logic:notEqual>
  </td>
  <td>
    <logic:equal name="numberIntValue"  value="90210.0" scope="request">
    equal
    </logic:equal>
    <logic:notEqual name="numberIntValue"  value="90210.0" scope="request">
    notEqual
    </logic:notEqual>
  </td>
  <td>
    <logic:equal name="numberDoubleValue"  value="90210.0" scope="request">
    equal
    </logic:equal>
    <logic:notEqual name="numberDoubleValue"  value="90210.0" scope="request">
    notEqual
    </logic:notEqual>
  </td>
  <td>
    <logic:equal name="nonnumberStringValue"  value="90210.0" scope="request">
    equal
    </logic:equal>
    <logic:notEqual name="nonnumberStringValue"  value="90210.0" scope="request">
    notEqual
    </logic:notEqual>
  </td>
</tr>
<tr>
  <td>
    90210a
  </td>
  <td>
    <logic:equal name="numberStringValue"  value="90210a" scope="request">
    equal
    </logic:equal>
    <logic:notEqual name="numberStringValue"  value="90210a" scope="request">
    notEqual
    </logic:notEqual>
```

LISTING 14.1 Continued

```
  </td>
  <td>
    <logic:equal name="numberIntValue"  value="90210a" scope="request">
    equal
    </logic:equal>
    <logic:notEqual name="numberIntValue"  value="90210a" scope="request">
    notEqual
    </logic:notEqual>
  </td>
  <td>
    <logic:equal name="numberDoubleValue"  value="90210a" scope="request">
    equal
    </logic:equal>
    <logic:notEqual name="numberDoubleValue"  value="90210a" scope="request">
    notEqual
    </logic:notEqual>
  </td>
  <td>
    <logic:equal name="nonnumberStringValue"  value="90210a" scope="request">
    equal
    </logic:equal>
    <logic:notEqual name="nonnumberStringValue"  value="90210a" scope="request">
    notEqual
    </logic:notEqual>
  </td>
</tr>
</table>
<table border="1" width="100%">
  <%--
  The following section shows less than and greater than.
  --%>
  <tr><td colspan="5" align="center">lessThan/greaterThan
  </td>
</TR>
<tr>
  <td align="left" >value
  </td>
  <td>
    String Value<BR>(090210)
  </td>
  <td>
    Int Value<BR>(90210)
```

LISTING 14.1 Continued

```
  </td>
  <td>
    Float Value<BR>(90210.0)
  </td>
  <td>
    NonNumber (90210a)
  </td>
</tr>
<tr>
  <td>
    90210
  </td>
  <td>
    <logic:lessThan name="numberStringValue"  value="90210" scope="request">
    lessThan
    </logic:lessThan>
    <logic:greaterThan name="numberStringValue"  value="90210" scope="request">
    greaterThan
    </logic:greaterThan> 
  </td>
  <td>
    <logic:lessThan name="numberIntValue"  value="90210" scope="request">
    lessThan
    </logic:lessThan>
    <logic:greaterThan name="numberIntValue"  value="90210" scope="request">
    greaterThan
    </logic:greaterThan> 
  </td>
  <td>
    <logic:lessThan name="numberDoubleValue"  value="90210" scope="request">
    lessThan
    </logic:lessThan>
    <logic:greaterThan name="numberDoubleValue"  value="90210" scope="request">
    greaterThan
    </logic:greaterThan> 
  </td>
  <td>
    <logic:lessThan name="nonnumberStringValue"  value="90210" scope="request">
    lessThan
    </logic:lessThan>
    <logic:greaterThan name="nonnumberStringValue"  value="90210" scope="request">
    greaterThan
```

LISTING 14.1 Continued

```
    </logic:greaterThan> 
  </td>
</tr>
<tr>
  <td>
    90210.0
  </td>
  <td>
    <logic:lessThan name="numberStringValue"  value="90210.0" scope="request">
    lessThan
    </logic:lessThan>
    <logic:greaterThan name="numberStringValue"  value="90210.0" scope="request">
    greaterThan
    </logic:greaterThan> 
  </td>
  <td>
    <logic:lessThan name="numberIntValue"  value="90210.0" scope="request">
    lessThan
    </logic:lessThan>
    <logic:greaterThan name="numberIntValue"  value="90210.0" scope="request">
    greaterThan
    </logic:greaterThan> 
  </td>
  <td>
    <logic:lessThan name="numberDoubleValue"  value="90210.0" scope="request">
    lessThan
    </logic:lessThan>
    <logic:greaterThan name="numberDoubleValue"  value="90210.0" scope="request">
    greaterThan
    </logic:greaterThan> 
  </td>
  <td>
    <logic:lessThan name="nonnumberStringValue"  value="90210.0" scope="request">
    lessThan
    </logic:lessThan>
  <logic:greaterThan name="nonnumberStringValue"  value="90210.0" scope="request">
    greaterThan
    </logic:greaterThan> 
  </td>
</tr>
<tr>
  <td>
```

LISTING 14.1 Continued

```
    90210a
  </td>
  <td>
    <logic:lessThan name="numberStringValue"  value="90210a" scope="request">
    lessThan
    </logic:lessThan>
    <logic:greaterThan name="numberStringValue"  value="90210a" scope="request">
    greaterThan
    </logic:greaterThan> 
  </td>
  <td>
    <logic:lessThan name="numberIntValue"  value="90210a" scope="request">
    lessThan
    </logic:lessThan>
    <logic:greaterThan name="numberIntValue"  value="90210a" scope="request">
    greaterThan
    </logic:greaterThan> 
  </td>
  <td>
    <logic:lessThan name="numberDoubleValue"  value="90210a" scope="request">
    lessThan
    </logic:lessThan>
    <logic:greaterThan name="numberDoubleValue"  value="90210a" scope="request">
    greaterThan
    </logic:greaterThan> 
  </td>
  <td>
    <logic:lessThan name="nonnumberStringValue"  value="90210a" scope="request">
    lessThan
    </logic:lessThan>
    <logic:greaterThan name="nonnumberStringValue"  value="90210a" scope="request">
    greaterThan
    </logic:greaterThan> 
  </td>
</tr>
</table>
<table border="1" width="100%">
  <%--
  The following section shows less than and greater than.
  --%>
  <tr><td colspan="5" align="center">lessEqual/greaterEqual
  </td>
```

LISTING 14.1 Continued

```
</TR>
<tr>
  <td align="left" >value
  </td>
  <td>
    String Value<BR>(090210)
  </td>
  <td>
    Int Value<BR>(90210)
  </td>
  <td>
    Float Value<BR>(90210.0)
  </td>
  <td>
    NonNumber (90210a)
  </td>
</tr>
<tr>
  <td>
    90210
  </td>
  <td>
    <logic:lessEqual name="numberStringValue"  value="90210" scope="request">
    lessEqual
    </logic:lessEqual>
    <logic:greaterEqual name="numberStringValue"  value="90210" scope="request">
    greaterEqual
    </logic:greaterEqual> 
  </td>
  <td>
    <logic:lessEqual name="numberIntValue"  value="90210" scope="request">
    lessEqual
    </logic:lessEqual>
    <logic:greaterEqual name="numberIntValue"  value="90210" scope="request">
    greaterEqual
    </logic:greaterEqual> 
  </td>
  <td>
    <logic:lessEqual name="numberDoubleValue"  value="90210" scope="request">
    lessEqual
    </logic:lessEqual>
    <logic:greaterEqual name="numberDoubleValue"  value="90210" scope="request">
```

LISTING 14.1 Continued

```
    greaterEqual
    </logic:greaterEqual> 
  </td>
  <td>
    <logic:lessEqual name="nonnumberStringValue"  value="90210" scope="request">
    lessEqual
    </logic:lessEqual>
    <logic:greaterEqual name="nonnumberStringValue"  value="90210" scope="request">
    greaterEqual
    </logic:greaterEqual> 
  </td>
</tr>
<tr>
  <td>
    90210.0
  </td>
  <td>
    <logic:lessEqual name="numberStringValue"  value="90210.0" scope="request">
    lessEqual
    </logic:lessEqual>
    <logic:greaterEqual name="numberStringValue"  value="90210.0" scope="request">
    greaterEqual
    </logic:greaterEqual> 
  </td>
  <td>
    <logic:lessEqual name="numberIntValue"  value="90210.0" scope="request">
    lessEqual
    </logic:lessEqual>
    <logic:greaterEqual name="numberIntValue"  value="90210.0" scope="request">
    greaterEqual
    </logic:greaterEqual> 
  </td>
  <td>
    <logic:lessEqual name="numberDoubleValue"  value="90210.0" scope="request">
    lessEqual
    </logic:lessEqual>
    <logic:greaterEqual name="numberDoubleValue"  value="90210.0" scope="request">
    greaterEqual
    </logic:greaterEqual> 
  </td>
  <td>
    <logic:lessEqual name="nonnumberStringValue"  value="90210.0" scope="request">
```

LISTING 14.1 Continued

```
    lessEqual
    </logic:lessEqual>
  <logic:greaterEqual name="nonnumberStringValue"  value="90210.0" scope="request">
    greaterEqual
  </logic:greaterEqual> 
  </td>
</tr>
<tr>
  <td>
    90210a
  </td>
  <td>
    <logic:lessEqual name="numberStringValue"  value="90210a" scope="request">
    lessEqual
    </logic:lessEqual>
    <logic:greaterEqual name="numberStringValue"  value="90210a" scope="request">
    greaterEqual
    </logic:greaterEqual> 
  </td>
  <td>
    <logic:lessEqual name="numberIntValue"  value="90210a" scope="request">
    lessEqual
    </logic:lessEqual>
    <logic:greaterEqual name="numberIntValue"  value="90210a" scope="request">
    greaterEqual
    </logic:greaterEqual> 
  </td>
  <td>
    <logic:lessEqual name="numberDoubleValue"  value="90210a" scope="request">
    lessEqual
    </logic:lessEqual>
    <logic:greaterEqual name="numberDoubleValue"  value="90210a" scope="request">
    greaterEqual
    </logic:greaterEqual> 
  </td>
  <td>
    <logic:lessEqual name="nonnumberStringValue"  value="90210a" scope="request">
    lessEqual
    </logic:lessEqual>
  <logic:greaterEqual name="nonnumberStringValue"  value="90210a" scope="request">
    greaterEqual
  </logic:greaterEqual> 
```

LISTING 14.1 Continued

```
  </td>
</tr>
</table>
</body>
</html:html>
```

All these tags follow essentially the same syntax. They perform a comparison between two values (one a constant, one a variable) and evaluate their contents if the test is true.

PERFORMING COMPARISONS BETWEEN NUMBERS AND STRINGS

One subtlety regarding the comparison tags: If both values can be successfully converted to numbers, the comparisons are done numerically rather than as literal strings. For example, `"90210.0"`, `"0090210"`, and `90210"` all compare as equal, and `"0090211"` compares as greater than `"90210"`, although the same zero-led string compares as less than `"90210a"` because one of the strings is nonnumeric.

All of these tags take their variable value from one of the following parameters:

- `cookie`—Looks for a cookie in the request with the specified name
- `header`—Looks for a request header value with the specified name
- `name`—Looks for a bean or bean property, if the `property` attribute is also set, of the specified `scope` (or any scope if the `scope` attribute isn't set)
- `parameter`—Looks for a request parameter (that is, a form value) of the specified name

If the specified variable doesn't exist or is null, the `value` is compared against a zero-length string.

The `<logic:equal>` and `<logic:notEqual>` Tags

The `equal` tag evaluates its contents if the variable equals the value, whereas the `notEqual` tag evaluates if the two differ. It's worth mentioning again that the comparison is numerical if both values can be converted to a double or a long.

The `<logic:lessThan>` and `<logic:greaterThan>` Tags

The `lessThan` and `greaterThan` tags evaluate their contents if the variable is (respectively) less or greater than the constant.

The <logic:lessEqual> and <logic:greaterEqual> Tags

These tags similar to the `lessThan` and `greaterThan` tags, but the tests here are less than or equal and greater than or equal.

Using Struts Logic Tags That Match Substrings

This section provides information about the following tags:

- `<logic:match>`—Evaluates its contents if the variable contains the value as a substring
- `<logic:notMatch>`—Evaluates its contents if the variable doesn't contain the value as a substring

This section uses the Logic Matching page at `/StrutsTaglibs/LogicMatch.do`. The rendered page is shown in Figure 14.3.

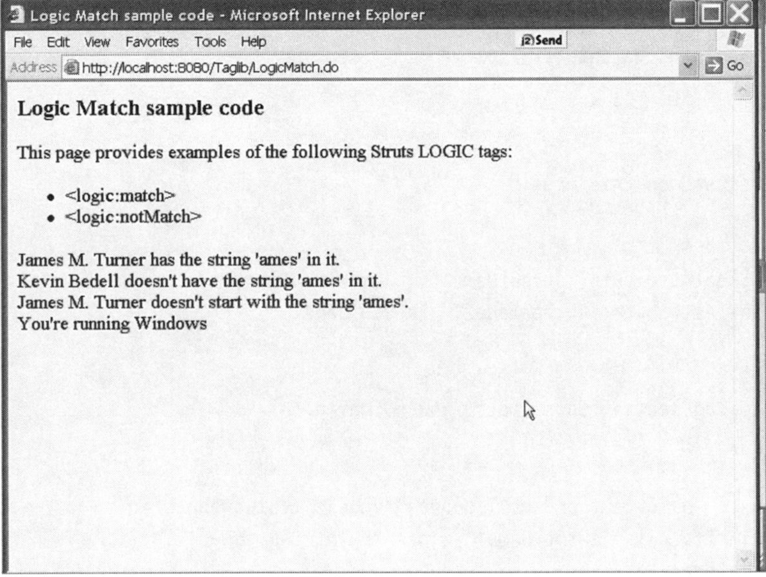

FIGURE 14.3 Logic Match page at `/StrutsTaglibs/LogicMatch.do`.

This page demonstrates a typical use of each of the tags. The source is shown in Listing 14.2.

LISTING 14.2 JSP File Demonstrating Use of Struts Logic Tags Looking for Substrings (LogicMatch.jsp)

```
<%@ page language="java" %>
<%@ taglib uri="/WEB-INF/struts-html.tld" prefix="html" %>
<%@ taglib uri="/WEB-INF/struts-bean.tld" prefix="bean" %>
<%@ taglib uri="/WEB-INF/struts-logic.tld" prefix="logic" %>
<%@ page import="java.util.Enumeration" %>
<html:html>
<head>
<title>Logic Match sample code</title>
</head>
<body bgcolor="white">

<h3>Logic Match sample code</h3>

<p>This page provides examples of the following Struts LOGIC tags:<br>
<ul>
<li>&lt;logic:match&gt;</li>
<li>&lt;logic:notMatch&gt;</li>
</ul>

<%--
Variables used on this page
--%>
<%
  request.setAttribute("authorName1", "James M. Turner");
request.setAttribute("authorName2", "Kevin Bedell");
%>
<%--
The following section shows match and notMatch.
--%>

<logic:match name="authorName1" scope="request" value="ames">
   <bean:write name="authorName1"/> has the string 'ames' in it.
</logic:match>
<logic:notMatch name="authorName1" scope="request" value="ames">
   <bean:write name="authorName1"/> doesn't have the string 'ames' in it.
</logic:notMatch>
<BR>
<logic:match name="authorName2" scope="request" value="ames">
   <bean:write name="authorName2"/> has the string 'ames' in it.
</logic:match>
```

LISTING 14.2 Continued

```
<logic:notMatch name="authorName2" scope="request" value="ames">
   <bean:write name="authorName2"/> doesn't have the string 'ames' in it.
</logic:notMatch>
<BR>
<logic:match name="authorName1" scope="request" value="ames" location="start">
   <bean:write name="authorName1"/> starts with the string 'ames'.
</logic:match>
<logic:notMatch name="authorName1" scope="request" value="ames" location="start">
   <bean:write name="authorName1"/> doesn't start with the string 'ames'.
</logic:notMatch>
<BR>
<logic:match header="user-agent" value="Windows">
   You're running Windows
</logic:match>
<logic:notMatch header="user-agent" value="Windows">
   You're not running Windows
</logic:notMatch>
<BR>
</body>
</html:html>
```

The `logic:match` and `logic:notMatch` Tags

These tags should be familiar to anyone who has ever used the `String` methods `indexOf`, `endsWith`, and `startsWith`. As with the comparison tags, you can specify `name`, `header`, `parameter`, or `cookie` as the source of the value to compare. However, unlike the comparison tags, a missing or null value throws a runtime exception.

With no other arguments, `match` looks for the `value` attribute anywhere inside the string returned from the variable. If the `location` attribute is `start`, the variable must start with the `value`; if it's `end`, the variable must end with the `value`.

This example also shows a nonbean lookup for the variable. The last two examples use the `user-agent` header value to check whether the client is running Microsoft Windows.

Using the Struts Logic Tags for Iteration

This section provides information about the following tag:

- `<logic:iterate>`—Loop over all the values of a collection and evaluate its contents

This section uses the Logic Iterate page at `/StrutsTaglibs/LogicIterate.do`. The rendered page is shown in Figure 14.4.

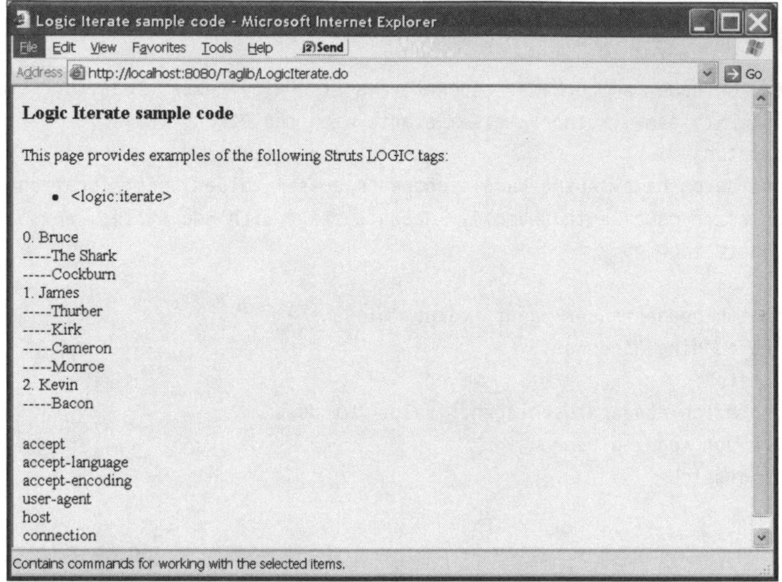

FIGURE 14.4 Logic Iterate page at `/StrutsTaglibs/LogicIterate.do`.

This page demonstrates a typical use of each of the tags. The source is shown in Listing 14.3.

LISTING 14.3 JSP File Demonstrating Use of Struts Logic Tag Iterating over Contents (`LogicIterate.jsp`)

```
<%@ page language="java" %>
<%@ taglib uri="/WEB-INF/struts-html.tld" prefix="html" %>
<%@ taglib uri="/WEB-INF/struts-bean.tld" prefix="bean" %>
<%@ taglib uri="/WEB-INF/struts-logic.tld" prefix="logic" %>
<%@ page import="java.util.HashMap" %>
<html:html>
<head>
<title>Logic Iterate sample code</title>
</head>
<body bgcolor="white">

<h3>Logic Iterate sample code</h3>

<p>This page provides examples of the following Struts LOGIC tags:<br>
```

LISTING 14.3 Continued

```
<ul>
<li>&lt;logic:iterate&gt;</li>
</ul>

<%--
Variables used on this page
--%>
<%
HashMap h = new HashMap();
String jameses[] = {"Joyce", "Thurber", "Kirk", "Cameron", "Monroe"};
String kevins[] = {"Spacey", "Bacon"};
String bruces[] = {"Willis", "The Shark", "Cockburn"};
h.put("James", jameses);
h.put("Kevin", kevins);
h.put("Bruce", bruces);
request.setAttribute("givenNames", h);
%>
<%--
The following section shows iterate.
--%>

<logic:iterate id="gname" indexId="ind" name="givenNames">
  <bean:write name="ind"/>. <bean:write name="gname" property="key"/><BR>
  <logic:iterate id="lname" name="gname" property="value" length="4" offset="1">
     -----<bean:write name="lname"/><BR>
  </logic:iterate>
</logic:iterate><P>
<logic:iterate id="header" collection="<%= request.getHeaderNames() %>">
   <bean:write name="header"/><BR>
</logic:iterate>
</body>
</html:html>
```

The `logic:iterate` Tag

The `iterate` tag is probably the most complicated one in the logic tag library, but also one of the most useful. At its heart, it's pretty simple. You specify a collection with the `name` or `name` and `property` attribute, and specify a bean to hold the individual members of the collection in `id`. The tag then loops over each member of the collection (which can either be an array, a `Collection`, `Enumeration`, `Iterator`, or `Map`), setting the `id` to the element and evaluating its contents.

If the collection is a map, the `id` is set to an object of class `java.util.Map.Entry`. These objects have two values: a `key` and a `value`.

Sometimes you want to iterate over a computed value rather than a bean property. In that case, you can use the `collection` attribute, as in the example in which the header names are displayed.

The `length` attribute limits the total number of items that are evaluated, and the `offset` attribute enables you to skip over values at the beginning of the collection.

Finally, you can get access to a counter (zero-based) that lets you know which iteration you're on by using the `indexed` attribute.

If the value of an iteration is null, no page-scoped value for `id` is established on that iteration and the item is skipped.

Using the Struts Logic Tags to Test for Absence or Presence of Values

This section provides information about the following tag:

- `<logic:empty>`—Evaluates its contents if the variable is null or an empty string
- `<logic:messagesPresent>`—Evaluates its contents if the message specified is available as an error or message
- `<logic:messagesNotPresent>`—Evaluates its contents if the message specified isn't available as an error or message
- `<logic:notEmpty>`—Evaluates its contents if the variable isn't null or an empty string
- `<logic:notPresent>`—Checks for the presence of the specified role, user, cookie, header, or bean and evaluates its contents if not found
- `<logic:present>`—Checks for the presence of the specified role, user, cookie, header, or bean and evaluates its contents if found

This section uses the Logic Presence page at `/StrutsTaglibs/LogicPresence.do`. The rendered page is shown in Figure 14.5.

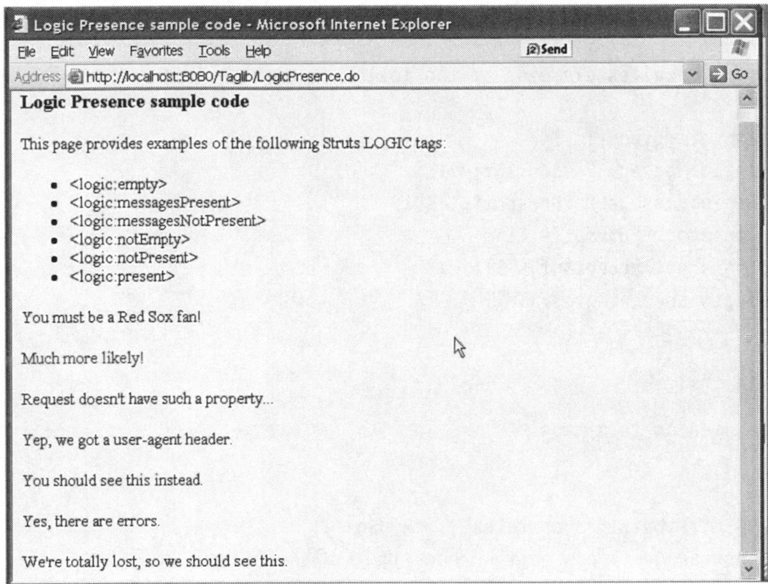

FIGURE 14.5 Logic Presence page at `/StrutsTaglibs/LogicPresence.do`.

This page demonstrates a typical use of each of the tags. The source is shown in Listing 14.4.

LISTING 14.4 JSP File Demonstrating Use of Struts Logic Tags Testing for the Presence of Values (`LogicPresence.jsp`)

```
<%@ page language="java" %>
<%@ taglib uri="/WEB-INF/struts-html.tld" prefix="html" %>
<%@ taglib uri="/WEB-INF/struts-bean.tld" prefix="bean" %>
<%@ taglib uri="/WEB-INF/struts-logic.tld" prefix="logic" %>
<%@ page import="java.util.HashMap" %>
<%@ page import="org.apache.struts.action.Action" %>
<%@ page import="org.apache.struts.action.ActionError" %>
<%@ page import="org.apache.struts.action.ActionErrors" %>
<html:html>
<head>
<title>Logic Presence sample code</title>
</head>
<body bgcolor="white">

<h3>Logic Presence sample code</h3>
```

LISTING 14.4 Continued

```
<p>This page provides examples of the following Struts LOGIC tags:<br>
<ul>
<li>&lt;logic:empty&gt;</li>
<li>&lt;logic:messagesPresent&gt;</li>
<li>&lt;logic:messagesNotPresent&gt;</li>
<li>&lt;logic:notEmpty&gt;</li>
<li>&lt;logic:notPresent&gt;</li>
<li>&lt;logic:present&gt;</li>
</ul>

<%--
Variables used on this page
--%>
<%
request.setAttribute("favoriteTeam", "RedSox");
ActionErrors errors = new ActionErrors();
errors.add("totallylost", new ActionError("application.totally.lost"));
request.setAttribute(Action.ERROR_KEY, errors);
request.setAttribute("goodThingsAboutTheYankees", "");
%>
<%--
The following section shows empty and notEmpty.
--%>

<logic:empty name="goodThingsAboutTheYankees">
   You must be a Red Sox fan!<P>
</logic:empty>
<logic:notEmpty name="goodThingsAboutTheYankees">
   New Yorker, eh?
</logic:notEmpty>
<P>
<%--
The following section shows present and notPresent.
--%>
<logic:present name="noSuchAttribute" property="noSuchProperty">
   Wow, someone defined it?
</logic:present>
<logic:notPresent name="noSuchAttribute" property="noSuchProperty">
   Much more likely!
</logic:notPresent>
<P>
```

LISTING 14.4 Continued

```
<logic:notPresent name="request" property="noSuchProperty">
   Request doesn't have such a property...
</logic:notPresent>
<P>
<logic:present header="user-agent">
   Yep, we got a user-agent header.
</logic:present>
<logic:notPresent header="user-agent">
   Odd, user-agent is a standard header property.
</logic:notPresent>
<P>
<%--
The following section shows messagesPresent and messagesNotPresent.
--%>
<logic:messagesPresent property="noSuchMessage">
   Should never see this.
</logic:messagesPresent>
<logic:messagesNotPresent property="noSuchMessage">
   You should see this instead.
</logic:messagesNotPresent>
<P>
<logic:messagesPresent>
   Yes, there are errors.
</logic:messagesPresent><P>
<logic:messagesPresent property="totallylost">
   We're totally lost, so we should see this.
</logic:messagesPresent>
<logic:messagesNotPresent property="totallylost">
      We're totally lost, so we shouldn't see this.
</logic:messagesNotPresent>

</body>
</html:html>
```

The `logic:empty` and `logic:notEmpty` Tags

If you want to check a bean or bean property to see whether it's null or a blank string or, in the case of a collection, whether the size of the collection is zero, you can use the `empty` and `notEmpty` tags.

The only interesting thing to note is that you can't really test for null on a bean itself because `getAttribute` returns null for both not present and null value, both of which cause an exception to be thrown. So, testing for null values is really useful only on properties of beans.

The `logic:present` and `logic:notPresent` Tags

If you want to check to see whether a bean, header, cookie, role, user, or parameter exists, you use `present` and `notPresent`. These tags evaluate based on the simple presence (or lack) of the specified value. In the case of a role or user, these tags evaluate whether the role or username is equal to the specified value.

The `logic:messagesPresent` and `logic:messagesNotPresent` Tags

The `<html:errors>` tag enables you to print out errors from an `Action`, but the `messagesPresent` tag enables you to check for their existence.

With no attributes, the `messagesPresent` tag evaluates (or doesn't evaluate) its contents if there are any `ActionErrors` in the current request scope. With a `property` attribute, `messagesPresent` checks for the existence of an error message for that specific property.

If the `messages` attribute is set to true, the tag checks the `Action.MESSAGE_KEY` bean value (where messages—as opposed to errors—are stored) instead of the normal `Action.ERROR_KEY` bean value. Alternatively, the `name` attribute enables you to explicitly specify the name of the bean.

Using the Struts Logic Tags to Transfer Control

Sometimes you need to transfer control to another page inside the current application or to an arbitrary URI entirely outside the application. Two tags in the logic library are designed to enable you to do this.

The `logic:forward` Tag

The `forward` tag causes a transfer of control using a global `ActionForward` defined in the Struts configuration file. It takes a single attribute, `name`, which is the name of the forward. For example:

```
<logic:forward name="badlogin"/>
```

The `logic:redirect` Tag

On its surface, the `redirect` tag seems complicated until you realize that all the attributes are the same as their namesakes in the `<html:link>` tag. The only difference is that whereas the `link` tag comes into effect when the link is clicked, the `redirect` tag takes effect immediately. Refer to the documentation on the `link` tag for details. Here's an example of this tag:

```
<logic:redirect href="http://www.cnn.com" paramId="userid" paramName="myUserId"/>
```

Conclusions

The Struts Logic library is the switchyard that controls the flow of your JSP document. By testing for the presence and absence of data or its value (by condition or pattern matching) and evaluating your JSP based on it, you can produce a highly customized page that varies greatly depending on tests. You can also use the library to redirect control either to another page in this application or entirely outside the application.

You can also use the Logic library to iterate over collections. The subject of the next chapter, the Nested Tag library, can be of great utility when used with `iterate`.

15

The Nested and Template Struts Tag Libraries: Handling Subproperties and Inserting Content

IN THIS CHAPTER

- Using the Struts Nested Tags
- Using the Struts Template Tags
- Conclusions

There are two other Struts tag libraries that are used in specific situations you might encounter during code development:

- The Nested tag library enables you to use many of the common tags from the other tag libraries, but apply them relative to an object.
- The Template library enables you to create Web pages based on a common template, with content passed in to the template to be inserted.

You can find all the files used here in the Taglib Web application. The main JSP page for this chapter, shown in Figure 15.1, is located at the URL `http://myAppServer/Taglib/misc.jsp`.

NOTE

In all URLs in the chapter, replace `myAppServer` with the hostname and port that you've configured your JSP server to run on. For Tomcat, this is usually localhost:8080.

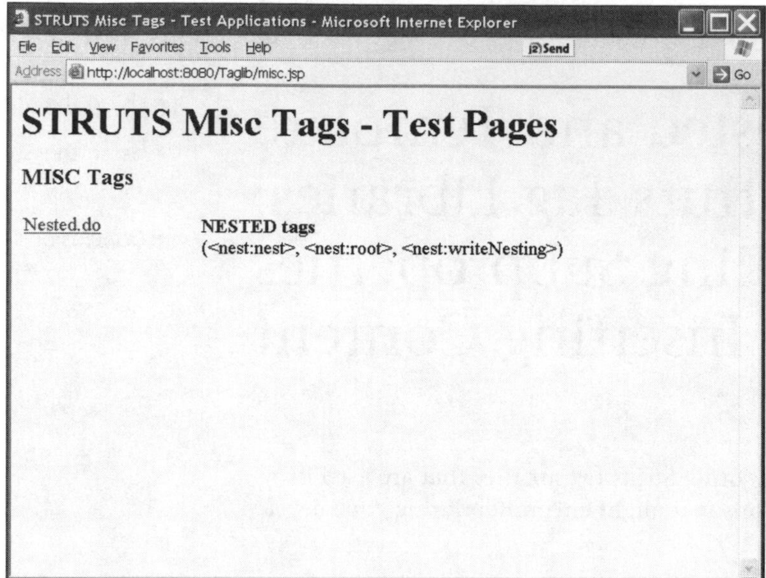

FIGURE 15.1 The sample application page for Struts nested and template tags.

Using the Struts Nested Tags

This section provides information about the following tags:

- `<nested:nest>`—Define a new level of nesting
- `<nested:root>`—Define the root level of a nested hierarchy
- `<nested:writeNesting>`—Send the current nesting level to the page

By using the `<nested:nest>` tag, you define the object relative to which all contained tags do their work.

The best way to demonstrate this is with an example. Examine the JSP shown in Listing 15.1.

LISTING 15.1 JSP File Demonstrating Use of Struts Nested Tags (`Nested.jsp`)

```
<%@ page language="java" %>
<%@ taglib uri="/WEB-INF/struts-html.tld" prefix="html" %>
<%@ taglib uri="/WEB-INF/struts-bean.tld" prefix="bean" %>
<%@ taglib uri="/WEB-INF/struts-logic.tld" prefix="logic" %>
<%@ taglib uri="/WEB-INF/struts-nested.tld" prefix="nested" %>
```

LISTING 15.1 Continued

```
<%@ page import="java.util.Vector" %>
<%@ page import="ch15.Person" %>
<%@ page import="ch15.Address" %>
<html:html>
<head>
<title>Misc Nested sample code</title>
</head>
<body bgcolor="white">

<h3>Misc Nested sample code</h3>

<p>This page provides examples of the following Struts NESTED tags:<br>
<ul>
<li>&lt;nested:nest&gt;</li>
<li>&lt;nested:select&gt;</li>
<li>&lt;nested:text&gt;</li>
<li>&lt;nested:writeNesting&gt;</li>
</ul>

<%--
The following section shows nest.
--%>
<html:form action="/showPerson">
<nested:nest property="person">
Last Name: <nested:text property="lastName"/><BR>
First Name: <nested:text property="firstName"/><BR>
Age: <nested:text property="age"/><BR>
Gender: <nested:select property="gender">
<html:option value="MALE">Male</html:option>
<html:option value="FEMALE">Female</html:option>
</nested:select><P>
<nested:nest property="address">
Current nesting is: <nested:writeNesting/><BR>
Street 1: <nested:text property="street1"/><BR>
Street 2: <nested:text property="street2"/><BR>
City: <nested:text property="city"/><BR>
State: <nested:text property="state"/><BR>
Postal Code: <nested:text property="postalCode"/><BR>
</nested:nest>
</nested:nest>
<html:submit/>
```

LISTING 15.1 Continued

```
</html:form>
</html:body>
</html:html>
```

This page implements a form in which some of the elements of the form are contained in one bean and some of the elements are contained in another bean that's a property of the first bean. In this case, the `Person` bean has a property called `address`, which itself contains another bean, the `Address` bean.

To understand this page better, you need to look at the definition of the `Person` and `Address` objects shown in Listings 15.2 and 15.3, respectively.

LISTING 15.2 Java Source for `Person` Object (`Person.java`)

```
package ch15;

public class Person {
  private String lastName;
  private String firstName;
  private String age;
  private String gender;
  private Address address;
  public String getLastName() {
    return lastName;
  }
  public void setLastName(String lastName) {
    this.lastName = lastName;
  }
  public void setFirstName(String firstName) {
    this.firstName = firstName;
  }
  public String getFirstName() {
    return firstName;
  }
  public void setAge(String age) {
    this.age = age;
  }
  public String getAge() {
    return age;
  }
```

LISTING 15.2 Continued

```
  public void setGender(String gender) {
    this.gender = gender;
  }
  public String getGender() {
    return gender;
  }
  public void setAddress(Address address) {
    this.address = address;
  }
  public Address getAddress() {
    return address;
  }

}
```

This is the same old bean format that should be old hat to you by now. The only thing to notice is that the `address` property contains another bean rather than a `String`.

LISTING 15.3 Source for `Address` Object (`Address.java`)

```
package ch15;

public class Address {
  private String street1;
  private String street2;
  private String city;
  private String state;
  private String postalCode;
  public String getStreet1() {
    return street1;
  }
  public void setStreet1(String street1) {
    this.street1 = street1;
  }
  public void setStreet2(String street2) {
    this.street2 = street2;
  }
  public String getStreet2() {
    return street2;
  }
```

LISTING 15.3 Continued

```
  public void setCity(String city) {
    this.city = city;
  }
  public String getCity() {
    return city;
  }
  public void setState(String state) {
    this.state = state;
  }
  public String getState() {
    return state;
  }
  public void setPostalCode(String postalCode) {
    this.postalCode = postalCode;
  }
  public String getPostalCode() {
    return postalCode;
  }
}
```

As you can see, the `Person` object defines the familiar list of attributes you'd associate with a person, such as last name and first name, as well as a pointer to a secondary `Address` object that stores the mailing address of the person.

The Struts configuration entry for the `showPerson` action is defined as

```
<action     path="/showPerson" name="NestedForm" type="ch15.NestedAction"
            validate="false" scope="request">
  <forward name="default"                 path="/showPerson.jsp"/>
</action>
```

This depends on the `NestedForm` form, defined as

```
<form-bean name="NestedForm" type="ch15.PersonForm"/>
```

Finally, `PersonForm` is defined in Listing 15.4.

LISTING 15.4 Source for `PersonForm` ActionForm (`PersonForm.java`)

```
package ch15;

import org.apache.struts.action.ActionForm;
import javax.servlet.http.HttpServletRequest;
```

LISTING 15.4 Continued

```
import org.apache.struts.action.ActionMapping;

public class PersonForm extends ActionForm {
  Person person = new Person();

  public void reset (ActionMapping mapping, HttpServletRequest request) {
    person = new Person();
    person.setAddress(new Address());
  }

  public Person getPerson() {
    return this.person;
  }

  public void setPerson(Person person) {
    this.person = person;
  }
}
```

With all this in place, you're ready to take a walk through the code. Going back to the JSP page, the action of the form specifies `showPerson`, which is looked up in the Struts configuration file. Struts determines that this action uses the `NestedForm` form, which is of type `ch15.PersonForm`. Struts then checks to make sure that this form doesn't already exist in the requested scope (by default, `request`), and because it doesn't, Struts creates a new form. As part of that creation, it calls the `reset` method, which causes the form to create a `Person` object and an `Address` object, and store the `Address` inside the `Person`.

Note that in this example, rather than the `ActionForm` containing individual bean properties for each field, it contains a single property that holds an object and the object has slots for all the fields.

Next, return to the JSP page. The next directive after the `<html:form>` tag is `<nested:nest>`. This tag directs that any reference made using a tag from the nested taglib be relative to the specified form property.

Following that, you see a series of fields using the `<nested:text>` tag. In fact, a large number of tags in the Nested library are simple extensions of their analogs in another taglib. The full list is as follows:

- `checkbox`
- `define`
- `empty`
- `equal`
- `errors`
- `file`
- `form`
- `greaterEqual`
- `greaterThan`
- `hidden`
- `image`
- `img`
- `iterate`
- `lessEqual`
- `lessThan`
- `link`
- `match`
- `message`
- `messages`
- `messagesNotPresent`
- `messagesPresent`
- `multibox`
- `notEmpty`
- `notEqual`
- `notMatch`
- `notPresent`
- `options`
- `optionsCollection`
- `password`
- `present`
- `radio`
- `select`
- `size`
- `submit`
- `text`
- `textarea`
- `write`

If you use any of these tags with the `nested` prefix rather than its native prefix (`<nested:text>` instead of `<html:text>`, for example), it works exactly the same as normal, except that the `property=` value has the current nesting value added to the front. That means when the first `<nested:text>` tag refers to `lastName`, it's really talking about `person.lastName`.

Later in the form, the `<nested:nest>` tag is used again, this time to fill in the values for the address, which is a child object of `Person`. By using another `<nested:nest>` inside the outer one, you create a reference to a subobject. In other words, nesting can be recursive.

The `<nested:writeNesting>` tag confirms this by displaying the nesting level as `person.address`. Figure 15.2 shows this page in action.

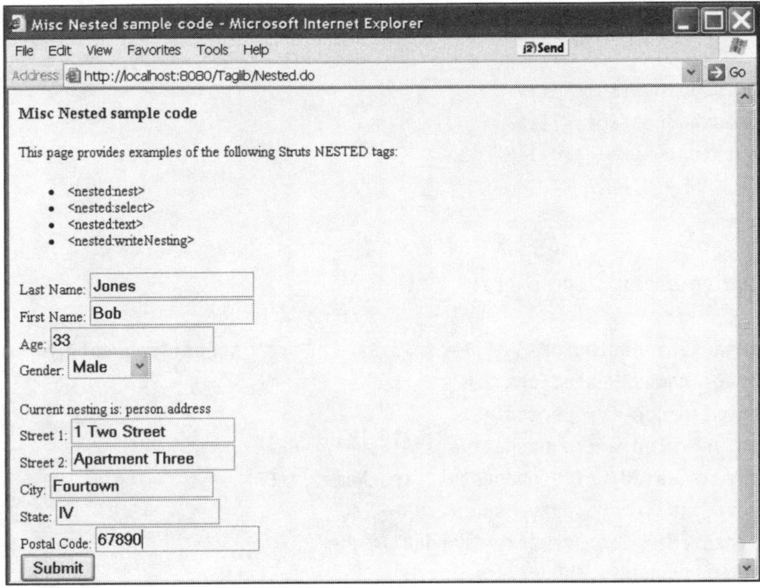

FIGURE 15.2 The first page of the nesting example at `/Taglib/Nested.do`.

When the form is submitted, control is handed to `showPerson.jsp` (shown in Listing 15.5).

LISTING 15.5 Displaying the Submitted Nested Values (`showPerson.jsp`)

```
<%@ page language="java" %>
<%@ taglib uri="/WEB-INF/struts-html.tld" prefix="html" %>
<%@ taglib uri="/WEB-INF/struts-bean.tld" prefix="bean" %>
<%@ taglib uri="/WEB-INF/struts-logic.tld" prefix="logic" %>
<%@ taglib uri="/WEB-INF/struts-nested.tld" prefix="nested" %>
<%@ page import="java.util.Vector" %>
<%@ page import="ch15.Person" %>
<%@ page import="ch15.Address" %>

<html:html>
<head>
<title>Misc NESTED sample code</title>
</head>
<body bgcolor="white">

<h3>Misc NESTED sample code</h3>

<p>This page provides examples of the following Struts NESTED tags:<br>
```

LISTING 15.5 Continued

```
<ul>
<li>&lt;nested:nest&gt;</li>
<li>&lt;nested:root&gt;</li>
<li>&lt;nested:write&gt;</li>
</ul>

<%--
The following section shows nest.
--%>
<jsp:useBean id="NestedForm" type="ch15.PersonForm" scope="request"/>
<nested:root name="NestedForm">
<nested:nest property="person">
Last Name: <nested:write property="lastName"/><BR>
First Name: <nested:write property="firstName"/><BR>
Age: <nested:write property="age"/><BR>
Gender: <nested:write property="gender"/><P>
<nested:nest property="address">
Street 1: <nested:write property="street1"/><BR>
Street 2: <nested:write property="street2"/><BR>
City: <nested:write property="city"/><BR>
State: <nested:write property="state"/><BR>
Postal Code: <nested:write property="postalCode"/><BR>
</nested:nest>
</nested:nest>
</nested:root>
</html:body>
</html:html>
```

This page shows one more useful tag: `<nested:root>`. By default, the `<nested:nest>` tag assumes that a form has been set up, and uses that form to look up the properties to nest on. The `<nested:root>` tag enables you to explicitly define the bean to be nested on. In this case, it's the submitted form. Figure 15.3 shows this page after submission.

Using the Struts Template Tags

This section provides information about the following tags:

- `<template:insert>`—Insert a template with passed content
- `<template:get>`—Retrieve template content
- `<template:put>`—Pass template content

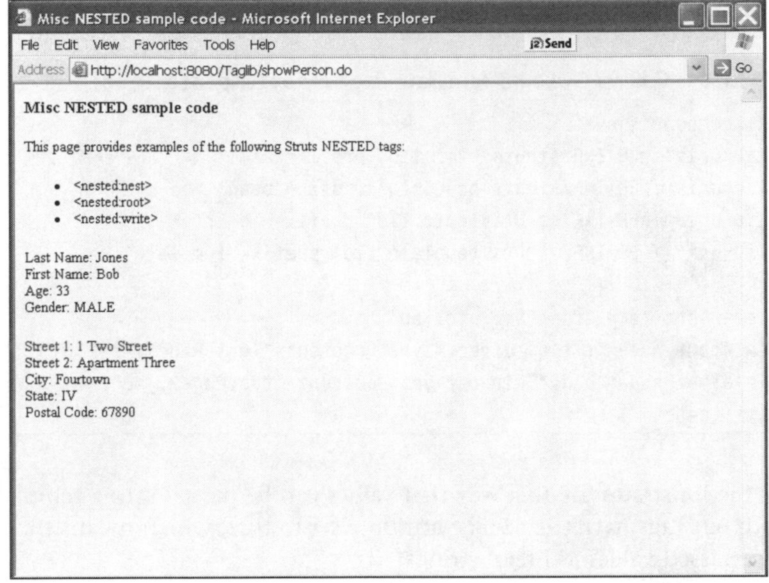

FIGURE 15.3 The submitted form at `/Taglib/showPerson.do`.

This section uses the testTemplate pages at `/Taglib/testTemplate[1-3].do`. Figure 15.4 shows the result of requesting `testTemplate1.do`.

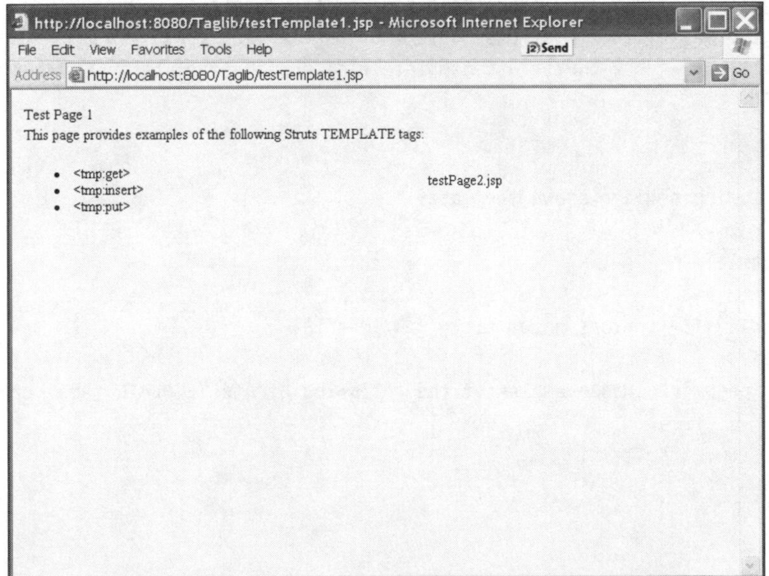

FIGURE 15.4 Test template page at `/Taglib/testTemplate1.do`.

The source to this page can be found in Listing 15.6.

LISTING 15.6 Calling Out to a Template Page (`testTemplate1.jsp`)

```
<%@ page language="java" %>
<%@ taglib uri="/WEB-INF/struts-html.tld" prefix="html" %>
<%@ taglib uri="/WEB-INF/struts-bean.tld" prefix="bean" %>
<%@ taglib uri="/WEB-INF/struts-logic.tld" prefix="logic" %>
<%@ taglib uri="/WEB-INF/struts-template.tld" prefix="template" %>

<template:insert template="Template.jsp">
  <template:put name="title" direct="yes" content="Test Page 1"/>
  <template:put name="body" direct="yes" content="testPage2.jsp"/>
</template:insert>
```

This JSP file illustrates the first way that values can be passed into a template. In this case, both `put` tags have the `direct` attribute set to true, which means that Struts treats the passed values as literal strings.

The template itself is found in Listing 15.7.

LISTING 15.7 Calling Out to a Template Page (`Template.jsp`)

```
<%@ page language="java" %>
<%@ taglib uri="/WEB-INF/struts-html.tld" prefix="html" %>
<%@ taglib uri="/WEB-INF/struts-bean.tld" prefix="bean" %>
<%@ taglib uri="/WEB-INF/struts-logic.tld" prefix="logic" %>
<%@ taglib uri="/WEB-INF/struts-template.tld" prefix="tmp" %>


<%--
The following section shows templates.
--%>
<html:html>
<body>
<TABLE><TR><TD><tmp:get name="title"/></TD></TR>
<TR><TD>
<p>This page provides examples of the following Struts TEMPLATE tags:<br>
<ul>
<li>&lt;tmp:get&gt;</li>
```

LISTING 15.7 Continued

```
<li>&lt;tmp:insert&gt;</li>
<li>&lt;tmp:put&gt;</li>
</ul>
</TD>
<TD><tmp:get name="body"/>
</TD>
</TR>
</TABLE>
</body>
</html:html>
```

Basically, wherever a `<template:get>` tag is used, it looks for the corresponding value to have been passed in using `<template:put>` in the calling `<template:insert>` tag.

In the second example, the `direct` attribute has been left off the second `<template:put>` tag. That means Struts looks for a Web resource with the `name` treated as a URI, and the contents are inserted. In this case (Listing 15.8), the requested page is the logic iteration example from the previous chapter. The results of requesting this page are shown in Figure 15.5.

LISTING 15.8 Inserting a Web Resource into a Template (`testTemplate2.jsp`)

```
<%@ page language="java" %>
<%@ taglib uri="/WEB-INF/struts-html.tld" prefix="html" %>
<%@ taglib uri="/WEB-INF/struts-bean.tld" prefix="bean" %>
<%@ taglib uri="/WEB-INF/struts-logic.tld" prefix="logic" %>
<%@ taglib uri="/WEB-INF/struts-template.tld" prefix="template" %>

<template:insert template="Template.jsp">
  <template:put name="title" direct="yes" content="Test Page 2"/>
  <template:put name="body"  content="testPage2.jsp"/>
</template:insert>
```

Finally, you can include content inside the body of a `<template:put>` tag instead of using the `content` attribute. If you do so, `direct` is automatically assumed to be true. Listing 15.9 shows this use of the tag, and Figure 15.6 shows what the page looks like.

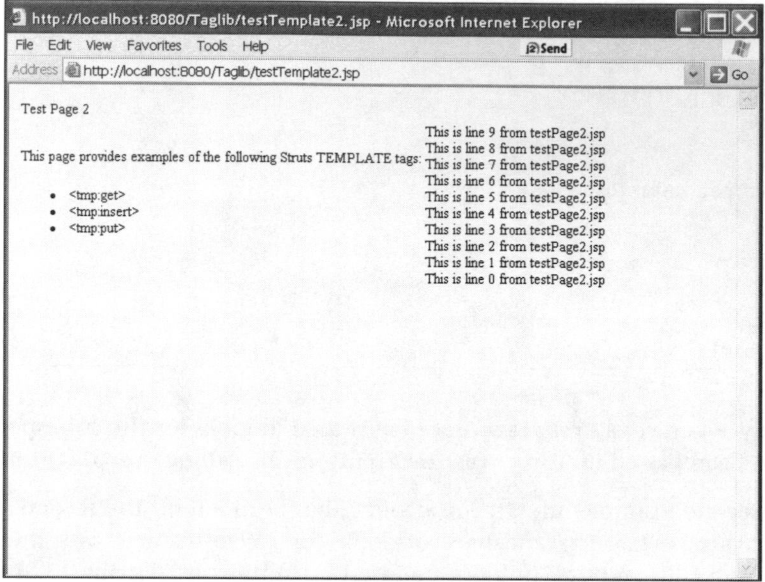

FIGURE 15.5 Test template page at `/Taglib/testTemplate2.do`.

LISTING 15.9 Inserting `put` Body Content into a Template (`testTemplate3.jsp`)

```
<%@ page language="java" %>
<%@ taglib uri="/WEB-INF/struts-html.tld" prefix="html" %>
<%@ taglib uri="/WEB-INF/struts-bean.tld" prefix="bean" %>
<%@ taglib uri="/WEB-INF/struts-logic.tld" prefix="logic" %>
<%@ taglib uri="/WEB-INF/struts-template.tld" prefix="template" %>

<template:insert template="Template.jsp">
  <template:put name="title" direct="yes" content="Test Page 1"/>
  <template:put name="body"><B>This is a test Body</B></template:put>
</template:insert>
```

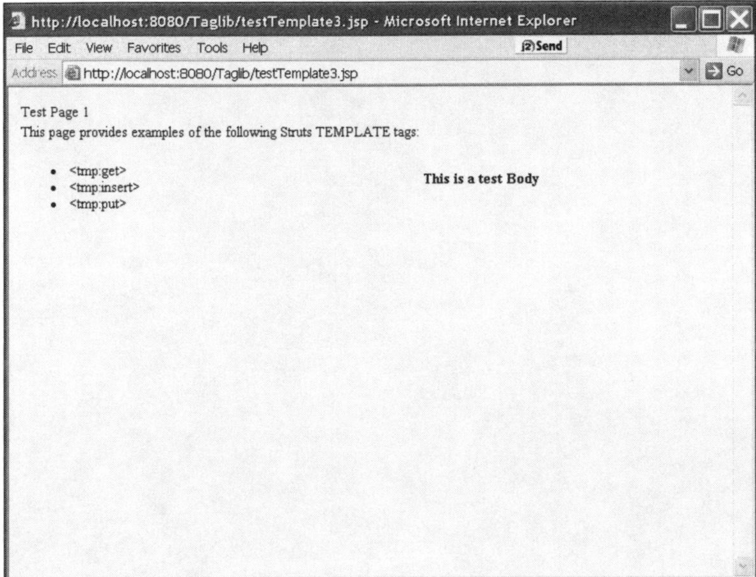

FIGURE 15.6 Test template page at `/Taglib/testTemplate3.do`.

Conclusions

Both the Nested and Template libraries can be very handy for specific situations. The Nested taglib is most convenient if you've adopted a development style in which your forms consist of a hierarchy of objects rather than a flat list of properties in a single simple form object. The Nested taglib has the advantage of enabling you to refer to properties simply, even if you're deep inside a set of concentric objects.

The Template taglib enables you to design a unified look and feel for your application, and to keep all the Web pages in sync by making changes to a single file instead of changing the same element on each page. However, the Template taglib is being overtaken by the newer Tiles template library, which is discussed in the next chapter. But a downside of the Tiles library is that it requires more setup, so you might want to stick with Template library tags for simple templating.

16

The Struts Tiles Tag Library: Creation Master Document Templates

IN THIS CHAPTER

- A Tiles Overview
- Enabling Tiles
- The Definitions Configuration File
- Writing JSP Files for Tiles
- Modifying Your Actions
- Putting It All Together
- Other Aspects of Tiles
- Conclusions

As you develop Web applications, you typically discover that each page has a core central element that changes, and is surrounded by relatively static elements such as the header, footer, and perhaps a side menu.

The Tiles taglib enables you to create a page template that you can use through your application, and which also enables you to define this structure in terms of a master XML template.

This chapter shows one possible way you could use Tiles to simplify your site design, but it isn't intended to be a complete guide to the library itself. For that, you should take a look at the API guide on the Jakarta Web site.

A Tiles Overview

In many ways, it's possible to consider Tiles as merely an extension of the Template tag library. But to do so would be to miss the real power of Tiles.

Using Tiles, you can define a base template page (called a *layout*), and then base your entire Web site on that layout. Because Struts is so closely integrated with Tiles, you can use layouts in place of JSP files in your Struts configuration file, as you'll see later in the chapter.

As with most things related to Struts, it's easier to see how Tiles works if you start by looking at an example. In this case, you'll see how the Stocktracker application that we used in Chapters 5 through 11 can be rewritten to leverage Tiles.

Enabling Tiles

Before you can use Tiles, you must make it available. If you merely want to use the Tiles tags in your JSP files, all you have to do is to insert the following line at the top of your JSP file:

```
<%@ taglib uri="/WEB-INF/struts-tiles.tld" prefix="tiles"%>
```

If you want to fully integrate Tiles into Struts, you need to add the following plug-in definition into your strutsconfig.xml file, as well:

```
<plug-in className="org.apache.struts.tiles.TilesPlugin" >
     <set-property property="definitions-config"
                   value="/WEB-INF/stocktrack-tiles.xml" />
     <set-property property="definitions-debug" value="2" />
     <set-property property="definitions-parser-details" value="2" />
     <set-property property="definitions-parser-validate" value="true" />
</plug-in>
```

The `definitions-debug` and `definitions-parser-details` properties define the level of debugging information that Tiles supplies, with a value of `0` being none and `2` being everything. The `definitions-parser-validate` property determines whether the layout configuration file is validated against the DTD.

The Definitions Configuration File

Now that Tiles is installed, you can write the definitions file. Listing 16.1 shows the definitions for the Stocktracker application.

LISTING 16.1 The Tiles Layout Definition File (`stocktrack-tiles.xml`)

```
<!DOCTYPE tiles-definitions PUBLIC
  "-//Apache Software Foundation//DTD Tiles Configuration//EN"
  "http://jakarta.apache.org/struts/dtds/tiles-config.dtd">

<tiles-definitions>
 <definition name="stocktrack.default" path="/layouts/stocktrackDefault.jsp">
  <put name="header" value="/header.jsp" />
  <put name="minibar" value="/minibar.jsp" />
 </definition>
 <definition name="stocktrack.index" extends="stocktrack.default">
  <put name="mainwindow" value="/home.jsp" />
  <put name="title" value="Welcome to Stock Tracker"/>
```

LISTING 16.1 Continued

```
 </definition>
 <definition name="stocktrack.portfolio" extends="stocktrack.default">
  <put name="mainwindow" value="/portfolio.jsp" />
  <put name="title" value="Portfolio View"/>
 </definition>
 <definition name="stocktrack.newUserName" extends="stocktrack.default">
  <put name="mainwindow" value="/newUserName.jsp" />
  <put name="title" value="Enter User Information"/>
 </definition>
 <definition name="stocktrack.newUserAddress" extends="stocktrack.default">
  <put name="mainwindow" value="/newUserAddress.jsp" />
  <put name="title" value="Enter User Address"/>
 </definition>
</tiles-definitions>
```

The file is composed of a number of `definition` tags bounded by a `tiles-definitions` tag. Each `definition` tag corresponds to a page in the application.

NOTE

The names of the definitions can be totally arbitrary. They don't need to correspond to any package definition or path. You could name a definition `starship.enterprise` if you wanted to. The definition's name merely serve as a unique identifier that you can use in place of JSP paths in a forward, input, or path directive.

However, that having been said, it makes sense to use some kind of hierarchical or package-based naming convention to keep things straight.

Writing JSP Files for Tiles

To begin, take a look at the `stocktrack.default` definition. It says that the JSP file that implements this layout can be found in `/layouts/stocktrackDefault.jsp`. Listing 16.2 shows the contents of this file.

LISTING 16.2 The Default JSP Layout File (*stocktrackDefault.jsp*)

```
<%@ taglib uri="/WEB-INF/struts-tiles.tld" prefix="tiles"%>

<tiles:importAttribute name="title"/>
<tiles:insert attribute="header">
  <tiles:put name="title" beanName="title" direct="true"/>
```

LISTING 16.2 Continued

```
</tiles:insert>
<table width="100%" BORDER="1" CELLPADDING="5">
<TR><TD WIDTH="250" VALIGN="TOP" HALIGN="LEFT">
<tiles:insert attribute="minibar"/>
</TD>
<TD VALIGN="TOP">
<tiles:insert attribute="mainwindow"/>
</TD></TR></TABLE>
</body>
</html>
```

If you look carefully, you'll see that this file looks pretty much like the generic page layout for the application, a header that's passed a title, a minibar on the left side of the window, and the main contents of the window on the right. The only differences between this page and the one you've already seen is that this page uses tile tags instead of using template tags, and the body of the page has been replaced with another `<tiles:insert>` tag.

Now go back and look at the definitions file. The `stocktrack.default` layout supplies two attributes using the `put` tag: the header and the minibar. These attributes define where the JSP files that provide that contents can be found. When `stocktrackDefault.jsp` does a `<tiles:get>` using the same name, the contents of this file are inserted, which is similar to how the template tags work.

You might already be asking, "How about the `mainwindow` content? The default layout doesn't supply a value for it." That's because the default layout isn't intended to be used directly. One of the features of Tiles is that a layout can inherit from another layout. In this case, the default layout is the parent of all the live layouts that are used in the application.

To see how this works, look at the `stocktrack.index` definition, which defines the entry page. This definition does not specify a `path`, but instead uses the `extends` property. This tells Tiles to base all the entries for this layout on the layout that it extends, unless a value is overridden.

The `mainwindow` and `title` of the page are defined in the body of the layout. This results in a fully implemented layout that can supply all the values that the `stocktrackDefault.jsp` template needs.

If you look at `home.jsp` (shown in Listing 16.3), you'll see that it's the old index page with all the templating removed (in other words, it's just the main body of the page).

LISTING 16.3 The Index Page (`home.jsp`)

```
<%@ taglib uri="/WEB-INF/struts-template.tld" prefix="tmp"%>
<H1><CENTER>Today's Economic News</CENTER></H1>
<TABLE WIDTH="100%" CELLPADDING="10"><TR><TD WIDTH="50%" VALIGN="TOP">
<tmp:insert template="mainstory.jsp"/>
<HR>
<tmp:insert template="substory1.jsp"/>
</TD><TD VALIGN="TOP">
<tmp:insert template="substory2.jsp"/>
<HR>
<tmp:insert template="substory3.jsp"/>
</TD></TR></TABLE>
```

All the other content pages have been similarly rewritten. In addition, `addTransaction.jsp` has been renamed as `portfolio.jsp`, which is a more appropriate name.

Going back for a moment to the `stocktrackDefault.jsp` file, you can see this bit of monkey business going on around the insertion of the header file:

```
<tiles:importAttribute name="title"/>
<tiles:insert attribute="header">
  <tiles:put name="title" beanName="title" direct="true"/>
</tiles:insert>
```

You need to get the title of the page to the header file from the layout definitions file. Unfortunately, Tiles attributes only go one file down (as of this writing). The `title` attribute defined for this page isn't available to pages that it in turn inserts. So, you must use the `importAttribute` tag to move the attribute into a bean, and then use a `put` tag inside the `insert` to supply the value to the header file. The `direct` flag says to pass the value as a string rather than looking for a file of that name and inserting its contents.

The `header.jsp` file (Listing 16.4) is almost identical to the old version.

LISTING 16.4 The New Header Content (`header.jsp`)

```
<%@ taglib uri="/WEB-INF/struts-tiles.tld" prefix="tiles"%>
<html>
<head>
<title>
<tiles:getAsString name="title"/>
</title>
</head>
<body>
```

LISTING 16.4 Continued

```
<table width="100%">
<tr><td align="CENTER"><H1>STOCK TRACKER</H1></td></tr>
<tr><td align="CENTER">Your Insider's View to Wall Street</td></tr>
</table><P>
```

Again the major difference is the use of Tiles tags instead of template tags. Also, to insert a value directly into the page content, you use the `<tiles:getAsString>` tag.

Modifying Your Actions

The final step in converting the application to use Tiles is to change the `action` tags in the application to use the Tiles layout names instead of JSP filenames. Listing 16.5 shows the new global forward and action sections of `struts-config.xml`.

LISTING 16.5 Modifications to `struts-config.xml`

```
<global-forwards type="org.apache.struts.action.ActionForward">
    <forward name="home" path="stocktrack.index" />
    <forward name="portfolio" path="stocktrack.portfolio"/>
    <forward name="newUserName" path="stocktrack.newUserName"/>
    <forward name="newUserAddress" path="stocktrack.newUserAddress"/>

</global-forwards>
<action-mappings type="org.apache.struts.action.ActionMapping">
    <action path="/index" forward="stocktrack.index" />
    <action path="/newaccount" forward="stocktrack.newUserName"/>
    <action path="/login" type="stocktrack.struts.action.LoginAction"
            name="loginForm" scope="request"/>
    <action path="/newUserName" type="stocktrack.struts.action.NewUserNameAction"
            name="newUserNameForm" scope="session" input="stocktrack.newUserName"/>
    <action path="/newUserAddress"
            type="stocktrack.struts.action.NewUserAddressAction"
            name="newUserAddressForm" scope="session"
            input="stocktrack.newUserAddress"/>
    <action path="/portfolio" type="stocktrack.struts.action.PortfolioAction"/>
    <action path="/addTransaction"
            type="stocktrack.struts.action.AddTransactionAction"
            name="addTransactionForm" scope="request"
            validate="true" input="stocktrack.portfolio">
      <forward name="home" path="stocktrack.portfolio"/>
    </action>
</action-mappings>
```

As you can see, a layout name can be freely used in place of a JSP pathname for a `forward`'s `path` attribute or `action`'s `input` attribute.

Putting It All Together

Now take a moment to walk through the entire flow of a page request using Tiles. Imagine that you request `/index.do`. Struts looks up the `action`, and finds that it should forward your request to the `stocktrack.index` layout. Tiles looks up that name and finds that it's an extension of the `stocktrack.default` layout. That layout uses the `stocktrackDefault.jsp` template file. So, Tiles combines the attributes from the two definitions and hands control over to the template file, which populates the contents from the various source files.

There are several advantages to using Tiles this way. For one thing, you can change the entire look of the site by adding a new template file and pointing the `stocktrack.default` layout at this new file.

Another advantage is that the content pages don't need to know anything about their surroundings. That means you can reuse the same content in several different layouts.

Also, using Tiles in this way totally removes any knowledge of the JSP filenames from the Struts configuration file. Everywhere in the application can refer to the logical names specified in the definitions file, and only the definitions file needs to actually know where the JSP files reside.

Other Aspects of Tiles

This chapter has shown one way to use Tiles—by using the plug-in and the layout definition file. You can also explicitly define layouts in your JSP by using the `<tiles:definition>` tag. The recommended strategy for using this tag is to put all of your definitions in one master file, and then have all your client pages include it.

In our opinion, this is a much less useful application of Tiles. You lose the ability to define a single common template and use the XML file to define the content of the layouts. It basically reduces Tiles to the level of a glorified template library.

As with most Struts tag libraries, there are a plethora of support tags and parameters that can be used for specific cases, but a good perusal of the API documentation for the library should answer most of your questions. Most, if not all, of them are intended for advanced applications using Tiles.

Conclusions

The Tiles tag library enables you to totally abstract your page layout by defining logical names in an XML layout file. Because layouts can be extended from other layouts, you define a foundation layout and base all the other page layouts on that one, only having to define what is different about the other pages.

To use Tiles effectively with Struts, you must use the Tiles plug-in. This enables you to use a logical Tiles layout name in place of a JSP filename anywhere in the `struts-config.xml` file.

17

DynaForms and the Validator

IN THIS CHAPTER

- DynaForms: Forms Without Java
- DynaBeans and Struts
- The Validator: Automating Field Checking
- Conclusions

It might sound like a comic book superhero, but a DynaForm can't leap a tall building in a single method invocation. On the other hand, it can reduce a lot of the drudgework of developing Struts applications.

Similarly, the Struts Validator framework can eliminate many common form validation tasks, leaving you to concentrate on the business logic. However, the validator must be used with care, because it doesn't handle all the more complex validations you could encounter during development.

By the end of this chapter, you'll have seen a few examples of how to create and use DynaForms, and how to integrate them with the Validator to create practically Java-less validating forms.

DynaForms: Forms Without Java

DynaForms are an extension of the Apache Commons Beanutils project. As part of the org.apache.commons.beanutils package, an interface called DynaBean was created. Unlike normal JavaBeans, which require explicit get*XXX*() and set*XXX*() methods to be written for each property, a DynaBean uses a generic get() and set() method with the property name as the first argument.

A fuller description of the DynaBean package can be found on the Jakarta Web site at http://jakarta.apache.org/commons/beanutils.html.

For example, in a traditional JavaBean, you would say

```
myBean.setType("kidneybean");
```

Using DynaBeans, you would say

```
myBean.set("type", "kidneybean");
```

This approach has both advantages and disadvantages. The major advantage is that you don't have to declare all your properties explicitly at compile-time; they can be loaded dynamically during execution. This can be very handy to quickly create new beans or new properties of beans.

The disadvantage is that you lose a lot of compile-time error checking. Let's say you are thick-fingered, and enter

```
myBean.set("tpye", "kidneybean");
```

The compiler won't catch this. As far as it's concerned, this is perfectly legal Java. It's not until run-time that you'll suddenly find yourself with a null pointer exception. Similarly, all `get()` and `set()` methods take and return the `Object` type, so you lose the strong type-checking of traditional beans.

DynaBeans and Struts

One place that DynaBeans make a lot of sense is in Struts. If you use DynaBeans correctly, you can reduce the size of your `ActionForms` by 80–90%. This is because you can use DynaBeans to eliminate all of your form getters and setters.

To see how this works, you'll rewrite the two `ActionForms` for the new account pages of the StockTrack application. To begin, take a look at one of the existing `ActionForms` and the same form rewritten with `DynaForms` (Listing 17.1 and 17.2).

LISTING 17.1 `NewUserAddressForm.java`

```
package stocktrack.struts.form;

import javax.servlet.http.*;
import org.apache.struts.action.ActionMapping;
import org.apache.struts.action.ActionErrors;
import org.apache.struts.action.ActionError;
import org.apache.struts.action.ActionForm;
import stocktrack.struts.form.BaseForm;

/**
 * stocktrack.struts.form.NewUserAddressForm class.
 * this class used by Struts Framework to store data from newUserAddressForm
 *
```

LISTING 17.1 Continued

```
 * struts-config declaration:
 * <form-bean name="newUserAddressForm"
 *         type="stocktrack.struts.form.NewUserAddressForm" />
 *
 * @see org.apache.struts.action.ActionForm org.apache.struts.action.ActionForm
 * Generated by StrutsWizard.
 */

public class NewUserAddressForm extends BaseForm {
  public void reset(ActionMapping mapping, HttpServletRequest request) {
    streetAddress1 = "";
    streetAddress2 = "";
    city = "";
    state = "";
    postalCode = "";
    homePhone = "";
    workPhone = "";
    workExt = "";
  }
  public ActionErrors validate(ActionMapping mapping,
                               HttpServletRequest request) {
    ActionErrors errors = new ActionErrors();
    if (this.isBlankString(streetAddress1)) {
        errors.add("streetAddress1",
                   new ActionError("stocktrack.newuser.required"));
    }
    if (this.isBlankString(city)) {
        errors.add("city", new ActionError("stocktrack.newuser.required"));
   }
    if (this.isBlankString(state)) {
        errors.add("state", new ActionError("stocktrack.newuser.required"));
   } else {
      if (!this.isValidState(state)) {
        errors.add("state",
                   new ActionError("stocktrack.newuser.invalid.state"));
      }
   }
    if (this.isBlankString(postalCode)) {
        errors.add("postalCode",
                    new ActionError("stocktrack.newuser.required"));
```

LISTING 17.1 Continued

```
    } else {
      if (!this.isValidPostalCode(postalCode)) {
          errors.add("postalCode",
                      new ActionError("stocktrack.newuser.invalid.postalCode"));
      }
    }
    if (this.isBlankString(homePhone)) {
        errors.add("homePhone", new ActionError("stocktrack.newuser.required"));
    } else {
        if (!this.isValidPhone(homePhone)) {
          errors.add("homePhone",
                      new ActionError("stocktrack.newuser.invalid.phone"));
        }
    }
    if (this.isBlankString(workPhone)) {
        errors.add("workPhone", new ActionError("stocktrack.newuser.required"));
    } else {
        if (!this.isValidPhone(workPhone)) {
          errors.add("workPhone",
                      new ActionError("stocktrack.newuser.invalid.phone"));
        }
    }
    return errors;
  }
  private String streetAddress1;
  private String streetAddress2;
  private String city;
  private String state;
  private String postalCode;
  private String homePhone;
  private String workPhone;
  private String workExt;
  public String getStreetAddress1() {
    return streetAddress1;
  }
  public void setStreetAddress1(String streetAddress1) {
    this.streetAddress1 = streetAddress1;
  }
  public String getStreetAddress2() {
    return streetAddress2;
  }
```

LISTING 17.1 Continued

```
  public void setStreetAddress2(String streetAddress2) {
    this.streetAddress2 = streetAddress2;
  }
  public String getCity() {
    return city;
  }
  public void setCity(String city) {
    this.city = city;
  }
  public String getState() {
    return state;
  }
  public void setState(String state) {
    this.state = state;
  }
  public String getPostalCode() {
    return postalCode;
  }
  public void setPostalCode(String postalCode) {
    this.postalCode = postalCode;
  }
  public String getHomePhone() {
    return homePhone;
  }
  public void setHomePhone(String homePhone) {
    this.homePhone = homePhone;
  }
  public String getWorkPhone() {
    return workPhone;
  }
  public void setWorkPhone(String workPhone) {
    this.workPhone = workPhone;
  }
  public String getWorkExt() {
    return workExt;
  }
  public void setWorkExt(String workExt) {
    this.workExt = workExt;
  }
}
```

LISTING 17.2 NewUserAddressForm.java as a DynaForm

```
package stocktrack.struts.form;

import javax.servlet.http.*;
import org.apache.struts.action.ActionMapping;
import org.apache.struts.action.ActionErrors;
import org.apache.struts.action.ActionError;
import org.apache.struts.action.ActionForm;
import stocktrack.struts.form.BaseForm;
import stocktrack.struts.form.BaseDynaForm;

/**
 * stocktrack.struts.form.NewUserAddressForm class.
 * this class used by Struts Framework to store data from newUserAddressForm
 *
 * struts-config declaration:
 * <form-bean name="newUserAddressForm"
 *         type="stocktrack.struts.form.NewUserAddressForm" />
 *
 * @see org.apache.struts.action.ActionForm org.apache.struts.action.ActionForm
 * Generated by StrutsWizard.
 */

public class NewUserAddressForm extends BaseDynaForm {

  public ActionErrors validate(ActionMapping mapping,
                               HttpServletRequest request) {
    ActionErrors errors = new ActionErrors();
    if (BaseForm.isBlankString(this.getString("streetAddress1"))) {
        errors.add("streetAddress1",
                   new ActionError("stocktrack.newuser.required"));
    }
    if (BaseForm.isBlankString(this.getString("city"))) {
        errors.add("city",
                   new ActionError("stocktrack.newuser.required"));
   }
    if (BaseForm.isBlankString(this.getString("state"))) {
        errors.add("state", new ActionError("stocktrack.newuser.required"));
   } else {
      if (!BaseForm.isValidState(this.getString("state"))) {
        errors.add("state",
                    new ActionError("stocktrack.newuser.invalid.state"));
```

LISTING 17.2 Continued

```
      }
    }
    if (BaseForm.isBlankString(this.getString("postalCode"))) {
        errors.add("postalCode",
                   new ActionError("stocktrack.newuser.required"));
    } else {
      if (!BaseForm.isValidPostalCode(this.getString("postalCode"))) {
          errors.add("postalCode",
                     new ActionError("stocktrack.newuser.invalid.postalCode"));
      }
    }
    if (BaseForm.isBlankString(this.getString("homePhone"))) {
        errors.add("homePhone", new ActionError("stocktrack.newuser.required"));
    } else {
        if (!BaseForm.isValidPhone(this.getString("homePhone"))) {
          errors.add("homePhone",
                     new ActionError("stocktrack.newuser.invalid.phone"));
        }
    }
    if (BaseForm.isBlankString(this.getString("workPhone"))) {
        errors.add("workPhone", new ActionError("stocktrack.newuser.required"));
    } else {
        if (!BaseForm.isValidPhone(this.getString("workPhone"))) {
          errors.add("workPhone",
                     new ActionError("stocktrack.newuser.invalid.phone"));
        }
    }
    return errors;
  }

}
```

The first thing to notice here is that the class has been changed from `BaseForm` (which, as you might recall, is simply `ActionForm` with a few helper functions added for validation) to `BaseDynaForm`, which is a different helper class that extends `DynaActionForm` instead. All the getters and setters have been removed, and the `validate` function now uses `this.getString` to get the values of the properties rather than accessing the local variables of the class.

getString() is in fact not a part of DynaActionForm, which only defines generic get() and set() methods that take and return Objects. However, rather than cast to String all the time, I've created BaseDynaForm, which adds the getString() versions. Listing 17.3 shows this simple class.

LISTING 17.3 BaseDynaForm.java

```
package stocktrack.struts.form;

import org.apache.struts.action.DynaActionForm;

public class BaseDynaForm extends DynaActionForm {
  public String getString(String name) {
    return (String) this.get(name);
  }

  public String getString(String name, int ind) {
    return (String) this.get(name, ind);
  }
}
```

In addition, now that the class no longer derives from BaseForm, you need to call out explicitly to BaseForm to get helper functions such as nullOrVoid. Because they were originally defined nonstatic, you must go into BaseForm and declare them static. I suppose that we could have copied the code from BaseForm to BaseDynaForm, but that would have meant maintaining the same code in two places.

The <form-property> Tag

So, if all the getters and setters have been removed from the class, how does the class know what its legal properties are? The answer lies in the form-bean tag in struts-config.xml.

Until now, the forms you've defined in the file looked like this:

```
<form-bean name="newUserAddressForm"
           type="stocktrack.struts.form.NewUserAddressForm" />
```

But now, you're going to add some new tags, form-property tags, to the form-bean (see Listing 17.4).

LISTING 17.4 The Rewritten newUserAddress Form

```
<form-bean name="newUserAddressForm" type="stocktrack.struts.form.NewUserAddress-
Form">
  <form-property name="streetAddress1" type="java.lang.String"/>
  <form-property name="streetAddress2" type="java.lang.String"/>
  <form-property name="city" type="java.lang.String"/>
  <form-property name="state" type="java.lang.String"/>
  <form-property name="postalCode" type="java.lang.String"/>
  <form-property name="homePhone" type="java.lang.String"/>
  <form-property name="workPhone" type="java.lang.String"/>
  <form-property name="workExt" type="java.lang.String"/>
</form-bean>
```

Inside the `form-bean`, all the properties have been listed along with their type. This allows the `DynaForm` to populate the fields. You can use pretty much any class you want in the `type` value, as well as primitives such as `int`, `Boolean`, and so on.

You can also specify initializations for properties via the `initial` keyword. For example, the following `form-property` sets up a property called `opt-in`, which defaults to true:

```
<form-property name="homePhone" type="boolean" initial="true"/>
```

The `initial` keyword is also the only way to create an array or list of a given size. Imagine that you have a form with 10 lines to fill in the names, ages, and genders of the user's dependents. You'd define it like so:

```
<form-property name="depName" type="java.lang.String[]"
   initial="{'','','','','','','','','',''}"/>
<form-property name="depAge" type="java.lang.String[]"
   initial="{'','','','','','','','','',''}"/>
<form-property name="depGender" type="java.lang.String[]"
   initial="{'','','','','','','','','',''}"/>
```

Whatever the type requested, if you want to specify an initial value, there must be a converter defined from `String` to that class in the Commons Beanutils package. You can add your own converters, so just about any class can be initialized via a `form-property` tag.

String (and other) arrays are accessed using `get()` and `set()`, the same as any other `DynaBean`. However, you use a second argument, which specifies the index into the array.

The Validator: Automating Field Checking

Using DynaBeans has enabled you to drastically reduce the size of the form bean, but wouldn't it be nice to get rid of it all together?

After moving all the properties out of the bean and into the DynaForm definition in struts-config.xml, the only thing left in the bean is the validate function. By using the Struts Validation framework, which ties into the Commons Validator package, you can remove this last piece of code and get rid of the form bean.

WHAT IS COMMONS?

Commons (or more formally, the Jakarta Commons project) is an effort to gather a lot of reusable Java code in one place.

The idea is that there are any number of commonly coded tasks that can be generalized and placed in one place, so that no one ever needs to reinvent the wheel again.

Commons is divided into two pieces: the Commons proper and the sandbox. The Commons proper is where well-tested robust packages live; they have release cycles and beta testing. The sandbox is where the "not ready for prime time" packages live while they undergo their initial development, and is a much less formal environment.

You'll find that many of the Jakarta projects, from Torque to Struts and beyond, depend on various Commons packages to work. You can learn more about the Commons project by visiting the Jakarta Web site at

http://Jakarta.apache.org/commons/

Adding validation to Struts forms is done in a few steps. To begin, you need to add the Validator plug-in to the struts-config.xml file. This is just a piece of boilerplate XML, shown in Listing 17.5.

LISTING 17.5 Adding the Validator Plug-In to Struts

```
<plug-in className="org.apache.struts.validator.ValidatorPlugIn">
  <set-property
  property="pathnames"
  value="/WEB-INF/validator-rules.xml,/WEB-INF/validation.xml"/>
</plug-in>
```

This plug-in should be the very last thing in the file before the </struts-config> tag.

The plug-in entry does two things. First, it notifies Struts that the validator should be made available. Secondly, it defines the locations of the validator rules files, which are used to define the validations that will be run over the forms. The validator-rules.xml file comes standard with the validator. It defines the most commonly used rules (such as credit cards, dates, strings, numbers, and so on). The `validation.xml` file is one that you will define, and contains specialized validations used by your application, as well as the actual validation-to-form field mappings.

First, take a look at a typical rule from `validator-rules.xml` as delivered by the Validator package (see Listing 17.6).

LISTING 17.6 A Rule from `validator-rules.xml`

```
<validator name="creditCard"
           classname="org.apache.struts.util.StrutsValidator"
           method="validateCreditCard"
           methodParams="java.lang.Object,
                         org.apache.commons.validator.ValidatorAction,
                         org.apache.commons.validator.Field,
                         org.apache.struts.action.ActionErrors,
                         javax.servlet.http.HttpServletRequest"
           depends=""
           msg="errors.creditcard">
   <javascript><![CDATA[
      function validateCreditCard(form) {
          var bValid = true;
          var focusField = null;
          var i = 0;
          var fields = new Array();
          oCreditCard = new creditCard();

          for (x in oCreditCard) {
              if ((form[oCreditCard[x][0]].type == 'text' ||
                   form[oCreditCard[x][0]].type == 'textarea') &&
                   form[oCreditCard[x][0]].value.length > 0) {
                 if (!luhnCheck(form[oCreditCard[x][0]].value)) {
                    if (i == 0)
                       focusField = form[oCreditCard[x][0]];

                    fields[i++] = oCreditCard[x][1];

                    bValid = false;
                 }
              }
          }

          if (fields.length > 0) {
             focusField.focus();
```

LISTING 17.6 Continued

```
            alert(fields.join('\n'));
        }

        return bValid;
    }

    /**
     * Reference: http://www.ling.nwu.edu/~sburke/pub/luhn_lib.pl
    */
    function luhnCheck(cardNumber) {
        if (isLuhnNum(cardNumber)) {
            var no_digit = cardNumber.length;
            var oddoeven = no_digit & 1;
            var sum = 0;
            for (var count = 0; count < no_digit; count++) {
                var digit = parseInt(cardNumber.charAt(count));
                if (!((count & 1) ^ oddoeven)) {
                    digit *= 2;
                    if (digit > 9) digit -= 9;
                };
                sum += digit;
            };
            if (sum == 0) return false;
            if (sum % 10 == 0) return true;
        };
        return false;
    }

    function isLuhnNum(argvalue) {
        argvalue = argvalue.toString();
        if (argvalue.length == 0)
           return false;
        for (var n = 0; n < argvalue.length; n++)
           if (argvalue.substring(n, n+1) < "0" || argvalue.substring(n,n+1) >
          ➥"9")
              return false;

        return true;
    }]]>
  </javascript>
</validator>
```

Unless you're a JavaScript wonk, only the first 10 lines of the definition are of any real importance to how the validator works with Struts. The first line of XML declares the official name of this validator—that's the name that other rules or field definitions will use to refer to it.

The next line of XML tells the validator which class defines the validation method for this rule. Unlike many Java-related (and especially JSP-related) tools, the validator doesn't call a standard method on each class. Instead, you can declare any number of methods in a single class and use different ones for different validations.

The `method` value tells the validator which method of the class that was just specified handles the validation for this rule. In this case, validation is handled by the aptly named `validateCreditCard()` method.

Adding to the ways in which the validator is different from everything else in Java, the validation method isn't defined as an interface or even a standard API. It can take a number of different arguments in a number of different orders. The validator code figures out which arguments go where by looking at the types of the arguments as specified in the `methodParams` arguments. They are

- `java.lang.Object`—The `ActionForm` that the value comes from, unless the property is a `String` array or `Collection`, (in which case it is the string itself).
- `org.apache.commons.validator.ValidatorAction`—The object created when the validation rules are parsed, one per rule.
- `org.apache.commons.validator.Field`—An object that holds information about the field being validated, such as its name.
- `org.apache.struts.action.ActionErrors`—The same old `ActionErrors` that you know and love; you add to it if there's a validation error.
- `javax.servlet.http.HttpServletRequest`—The request being processed.
- `org.apache.commons.validator.Validator`—Gives you a handle to the Validator itself, useful for accessing other fields values.

Given all that information, the method should be able to figure out whether there was a validation error or not, eh?

Next, the `depends` tag specifies any other rules that should be run before this rule runs. In this case, the file used to say that the `required` rule should be run first. But, in my opinion, that was wrong. It would mean that you couldn't have a form with both a credit card and bank account field and let the user fill out one or the other, because credit card would be a required field. Luckily, I was able to convince the Struts folks to remove these dependencies, so now you need to explicitly use the `"required"` tag if you need a field to be `required`.

Finally, the `message` tag enables you to define the error message, which will be drawn from the default `Resource`, to use for this validation error.

The remainder of the file defines the JavaScript that's used to provide client-side validation of the field, if requested. It's optional, and those who are interested are welcome to refer to the documentation for the validator to learn more.

Adding the Validator to NewUserAddress

By using the validator, you can completely eliminate the need to create an ActionForm. This can be demonstrated with the same NewUserAddress action you converted to DynaBeans in the first half of this chapter.

To start, you need to create a validation.xml file, which goes into the same directory (WEB-INF) as the validator-rules.xml file. Listing 17.7 shows the file with only the rules for this form placed in it.

LISTING 17.7 validation.xml

```
<form-validation>
 <global>
  <constant>
   <constant-name>phone</constant-name>
   <constant-value>^\(?(\d{3})\)?[-| ]?(\d{3})[-| ]?(\d{4})$</constant-value>
  </constant>
  <constant>
    <constant-name>states</constant-name>
    <constant-value>^(AL|AK|AS|AZ|AR|CA|CO|CT|DE|DC|FM|FL|GA|
➥GU|HI|ID|IL|IN|IA|KS|KY|LA|ME|MH|MD|MA|MI|MN|MS|MO|MT|NE|NV|NH|
➥NJ|NM|NY|NC|ND|MP|OH|OK|OR|PW|PA|PR|RI|SC|SD|TN|TX|UT|VT|VI|VA
➥|WA|WV|WI|WY)$</constant-value>
  </constant>
  <constant>
    <constant-name>zip</constant-name>
    <constant-value>^\d{5}(-\d{4})?$</constant-value>
  </constant>
 </global>
 <formset>
  <form name="newUserAddressForm">
   <field
     property="streetAddress1"
     depends="required">
     <arg0 key="newUserAddressForm.streetAddress1.label"/>
   </field>
   <field
     property="city"
     depends="required">
```

LISTING 17.7 Continued

```
      <arg0 key="newUserAddressForm.city.label"/>
    </field>
    <field
      property="state"
      depends="required,mask">
      <arg0 key="newUserAddressForm.state.label"/>
      <var>
        <var-name>mask</var-name>
        <var-value>${states}</var-value>
      </var>
    </field>
    <field
      property="postalCode"
      depends="required,mask">
      <arg0 key="newUserAddressForm.postalCode.label"/>
        <var>
          <var-name>mask</var-name>
          <var-value>${zip}</var-value>
        </var>
    </field>
  <field
      property="workPhone"
      depends="required,mask">
      <arg0 key="newUserAddressForm.workPhone.label"/>
        <var>
          <var-name>mask</var-name>
          <var-value>${phone}</var-value>
        </var>
    </field>
   <field
      property="homePhone"
      depends="required,mask">
    <arg0 key="newUserAddressForm.homePhone.label"/>
        <var>
          <var-name>mask</var-name>
          <var-value>${phone}</var-value>
        </var>
    </field>
  </form>
  </formset>
</form-validation>
```

This file is broken into two main sections. The top section (inside the `globals` tag) is a place to define any global values that will be used throughout the file. Normally, these are strings that will be used for the `mask` validation, but they could also be used in other places, such as for key values.

In this case, you're defining three constants, which are Perl-style regular expressions that will be used to validate phone numbers, ZIP codes, and states.

After the `globals` section comes the `formset` section. Each `form` begins with a `form` tag containing a single attribute, which is the name of the form (and must match the name as defined in `struts-config.xml`).

Inside the `form` tag are a number of `field` tags. This tag has several attributes. The first is the property of the form that this entry validates, which must match a `form-property`. Next is the `depends` attribute, which specifies one or more validations that must be confirmed for this field to pass. For example, because the `postalCode` field has `required,mask` for a `depends`, both the `required` and `mask` validation must pass for this field to validate.

Inside the `form` tag, two types of values are commonly defined. The `arg`*x* (that is, `arg0`, `arg1`, and so on) tags are used to provide values to the error message if one is generated. Usually, all that's done here is to provide the key that corresponds to the name of the field in the `Resource` file.

The second tag, `var`, is used to pass arguments to the validators themselves. In this example, the `mask` validation is handed several different masks, depending on which field is being validated. By using the `${var}` syntax, values defined in the `globals` section can be used here.

For the error messages to work, a number of strings must be put in the `ApplicationResources.properties` file (see Listing 17.8).

LISTING 17.8 Additions to `ApplicationResources.properties`

```
# Validator errors
errors.required={0} is required.
errors.minlength={0} can not be less than {1} characters.
errors.maxlength={0} can not be greater than {1} characters.
errors.invalid={0} is invalid.
errors.byte={0} must be an byte.
errors.short={0} must be an short.
errors.integer={0} must be an integer.
errors.long={0} must be an long.
errors.float={0} must be an float.
errors.double={0} must be an double.
errors.date={0} is not a date.
```

LISTING 17.8 Continued

```
errors.range={0} is not in the range {1} through {2}.
errors.creditcard={0} is not a valid credit card number.
errors.email={0} is an invalid e-mail address

#New user address form
newUserAddressForm.streetAddress1.label=Street Address
newUserAddressForm.city.label=City
newUserAddressForm.state.label=State
newUserAddressForm.postalCode.label=Postal Code
newUserAddressForm.homePhone.label=Home Telephone
newUserAddressForm.workPhone.label=Work Telephone
```

The top section of strings is the generic validator error messages. You're free to alter them as you want; these are just the ones suggested in the code. The `{0}` will be replaced with the `arg0` value defined in the `field` tag, as will the others by other arguments (for example, the `{1}` will be replaced by the minimum required length in the `minlength` validation).

The lower section simply defines the labels (names) that were used as keys to the field names in the `validation.xml` file. You can also used them with the `bean:message` tag in your JSP to internationalize your forms.

A few more steps are needed to complete the transition. The `type` attribute of `newUserAddressForm` in `struts-config.xml` must be changed to `org.apache.struts.validator.DynaValidatorForm`. Similarly, the line in `NewUserAddressAction` where the Form is cast to from a generic form must be changed to read:

```
DynaValidatorForm uf = (DynaValidatorForm) form;
```

With those changes, you can start the application and test it. You can also delete `NewUserAddressForm.java` because you've totally eliminated it.

Last Minute Validator News

One of the frustrations I (James speaking here) had with Struts was that the validator was languishing for lack of development. Specifically, there was no way to say "validate the checking account number only if the Use Checking Account button is pushed," short of doing those validations in the action.

Also, the Commons Validator package, which is what the Struts Validator Framework depends on, had stalled short of a 1.0 release. I (and a lot of other Struts developers) felt nervous about depending on a package that hadn't even gotten out of the Commons Sandbox.

As this book was being completed, I was accepted as a committer for the Commons Validator package, and volunteered to spearhead a 1.0 release, which is currently scheduled for November of 2002. In addition, I refactored some of the underlying Validator code and added the needed hooks so that cross-form dependencies can be implemented. With that in mind, I submitted a patch against the Struts Validator that added a "requiredif" dependency rule, and which is now part of the core Struts Validator Framework.

Defining a New Validation

Before we leave the topic, it's a useful exercise to see how a new validation type could be written. A good example is the validation done on bank account routing numbers, known in the industry as the ACH (automated clearing house) routing number.

The basic algorithm for this validation is similar to the one done on credit card numbers, in that it's a simple checksum. The number itself is nine digits long. The digits are handled in groups of three starting from the left. For each group of three, the first digit is multiplied by thee, the second by seven, and the third left as is. All the results are added together, and if the resulting number is evenly divisible by 10, the number passes.

To implement this check, you must first define a new class, which in turn defines a method that does the check. Listing 17.9 shows this file.

LISTING 17.9 ACHCheck.java

```
package stocktrack.validator;

import java.io.Serializable;
import javax.servlet.http.HttpServletRequest;
import org.apache.commons.validator.Field;
import org.apache.commons.validator.ValidatorAction;
import org.apache.struts.action.ActionErrors;
```

LISTING 17.9 Continued

```
import org.apache.commons.validator.GenericValidator;
import org.apache.commons.validator.ValidatorUtil;
import org.apache.struts.util.StrutsValidatorUtil;

public class ACHCheck implements Serializable {

    public static boolean validateACHRouting(Object bean,
                         ValidatorAction va, Field field,
                         ActionErrors errors,
                         HttpServletRequest request) {

      String value = null;
      boolean results = false;

      if (isString(bean)) {
          value = (String) bean;
      } else {
          value = ValidatorUtil.getValueAsString(bean, field.getProperty());
      }

       if (GenericValidator.isBlankOrNull(value)) {
        return true;
      }

      if (value.length() != 9) {
        errors.add(field.getKey(),
                  StrutsValidatorUtil.getActionError(request, va, field));
        return false;
      }

      int n = 0;
      for (int i = 0; i < value.length(); i += 3) {
        n += CharToInt(value.charAt(i)) * 3
                         +  CharToInt(value.charAt(i + 1)) * 7
                         +  CharToInt(value.charAt(i + 2));
      }
```

LISTING 17.9 Continued

```
      // If the resulting sum is an even multiple of ten (but not zero),
      // the aba routing number is good.

      if (n != 0 && n % 10 == 0)
          return true;
     else {
        errors.add(field.getKey(),
                   StrutsValidatorUtil.getActionError(request, va, field));
        return false;
          }
   }

   public static int CharToInt(char chr)
    {
      return Integer.parseInt(CharToString(chr));
    }

  public static String CharToString(char chr)
    {
      return String.valueOf(chr);
    }

  private static Class stringClass = new String().getClass();

  private static boolean isString(Object o) {
    if (o == null) return true;
    return (stringClass.isInstance(o));
  }

}
```

The first thing to notice is that the arguments to the validation function should look very familiar because they're the same types as the values of the `methodParams` attribute in the `validator-rules.xml` file. That's because you're now defining the method that will be called by the validator and will follow the template described in the `validator` tag.

The first thing to do is see whether the bean value passed in is a string. If it is not a string, the function must have been called during validation of a string array.

If it's not a string (or null), the function must look up the property name in the bean. `ValidatorUtil` has a nice helper function to do this.

After the function has the value, it checks whether it's of the right length, and if so, whether it passes the checksum. If it fails, a helper function from `StrutsValidatorUtil` is used to generate the appropriate `ActionError` for the property.

In addition to adding to the `ActionErrors` variable, the method must also return true or false because the validator depends on this to determine whether further validations should be run on this field.

Next, you must add the validation rule. Technically, it could go in either `validation.xml` or `validator-rules.xml` because both files are the same format (and, in fact, you can load an arbitrary number of these files by changing the list in `struts-config.xml`). However, it's a good idea to put local extensions into `validation.xml` because the other file comes with Struts, and might be overwritten. Here are the additional lines of XML, placed right after the `global` tag:

```
<validator name="achRouting"
     classname="stocktrack.validator.ACHCheck"
     method="validateACHRouting"
     methodParams="java.lang.Object,
                   org.apache.commons.validator.ValidatorAction,
                   org.apache.commons.validator.Field,
                   org.apache.struts.action.ActionErrors,
                   javax.servlet.http.HttpServletRequest"
     depends=""
     msg="errors.achRouting"/>
```

Now you can add a new property to the new address form for testing:

```
<form-property name="bankRouting" type="java.lang.String"/>
```

Of course, there are new resource strings, too:

```
errors.achRouting={0} is not a valid routing number.
newUserAddressForm.bankRouting.label=Bank Routing Number
```

And, finally, the form itself needs to handle the field:

```
<tr>
  <td>Bank Routing</td><td>
      <html:text property="bankRouting" maxlength="9" size="9"/></td>
  <td><html:errors property="bankRouting"/></td>
</tr>
```

With all that work in place, you can now validate bank routing numbers. If you want a good one, 123123123 will pass.

IS THE VALIDATOR WORTH IT?

I have to say that I'm honestly of two minds in regards to the validator. On one hand, I like the way it enables you to eliminate many `FormAction` classes altogether.

On the other hand, you end up writing a lot of boilerplate XML for every form, and for every field of every form. In fact, a rough estimate showed that a 20-line Java class file that implemented the validations in a `FormAction` might be replaced by 40 or more lines of XML and properties to do the same thing.

On the other other hand, the validator does reduce the amount of validation logic you have to write. So, I can't say that there's a good answer one way or the other.

Conclusions

Using `DynaBeans` and the Validator framework, you can reduce or even eliminate the need to write an `ActionForm`. `DynaForms` enable you to define the properties of a form in the `struts-config.xml` file, rather than in the form bean itself. You then use generic `get` and `set` operations on the form, rather than explicitly defined accessors.

The Validator framework integrates Struts with the Commons Validator project. The validator enables you to define validation rules in XML files, and automatically run them against the form during submission. This eliminates the need for the `validate` method on the `Form`, and in combination with a `DynaForm`, it eliminates the need for a distinct class.

Because the framework doesn't handle all types of validations, it might be necessary to handle some of them in the `Action`, although this can confuse the user by presenting errors in two stages.

The Framework can also be extended by writing new validation rules, which are defined in one of the XML configuration files and implemented in a new class and method.

18

Using Struts with Enterprise JavaBeans

IN THIS CHAPTER

In many organizations and for many types of applications, it's common to use Enterprise JavaBeans (EJBs). EJBs are useful for isolating business logic, interfacing to databases, and many other types of applications—especially those that can benefit from the services provided by EJB containers, such as transactional management and database connection pooling. Upcoming revisions to the EJB specifications will make it even easier to use EJBs to implement Web Services. As a technology, EJBs have matured significantly from where they began a few years ago.

This chapter examines how EJBs fit in the overall Struts framework. It offers design strategies as well as sample code to assist you in getting a Struts/EJB-based application off the ground quickly.

EJBs Fit with Model Components

As discussed earlier, Struts is a framework based on the Model-View-Controller (MVC) design pattern. It's also been pointed out that one of the great strengths of MVC is the flexibility you have for implementing Model components. This explains why Struts has tag libraries for building View components and `Action` classes for building Controller components, but no specific classes for extending or implementing Model components.

That means you'll most likely incorporate EJBs into your Struts project by accessing them as Model components from within your `Action` classes. You can access them directly from the `Action` class or you can build helper classes that hide the details of EJB access from the `Action` class—there's no single right answer for how to incorporate them.

It should be pointed out that it's possible to access EJBs directly from the JSP files (View components) using scriptlets or via bean help classes or custom tags. In general, this practice is strongly discouraged. It's a misuse of the framework and will very likely require you to put code in your JSP file that really belongs in a Controller component.

For example, what if the EJB container is unavailable or throws you a `RemoteException`? In that case, you must make decisions on what to show the user based on whether this error condition occurs—and that decision is better made in an `Action` class where you have the ability to forward the user to an appropriate error page.

In addition, it's likely that you'll want to implement business logic to display different information or take different actions based on data you retrieve through the EJB. This logic is best put in the Controller components. Even if your initial requirements call for simply retrieving and displaying data through the EJB, you can be sure that your customers will change their minds over time and you'll have to implement new functionality by encoding business logic based on data in the EJBs. Do yourself a favor: *Work with the framework* and access the EJBs from your `Action` classes from the beginning.

So, why is the name of this section "EJBs *Fit with* Model Components" instead of "EJBs *Are* Model Components"? Basically, it's worded that way to emphasize all the flexibility you have. The best way to meet your system requirements might be to treat EJBs exactly as model components or it might not. Some best practice approaches are presented in this chapter, but what you do in the end might differ, depending on your need. This section gets you started, but your end design will vary based on what works for you.

Quick Review of EJB Technologies

Hold on to your hat—this is going to be fast. There are already many good books about EJBs, so this section is going to skim and provide just the information you need to know. Fasten your seatbelt; we're on our way to 30,000 feet!

EJBs Live in an EJB Container

EJBs are defined by the J2EE specifications. These specifications also define the requirements for EJB containers. EJBs containers provide the system services and API support that are required to allow EJBs to run. That is, an EJB without an EJB container is like an engine without a car to put it in—you're not going anywhere.

Formally, an EJB container is a software application that can host EJBs because it supports all the APIs defined by the EJB specifications. Among the APIs that must be supported are JNDI, Java Mail, JDBC, and a number of others. If a container is EJB compliant (so the story goes), an EJB developed for one container should be easy to move to another container. The truth is, of course, that this depends on a number of things, including the particular container you choose and how you go about developing your code.

At JavaWorld 2002, the three top EJB containers selected by judges were JBoss, BEA WebLogic, and IBM WebSphere. Other popular containers are JRun from Macromedia, Orion Application Server, Borland Enterprise Server, and ATG Dynamo. Users of the SAP ERP system can host applications on the SAP Web Application Server (formerly In-Q-My J2EE Application Server). Oracle users can deploy EJBs either in Oracle Application Server or directly in the Oracle database itself. In addition to JBoss, OpenEJB on SourceForge provides another viable open source option. (Of course, we've now likely offended someone by leaving his favorite container off this abbreviated list!)

As you can see, there's no shortage of options when it comes to EJB containers. For the sample applications in this chapter, we use JBoss 3.0.3. You can acquire it by downloading it for free at `http://www.jboss.org`. It is also included on the companion CD.

Because your Struts code is servlet-based, it can't live in the EJB container itself. For Struts to run, it needs a Web container (also defined by the J2EE specifications). In the examples throughout this book, the Web container is always Jakarta Tomcat.

Struts lives in the Web container (Tomcat) and EJBs live in the EJB container (JBoss), so the Struts code must connect to the EJB container to access the EJBs. The details of how to do all this are covered in later sections.

Anatomy of an EJB

Creating and using an EJB requires coding a number of classes as well as making a few important deployment decisions. The required classes are

- Home interface—This interface defines the methods in the EJB bean class that are used to find, create, and delete EJB instances. All EJB access done in Struts is initiated by first acquiring the home interface for the EJB you need. This is done via a JNDI lookup and is covered later in more detail. An EJB home interface must extend `javax.ejb.EJBHome`.
- Remote interface—Any business logic methods implemented in the EJB bean class must be defined in the remote interface for the container to allow access to them. Examples of methods defined in the remote interface might be `calculateAverage()` or `getCustomerName()`. These are the methods you invoke on the EJBs after you locate or create them using the home interface. A remote interface must extend `javax.ejb.EJBObject`.

- EJB bean class—The EJB bean class is the actual class that implements all the methods defined in both the home interface and the remote interface. After your Struts code locates or creates an EJB instance using the EJBs home interface, it invokes the methods exposed by the remote interface. Those methods are actually implemented in the EJB bean class. The bean class must extend `javax.ejb.SessionBean`, `javax.ejb.EntityBean`, or (beginning in EJB 2.0) `javax.ejb.MessageDrivenBean`.
- Optional value object—Value objects aren't defined by, or even a part of, the J2EE specifications. Many applications don't use them. Different people may define value objects differently, but for this book, value objects are defined as simple, non-EJB bean classes that allow information to be passed to and from an EJB "one bean at a time" instead of "one property at a time." Passing data to/from the EJB container this way helps your Struts application use EJBs efficiently.

In addition to creating these classes, you must also create deployment descriptors for your EJBs. There are usually at least two deployment descriptors: the standard `ejb-jar.xml` that's defined by the EJB specification, and a container-specific descriptor used by the particular EJB container you're using (for JBoss, this descriptor is named `jboss.xml`). Among the information in these files is the JNDI name that's needed for Struts to access the EJBs from the Web container.

Using Different EJB Types with Struts

This section examines the four main types of available EJBs and how they might fit in with Struts. Although in any situation, as the old Perl adage goes, TIMTOWTDI ("There is more than one way to do it!"), it's possible to generalize. These recommendations might not exactly fit what you're doing, but they provide a starting point and give you a good idea of how EJB technology fits with Struts.

Entity Beans

Entity beans are primarily used as an interface to a database. They enable the developer to work with database data at a business-object level and not worry about low-level management of the database. The actual JDBC calls as well as the code are taken care of by the entity bean and the EJB container.

Because of their tight integration with the database, entity beans aren't intended to contain a great deal of business logic. In fact, the majority of entity bean implementations (especially those using container-managed persistence [CMP]) have virtually no business logic in them; they exist only as an interface to the database.

Given these characteristics, the following general rules are appropriate for using entity beans in Struts:

- Entity beans should be very thin. That is, entity beans should provide minimal formatting or other logic in front of the database fields they provide access to. Any business logic that might cause different View components to be presented to the user should usually be moved into the `Action` class. Also, use value objects rather than setting/getting individual properties.
- An `Action` class should interact with no more than one or two entity beans. If more than one or two entity beans are required, consider using a stateless session bean as a facade in front of them. This has the advantages of both minimizing traffic between the Web and EJB containers and simplifying the `Action` class.
- Minimizing the number of entity beans your `Action` class deals with is easier if you make the entity beans represent business-level objects rather than just map them directly to tables in your database. This is sometimes called designing them to be *coarse grained*. For example, having a `Customer` entity bean that has the customer's personal and address information might be better than having a `Customer` entity bean that maps to the Customer table and an `Address` entity bean that maps to the Address table.

Stateless Session Beans

Stateless session beans are ideal for many uses in Struts applications. They have the advantage of being relatively lightweight objects in your EJB container as well as providing a lot of flexibility. Stateless session beans should be considered for use when

- Multiple entity bean or other database accesses can be hidden behind the facade of a single session bean.
- If two systems need to be updated as part of a single transaction, wrap them in a single stateless session bean. For example, if a stock purchase must be recorded in both a customer information system as well as sent through a purchase clearing system, have your `Action` class access a stateless session bean and have it coordinate the other transactions. That way you have the EJB container to manage transaction commit and rollback if needed.

The reality is that stateless session beans are the most versatile of all the EJB forms. You can do about anything with them.

It's the best practice to create the session bean just before you need to access it and then remove it immediately after you're done. This minimizes the load on the EJB server. You should never store a reference to a stateless session bean for reuse.

Stateful Session Beans

Stateful session beans are similar to stateless session beans except that they remain stateful with the user's session in the EJB server. That is, they aren't directly related to the session information in Struts (that information is stored in the session context of the Web container). Remember: Both the Web container and the EJB container maintain their own session information.

Stateful session beans can maintain the user's conversational state. For example, they can be used to hold items in a user's shopping cart between requests. However, this comes at a price. The price is that the EJB container has to dedicate resources to maintain the stateful session beans until the session on the EJB container ends. If you have many users, maintaining the pool of stateful session beans can take up a lot of resources. In addition, when clustering EJB servers, some implementations require all stateful beans to be replicated between servers in case a failover occurs.

When you consider that Struts and the Web container automatically maintain stateful information anyway, using stateful session beans seems like a bad idea unless you really need them. For this reason, we recommend against their use. If you can, use stateless session beans and store stateful information in the session context of the Web container.

One situation in which stateful session beans make sense is when a transaction in the back-end system requires multiple requests to complete. If this occurs and you need the EJB container to manage the transaction, use stateful session beans—just keep them as small as possible and remove them as soon as you can.

Message-Driven Beans

The newest breed of EJBs (since the EJB 2.0 specification) is message-driven beans. Message-driven beans essentially wrap a JMS (Java Message Service) queue and allow the full power of JMS to be used, while enabling you to write code to interact with the JMS queue as if it were an EJB instead of having to learn to write JMS client code.

Message-driven beans are useful in the same places that JMS is useful. For example

- When you need to pass information to a back-end messaging system such as MQSeries.
- In a situation in which you're working asynchronously when there might be a lag between the time you send in a transaction and the time the response comes back. For example, you might send a customer address change into a back-end system where the change occurs overnight. Using a message-driven bean, you can originate the transaction and look for the response later (or some other process can look for responses).

Summary of the Rules for Using Struts with EJBs

In summary, EJBs fit in with Struts in the following ways:

- EJBs fit with Struts Model components. Generally, they should be called only from the Struts `Action` class.
- If you have more than one (or maybe two) EJB to access from your `Action` class, consider implementing a stateless session bean (or even a non-EJB helper class that's called from your `Action` class) to act as a facade and simplify your `Action` class.
- Entity beans should be coarse grained to minimize the number of beans created and to isolate the `Action` class from changes in the table structure of the underlying database.
- Use value objects and pass data to and from the EJB "one bean at a time" rather than "one property at a time."
- Avoid using stateful session beans. Use stateless session beans instead and maintain stateful information in Struts using the session context of the Web container.
- Use stateful session beans only if you have transactions that span more than one user request and you need the EJB container to manage committing or rolling back the transaction.

Future Directions for Struts and EJBs

EJB technology isn't standing still. The EJB 2.0 and 2.1 specifications added a great deal of capability to EJBs. In addition, many corporations have adopted a J2EE-compliant application server such as WebLogic, WebSphere, iPlanet, or JBoss as their corporate standard for new application development.

The widespread adoption of J2EE and EJB technologies has ensured that this technology will be around for a long time. So, what changes are coming?

The EJB 2.0 and 2.1 specifications are adding a great deal of capability. Message-driven beans were added in 2.0 and will be enhanced in 2.1. A timer service will be available for EJBs to have the container call their methods at specific time intervals. But the biggest changes to come center around making EJBs easier to use with Web services. Session beans will be used to publish JAX-RPC–style Web services and message-driven beans will be used to publish JAX-M–style Web services. This support will be a requirement in EJB 2.1.

What does this mean for Struts? Mainly this: You can safely build your Struts applications today to interact with EJBs and be confident that EJB support will be available through the life of the application.

A Struts/EJB Sample Application

Now it's time to move from theory to practice. This sample application is intended to illustrate a collection of what we consider to be best practices in regard to using Struts with EJBs.

It's our hope that you can take this core application and use it as a base for building actual, real Struts/EJB applications. We've used these basic principles in numerous projects and are confident they'll work for you.

This application is developed using Tomcat as our servlet/JSP container and JBoss 3.0.3 as a container for the EJBs. Basic configuration information is provided directly in the chapter as the need for it arises.

Due to differences between EJB containers (or even between different releases of JBoss), any configuration information provided here might differ slightly (or dramatically!) from your specific situation. In that case, refer to the documentation for the application servers you're using.

The Application: Updating Customer Information

In this basic application, a simple form is provided to allow information about a customer to be updated. Like any Struts form, the information is populated into a form bean when it's submitted. The form bean is then passed to an `Action` class for processing. After processing, an `ActionForward` is called to indicate which JSP file to display the results with.

This processing is all very basic and should be ingrained in your memory by now. But there's a twist this time: The customer information is managed using an EJB inside an EJB container (JBoss, in this case). The `Action` class must update the customer information by invoking methods on the EJB that manages the customer information.

Figure 18.1 shows the form used to enter the information.

When you submit the form, the address of the customer changes. That's all. No magic, smoke, or mirrors. The EJB that generates this new address simply chooses randomly between three hard-coded addresses and returns one.

The purpose of this application isn't to be fancy; it's to provide a working application that demonstrates good design fundamentals that you can copy and reuse.

In covering this sample application, you'll first go over configuring the system and building the application. Following that, you'll go through the application code itself.

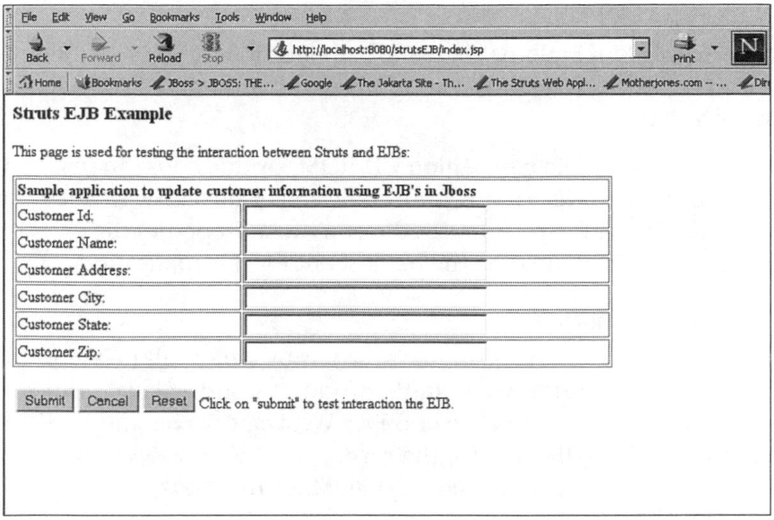

FIGURE 18.1 The EJB sample application—`/strutsEJB/index.jsp`.

Because a big part of using EJBs with Struts has to do with configuration of the Web container and the EJB container, we feel this is appropriate material to include in this book. If you've already got a working configuration, please skip the following sections.

Also, be forewarned that although we've done our best to make this accurate, changes in JBoss and/or Tomcat could render parts of this section obsolete. Even if this is this case, the overall approach should still be instructive. To ensure that this sample application goes as smoothly as possible, we recommend using the particular versions of JBoss, Tomcat and XDoclet that are included on the companion CD-ROM that came with this book. These particular versions have been thoroughly tested with the sample application.

Configuring and Building the Application

The following sections lay out the specifics of how to configure the Web container (Tomcat) and the EJB container (JBoss) to work together and how to build the application. If you're using different Web or EJB containers, the basic steps might vary somewhat but should be basically the same.

NOTE

It's important that you follow the steps in this section closely. If you run into problems, the best thing to do is to back up a step and make sure that you did everything correctly. We worked hard to make this process as clear as possible!

Installing XDoclet

XDoclet is required for building the sample application. If you're familiar with JBoss, you've probably already used XDoclet; it's very common to use XDoclet for developing EJBs with JBoss.

XDoclet is included on the companion CD-ROM for this book. To install it, simply extract the `xdoclet-1.1.2.zip` file into a convenient directory. In a later section, you are asked to enter the path to this directory in a properties file (`.ant.properties`) that's used by the build script for the application.

The EJB Container: JBoss 3.0.3

JBoss (available free at `http://www.jboss.org`) is by almost all measures the most widely used J2EE application server in the world. It won the JavaWorld 2002 Editor's Choice as Best Java Application Server (BEA's WebLogic Server and IBM's WebSphere finished just behind it). JBoss 3.0.3, the version used during development of this book, is contained on the companion CD-ROM for this book.

NOTE

Note that the companion CD-ROM for this book contains the Sun JDK version 1.4. However, at the time of this writing, there are a number of known issues running JBoss 3.0.3 with this version of JDK. As a result, I recommend that you use JDK 1.3.1 with the JBoss version 3.0.3 that comes with this book. This is the JDK version that the sample application was developed and tested with.

Installing JBoss

Installing JBoss is extremely simple. You can simply extract it from the companion CD-ROM into a convenient directory. (During development of the book, I used `c:\dev\jboss`.) From here to the end of the chapter, this directory is referred to as `JBOSS_HOME`. After this step is complete, start JBoss by changing into the directory `JBOSS_HOME/bin` and typing run. You must make sure that you've defined the environment variable `JAVA_HOME` to point to the top directory of the Java SDK you're using.

You should now see startup messages indicating that JBoss is starting all its services.

Moving the JBoss Web Container (Jetty) Out of the Way

JBoss comes with an embedded servlet/JSP engine called Jetty. Because the sample application (like all applications in this book) is run under Jakarta Tomcat, Jetty isn't needed. The fact that it's there isn't a problem; it can be safely ignored. However, if you're running both Tomcat and Jetty, you should know that they have the same default port (port 8080). This will cause problems, so it must be fixed.

How to fix this problem depends on the exact release of JBoss you have. What you must do is find the `jboss-service.xml` file for the Jetty service and change the `jetty.port` property from its default value of 8080 to some other value (for example, 8081). The tricky part is finding the Jetty service.

All services installed in your JBoss server are, by default, located in the directory `JBOSS_HOME/server/default/deploy`. To deploy a new application in JBoss, you just copy the application file (`.war`, `.jar`, `.ear`, and so on) into this directory. JBoss immediately finds and installs it. The only question is this: Which file (or subdirectory) is the Jetty service defined in?

In JBoss 3.0.3, the `jboss-service.xml` file that controls the Jetty service is located in the `JBOSS_HOME\server\default\deploy\jbossweb.sar\META-INF` directory. In a different release, it might be located somewhere else. Look around; there aren't that many default components and you should be able to find Jetty with a minimal amount of effort. After you locate this file, edit it and look for the line

```
<SystemProperty name="jetty.port" default="8080"/>
```

To move Jetty to a different port, simply change this port to some other number (for example, `"8081"`) and then close and save the file. JBoss automatically redeploys the Jetty service to listen on the new port. You should now be able to run Tomcat on its default 8080 port with no problem.

NOTE

Depending on your version of JBoss and your comfort level working with it, there are a number of other ways to resolve this issue. For example, you might find it easier to simply remove the Jetty service or you may even deploy your Struts application into the Jetty service instead of Tomcat. This approach chosen in this chapter was taken because it is straightforward and easy to explain and understand.

One problem with simply moving Jetty to another port is that Jetty also has a listener for the Apache Jserv Protocol (AJP). This is on port 8009 by default for both Jetty and Tomcat, so there's a conflict for this protocol similar to the conflict with the HTTP protocol on the 8080 port. This isn't a problem if all you're doing is installing JBoss to run this sample application. However, if you're installing and running this application in an existing environment, you should know that this could cause problems for you.

If you believe this might cause a problem, then you can disable this protocol or move it to a different port number by modifying its entry in the same `jboss-service.xml` file that you modified earlier to change the default Jetty port (8080). Simply locate the entry for the AJP protocol and move it to a new port, or comment it out to keep it from running at all.

Installing the Sample Application

The sample application for this chapter is provided on the companion CD-ROM for this book. It is contained in the `strutsEJB.zip` file. To install it, simply extract it into a directory where you can work on it. For the development of this application, we put it directly in the `JBOSS_HOME` directory (at the location `JBOSS_HOME/strutsEJB`).

For the rest of the chapter, directories that are part of the build process are referred to using their parameter names as defined in the Ant `build.xml` file that's provided with the sample application.

After the sample application is installed, you can move to the next step.

> **NOTE**
>
> Although most of the following steps will have been already completed in the sample application, this chapter proceeds as if they haven't. This is done so that you can understand how the application was built. Please follow all the steps closely!

Configuring Classpaths and Libraries

For your Struts application to be able to communicate with the JBoss server, a number of libraries (`.jar` files) are required by the Struts application. This section tells you which `.jar` files you need, where to find them, and where to put them in the Struts application to make things work.

In the strutsEJB application you just installed, there's a `lib` directory just under the main `strutsEJB` directory. This directory is referred to in the `build.xml` file as the `struts.libs.dir` and it's defined by a property in the `.ant.properties` file.

In this directory there must be two sets of files: all the files required for Struts, and all the files required for communications with JBoss. The Struts libraries are all the JAR files that came with your Struts distribution. The files required for JBoss communication are

- `jboss.jar`
- `jboss-common-client.jar`
- `jboss-j2ee.jar`
- `jbosssx-client.jar`
- `jnet.jar`
- `log4j.jar`

You can copy all these files from the JBOSS_HOME/client directory except for the jboss.jar file. The jboss.jar file is located in the directory JBOSS_HOME/server/default/lib.

After all these library files are copied into the strutsEJB/lib directory, you're ready to proceed to the next step and build the application.

Building the Application

This application was adapted from the default application template provided with JBoss. This was done intentionally in order to be useful to those familiar with JBoss. If your background is with some other EJB container, this build process should still be useful, but will probably require modifications to work in your environment.

You should now have JBoss and the sample application installed on your machine, and all the library files should be in place in the strutsEJB/lib directory.

NOTE

This section makes the assumption that you have a basic understanding of the Jakarta Ant utility and at least some experience in its use. If this isn't the case, we recommend that you become familiar with Ant before you proceed. Jakarta Ant is available at http://jakarta.apache.org/ant as well as on the companion CD-ROM for this book.

Because the application is built using the Jakarta Ant utility, a build.xml file is provided. The build process is customized to your specific environment by modifying parameters in the .ant.properties file that's also provided. These files are versions of the standard JBoss application build files that have been modified to work with Struts.

The build.xml file won't be reviewed in detail here, but the .ant.properties file is shown in Listing 18.1.

LISTING 18.1 Struts and JBoss Properties for the Sample Application (.ant.properties)

```
# This file has been modified from the original sample provided with JBoss.
#
# Some parameters have been left alone and are unchanged from the
# original example template. Others have been added or modified from
# the original file.
#
# Entries in this file may override properties set in the build.xml file.
#
```

LISTING 18.1 Continued

```
# The following properties are unchanged. These properties may not be
# used, but there is no reason to delete them unless you have a need to.

jboss.configuration=default
xdoclet.force=false
ejb.version=2.0
jboss.version=3.0
type.mapping=Hypersonic SQL
datasource.name=java:/DefaultDS

# The following properties have been added or changed from the original
# example provided with JBoss.
#
# THESE MUST BE MODIFIED FOR YOUR ENVIRONMENT OR THE APP WILL NOT WORK!
#

# A property identifying the path to the jboss-j2ee.jar file
servlet-lib.path=C:\\dev\\jboss\\server\\default\\lib\\jboss-j2ee.jar

# The top directory of your Tomcat installation
tomcat.home=c:\\dev\\tomcat

# The directory containing struts.jar and other struts libs
struts.libs.dir=c:\\dev\\jboss\\strutsEJB\\lib

# The Ant home directory
ant.home=c:\\dev\\ant

# The JBoss home directory. Used to locate libs and for deployment
jboss.home=C:\\dev\\jboss

# The Xdoclet home directory. Needed to use XDoclet.
xdoclet.home=C:\\dev\\xdoclet
```

It's very important that you modify this file and set all the properties to reflect your environment configuration. If you find yourself running into trouble getting the application to work, make sure that you review this file in detail to confirm that all the settings are correct.

Most of the properties in the `.ant.properties` file are used in the JBoss build process. The only two properties that have been added to modify it for use with Struts are

- `tomcat.home`—The home directory for your Tomcat installation.
- `struts.libs.dir`—The directory containing all the Struts `.jar` files and the JBoss `.jar` files required for communications between Struts and JBoss. This was covered in the previous section.

After the build properties are configured properly, proceed with building the application. The result of the build is two archives:

- `strutsEJB.jar`—A JAR file suitable for deployment in JBoss.
- `strutsEJB.war`—A WAR file suitable for deployment in Tomcat.

Running the build is done by simply typing the command `ant` in the `strutsEJB` main directory. A successful build will have output similar to Listing 18.2.

LISTING 18.2 Output from Running the `ant` Command to Build the strutsEJB Sample Application

```
C:\dev\jboss\strutsEJB>ant
Buildfile: build.xml

check-environment:

check-jboss:

wrong-jboss:

check-xdoclet:

wrong-xdoclet:

init:
     [echo] build.compiler = ${build.compiler}
     [echo] user.home = C:\Documents and Settings\a
     [echo] java.home = C:\jdk1.3.1_01\jre
     [echo] ant.home = c:\dev\ant
     [echo] jboss.home = C:\dev\jboss
     [echo] xdoclet.home = C:\dev\xdoclet
     [echo] jboss.client = C:\dev\jboss/client
```

LISTING 18.2 Continued

```
    [echo] tomcat.home = c:\dev\tomcat

xdoclet-generate:
    [ejbdoclet] Generating Javadoc
    [ejbdoclet] Javadoc execution
    [ejbdoclet] Loading source file
➥C:\dev\jboss\strutsEJB\src\main\jboss\ch18\session\CustomerSessionBean.java
    [ejbdoclet] Constructing Javadoc information...
    [ejbdoclet] Running <homeInterface/>
    [ejbdoclet]   Generating Home interface
    ➥        for 'jboss.ch18.session.CustomerSessionBean'.
    [ejbdoclet] Running <remoteInterface/>
    [ejbdoclet]   Generating Remote interface
    ➥        for 'jboss.ch18.session.CustomerSessionBean'.
    [ejbdoclet] Running <dataobject/>
    [ejbdoclet] Running <deploymentDescriptor/>
    [ejbdoclet]   Generating EJB deployment descriptor.
    [ejbdoclet] Running <jboss/>
    [ejbdoclet]   Generating jboss.xml.

compile:

compile:
    [echo] Compilation Path = C:\dev\ant\lib\ant.jar;
    ➥C:\dev\xdoclet\lib\xdoclet.jar;
    ➥C:\dev\jboss\client\log4j.jar;
    ➥C:\dev\jboss\strutsEJB\lib\commons-beanutils.jar;
    ➥C:\dev\jboss\strutsEJB\lib\commons-collections.jar;
    ➥C:\dev\jboss\strutsEJB\lib\commons-dbcp.jar;
    ➥C:\dev\jboss\strutsEJB\lib\commons-digester.jar;
    ➥C:\dev\jboss\strutsEJB\lib\commons-fileupload.jar;
    ➥C:\dev\jboss\strutsEJB\lib\commons-lang.jar;
    ➥C:\dev\jboss\strutsEJB\lib\commons-logging.jar;
    ➥C:\dev\jboss\strutsEJB\lib\commons-pool.jar;
    ➥C:\dev\jboss\strutsEJB\lib\commons-resources.jar;
    ➥C:\dev\jboss\strutsEJB\lib\commons-services.jar;
    ➥C:\dev\jboss\strutsEJB\lib\commons-validator.jar;
    ➥C:\dev\jboss\strutsEJB\lib\jakarta-oro.jar;
    ➥C:\dev\jboss\strutsEJB\lib\jdbc2_0-stdext.jar;
    ➥C:\dev\jboss\strutsEJB\lib\struts.jar;
    ➥C:\dev\jboss\lib\concurrent.jar;
```

LISTING 18.2 Continued

```
    ➥C:\dev\jboss\lib\crimson.jar;
    ➥C:\dev\jboss\lib\getopt.jar;
    ➥C:\dev\jboss\lib\gnu-regexp.jar;
    ➥C:\dev\jboss\lib\jaxp.jar;
    ➥C:\dev\jboss\lib\jboss-boot.jar;
    ➥C:\dev\jboss\lib\jboss-common.jar;
    ➥C:\dev\jboss\lib\jboss-jmx.jar;
    ➥C:\dev\jboss\lib\jboss-system.jar;
    ➥C:\dev\jboss\lib\log4j-boot.jar;
    ➥C:\dev\jboss\server\default\lib\javax.servlet.jar;
    ➥C:\dev\jboss\server\default\lib\jboss-j2ee.jar;
    ➥C:\dev\ant\lib\optional.jar;
    ➥C:\dev\ant\lib\xercesImpl.jar;
    ➥C:\dev\ant\lib\xml-apis.jar;
    ➥C:\dev\jboss\strutsEJB\build\classes
    [mkdir] Created dir: C:\dev\jboss\strutsEJB\build\classes
    [javac] Compiling 13 source files to C:\dev\jboss\strutsEJB\build\classes

jboss-jar:
    [mkdir] Created dir: C:\dev\jboss\strutsEJB\build\classes
    [javac] Compiling 13 source files to C:\dev\jboss\strutsEJB\build\classes

jboss-jar:
    [mkdir] Created dir: C:\dev\jboss\strutsEJB\build\jbossdeploy
      [jar] Building jar: C:\dev\jboss\strutsEJB\build\jbossdeploy\strutsEJB.jar

struts-war:
     [copy] Copying 1 file to C:\dev\jboss\strutsEJB\build\classes
    [mkdir] Created dir: C:\dev\jboss\strutsEJB\build\strutsdeploy
      [war] Building war: C:\dev\jboss\strutsEJB\build\strutsdeploy\strutsEJB.war
      [war] Warning: selected war files include a WEB-INF/web.xml
      ➥which will be ignored (please use webxml attribute to war task)
      [war] Warning: selected war files include a WEB-INF/web.xml
      ➥which will be ignored (please use webxml attribute to war task)

deploy-server:
     [copy] Copying 1 file to C:\dev\jboss\server\default\deploy
     [copy] Copying 1 file to C:\dev\tomcat\webapps

BUILD SUCCESSFUL
Total time: 19 seconds
```

NOTE

The preceding build was run using a freshly installed copy of Jakarta Ant version 1.5.1 with no additional libraries added. If you have problems building the application, try using the version of Ant that's included on the companion CD-ROM with this book.

Now that the archive files for both JBoss and Tomcat have been built and deployed, you should be able start your JBoss and Tomcat servers and see the application run! To run the application, simply start JBoss and Tomcat and point your browser to `http://localhost:8080/strutsEJB/Customer.do`.

Reviewing the Sample Application Source Files

This section of the chapter is dedicated to reviewing the sample application code. The goal of this section is to provide you with an understanding of how to use Struts to interact with an EJB container. This design isn't the only one possible, but it's one we consider to be a best practice.

The Value Object: `CustomerValueObject.java`

A good place to begin with is with the value object. As discussed earlier, a value object is nothing more than a simple bean used to pass data between the Web container and the EJB container. Because a lot of effort is spent encoding and decoding the data (as well as coordinating the transfer) each time data is passed between the two containers, trying to minimize this overhead is good.

The sample application minimizes the overhead related to sending/receiving data by sending the data one bean at a time rather than one property at a time.

`CustomerValueObject.java` is the value object used in this sample application. Its source code is shown in Listing 18.3.

LISTING 18.3 The `CustomerValueObject.java` Source Listing

```
package struts.ch18.client;

import jboss.ch18.interfaces.AbstractData;

/**
 * Example Value Object for showing integration of Struts with EJBs
 *
 * @author Kevin Bedell & James Turner
 * @version 1.0
 */
public class CustomerValueObject extends AbstractData {
```

LISTING 18.3 Continued

```
public CustomerValueObject () {

    this.name     = "";
    this.custId   = "";
    this.address  = "";
    this.city     = "";
    this.state    = "";
    this.zip      = "";
}

public CustomerValueObject (String name,
                            String custId,
                            String address,
                            String city,
                            String state,
                            String zip
                           ) {

    this.name     = name;
    this.custId   = custId;
    this.address  = address;
    this.city     = city;
    this.state    = state;
    this.zip      = zip;
}

private String name;
public String getName() { return this.name; }
public void setName(String nameus) { this.name = name; }

private String custId;
public String getCustId() { return this.custId; }
public void setCustId(String custId) { this.custId = custId; }

private String address;
public String getAddress() { return this.address; }
public void setAddress(String address) { this.address = address; }

private String city;
public String getCity() { return this.city; }
public void setCity(String city) { this.city = city; }
```

LISTING 18.3 Continued

```
  private String state;
  public String getState() { return this.state; }
  public void setState(String state) { this.state = state; }

  private String zip;
  public String getZip() { return this.zip; }
  public void setZip(String zip) { this.zip = zip; }

}
```

As you can see from this listing there's nothing fancy about value objects. They simply hold properties for communications between containers.

You might have noticed that this class extends the class `AbstractData`. `AbstractData` is an `abstract` class defined in the template application provided with JBoss. It doesn't require JBoss to be used and its source code is provided. `AbstractData` is simply a class recommended by the JBoss developers for use with value objects.

The Form Bean: `CustomerForm.java`

The form bean used with the sample application is similar to the other form beans you've used throughout this book. The only difference is that support has been added to enable it to work easily with value objects.

This added support takes the form of adding set/get methods that accept and return `CustomerValueObjects`. You'll see how this simplifies things a bit later when you review the form bean.

When the Model portion of your application uses EJBs, one of the primary functions of the `Action` class is to manage communications with the EJB container. Designing your form bean to make it easy for the `Action` class to interact with it using value objects is a best practice that you'll want to follow.

`CustomerForm.java` is the form bean used in this sample application. Its source code is shown in Listing 18.4.

LISTING 18.4 The `CustomerForm.java` Source Listing

```
package struts.ch18.client;

import org.apache.struts.action.ActionForm;
import org.apache.struts.action.ActionMapping;

import javax.servlet.http.HttpServletRequest;
```

LISTING 18.4 Continued

```
import struts.ch18.client.CustomerValueObject;

/**
 * Form bean class to demonstrate EJB Integration with Struts
 *
 * @author Kevin Bedell & James Turner
 * @version 1.0
 */
public class CustomerForm extends ActionForm {

  // Default bean constructor
  public CustomerForm() { }

  private String name;
  public String getName() { return this.name; }
  public void setName(String name) { this.name = name; }

  private String custId;
  public String getCustId() { return this.custId; }
  public void setCustId(String custId) { this.custId = custId; }

  private String address;
  public String getAddress() { return this.address; }
  public void setAddress(String address) { this.address = address; }

  private String city;
  public String getCity() { return this.city; }
  public void setCity(String city) { this.city = city; }

  private String state;
  public String getState() { return this.state; }
  public void setState(String state) { this.state = state; }

  private String zip;
  public String getZip() { return this.zip; }
  public void setZip(String zip) { this.zip = zip; }

  /*
   *  Allow the form bean to work with Value Objects.
   */
  public CustomerValueObject getValueObject () {
```

LISTING 18.4 Continued

```
    return new CustomerValueObject(   this.name,
                                      this.custId,
                                      this.address,
                                      this.city,
                                      this.state,
                                      this.zip  );
  }

  public void  setValueObject (CustomerValueObject vo) {

      this.setName(    vo.getName()     );
      this.setCustId(  vo.getCustId()   );
      this.setAddress( vo.getAddress()  );
      this.setCity(    vo.getCity()     );
      this.setState(   vo.getState()    );
      this.setZip(     vo.getZip()      );

  }

  public void reset(ActionMapping mapping, HttpServletRequest request) {

      this.name = "";
      this.custId = "";
      this.address = "";
      this.city = "";
      this.state = "";
      this.zip = "";
  }

}
```

The Action Class: `CustomerAction.java`

The value of all this design and organization really shows itself in the `Action` class. What could otherwise be a complicated class is actually pretty simple.

The first simplifying feature comes from creating the value object and writing the form bean to make use of it. As a result, the `Action` class can retrieve all the values it needs from the form bean with a single method call. It can also update the form bean with the results from the EJB container in a single method call. This is the benefit of using value objects in the design.

Another important benefit of value objects is the impact doing so has on maintaining the application. Over the life of the application, properties will likely be added and changed. When that happens, the form bean and value objects must change, but the `Action` class doesn't. By having the `Action` class work with the properties one bean at a time, changes inside the value object itself have no impact on it.

The second simplifying feature comes from burying the details of interacting with the EJB container inside a facade class. Because the Action class is primarily concerned with coordinating program flow and directing the processing, the details of interacting with the EJB container aren't really important to it.

The `Action` class really needs to know only whether the update was successful. In its role as the Controller in the MVC architecture, it doesn't need the details—it only needs to know how to direct processing.

As part of burying the EJB container interactions inside the facade, all exceptions that can occur as part of the communications also should be buried there. This is done by having the facade throw only an application-specific exception (`CustomerUpdateException`). The facade catches any exceptions that can occur when interacting with the EJB container and rethrows them as `CustomerUpdateException`. Therefore, any changes in how the facade handles exceptions are isolated from the `Action` class.

`CustomerAction.java` is the `Action` class used in this sample application. Its source code is shown in Listing 18.5.

LISTING 18.5 The `CustomerAction.java` Source Listing

```
package struts.ch18.client;

import javax.servlet.http.HttpServletRequest;
import javax.servlet.http.HttpServletResponse;
import org.apache.struts.action.Action;
import org.apache.struts.action.ActionForm;
import org.apache.struts.action.ActionForward;
import org.apache.struts.action.ActionMapping;

import struts.ch18.client.CustomerValueObject;

/**
 * Action class to demonstrate EJB Integration with Struts
 *
 * @author Kevin Bedell & James Turner
 * @version 1.0
 */
```

LISTING 18.5 Continued

```
public class CustomerAction extends Action {

    /**
     * Update the customer's address.
     *
     * @param mapping The ActionMapping from this struts-config.xml entry
     * @param actionForm The ActionForm to process, if any
     * @param request The JSP request object
     * @param response The JSP response object
     *
     * @exception Exception if business logic throws an exception
     */
    public ActionForward execute(ActionMapping mapping,
                                 ActionForm form,
                                 HttpServletRequest request,
                                 HttpServletResponse response)
        throws Exception {

        /*
         * Cast the form bean to CustomerForm
         */
        CustomerForm cf = (CustomerForm) form;

        /*
         * Instantiate the facade - it hides the details
         * for us and simplifies the Action class.
         */
        CustomerEJBFacade facade = new CustomerEJBFacade();

        /*
         * The Value Object allows us to pass data "a bean at a time".
         * This increases speed, reduces maintenance and simplifies
         * tha Action class as well. Add methods to the form bean to
         * allow it to work with Value Objects too.
         */
        CustomerValueObject cvo = cf.getValueObject();

        try {
          /*
           * Pass in a value object, and get one in return
           */
```

LISTING 18.5 Continued

```
        cvo = facade.addressChange( cvo );
      } catch (CustomerUpdateException cue) {
        //  In a real application, this exception would be handled better.
        //  return (mapping.findForward("CustUpdateError"));
      }

      /*
       * Update the form bean with all values returned at once.
       */
      cf.setValueObject(cvo);

      return (mapping.findForward("default"));
    }
}
```

The Facade: `CustomerEJBFacade.java`

As discussed in the previous section, the facade class coordinates interaction with the EJB container and provides a simple interface for the action class to work with. It also handles exception processing and rethrows any exceptions it can't handle as the application-specific exception `CustomerUpdateException`.

The main points regarding the functioning of this facade class are

- The first thing it does is create an `InitialContext` to allow it to connect with the EJB container. Although this is a requirement for any EJB container, the details of how it's done are dependent on the specific EJB container you're using.
- Another point is that, like the `Action` class, the facade class communicates to the EJB container using value objects. This simplifies processing in addition to making the communications more efficient.
- The EJB that this class creates to work with is a stateless session bean. This is the preferred type of bean to work with. If the application requires information to be kept in session, this should be kept in session in the Web container while all EJBs remain stateless, if possible.
- The stateless EJB is created just prior to use and removed as soon as the need for it is gone. This helps the EJB container manage its resources most efficiently.
- The only exception thrown is the application-specific exception, `CustomerUpdateException`.

`CustomerEJBFacade.java` is the facade used in this sample application. Its source code is shown in Listing 18.6.

LISTING 18.6 The `CustomerEJBFacade.java` Source Listing

```
package struts.ch18.client;

import java.util.Properties;

import javax.naming.Context;
import javax.naming.InitialContext;

import jboss.ch18.interfaces.AbstractData;
import jboss.ch18.interfaces.CustomerSession;
import jboss.ch18.interfaces.CustomerSessionHome;

/**
 * Example facade which hides interactions with the back-end servers
 *
 * @author Kevin Bedell & James Turner
 * @version 1.0
 */
public class CustomerEJBFacade {

  public CustomerEJBFacade () { }

  /**
   *  This method sends the value object to the EJB server
   *  for it to process. It's goal is to hide the implementation
   *  details of interacting with the EJB server.<p>
   *
   *  Note that this method captures any EJB-access related Exceptions
   *  and rethrows them as "application-specific" Exceptions
   *  (CustomerUpdateException). This helps to "decouple" the
   *  application from the EJB-backend.
   *
   * @param cvo_in
   * @return CustomerValueObject
   * @throws CustomerUpdateException
   */
  public CustomerValueObject addressChange( CustomerValueObject cvo_in )
  throws CustomerUpdateException
```

LISTING 18.6 Continued

```
{
    try {

        /*
         * The first section of code is to connect the servlet engine
         * (Tomcat in this case) to the EJB server. Details are
         * available in the JBoss code.
         */

        Properties props = new Properties();
        props.put(Context.INITIAL_CONTEXT_FACTORY,
                  "org.jnp.interfaces.NamingContextFactory" );
        props.put(Context.PROVIDER_URL,  "localhost:1099" );
        props.put(Context.URL_PKG_PREFIXES,
                  "org.jboss.naming:org.jnp.interfaces" );
        props.put("jnp.socketFactory",
                  "org.jnp.interfaces.TimedSocketFactory" );
        InitialContext csContext = new InitialContext(props);

        /*
         * We now have an InitialContext - we can access EJBs through it;
         * To access an EJB, first look up the Home Interface of the bean.
         */

        CustomerSessionHome csHome = (CustomerSessionHome)
               csContext.lookup( "ejb/jboss/ch18/CustomerSession" );

        /*
         * We now have the Bean's Home Interface. Now let's create a bean.
         */
        CustomerSession csBean = csHome.create();

        /*
         * We now have a bean. Pass the value object to the addressChange()
         * method. It passes an updated one back.
         */
        CustomerValueObject cvo_return = csBean.addressChange(cvo_in);

        /*
         * Since the bean is stateless and will not be reused after this
         * "action", go ahead and let the container know we are through
         * and don't need it anymore.
```

LISTING 18.6 Continued

```
         */
        csBean.remove();

        /*
         * Send back the updated value bean.
         */
        return cvo_return;

      } catch( Exception e ){
        throw new CustomerUpdateException(e.toString());
      }
   }

}
```

The Application Exception: `CustomerUpdateException.java`

Creating application-specific exceptions is a common way to have applications control and manage exceptions that can occur during processing. This is a best practice that, in this case, allows the `Action` class to be isolated from handling any of the variety of exceptions that have to do with EJB processing.

The `CustomerUpdateException.java` class is an application-specific exception that can be copied and modified for use with any application you're building. Its source code is shown in Listing 18.7.

LISTING 18.7 The `CustomerUpdateException.java` Source Listing

```
package struts.ch18.client;

/**
 * An application exception that wraps any exceptions that could occur when
 * updating customer information.<p>
 *
 * It is expected that the CustomerEJBFacade will throw only this exception.
 * All exceptions behind the facade should either catch and handle
 * exceptions or re-throw them as CustomerUpdateException.<p>
 *
 * @author Kevin Bedell & James Turner
 * @version 1.0
 */
```

LISTING 18.7 Continued

```
public class CustomerUpdateException extends java.lang.Exception {

    /**
     * Constructs a CustomerUpdateException with the specified detail message.
     *
     * @param msg - The detail message.
     */
    public CustomerUpdateException( String msg ) {
        super( msg );
    }

    /**
     * Constructs a CustomerUpdateException with no detail message.
     *
     */
    public CustomerUpdateException() {
        super();
    }
}
```

The EJB: `CustomerSessionBean.java`

Finally, the EJB chapter actually presents an EJB! I hope it was worth the wait!

To be honest, you're probably going to be disappointed. After all, this is a book about Struts, so the real value that we tried to add is in how to design and build the Struts portion of the code. The EJB itself is actually pretty straightforward.

The only really important point with regard to the design that has been presented in this chapter is that the EJB, like all the Struts code, also works with our value object, `CustomerValueObject`.

This EJB was modified from one of the EJBs provided in the template application provided with JBoss. Because the JBoss developers recommend using XDoclet to generate home and remote interfaces as well as deployment descriptors, that's what the sample application does. More information about EJBs, JBoss, and XDoclet isn't provided here because there are other better sources for that information.

The `CustomerSessionBean.java` class is the stateless session bean used with this application. Its source code is shown in Listing 18.8.

LISTING 18.8 The `CustomerSessionBean.java` Source Listing

```
/*
* JBoss, the OpenSource J2EE webOS
*
* Distributable under LGPL license.
* See terms of license at gnu.org.
*/
package jboss.ch18.session;

import java.util.Random;

import java.rmi.RemoteException;
import javax.ejb.CreateException;
import javax.ejb.EJBException;
import javax.ejb.FinderException;
import javax.ejb.RemoveException;
import javax.ejb.SessionBean;
import javax.ejb.SessionContext;
import javax.naming.Context;
import javax.naming.InitialContext;
import javax.naming.NamingException;
import javax.rmi.PortableRemoteObject;

import jboss.ch18.interfaces.InvalidValueException;

import struts.ch18.client.CustomerValueObject;

/**
 * Session Bean for Customer information updating. This is a modification
 * of the session bean that comes with the JBoss template project.
 *
 * It uses XDoclet to create the Remote and Home interfaces as well as
 * to create the ejb-jar.xml and jboss deployment descriptors.
 *
 * ATTENTION: Some of the XDoclet tags are hidden from XDoclet by
 *            adding a "--" between @ and the namespace. Please remove
 *            this "--" to make it active or add a space to make an
 *            active tag inactive.
 *
 * @ejb:bean name="jboss/ch18/CustomerSession"
 *           display-name="Customer Test Session Bean"
 *           type="Stateless"
```

LISTING 18.8 Continued

```
 *           transaction-type="Container"
 *           jndi-name="ejb/jboss/ch18/CustomerSession"
 *
 ***/
public class CustomerSessionBean
   implements SessionBean
{

   // -------------------------------------------------------------------------
   // Static
   // -------------------------------------------------------------------------

   // -------------------------------------------------------------------------
   // Members
   // -------------------------------------------------------------------------

   private SessionContext mContext;

   // -------------------------------------------------------------------------
   // Methods
   // -------------------------------------------------------------------------

   // -------------------------------------------------------------------------
   // Methods
   // -------------------------------------------------------------------------

   /**
    * Change the address property in the value object. This method randomly
    * chooses one of three addresses and changes the value object address
    * to that address.
    *
    * @param CustomerValueObject A value object which containing the
    * current customer information.
    *
    * @return CustomerValueObject containing the updated address
    *
    * @throws RemoteException
    *
    * @ejb:interface-method view-type="remote"
    * @ejb:transaction type="NotSupported"
    **/
```

LISTING 18.8 Continued

```
public CustomerValueObject addressChange( CustomerValueObject cvo )
   throws  RemoteException
{

   Random r = new Random();

   switch (r.nextInt(3)) {

       case 0:
         cvo.setAddress("1313 Mockingbird Lane");
         break;
       case 1:
         cvo.setAddress("Corner of Michigan and Trumble");
         break;
       case 2:
         cvo.setAddress("62 Hauser Street");
         break;

   }

   /*
    *  This allows us to watch activity in the JBoss console log.
    */
   System.out.println( "CustomerSessionBean.addressChange() called." +
                       " Set address to: " + cvo.getAddress() );

   return cvo;

}

/**
* Create the Session Bean
*
* @throws CreateException
*
* @ejb:create-method view-type="remote"
**/
public void ejbCreate()
   throws
      CreateException
{
```

LISTING 18.8 Continued

```
      System.out.println( "CustomerSessionBean.ejbCreate() called" );
   }

   /**
   * Describes the instance and its content for debugging purpose
   *
   * @return Debugging information about the instance and its content
   **/
   public String toString()
   {
      return "CustomerSessionBean [ " + " ]";
   }


   // -------------------------------------------------------------------------
   // Framework Callbacks
   // -------------------------------------------------------------------------

   public void setSessionContext( SessionContext aContext )
      throws
         EJBException
   {
      mContext = aContext;
   }

   public void ejbActivate()
      throws
         EJBException
   {
   }

   public void ejbPassivate()
      throws
         EJBException
   {
   }

   public void ejbRemove()
      throws
         EJBException
   {
```

LISTING 18.8 Continued

```
        System.out.println( "CustomerSessionBean.ejbRemove() called" );
    }
}
```

Conclusions

The goal of this chapter was to provide information on using Struts with EJBs. This was accomplished in three steps:

- First, EJB technology was reviewed. General best practices and rules of thumb were presented to give you an understanding of how Struts and EJB technologies can be used together.
- A sample application was presented. The first part of this presentation covered configuration issues related to integrating Struts with an EJB container. This was presented with the understanding that although the general steps are likely to be similar, the specific steps are highly dependent on the particular Web containers and EJB containers (or even versions of these) that you're using.
- Finally, the source code of the sample application was reviewed with particular attention paid to the rules of thumb and design strategies that are recommended in this chapter.

Struts is an excellent technology for use in building the client-facing portions of applications that use EJBs and EJB containers for back-end processing. We hope that you can take the ideas and sample code presented in this chapter and apply them in your own applications.

19

Using Struts with Web Services

IN THIS CHAPTER

Web Services are more than just the latest cool technology on the block. They represent a real change. Web Services represent an opportunity to significantly reduce the effort required to get two systems to communicate.

Web Services accomplish this by encoding the data transferred in XML (extensible markup language). XML isn't dependent on any particular technology, so any programming language or platform can use it. This openness means that if a programming language can encode information and communicate using XML, it can participate in Web Services communications.

Although Web Services can be used for much more than just making two applications communicate, this is the most widely adopted Web Service application. In addition, it's the most likely application where Struts will be used with a Web Service.

Some material in this chapter is similar to the previous chapter on integrating EJBs with Struts. This is done deliberately, for two reasons:

- Web Services are most likely to be used with Struts in a manner similar to the way EJBs are used with Struts. That is, the front end of the application is most likely built using Struts, whereas the Web Service is behind the scenes providing information and data for the Struts application to use.
- This approach makes it easier to compare the differences between using EJBs with Struts and using Web Services with Struts. In turn, this makes it easier to see the strengths and weaknesses of each approach.

The chapter begins by discussing Web Services in general and then moves on to discuss the specifics of how Web Services can be used with Struts. Following that, a sample application is presented to illustrate the points made. We intend for the sample application to form the basis of an actual application that you could develop.

NOTE

All command files in this chapter are built and tested on Windows-based system. They can be easily adopted for Unix by converting them from Windows `.cmd` files into shell scripts written for the shell of your choice.

Struts (and Axis, and the other programs used in this chapter) should all work with little or no modification in a Unix environment.

Web Services Fit with Struts Model Components

NOTE

Material contained in this section is largely repeated from the previous chapter. This is because EJBs and Web Services are accessed from Struts in a similar manner.

This duplication is intentional to allow this chapter to read as standalone by readers who aren't interested in reading the previous chapter.

If you read the previous chapter, we recommend skimming these sections both as a review and because the material isn't completely identical.

Struts is a framework based on the Model-View-Controller (MVC) design pattern. One of the strengths of MVC, as you recall, is the flexibility you have for implementing Model components. This explains why Struts has tag libraries for building View components, and `Action` classes for building Controller components, but no specific classes to extend to implement Model components.

That means you'll most likely incorporate Web Services into your Struts project by accessing them as Model components from within your `Action` classes. You may access them directly from the `Action` class or you may build helper classes that hide the details of the Web Service from the `Action` class.

Although it's possible to access a Web Service directly from the JSP files (View components) using scriptlets or via bean helper classes or custom tags, this practice is strongly discouraged. Such an approach is a misuse of the framework and will likely require you to put code in your JSP file that really belongs in a Controller component.

For example, what if the Web Service is unavailable or throws an `Exception` when you access it? If this happens you will need to make decisions on what to show the user based on whether or not the `Exception` is thrown. This decision is better made in an `Action` class in which you have the ability to forward the user to the appropriate error page.

In addition, its likely that you'll want to implement business logic to display different information or take different actions based on data you retrieve through the Web Service. This logic is best put in Controller components. Even if your initial requirements call for simply retrieving and displaying data through the Web Service, you can be sure that your business requirements will change over time and you'll have to implement new functionality by encoding business logic based on data in the Web Service. Do yourself a favor: *Work with the framework* and access the Web Service from your `Action` classes from the beginning.

So, why is the name of this section, "Web Services *Fit* with Struts Model Components" instead of "Web Services *Are* Struts Model Components"? Basically, the wording is to emphasize all the flexibility you have. The best way to meet your system requirements might be to treat the Web Service exactly as a model component, or it might not. Some best practice approaches are presented in this chapter, but what you do in the end might differ depending on your need. This section gets you started, but your end design will vary based on what works for you.

A Quick Review of Web Service Technologies

A number of great books about Web Services are available, so the material presented here is intended to just be an overview.

NOTE

If you're interested in more details on Web Services technology, please refer to the following books:

Java Web Services Unleashed (ISBN: 067232363X) by Robert, J. Brunner, Frank Cohen, et al; Sams Publishing

Building Web Services with Java: Making Sense of XML, SOAP, WSDL, and UDDI (ISBN: 0672321815) by Steve Graham, et al; Sams Publishing

How Web Services Communications Work

The concept that Web Services communicate using XML was introduced at the beginning of the chapter. It's worth expanding on here. In case you've never seen XML, here's a sample:

```
<customer>
        <name>Fred Flintstone</name>
        <address>123 Main Street</address>
        <city>Bedrock City</city>
</customer>
```

As you can see, XML representation of data is independent of any particular language. It's usually readable English and is extremely flexible in the ways you can use it to represent information. This XML fragment represents a customer and contains the customer's name, address, and city.

The key to Web Services communications using XML revolves around three high-level ideas:

- **Converting the data you need to send into XML.** The Web Services client (which is Struts in this case) must turn the data into an XML format to send it. This is easy if the data you're sending are simple strings. It becomes more challenging if you want to send complex objects. This process of converting the data into an XML format is called *serializing* the data.
- **Communicating the data to the Web Service server and retrieving the response.** This communication is usually done using HTTP (although other protocols can be used). Data is communicated between the client and server using a protocol called SOAP (Simple Object Access Protocol). During this process, the data being communicated is generally transferred in character strings encoded using XML.
- **Converting the data back into a useable format on the server.** This process is referred to as *deserializing* the data. The program running in the server doesn't need to be written using the same language as the program running on the client. As long as the program on the server can deserialize the data that the client sends it, the conversion can work.

This is how Web Services makes it possible to easily connect two systems together. It doesn't matter if the client and server run on different platforms. By using Web Services, both sides just need to know how to communicate using SOAP and how to serialize and deserialize each other's data.

Comparing the EJB and Web Services Approaches

Comparing this to the EJB technology presented in previous chapter, here are some highly generalized comparisons:

- Web Services are more flexible for communications between languages or platforms. EJBs are by definition Java specific.

- Using Web Services, the contract between client and server is defined by specifying the XML that can be sent between them. For EJBs, the equivalent is specifying the home and remote interfaces (which are Java-specific and more difficult for non-programmers to understand). One important benefit here is that nonprogrammers (for example, business analysts, program managers, and so on) might be able to coordinate the development of XML specifications. Specifying the interface between two systems using EJB technologies is not as straightforward.
- EJBs can be counted on to have certain container services supporting them. For example, they can be made transaction-aware if required. These types of container services aren't necessarily available in Web Services, although they might be, depending on your Web Services implementation.
- Web Services are generally sent over HTTP, although they aren't tied to it. This provides a great deal more flexibility when it comes to protocol support. EJB implementations are tightly tied to both JNDI and RMI technologies, which are more restrictive. The ability to use HTTP also makes Web Services more firewall-friendly.
- Because Web Services use XML for communications, sending complex objects between systems might require developing complicated serializers and deserializers. If you're using Java on both the client and server, you can send complex objects much easier by using EJBs.

In summary, Web Services are more flexible and make interfaces between different systems easier to both specify and develop. EJBs are less flexible, but come with more sophisticated container support (for example, sophisticated transactional support). Also, sending complex objects directly between systems is easier using EJBs. Sending complex data using Web Services is possible as well, but might require custom serializers/deserializers to be written for both client and server.

Anatomy of a Web Service

Based on the previous section, here are the pieces of the puzzle that we need to use Struts with a Web Service:

- Web Service client software. This is the software that understands the SOAP protocol and knows how to serialize and deserialize the data.
- Web Service server software. This is the software that runs on the server that the client communicates with. It communicates using SOAP as well, and must know how to serialize and deserialize the specific data types you're sending to it.

- Business logic code inside the Web Service server. After Struts can communicate with the server, there must be something for it to do!

For the sample application in this chapter, you use Apache Axis. Apache Axis, according to its developers, is "the third generation of Apache Soap!" They refer to it as "essentially a *SOAP engine*—a framework for constructing SOAP processors such as clients, servers, gateways, etc."

Apache Axis is among the fastest growing open source Web Services. The sample application in this book gets you up and running with a basic Web Service application based on Struts and Apache Axis. We hope that this basic application can provide a foundation for building production applications using these technologies.

How to Use Struts with a Web Service

The title of this section is a bit misleading. It seems to imply that there might be a single best way of using Struts with a Web Service. This isn't the case. There are many options that could make sense based on your specific environment and application. However, that being said, this chapter provides a specific recommended approach.

This recommended approach is illustrated in the sample application presented in the next section. But first, here are some key points to the design:

- **The Web Service is called from the `Action` class.** The need to manage `Exceptions` and to coordinate different views based on the Web Service response makes the `Action` class the appropriate place for calling the Web Service.
- **A value object is used to transfer data to and from the Web Service.** Value objects are simple JavaBeans that are used to hold properties as a group. The benefit of using value objects is that doing so enables you to send data to the Web Service "one bean at a time" instead of "one property at a time." This makes the communications much more efficient and simplifies processing in the `Action` class.
- **Details of the Web Service communications are hidden using a facade pattern.** A *facade* is nothing more than a class designed to expose an easy-to-use set of methods while hiding complex code inside. A facade can hide access with a single Web Service or it might manage communications with more than one. As you'll see in the sample application, applying a facade greatly simplifies both development and maintenance of your `Action` class.

If you read the previous chapter regarding integration of EJBs with Struts, this should all sound familiar. In fact, you'll see that the sample applications in these two chapters are virtually identical except that the facade class developed in the previous chapter is replaced with a different facade class.

By isolating the communications in the `Action` class and using a facade class to hide the implementation details, the design itself has actually been validated! The entire back-end system has changed, but the only portion of the Struts code that has to be modified is a single facade class!

In reality, it's not quite that simple and you'll still need to understand how to implement things on the server side. But the point remains that this design is solid and could be used as the basis for a larger, production application.

A Struts/Web Service Sample Application

Now it's time to move from theory to practice. This sample application is intended to illustrate a collection of what we consider to be best practices with regard to using Struts with Web Services.

This application is developed using Tomcat as our servlet/JSP container and Apache Axis as a Web Services server. Basic configuration information is provided directly in the chapter as the need for it arises.

Because Web Service implementations differ in the specifics of how they implement the SOAP protocol, it's possible that the code you develop here might need modification before it works with any other Web Services server—for example, a .NET implementation. On the other hand, things might work with little or no modification. One of the benefits of using Axis in the sample application is that its adoption rate is accelerating and it's likely that if you use Struts to access Web Service, that service might be Axis-based.

To demonstrate this application, you'll walk through all the steps required to build similar applications on your own.

The Application: Updating Customer Information

In this basic application, a simple form is provided to allow information about a customer to be updated. Like any Struts form, the information is populated into a form bean when it's submitted. The form bean is then passed to an `Action` class for processing. After processing, an `ActionForward` is called to indicate which JSP file to display the results with.

All this processing is very basic and should be ingrained in your memory by now. The changes related to integrating with the Web Service are isolated in the `Action` class. The `Action` class must update the customer information by calling the Web Service that manages the customer information.

Figure 19.1 shows the form used to enter the information.

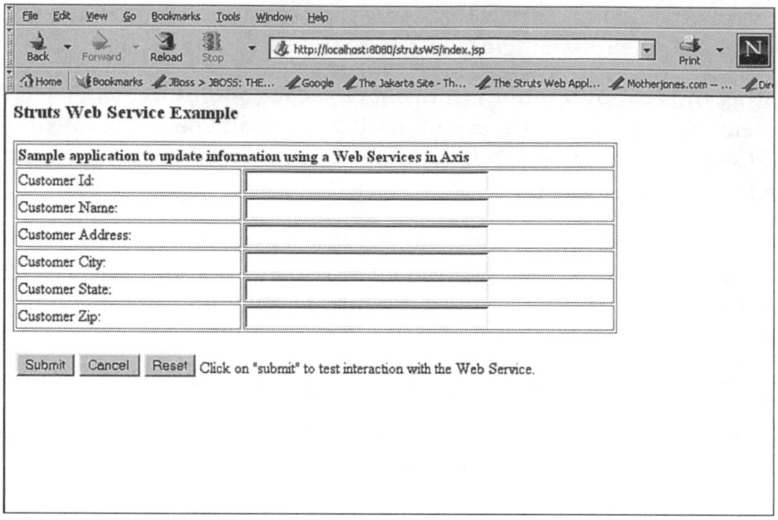

FIGURE 19.1 The sample Web Services application—`/strutsWS/index.jsp`.

When you submit the form, the address of the customer changes. That's all. No magic, smoke, or mirrors. The Web Service that generates this new address simply chooses randomly between three hard-coded addresses and returns one.

The purpose of this application isn't to be fancy; it's to provide a working application that demonstrates good design fundamentals that you can copy and reuse.

In reviewing this sample application, you first go over configuring the system and building the application. Following that, you look through the application code itself.

Be forewarned that although we've done our best to make the configuration and build steps in this chapter accurate, updated versions of Axis, Tomcat, or Struts might make these directions obsolete. But even if this is this case, the overall approach should still be instructive.

Installing the Sample Application File

The sample application for this chapter is provided on the companion CD-ROM for this book. It's contained in the file `strutsWS.zip`. To install it, simply extract it into a directory where you can work on it.

For the rest of the chapter, directories that are a part of the build process are referred to using their parameter names as defined in the Ant `build.xml` file that's provided with the sample application.

After the sample application is installed, you can move to the next step and begin the process of building, deploying, and running the sample application.

NOTE

Although most of the following steps have already been completed in the sample application, this chapter proceeds as if they haven't. This is done so that you can understand how the application was built. Please follow all the steps closely!

COMPARING BUILDING AND DEPLOYING EJBS VERSUS WEB SERVICES

It's worth a few paragraphs to discuss a bit about the complexity of building and deploying Web Services versus building and deploying EJBs.

If you read the previous chapter on Struts/EJB integration, you'll notice that configuration of the Web Service server (Axis) is much simpler than configuration of the EJB Container (even though we used JBoss, among the easiest to use EJB containers around). The overall configure/build/deploy process for Axis is simpler than using an EJB container.

Of course, this simplification is somewhat dependent on your Web Services server. In this case, you're using Axis for development of both the client and the server code. Using the same SOAP implementation for both ends of the SOAP communications minimizes a lot of potential problems. You're not required to do this—after all, SOAP implementations over HTTP should be interchangeable. To a great extent, this actually is the case.

In addition, deploying Web Services applications with Axis is relatively easy, as you'll see when we get into the application. Using WebLogic Server, for example, you're required to implement a Web Service as a session bean in the WebLogic EJB container—an Ant task is available that takes your session bean and implements a Web Service based on it. (Of course, if you're already using WebLogic, implementing session beans is something you probably do all the time anyway, so it's not likely to be a problem for you.)

The EJB 2.1 specification (viewable at `http://www.jcp.org/jsr/detail/153.jsp`), makes it a requirement that every EJB container expose session beans as Web Services. After the leading EJB containers implement this standard, the effort to implement a Web Service or an EJB will be virtually the same!

Axis 1.0: A Flexible, Extensible Web Services Framework

When the first Apache Axis 1.0 release candidate was announced, the Axis team posted an email to the axis-user email list server. In it, they said that Axis

- Is a flexible, extensible Web Services framework for Java developers
- Has a complete implementation of Sun's JAX-RPC (Java API for XML-Based RPC) and SAAJ (SOAP with Attachments API for Java) specifications

- Has successfully passed the JAX-RPC and SAAJ TCK (Technology Compatibility Kit) test suites
- Is easy to use (including instant deployment, by dropping a Java source file into a Web app)
- Supports bidirectional WSDL (Web Service Definition Language)<->Java generation, both via command-line tools and automatically in the runtime
- Contains support for the new version of the DIME (Direct Internet Message Encapsulation) specification for attachments
- Contains preliminary SOAP 1.2 support

Axis is freely available from its Web site (part of the Apache XML project at `http:// xml.apache.org/axis`). A copy of Axis 1.0 is also included on the companion CD-ROM for this book.

Our sample application uses a number of features of Axis, including

- Axis software is used as the Web Service client software for communicating from Struts to a Web Service server using the SOAP protocol.
- Axis software is used as the Web Service server software for communicating from the Web Service server back to Struts using the SOAP protocol.
- Axis software is used to serialize and deserialize a value object containing a series of properties. This is a step up in complexity from sending individual properties via SOAP. This additional complexity is added to make the application more useful and to leverage the value object design introduced in the previous chapter and continued here.
- The Axis WSDL2Java tool is used to assist in generating all the classes required to take advantage of Axis. This tool makes using Axis simpler by automating a number of important steps for you.

The Web Services Server: Installing the Axis Server

In a Web Services application, there are both client and server components. In the sample application, both of these are based on Axis. The client portion of the sample application is the Struts application. The server portion of the application is based on Axis as well and is deployed in Tomcat as a separate Web application.

As a result, you have *two* Web applications: the Struts application acting as the Web Service client and the Axis server application.

The 1.0 release of Axis is included on the companion CD-ROM for this book. Begin the installation process by unzipping it into a convenient directory. When that's complete, the first major step is to install the Axis server application (without the sample application code to begin with) and validate that it's working correctly. Following are the steps to accomplish this first step:

- Under the main Axis installation directory (`xml-axis-10`) is a `webapps` subdirectory. In this subdirectory is the `axis` subdirectory. Copy the `axis` subdirectory (including all files and directories beneath it) into your Tomcat `webapps` directory. This installs a clean copy of the Axis server code. At this point, you might need to start (or restart) Tomcat.
- Now open a browser and point it to `http://localhost:8080/axis/index.html`. If you don't see a simple HTML page with the phrase, "Hello! Welcome to Apache-Axis.", check to make sure that Tomcat is running and that you have the correct host and port number.
- When you can see a page at `http://localhost:8080/axis/index.html`, click on the link that says "Validate the local installation's configuration." This executes the JSP page `http://localhost:8080/axis/happyaxis.jsp` or what's known as the *Happy Axis* page. The Happy Axis page looks through your environment to determine whether you have all the required libraries.

Listing 19.1 presents the output from the Happy Axis page on my system at the time of this writing. (Note: All the formatting has been removed, but you can still look at the text to see how I have my system configured.)

If you have any problems making the Happy Axis page happy, check the locations of each library (`.jar`) file in Listing 19.1. Of course, you don't have to configure your system identically—the only goal is to make the Happy Axis page happy!

LISTING 19.1 Output from the Happy Axis Page

```
Examining webapp configuration

Needed Components
Found SAAJ API (javax.xml.soap.SOAPMessage) at
  ➥C:\dev\tomcat\webapps\axis\WEB-INF\lib\saaj.jar
Found JAX-RPC API (javax.xml.rpc.Service) at
  ➥C:\dev\tomcat\webapps\axis\WEB-INF\lib\jaxrpc.jar
Found Apache-Axis (org.apache.axis.transport.http.AxisServlet) at
  ➥C:\dev\tomcat\webapps\axis\WEB-INF\lib\axis.jar
Found Jakarta-Commons Discovery (org.apache.commons.discovery.Resource) at
  ➥C:\dev\tomcat\webapps\axis\WEB-INF\lib\commons-discovery.jar
```

LISTING 19.1 Continued

```
Found Jakarta-Commons Logging (org.apache.commons.logging.Log) at
  ➥C:\dev\tomcat\webapps\axis\WEB-INF\lib\commons-logging.jar
Found IBM's WSDL4Java (com.ibm.wsdl.factory.WSDLFactoryImpl) at
  ➥C:\dev\tomcat\webapps\axis\WEB-INF\lib\wsdl4j.jar
Found JAXP implementation (javax.xml.parsers.SAXParserFactory) at
  ➥C:\dev\tomcat\common\endorsed\xmlParserAPIs.jar
Found Activation API (javax.activation.DataHandler) at
  ➥C:\dev\tomcat\common\lib\activation.jar
Optional Components
Found Mail API (javax.mail.internet.MimeMessage) at
  ➥C:\dev\tomcat\common\lib\mail.jar

Warning: could not find class org.apache.xml.security.Init from file xmlsec.jar
XML Security is not supported
See http://xml.apache.org/security/

The core axis libraries are present. 1 optional axis library is missing
Note: On Tomcat 4.x, you may need to put libraries that
contain java.* or javax.* packages into CATALINA_HOME/commons/lib

Note: Even if everything this page probes for is present, there is no
guarantee your web service will work, because there are many configuration
options that we do not check for. These tests are necessary but not sufficient
Examining Application Server
Servlet version 2.3
XML Parser org.apache.xerces.jaxp.SAXParserImpl
Examining System Properties

java.runtime.name=Java(TM) 2 Runtime Environment, Standard Edition
sun.boot.library.path=C:\jdk1.3.1_01\jre\bin
java.vm.version=1.3.1_01
java.vm.vendor=Sun Microsystems Inc.
java.vendor.url=http://java.sun.com/
path.separator=;
java.vm.name=Java HotSpot(TM) Client VM
file.encoding.pkg=sun.io
java.vm.specification.name=Java Virtual Machine Specification
user.dir=C:\dev\tomcat\bin
java.runtime.version=1.3.1_01
java.awt.graphicsenv=sun.awt.Win32GraphicsEnvironment
java.endorsed.dirs=c:\dev\tomcat\bin;c:\dev\tomcat\common\endorsed
```

LISTING 19.1 Continued

```
os.arch=x86
java.io.tmpdir=c:\dev\tomcat\temp
line.separator=

java.vm.specification.vendor=Sun Microsystems Inc.
java.awt.fonts=
java.naming.factory.url.pkgs=org.apache.naming
os.name=Windows 2000
java.library.path=C:\jdk1.3.1_01\bin;.;C:\WINDOWS\System32;C:\WINDOWS;
➥c:\mysql\bin;C:\jdk1.3.1_01\bin;c:\dev\ant\bin;C:\WINDOWS\system32;
➥C:\WINDOWS;C:\WINDOWS\System32\Wbem;c:\emacs-20.7\bin;c:\dev\cygwin\bin;
➥c:\dev\maven\bin
java.specification.name=Java Platform API Specification
java.class.version=47.0
os.version=5.1
user.home=C:\Documents and Settings\a
user.timezone=America/New_York
catalina.useNaming=true
java.awt.printerjob=sun.awt.windows.WPrinterJob
file.encoding=Cp1252
java.specification.version=1.3
catalina.home=c:\dev\tomcat
user.name=a
java.class.path=C:\jdk1.3.1_01\lib\tools.jar;c:\dev\tomcat\bin\bootstrap.jar
java.naming.factory.initial=org.apache.naming.java.javaURLContextFactory
java.vm.specification.version=1.0
java.home=C:\jdk1.3.1_01\jre
java.specification.vendor=Sun Microsystems Inc.
user.language=en
awt.toolkit=sun.awt.windows.WToolkit
java.vm.info=mixed mode
java.version=1.3.1_01
java.ext.dirs=C:\jdk1.3.1_01\jre\lib\ext
sun.boot.class.path=C:\jdk1.3.1_01\jre\lib\rt.jar;
➥C:\jdk1.3.1_01\jre\lib\i18n.jar;C:\jdk1.3.1_01\jre\lib\sunrsasign.jar;
➥C:\jdk1.3.1_01\jre\classes
java.vendor=Sun Microsystems Inc.
catalina.base=c:\dev\tomcat
file.separator=\
java.vendor.url.bug=http://java.sun.com/cgi-bin/bugreport.cgi
sun.cpu.endian=little
```

LISTING 19.1 Continued

```
sun.io.unicode.encoding=UnicodeLittle
user.region=US
sun.cpu.isalist=pentium i486 i386

Platform: Apache Tomcat/4.1.12
```

Don't worry if your output is different than in the preceding listing. Many of the properties should be different because file locations on your machine will likely be different than mine. By default, the basic installation has all the library files you need for the sample application, so you should be ready to proceed.

You might have noticed in this listing that one of the optional libraries (`xmlsec.jar`) wasn't found. That's fine—it isn't required for the sample application.

After your Happy Axis page is happy, your Web Services server is configured correctly and you're ready to move on to the next step : configuring and building the client application.

Configuring Axis in the Build Environment

Now that you've validated the basic Axis installation, it's time to build and deploy the sample Struts application. This isn't complex, but it takes a number of steps. All these steps are described in the following sections.

Copy the Axis Web Application into the Build Environment

The first step in preparing the build environment is to copy the axis Web application you just validated into the sample application build directory (this has actually already been done for you in the strutsWS application).

This step is required because a part of the sample application includes the business logic that lives in the Axis server. After all, there's not much use invoking a Web Service unless it actually does something!

To accomplish this, copy the `axis` Web application into the sample application main directory (into the directory `strutsWS/axis`).

Configure the Build Parameters in the `build.properties` File

A build script (`build.xml`) has been provided for use with the Jakarta Ant build tool to build the application. The `build.xml` file is located in the top directory of the sample application. In addition, a `build.properties` file is also provided that has two properties that must be configured for your environment:

- **`tomcat.home`**—This is the top directory of your Tomcat installation. It's required for the build process to know where to deploy the application to.
- **`webapps.home`**—This points to the `webapps` directory that's directly beneath the `tomcat.home`. The build script copies `.war` files into this directory to deploy them.

After these two properties are set for your system, save the file and exit. Your environment is now set. The next steps have to do with using Axis to define and build a Web Service application.

The Web Services Client: Struts and Axis Integrated

Here's a review of the overall application and how you're going to integrate Axis code with Struts:

- The application itself has a single data entry form as its only page. On this form there are six fields relating to a customer record: Id, Name, Address, City, State, and Zip.
- When the form is posted, these values are posted to a form bean. The form bean is passed into the `Action` class so that the input can be processed.
- The first important design element relating to this design is a value object, `CustomerValueObject.java`. Both the form bean (`CustomerForm.java`) and the `Action` class (`CustomerAction.java`) have been written to take advantage of the value object. For example, the form bean has two methods, `getValueObject` and `setValueObject`, that allow it to work with data a bean at a time. (Because these files are virtually identical to the same files presented in the previous chapter, they aren't reviewed again here.)
- The `Action` class communicates with the Web Service in Axis using a facade class (`CustomerWSFacade.java`). Details of interacting with the Web Service are hidden inside this facade class. The `Action` class simply passes in a value object and receives an update value object back from the Web Service.

Note that this design is virtually identical to the design in the previous chapter. Because of the design modularity, all that had to be done to change the application from using an EJB server to using a Web Service for back-end processing was to replace the facade class.

Details of the facade class are provided later in the chapter after the code needed to interact with the Web Service has been explained.

Java2WSDL and WSDL2Java: Automating Axis Code Development

The Axis developers provide two invaluable utilities to help you build Web Services applications: `Java2WSDL` and `WSDL2Java`. You'll see how valuable they are in the next few sections as we go through the steps to build the sample application.

WSDL stands for Web Services Description Language and is used to provide a program language-independent description of a Web Service. WSDL is written using XML and provides information about the data types, operations, and access locations that make up the Web Service. This chapter doesn't provide detailed information about WSDSL—you can refer to one of the many good books available on SOAP and Web Services for that. However, the chapter presents the WSDL for the service you're building and provides an overview of it that should get you started.

At a high level, the process that you follow for building your Web Service code is

- Create some basic Java classes and use them to generate WSDL using `Java2WSDL`.
- Use `WSDL2Java` to create the Web Service client software. This code is integrated into Struts in a later step.
- After that, use `WSDL2Java` again to generate the Web Service server classes that will be deployed in the Axis server.
- After the code is all generated, the next step is to compile everything and then deploy the server code into Axis. The step will finish by validating that the web service is installed and working.
- Finally, after the Web Service communications code is generated, compiled, deployed and working, the final step is to integrate the code into the Struts application.

Now let's dive in and start building the application!

Step 1: Generate the WSDL for the Application

NOTE

It's important to note that some steps in development of this sample application involve generating code automatically using the `Java2WSDL` and `WSDL2Java` utilities that are a part of Axis. These utilities are destructive in that every time they run, they overwrite all files they generate. For this reason, you should be very careful each time you run them that any files you want to keep are backed up in a safe location!

In this step, you use the Axis `Java2WSDL` utility to generate WSDL for the application. To do so, you must first create some Java for it to use to generate the WSDL.

The Java you must create consists of two classes. The first is the value object you're using. `Java2WSDL` determines the properties of the value object and generates the WSDL to allow it to be transferred using the Web Service. Remember that the Web Service server you're communicating with need not be written in Java. The WSDL generated here must carry all the information about the data being sent so that program at the other end can understand how to deserialize it.

The second class you must create is a simple, Java interface file. This interface file (similar to the remote interface for an EJB) defines the business methods that the Web Service exposes.

`CustomerWSValueObject.java` is the value object form bean used in this sample application. It's virtually identical to the value object from the previous chapter except for the class name and package. Its source code is shown in Listing 19.2.

LISTING 19.2 The `CustomerWSValueObject.java` Source Listing

```
package struts.ch19.customer;

/**
 * Example Value Object for showing integration of Struts with Web Services
 *
 * @author Kevin Bedell & James Turner
 * @version 1.0
 */
public class CustomerWSValueObject {

  public CustomerWSValueObject () {

      this.name     = "";
      this.custId   = "";
      this.address  = "";
      this.city     = "";
      this.state    = "";
      this.zip      = "";
  }

  public CustomerWSValueObject (String name,
                                String custId,
                                String address,
                                String city,
                                String state,
                                String zip
                               ) {
```

LISTING 19.2 Continued

```
        this.name     = name;
        this.custId   = custId;
        this.address  = address;
        this.city     = city;
        this.state    = state;
        this.zip      = zip;
    }

    private String name;
    public String getName() { return this.name; }
    public void setName(String nameus) { this.name = name; }

    private String custId;
    public String getCustId() { return this.custId; }
    public void setCustId(String custId) { this.custId = custId; }

    private String address;
    public String getAddress() { return this.address; }
    public void setAddress(String address) { this.address = address; }

    private String city;
    public String getCity() { return this.city; }
    public void setCity(String city) { this.city = city; }

    private String state;
    public String getState() { return this.state; }
    public void setState(String state) { this.state = state; }

    private String zip;
    public String getZip() { return this.zip; }
    public void setZip(String zip) { this.zip = zip; }

}
```

As you can see, this is a basic value object for use in storing information about a customer.

The Java interface used in the sample application exposes only a single business method that's used to process address changes. The `CustomerWS.java` class is the Java interface used with this application to assist in generating the Web Service communications files. Its source code is shown in Listing 19.3.

LISTING 19.3 The `CustomerWS.java` Source Listing

```
package struts.ch19.customer;

import struts.ch19.customer.CustomerWSValueObject;

/**
 * Interface describing a web service to process customer information changes
 **/
public interface CustomerWS {
    public CustomerWSValueObject addressChange( CustomerWSValueObject cvo );
}
```

As you can see in the listing, the `addressChange` method accepts and returns a `CustomerWSValueObject`. This is how the Web Service is defined to allow passing data a bean at a time instead of a property at a time. After you run `Java2WSDL` next, you'll be able to see how this is defined in the WSDL.

To simplify the running of the `Java2WSDL` utility, Listing 19.4 provides a batch program that configures the environment and runs Java2WSDL. For details about all the options for `Java2WSDL` and `WSDL2Java`, see the Reference Guide included in the Axis documentation.

NOTE

Prior to running `java2WSDL`, the two Java files used here must be compiled. To simplify this, a command file—`compile.cmd`—has been provided. This file is provided as a convenience and isn't discussed further. Any method of compiling these files will do as long as

- The class files are output in the same directory as would be used by the `compile.cmd` file. For this example, the output directory is required to be the same as the source directory. When you're done compiling, you should have both `.java` and `.class` files in the source directory.
- The files must be compiled with the debug option on. This compiles symbols into the `.class` files that `Java2WSDL` uses to create the WSDL and an Axis-friendly value object.

LISTING 19.4 The `StrutsCh19Step1.cmd` File for Generating WSDL

```
@ECHO OFF

set JAVA_HOME=C:\jdk1.3.1_01
set JAVAC=%JAVA_HOME%\bin\javac.exe
set JAVA=%JAVA_HOME%\bin\java.exe
set AXIS_LIBS=.\axis\WEB-INF\lib
set XERCES=.\lib\xerces.jar
set AXIS_SRC=.\src

REM Build out the classpath
set LCP=.;%JAVA_HOME%\lib\tools.jar

REM Add Axis jars to the classpath
set LCP=%LCP%;%AXIS_LIBS%\axis.jar
set LCP=%LCP%;%AXIS_LIBS%\axis-ant.jar
set LCP=%LCP%;%AXIS_LIBS%\commons-discovery.jar
set LCP=%LCP%;%AXIS_LIBS%\commons-logging.jar
set LCP=%LCP%;%AXIS_LIBS%\jaxrpc.jar
set LCP=%LCP%;%AXIS_LIBS%\log4j-1.2.4.jar
set LCP=%LCP%;%AXIS_LIBS%\saaj.jar
set LCP=%LCP%;%AXIS_LIBS%\wsdl4j.jar

REM Xerces Parser
set LCP=%LCP%;%XERCES%

REM Add the app class files to the classpath
set LCP=%LCP%;%AXIS_SRC%

%JAVA% -cp %LCP% org.apache.axis.wsdl.Java2WSDL
  ➥-o %AXIS_SRC%\struts\ch19\customer\customer.wsdl
  ➥-l"http://localhost:8080/axis/services/Customer"
  ➥-n  "urn:Customer" -p"struts.ch19.customer" "urn:Customer"
  ➥struts.ch19.customer.CustomerWS
```

NOTE

This file is located in the `strutsWS` main directory (along with all the other command files for this chapter!). To run it, simply change to that directory and type its name.

Prior to running this file, you must edit it and modify the `JAVA_HOME` parameter to point to the JDK you're using.

Running this file batch file generates a WSDL file named `customer.wsdl` in the `strutsWS/src/struts/ch19/customer` directory. This file is shown in Listing 19.5.

LISTING 19.5 The `customer.wsdl` WSDL File

```
<?xml version="1.0" encoding="UTF-8"?>
<wsdl:definitions targetNamespace="urn:Customer"
 ➥xmlns="http://schemas.xmlsoap.org/wsdl/"
 ➥xmlns:apachesoap="http://xml.apache.org/xml-soap"
 ➥xmlns:impl="urn:Customer" xmlns:intf="urn:Customer"
 ➥xmlns:soapenc="http://schemas.xmlsoap.org/soap/encoding/"
 ➥xmlns:wsdl="http://schemas.xmlsoap.org/wsdl/"
 ➥xmlns:wsdlsoap="http://schemas.xmlsoap.org/wsdl/soap/"
 ➥xmlns:xsd="http://www.w3.org/2001/XMLSchema">
 <wsdl:types>
  <schema targetNamespace="urn:Customer" xmlns="http://www.w3.org/2001/XMLSchema">
   <import namespace="http://schemas.xmlsoap.org/soap/encoding/"/>
   <complexType name="CustomerWSValueObject">
    <sequence>
     <element name="address" nillable="true" type="xsd:string"/>
     <element name="name" nillable="true" type="xsd:string"/>
     <element name="zip" nillable="true" type="xsd:string"/>
     <element name="custId" nillable="true" type="xsd:string"/>
     <element name="state" nillable="true" type="xsd:string"/>
     <element name="city" nillable="true" type="xsd:string"/>
    </sequence>
   </complexType>
   <element name="CustomerWSValueObject" nillable="true"
    ➥type="impl:CustomerWSValueObject"/>
  </schema>
 </wsdl:types>
   <wsdl:message name="addressChangeResponse">
      <wsdl:part name="addressChangeReturn" type="intf:CustomerWSValueObject"/>
   </wsdl:message>
   <wsdl:message name="addressChangeRequest">
      <wsdl:part name="in0" type="intf:CustomerWSValueObject"/>
   </wsdl:message>
   <wsdl:portType name="CustomerWS">
      <wsdl:operation name="addressChange" parameterOrder="in0">
         <wsdl:input message="intf:addressChangeRequest"
            ➥name="addressChangeRequest"/>
         <wsdl:output message="intf:addressChangeResponse"
             ➥name="addressChangeResponse"/>
```

LISTING 19.5 Continued

```
      </wsdl:operation>
   </wsdl:portType>
   <wsdl:binding name="CustomerSoapBinding" type="intf:CustomerWS">
      <wsdlsoap:binding style="rpc"
        ➥transport="http://schemas.xmlsoap.org/soap/http"/>
      <wsdl:operation name="addressChange">
         <wsdlsoap:operation soapAction=""/>
         <wsdl:input name="addressChangeRequest">
            <wsdlsoap:body encodingStyle=
                   ➥"http://schemas.xmlsoap.org/soap/encoding/"
                   ➥namespace="urn:Customer" use="encoded"/>
         </wsdl:input>
         <wsdl:output name="addressChangeResponse">
            <wsdlsoap:body encodingStyle=
                   ➥"http://schemas.xmlsoap.org/soap/encoding/"
                   ➥namespace="urn:Customer" use="encoded"/>
         </wsdl:output>
      </wsdl:operation>
   </wsdl:binding>
   <wsdl:service name="CustomerWSService">
      <wsdl:port binding="intf:CustomerSoapBinding" name="Customer">
         <wsdlsoap:address location=
                   ➥"http://localhost:8080/axis/services/Customer"/>
      </wsdl:port>
   </wsdl:service>
</wsdl:definitions>
```

If you're not used to reading WSDL, don't worry about it for now. Two important parts are highlighted in **bold**. These pieces are repeated in XML fragments below as they're explained.

Here's the first XML fragment, which defines the value object:

```
<complexType name="CustomerWSValueObject">
  <sequence>
   <element name="address" nillable="true" type="xsd:string"/>
   <element name="name" nillable="true" type="xsd:string"/>
   <element name="zip" nillable="true" type="xsd:string"/>
   <element name="custId" nillable="true" type="xsd:string"/>
   <element name="state" nillable="true" type="xsd:string"/>
   <element name="city" nillable="true" type="xsd:string"/>
  </sequence>
</complexType>
```

As you can see, the WSDL created provides a language-independent description of the CustomerWSValueObject. Any other Web Services client could read this and understand how to deserialize the data, which is the key to Web Services interoperability, after all.

The next fragment to review is where the WSDL defines the operations that the Web Service supports:

```
<wsdl:message name="addressChangeResponse">
   <wsdl:part name="addressChangeReturn" type="intf:CustomerWSValueObject"/>
</wsdl:message>
<wsdl:message name="addressChangeRequest">
   <wsdl:part name="in0" type="intf:CustomerWSValueObject"/>
</wsdl:message>
<wsdl:portType name="CustomerWS">
   <wsdl:operation name="addressChange" parameterOrder="in0">
      <wsdl:input message="intf:addressChangeRequest"
         ➥name="addressChangeRequest"/>
      <wsdl:output message="intf:addressChangeResponse"
         ➥name="addressChangeResponse"/>
   </wsdl:operation>
</wsdl:portType>
```

This fragment identifies two types of elements: Two message elements and a single portType element. Although it might seem out of order, let's discuss the portType element first.

A portType defines a collection of operation elements. The portType defined here is named CustomerWS after the CustomerWS.java file that Java2WSDL was run against. Within the portType element are defined one or more operation elements that specify the operations that the Web Service supports. In this case, there's only a single operation, named addressChange. It also specifies that addressChange takes a single input parameter, in0. You'll see in a minute that in0 is a CustomerWSValueObject.

The message elements in this fragment provide definitions that are needed by the operation element that we just discussed. You can look at the fragment to see how this works: The message elements are defined and then the operation elements refer to them. In this case, two message elements define the input and output (or request and response) required by the addressChange operation. If you look at the part elements enclosed by each of the message elements, you'll see that the input and return parameters (named in0 and addressChangeReturn, respectively) are both of type CustomerWSValueObject.

To be honest, this is really all you need to know about WSDL for now. You can read the rest of the WSDL if you want, but it's not required to move forward with the sample application. The main thing to take away from this is to remember that WSDL provides an XML description of the Web Service that's language and platform independent.

Step 2: Generate the Web Service Client Code

The next step is to create the Java class files that are eventually incorporated into Struts to allow it to communicate with the Web Service server. Fortunately, Axis provides another utility to help with this.

The Axis `WSDL2Java` utility performs a transformation opposite to the one performed in the previous step 1. `WSDL2Java` takes the WSDL that was just created and uses it to generate a series of Java class files that can be used to communicate with the Web Service that the WSDL describes. (In addition to generating Java class files for use in communicating to a Web Service server, `WSDL2Java` can also generate the Java class files needed by the server, but that's skipping ahead to step 3!)

Another batch program is provided to assist you in running step 2. Listing 19.6 presents `StrutsCh19Step2.cmd`, a batch file that configures the environment that executes `WSDL2Java` to generate the code that runs in the Web Service client. For details about all the options for `Java2WSDL` and `WSDL2Java`, see the Reference Guide included in the Axis documentation.

LISTING 19.6 `StrutsCh19Step2.cmd` Creates Java Classes for Accessing the Web Service Server

```
@ECHO OFF

set JAVA_HOME=C:\jdk1.3.1_01
set JAVAC=%JAVA_HOME%\bin\javac.exe
set JAVA=%JAVA_HOME%\bin\java.exe
set AXIS_LIBS=.\axis\WEB-INF\lib
set XERCES=.\lib\xerces.jar
set AXIS_SRC=.\src

REM Build out the classpath
set LCP=.;%JAVA_HOME%\lib\tools.jar

REM Add Axis jars to the classpath
set LCP=%LCP%;%AXIS_LIBS%\axis.jar
set LCP=%LCP%;%AXIS_LIBS%\axis-ant.jar
set LCP=%LCP%;%AXIS_LIBS%\commons-discovery.jar
set LCP=%LCP%;%AXIS_LIBS%\commons-logging.jar
```

LISTING 19.6 Continued

```
set LCP=%LCP%;%AXIS_LIBS%\jaxrpc.jar
set LCP=%LCP%;%AXIS_LIBS%\log4j-1.2.4.jar
set LCP=%LCP%;%AXIS_LIBS%\saaj.jar
set LCP=%LCP%;%AXIS_LIBS%\wsdl4j.jar

REM Xerces Parser
set LCP=%LCP%;%XERCES%

REM Add the app class files to the classpath
set LCP=%LCP%;%AXIS_SRC%

%JAVA% -cp %LCP% org.apache.axis.wsdl.WSDL2Java -o %AXIS_SRC%
➥-p struts.ch19.customer.client customer.wsdl
```

NOTE

This file is located in the `strutsWS` main directory (along with all the other command files for this chapter!). To run it, simply change to that directory and type its name.

Prior to running this file, you must edit it and modify the `JAVA_HOME` parameter to point to the JDK you're using.

Running this file causes a number of Java source files to be created. Notice that the last command in the file specifies a package (`struts.ch19.customer.client`) that's different from the one in the initial `CustomerWS.java` and `CustomerWSValueObject.java` files (in case you don't remember, that was `struts.ch19.customer`). This is to make it easy to keep the files required for the Web Service client separate from all the other files. It also makes your code more organized and easier to understand.

Following is a list of these files with a short description of what each is used for:

- `CustomerWSValueObject.java`—A new version of the value object defined earlier. WSDL2Java creates its own version of this file that is a little more formal and predictable for the Axis code to use.
- `CustomerWS.java`—A new version of the `CustomerWS.java` Java interface that you began with. WSDL2Java creates its own version of this file as well.
- `CustomerWSServiceLocator.java`—This generated Java file is the one you use to get a handle to the actual Web Service. This class is the one used in the Struts application to locate the Web Service and allow you to communicate with it.

- CustomerWSService.java—An interface that extends the JAX-RPC Service interface (javax.xml.rpc.Service). According to Sun's Javadoc, the service interface "acts as a factory of the following: Dynamic proxy for the target service endpoint." In other words, you can use this as a factory class to create a JAX-RPC service object. Use of this class is beyond the scope of this example.
- CustomerSoapBindingStub.java—Handles some of the guts of the actual SOAP communications. Use of this class is beyond the scope of this example.

This step in the process was just to generate these files. Actually using them comes later, in step 5, when you integrate them into the sample Struts application.

Step 3: Generate the Web Service Server Code

Now that you've created the Web Service client code, it's time to generate the corresponding code to run on the Web Service server.

Why do you need to do this? Why can't the server just know how to accept all the data that you send it? The answer is really in two parts.

The first part of the answer goes back to the earlier discussion about serialization/deserialization and knowing what data types to expect. This is one of the fundamental issues with Web Services: The code running on the server has to know what kinds of arguments to accept and how to deserialize them into meaningful data again after it receives them. So, the first reason to generate the server code is to handle communication of the data.

The second reason is because the Web Service server code must provide you with a place to tie in to so that you can create a Web Service that actually does something. It also must connect the code where you tie in your business logic back to the portTypes and operations that the Web Service exposes to the client code.

Now that you have a basic idea of what must be done, here's how to do it. Listing 19.7 presents StrutsCh19Step3.cmd, a batch file that configures the environment that executes the WSDL2Java to generate the code that runs on your Web Service server. For details about all the options for Java2WSDL and WSDL2Java, see the Reference Guide included in the Axis documentation.

LISTING 19.7 StrutsCh19Step3.cmd Creates Java Classes for Use by the Web Service Server

```
@ECHO OFF

set JAVA_HOME=C:\jdk1.3.1_01
set JAVAC=%JAVA_HOME%\bin\javac.exe
set JAVA=%JAVA_HOME%\bin\java.exe
set AXIS_LIBS=.\axis\WEB-INF\lib
```

LISTING 19.7 Continued

```
set XERCES=.\lib\xerces.jar
set AXIS_SRC=.\src

REM Build out the classpath
set LCP=.;%JAVA_HOME%\lib\tools.jar

REM Add Axis jars to the classpath
set LCP=%LCP%;%AXIS_LIBS%\axis.jar
set LCP=%LCP%;%AXIS_LIBS%\axis-ant.jar
set LCP=%LCP%;%AXIS_LIBS%\commons-discovery.jar
set LCP=%LCP%;%AXIS_LIBS%\commons-logging.jar
set LCP=%LCP%;%AXIS_LIBS%\jaxrpc.jar
set LCP=%LCP%;%AXIS_LIBS%\log4j-1.2.4.jar
set LCP=%LCP%;%AXIS_LIBS%\saaj.jar
set LCP=%LCP%;%AXIS_LIBS%\wsdl4j.jar

REM Xerces Parser
set LCP=%LCP%;%XERCES%

REM Add the app class files to the classpath
set LCP=%LCP%;%AXIS_SRC%

%JAVA% -cp %LCP% org.apache.axis.wsdl.WSDL2Java -o %AXIS_SRC% -s -S true
➥ -p struts.ch19.customer.server customer.wsdl
```

NOTE

This file is located in the `strutsWS` main directory (along with all the other command files for this chapter). To run it, simply change to that directory and type its name.

Prior to running this file, you must edit it and modify the `JAVA_HOME` parameter to point to the JDK you're using.

Notice that the package (denoted by the `-p` option) is `struts.ch19.customer.server`. This makes it easier to isolate the files generated for the server.

Looking at the generated files, you can see that most of them are duplicates of the files that were generated for the client. Some of the files aren't used by the server, and some are. But it's best to deploy all the files with the server code just to be sure. The following are the four new files:

- `CustomerSoapBindingSkeleton.java`—This file coordinates low-level SOAP communications and is beyond the scope of this example.
- `CustomerSoapBindingImpl.java`—This is where you implement the Web Service server functionality. It's an empty implementation of the `CustomerWS.java` interface we started with. In this case, it contains a single method, `addressChange`, that you use to implement business logic to implement the address change function. You'll implement this functionality in step 5.
- `deploy.wsdd`—The Web Service Deployment Descriptor (hence, the `.wsdd` extension). Web Service files in Axis need deployment descriptors just as EJBs do in an EJB container.
- `undeploy.wsdd`—An undeploy descriptor. Use this when you need to remove a Web Service from Axis.

This step in the process was just to generate these files.

Step 4: Compile, Deploy, and Test the Web Service Server Code

Now that you've generated all the files, the next step is to compile everything and make sure that you can deploy the files into your Axis server and get them to run correctly.

Step 4 doesn't involve incorporating your Struts code or any code in the server that implements business logic. To begin, first make sure that you can deploy and access the Web Service. After that's done, you can move on to integrating your Struts code in Step 5.

To accomplish this build process, a `build.xml` Ant script has been provided. Assuming that you edited the `build.properties` file earlier in the chapter, you should be able to go ahead and just run the build process now.

To run the build, simply type **`ant deploy`**. You should see Ant compiling all the files and deploying two `.war` files—`strutsWS.war` and `axis.war`—into your Tomcat `webapps` directory.

The output from the build process is presented in Listing 19.8.

LISTING 19.8 Output from a Successful Ant Build Process

```
C:\dev\apps\strutsWS>ant deploy
Buildfile: build.xml

prepare:
     [echo] Tomcat Home  = c:/dev/tomcat
     [echo] webapps Home = c:\dev\tomcat\webapps
```

LISTING 19.8 Continued

```
compile:
    [javac] Compiling 13 source files to C:\dev\apps\strutsWS\object
     [copy] Copying 13 files to C:\dev\apps\strutsWS\src

build:
     [copy] Copying 13 files to C:\dev\apps\strutsWS\build\WEB-INF\classes
     [copy] Copying 8 files to C:\dev\apps\strutsWS\build\WEB-INF\lib
      [jar] Building jar: C:\dev\apps\strutsWS\deploy\strutsWS.war
     [copy] Copying 20 files to C:\dev\apps\strutsWS\axis\WEB-INF\classes
      [jar] Building jar: C:\dev\apps\strutsWS\deploy\axis.war

deploy:
     [copy] Copying 1 file to C:\dev\tomcat\webapps
     [copy] Copying 1 file to C:\dev\tomcat\webapps

BUILD SUCCESSFUL
Total time: 27 seconds
```

NOTE

The `build.xml` file is located in the `strutsWS` main directory (along with all the other command files for this chapter). To run it, simply change to that directory and type `ant deploy`.

Prior to running this file, you must edit the `build.properties` file and update it with the paths for your Tomcat home directory and your Tomcat `webapps` directory.

The output of the build process is two `.war` files (`axis.war` and `strutsWS.war`) that are copied into your Tomcat `webapps` directory.

Note that after the build process is complete, you might need to restart Tomcat to get the new `.war` files to deploy and run. In fact, some users have had to stop Tomcat, delete the existing `axis` and `strutsWS` subdirectories in their Tomcat `webapps` directory, and then restart to get the updated `.war` files to deploy.

After the build is complete, Tomcat is running, and the `.war` files have been successfully deployed in Tomcat, you're ready for the last major piece in step 4: deploying the files into the Axis server.

Deploying the Web Service is the process of registering it with the Web Service server and providing the details of how it should be accessed and how to process the data associated with it. When you ran `WSDL2Java` the last time, a deployment descriptor was generated and named `deploy.wsdd`. This file, which is located in the `strutsWS/src/struts/ch19/customer/server` directory, is presented in Listing 19.9.

LISTING 19.9 `deploy.wsdd`—The Web Service Deployment Descriptor for the CustomerWS Web Service

```
!-- Use this file to deploy some handlers/chains and services      -->
<!-- Two ways to do this:                                           -->
<!--   java org.apache.axis.client.AdminClient deploy.wsdd          -->
<!--      after the axis server is running                          -->
<!-- or                                                             -->
<!--   java org.apache.axis.utils.Admin client|server deploy.wsdd   -->
<!--      from the same directory that the Axis engine runs         -->

<deployment
    xmlns="http://xml.apache.org/axis/wsdd/"
    xmlns:java="http://xml.apache.org/axis/wsdd/providers/java">

  <!-- Services from CustomerWSService WSDL service -->

  <service name="Customer" provider="java:RPC">
      <parameter name="wsdlTargetNamespace" value="urn:Customer"/>
      <parameter name="wsdlServiceElement" value="CustomerWSService"/>
      <parameter name="wsdlServicePort" value="Customer"/>
      <parameter name="className"
       ➥ value="struts.ch19.customer.server.CustomerSoapBindingSkeleton"/>
      <parameter name="wsdlPortType" value="CustomerWS"/>
      <parameter name="allowedMethods" value="*"/>

      <typeMapping
        xmlns:ns="urn:Customer"
        qname="ns:CustomerWSValueObject"
        type="java:struts.ch19.customer.server.CustomerWSValueObject"
        serializer="org.apache.axis.encoding.ser.BeanSerializerFactory"
        deserializer="org.apache.axis.encoding.ser.BeanDeserializerFactory"
        encodingStyle="http://schemas.xmlsoap.org/soap/encoding/"
      />
  </service>
</deployment>
```

As you can see, the Web Service deployment descriptor provides the Web Service server with the details for how to expose the Web Service, including how it's to be addressed by the client and how the data is to be serialized and deserialized.

Note the `serializer` and `deserializer` attributes to the `typeMapping` element. These attributes reference the `BeanSerializerFactory` and `BeanDeserializerFactory` classes. These are classes that are Axis-specific and make it easy to send simple JavaBeans as parameters across an Axis-based Web Service. This support for serializing/deserializing JavaBeans is built into Axis and is one of the reasons for its popularity. They might not be recognizable by other Web service implementations, however, so they should be used with caution.

To perform the deployment, a command file is provided. This file is named `deployServer.cmd` and it's shown in Listing 19.10.

LISTING 19.10 `deployServer.cmd`—A Command File to Deploy the CustomerWS Web Service

```
@ECHO OFF

set JAVA_HOME=C:\jdk1.3.1_01
set JAVAC=%JAVA_HOME%\bin\javac.exe
set JAVA=%JAVA_HOME%\bin\java.exe
set AXIS_LIBS=.\axis\WEB-INF\lib
set XERCES=.\lib\xerces.jar
set AXIS_SRC=.\src

REM Build out the classpath
set LCP=.;%JAVA_HOME%\lib\tools.jar

REM Add Axis jars to the classpath
set LCP=%LCP%;%AXIS_LIBS%\axis.jar
set LCP=%LCP%;%AXIS_LIBS%\axis-ant.jar
set LCP=%LCP%;%AXIS_LIBS%\commons-discovery.jar
set LCP=%LCP%;%AXIS_LIBS%\commons-logging.jar
set LCP=%LCP%;%AXIS_LIBS%\jaxrpc.jar
set LCP=%LCP%;%AXIS_LIBS%\log4j-1.2.4.jar
set LCP=%LCP%;%AXIS_LIBS%\saaj.jar
set LCP=%LCP%;%AXIS_LIBS%\wsdl4j.jar

REM Xerces Parser
set LCP=%LCP%;%XERCES%

REM Add the app class files to the classpath
set LCP=%LCP%;%AXIS_SRC%

set ADMIN=org.apache.axis.client.AdminClient

%JAVA% -classpath %LCP% %ADMIN% %AXIS_SRC%\struts\ch19\customer\server\deploy.wsdd
```

NOTE

The `deployServer.cmd` file is located in the `strutsWS` main directory (along with all the other command files for this chapter). To run it, simply change to that directory and type `deployServer.cmd`.

Prior to running this file, you must make sure that Tomcat is running and that the `axis` and `strutsWS .war` files have been properly deployed.

You'll know the deployment went correctly if you see the results:

```
C:\dev\apps\strutsWS>deployserver
- Processing file .\src\struts\ch19\customer\server\deploy.wsdd
- <Admin>Done processing</Admin>
```

After the Web Service is deployed, you should verify that the Web Service server shows it to be available. With Axis, this is a simple task. Just point your browser to

```
http://localhost:8080/axis/index.html
```

This is the same main page you used earlier to access the Happy Axis! page. This time, choose the option to "View the list of deployed Web services." In it, you should see your deployed `Customer` service. This means the deployment worked correctly. Clicking on the "wsdl" link brings back the WSDL for the Web Service.

After you've validated that the `Customer` Web Service is correctly deployed to Axis, you're ready to move to the final step!

NOTE

If you don't see the service deployed, make sure that the `axis.war` file that the build process generated is loaded correctly. You might have to stop Tomcat, manually remove the `axis` directory from Tomcat's `webapps` directory, and then restart Tomcat.

Step 5: Integrating with Struts and Building the Business Logic on the Server

If the steps so far seemed complicated, they're really not that bad. After you get into development and go through this cycle a few times, the process goes much smoother. Almost everything you've done so far is the one-time setup and learning that enables you to get up and running.

So, now that you've deployed and tested your Web Service server code, it's time for the last step: Actually integrating the code into your Struts application.

There are two parts to performing the integration: integrating the Axis code with your Struts classes for the Web Service client code and adding business logic to the Web Services server classes. Let's start by integrating the Web Services code with the Struts code.

The design of the Struts sample application makes it easy to complete the integration. Here's a quick overview:

- The user enters her data and clicks the submit button.
- After the form is submitted, the data is populated into the form bean.
- The form bean is passed to the `Action` class.
- The `Action` class extracts the data from the form bean in the form of a value object (using the class `struts.ch19.customer.CustomerValueObject`).
- The `Action` class sends the value object to the Web Service using a facade class. The facade class returns an updated value object back to the `Action` class from the Web Service.
- All the code to communicate with the Axis server is hidden inside the facade class.

This design is identical to the design used to communicate with the JBoss EJB server in the previous chapter. In fact, virtually the only changes (other than changing the Java package names and a few of the actual Java class file names) are modifications to the facade class. Everything else is identical.

Speaking of changing Java package names, all the Struts code is in the package `struts.ch19.customer.struts`. This is parallel to the Axis client code in `struts.ch19.customer.client` and the Axis server code in `struts.ch19.customer.server`.

Before jumping into the facade class, it's good to review the `Action` class so that you can understand how the facade is used. Listing 19.11 presents the file `CustomerAction.java` file.

LISTING 19.11 `CustomerAction.java`—The `Action` Class for the Sample Struts/Axis Application

```
package struts.ch19.customer.struts;

import javax.servlet.http.HttpServletRequest;
import javax.servlet.http.HttpServletResponse;
import org.apache.struts.action.Action;
import org.apache.struts.action.ActionForm;
import org.apache.struts.action.ActionForward;
import org.apache.struts.action.ActionMapping;

import struts.ch19.customer.struts.CustomerValueObject;
```

LISTING 19.11 Continued

```
/**
 * Action class to demonstrate EJB Integration with Struts
 *
 * @author Kevin Bedell & James Turner
 * @version 1.0
 */

public class CustomerAction extends Action {


    /**
     * Update the customer's address.
     *
     * @param mapping The ActionMapping from this struts-config.xml entry
     * @param actionForm The ActionForm to process, if any
     * @param request The JSP request object
     * @param response The JSP response object
     *
     * @exception Exception if business logic throws an exception
     */
    public ActionForward execute(ActionMapping mapping,
                                 ActionForm form,
                                 HttpServletRequest request,
                                 HttpServletResponse response)
        throws Exception {

        /*
         * Cast the form bean to CustomerForm
         */
        CustomerForm cf = (CustomerForm) form;

        /*
         * Instantiate the facade - it hides the details
         * for us and simplifies the Action class.
         */
        CustomerWSFacade facade = new CustomerWSFacade();

        /*
         * The Value Object allows us to pass data "a bean at a time".
         * This increases speed, reduces maintenance and simplifies
         * tha Action class as well. Add methods to the form bean to
```

LISTING 19.11 Continued

```
         * allow it to work with Value Objects too.
         */
        CustomerValueObject cvo = cf.getValueObject();

        try {
          /*
           * Pass in a value object, and get one in return
           */
          cvo = facade.addressChange( cvo );
        } catch (CustomerUpdateException cue) {
          //  In a real application, this exception would be handled better.
          //  return (mapping.findForward("CustUpdateError"));
            cue.printStackTrace();
        }

        /*
         * Update the form bean with all values returned at once.
         */
        cf.setValueObject(cvo);

        return (mapping.findForward("default"));
    }
}
```

The critical things here to note are the use of the facade class and the value object. This approach simplifies the design of the `Action` class a great deal.

Also notice that the value object used in the `Action` class is the Axis-independent version. It's identical to the original value object we used with `Java2WSDL` to create the original WSDL way back in step 1. This was done to make sure that the value object was independent of Axis in case we want to switch to a new architecture later. (Don't worry, you'll see the `WSDL2Java`-generated value object later when we review the facade class.)

Now that you've reviewed the `Action` class, it's time to review the facade class and understand exactly how the Struts/Axis integration works. The facade class, `CustomerWSFacade.java`, is presented in Listing 19.12.

LISTING 19.12 `CustomerWSFacade.java`—The Facade That Actually Performs the Struts/Axis Integration

```
package struts.ch19.customer.struts;

import java.util.Properties;

import struts.ch19.customer.client.CustomerWS;
import struts.ch19.customer.client.CustomerWSServiceLocator;
import struts.ch19.customer.client.CustomerWSValueObject;

/**
 * Example facade which hides interactions with the back-end web service
 *
 * @author Kevin Bedell & James Turner
 * @version 1.0
 */
public class CustomerWSFacade {

  public CustomerWSFacade () { }

  /**
   *  This method sends the value object to the Web Service
   *  for it to process. It's goal is to hide the implementation
   *  details of interacting with the Web Service.<p>
   *
   *  Note that this method captures any Web Service related Exceptions
   *  and rethrows them as "application-specific" Exception
   *  (CustomerUpdateException). This helps to "decouple" the
   *  application from the web service backend.
   *
   * @param cvo_in
   * @return CustomerValueObject
   * @throws CustomerUpdateException
   */
  public CustomerValueObject addressChange( CustomerValueObject cvo_in )
  throws CustomerUpdateException

  {
      try {

          // Use the web service locator created by WSDL2Java
          CustomerWSServiceLocator servLoc = new CustomerWSServiceLocator();
```

LISTING 19.12 Continued

```
          CustomerWS custService = servLoc.getCustomer();

          // Create a WS value object - WS val obj is created by WSDL2Java
          CustomerWSValueObject wsCustVO = new CustomerWSValueObject();
          wsCustVO.setName(cvo_in.getName());
          wsCustVO.setCustId(cvo_in.getCustId());
          wsCustVO.setAddress(cvo_in.getAddress());
          wsCustVO.setCity(cvo_in.getCity());
          wsCustVO.setState(cvo_in.getState());
          wsCustVO.setZip(cvo_in.getZip());

          wsCustVO = custService.addressChange(wsCustVO);

          cvo_in.setName(wsCustVO.getName());
          cvo_in.setCustId(wsCustVO.getCustId());
          cvo_in.setAddress(wsCustVO.getAddress());
          cvo_in.setCity(wsCustVO.getCity());
          cvo_in.setState(wsCustVO.getState());
          cvo_in.setZip(wsCustVO.getZip());

          return cvo_in;

      } catch( Exception e ){
        throw new CustomerUpdateException(e.toString());
      }
   }
}
```

To summarize how the facade works, it follows this path:

- It first creates a service locator using the `WSDL2Java`-generated class `CustomerWSServiceLocator`, and then uses it to locate the `CustomerWS` Web Service.
- After it's obtained the `CustomerWS` interface to the Web Service, it creates a value object for use with the Web Service and copies properties into it from the value object it received from the `Action` class. (The reason there are two value objects is explained later.)
- It then calls the Web Service and invokes the `addressChange` operation. It passes a value object to the Web Service and receives an updated one in return.

- The updated value object it received from the Web Service has its properties copied into the value object that will be returned to the `Action` class.
- If any exceptions are caught, they're rethrown as the application-specific exception `CustomerUpdateException`. This ensures that the exception processing in the `Action` class doesn't have to handle any Web Service-specific exceptions. In this way the `Action` class doesn't know it's talking to a Web Service—it only knows about the facade!

The fact that two kinds of value objects are used warrants a bit further explanation. The two types of value objects are `struts.ch19.customer.struts.CustomerValueObject` and `struts.ch19.customer.client.CustomerWSValueObject`. These two objects are actually very similar, but there's a good reason for having two. The reason for using two similar value objects is that doing so allows the Struts application to be completely isolated from the Axis code. This ensures that as the Axis code is modified or completely removed, little or no maintenance is required in the `Action` class or anywhere else in the Struts application.

This is borne out by looking at the changes to the application from Chapter 18 to now. Because the application uses a facade class and a value object that's independent of the back-end system, the only thing that had to be done when the application changed from using JBoss to using Axis as its back-end server was to change the facade. Even the value object didn't have to change—it's still the same as it was previously.

The final thing we must do to finish the integration between Struts and the Axis Web Service is to tie in the business logic on the Web Service server. This is straightforward as well.

When the Axis `WSDL2Java` utility generated the Web Service server code back in step 3, it created an empty class for you to put your business logic in. The class's name is `CustomerSoapBindingImpl.java`.

To demonstrate this, we'll use a before-and-after approach. First you'll be shown the file just as the `WSDL2Java` utility created it, and then you'll be shown the same file with the business logic code inserted.

Listing 19.13 contains the `CustomerSoapBindingImpl.java` file just as it was generated by the `WSDL2Java` utility.

LISTING 19.13 `CustomerSoapBindingImpl.java` as It Was Created by `WSDL2Java`

```
/**
 * CustomerSoapBindingImpl.java
 *
 * This file was auto-generated from WSDL
 * by the Apache Axis WSDL2Java emitter.
 */

package struts.ch19.customer.server;

public class CustomerSoapBindingImpl implements
➥struts.ch19.customer.server.CustomerWS{
    public struts.ch19.customer.server.CustomerWSValueObject
addressChange(struts.ch19.customer.server.CustomerWSValueObject in0)
➥throws java.rmi.RemoteException {
        return null;
    }
}
```

As you can see, there's not much there. It's just a stub class that returns a `null`. Listing 19.14 presents the same file after the business logic for this application has been added.

LISTING 19.14 `CustomerSoapBindingImpl.java` with Business Logic Added

```
/**
 * CustomerSoapBindingImpl.java
 *
 * This file was auto-generated from WSDL
 * by the Apache Axis WSDL2Java emitter.
 *
 * Following being automatically created by the Apache Axis WSDL2Java emitter,
 * it was modified with the actual web service business logic required.
 */

package struts.ch19.customer.server;

import java.util.Random;

public class CustomerSoapBindingImpl
➥ implements struts.ch19.customer.server.CustomerWS {
```

LISTING 19.14 Continued

```
    public struts.ch19.customer.server.CustomerWSValueObject
➥addressChange(struts.ch19.customer.server.CustomerWSValueObject in0)
➥ throws java.rmi.RemoteException {

        Random r = new Random();

        switch (r.nextInt(3)) {

            case 0:
              in0.setAddress("Downing Street");
              break;
            case 1:
              in0.setAddress("Via Del Museo De Prado");
              break;
            case 2:
              in0.setAddress("The Outback Road");
              break;

        }

        /*
         *  This allows watching activity in the Tomcat window (if one exists)
         */
        System.out.println( "CustomerSoapBindingImpl.addressChange() called." +
                            " Set address to: " + in0.getAddress() );

        return in0;

    }

}
```

You can see that some simple logic was added to Listing 19.14 just to send back a random address and print a message to the standard output when the method was called. In practice, you'd more likely build the business logic in some other class and have this class simply parse the input parameters and then call other classes that would perform the actual work.

After you have modified this class with the preceding lines, re-run the Ant build process to deploy the new code to Tomcat. You might have to restart Tomcat again before testing the application.

After this final step is complete, you should be able to point your browser to the address `http://localhost:8080/strutsWS/Customer.do` to test the final application.

NOTE

If you run into problems at this point, it may be useful to try the following:

- Verify that the Web Service is deployed by pointing your browser to `http://localhost:8080/axis/index.html` and viewing the installed services.
- Try stopping Tomcat, deleting one or both of the `axis` and `strutsWS` subdirectories in the Tomcat `webapps` directory, and then restarting Tomcat.

Conclusions

This chapter presented a detailed analysis and sample application to demonstrate integrating Struts with a Web Services application.

Among the important points of the chapter were

- Web Services fit with Struts Model components. That is, they should be called from the Struts `Action` class and likely represent an interface to some data or business logic in a remote system.
- Web Services are a technology based on communication and encoding of data in XML. The SOAP protocol is used for communications of data.
- Serializing data is the process of converting data in your program into an XML representation that's independent of any particular computer language or platform. Deserialization is the opposite: It's the process of taking data in an XML format and converting it into a format useful for your program to use.
- Axis is a Java-based Web Service framework and SOAP engine. It's open source and developed under the umbrella of the Apache XML Project. Its home page is `http://xml.apache.org/axis`.
- Java2WSDL and WSDL2Java are two utilities made available as part of Axis that provide significant support in terms of automating the development of Web Services applications using Axis.
- By utilizing a Struts application design based on the use of value objects to carry data one bean at a time and also the use of a facade class to isolate the `Action` class from the details of the actual Web Services communications, it's possible to greatly simplify the development and maintenance of Struts applications based on Web Services.

20

Building, Deploying, and Testing Struts Applications

IN THIS CHAPTER

- An Integrated and Incremental Build/Test Cycle: It's Extreme!
- Building and Deploying Struts Applications Using Jakarta Ant
- Developing a `build.xml` File for Building Struts Applications Using Ant
- Extreme Struts Development with Integrated and Ongoing Testing
- Mock Object Testing Using JUnit, StrutsTestCase, and Ant
- In-Container Testing Using Cactus, JUnit, StrutsTestCase, and Ant
- Conclusions

Beginning with Apache Tomcat and continuing through today, The Jakarta Project has provided an astonishing array of open source, no-charge applications for the Java platform. Its impact on software development has been amazing. At last count, there are nearly 25 subprojects operating under The Jakarta Project, including Struts, Tomcat, Log4J, and many others.

One of the biggest impacts that The Jakarta Project has had on developers has been by providing tools to make their jobs easier. With those tools has come a series of best practices for development.

In this chapter, you're introduced to a process for building, deploying, and testing applications that has evolved through use on numerous Jakarta projects. This development process involves using the Ant build tool and incorporating incremental and ongoing testing using JUnit and the Cactus Framework.

An Integrated and Incremental Build/Test Cycle: It's Extreme!

The fundamental principles involved here are simple and intuitive. And, amazingly, they work *extreme*ly well!

In case you haven't picked it up by now, the *extreme* references have to do with Extreme Programming (XP), a style of programming that was developed in the mid-1990s. XP stresses simplicity of design, frequent small releases, aggressively creating opportunities for communications, and—in case you wondered when this section would discuss it—testing.

XP tells you to test early and test often. In XP, it's not considered to be too early if you write the unit test even before you write the code!

This chapter isn't about XP or development methodologies. But the integrated build/deploy/test cycle that this chapter introduces is a big part of XP.

It's also important to know that these features weren't adopted because various Jakarta subprojects decided they want to "go XP." These approaches were developed and polished by teams of developers constantly looking for new and better ways to work together. The fact that the end result has characteristics of XP is really just a validation that those features of XP are useful.

To summarize: This chapter covers a build/deploy/test process that's used on a number of Jakarta subprojects and incorporates some elements of Extreme Programming. These processes involve using open source tools that have been developed and polished for just this purpose.

FOR MORE ABOUT EXTREME PROGRAMMING

Extreme Programming is a popular and spreading approach to software development. If you haven't been exposed to it, it's worth your time to learn more about it. Adopting just some of its processes can be useful.

A good place to begin would be at one of the many Web sites devoted to it. Two sites that we can recommend are

A Gentle Introduction to Extreme Programming at

```
http://www.extremeprogramming.org
```

and The Extreme Programming Roadmap at

```
http://c2.com/cgi/wiki?ExtremeProgrammingRoadmap
```

Sams Publishing has also recently released what looks to be a good book on this topic: *Sams Teach Yourself Extreme Programming in 24 Hours* (ISBN:0672324415) by Stewart Baird.

Building and Deploying Struts Applications Using Jakarta Ant

You might have been using Ant all through the book. At least a few previous chapters came with Ant build files. But we felt it was important to dedicate some space to Ant directly because of its importance and because many readers probably haven't used it to a great extent.

In this section, you revisit the original Hello World application from back in Chapter 3. It's a simple, basic application and is just right for demonstrating the process of creating an Ant build file.

To begin with, you need two directory structures. The first is the development structure where the files are kept while you're working on them. The second directory structure is the one you have to deploy the application into after you compile your code. Both are described in the next sections.

A Recommended Directory Structure for Development

How you structure your files during development is many times a personal thing. But after you standardize on a build process, everyone has to do things the same way for the build files to work. There are many different ways you could store your files during development, and each of them has its own benefits and drawbacks. The directory structure used in this chapter is

```
app.home --+                    - Top level directory
           |
           +-- build            - Top of build/assemble area
           |
           +-- deploy           - Generate the WAR file into here
           |
           +-- doc              - Javadoc is generated below here
           |
           +-- lib              - Store all JARs and so on here
           |
           +-- object           - Holds compiled .class files
           |
           +-- src              - Java source top directory
           |
           +-- web              - Top of your JSP directory
                  |
                 +--WEB-INF     - web.xml, struts-config.xml, tld
```

Here's a list of what each is used for and what generally goes in each directory:

- `app.home`—The top of the development directory tree. For this application, the only files in this directory are the `build.xml` file (the default Ant build file) and the `build.properties` file (which contains properties that are specific to this particular host). We'll talk more about these files later.

- `build`—This directory is the place you build the WAR file in preparing it for deployment. Beneath it is built a direct image of what must go in the WAR file (which is discussed in more detail in the next section). Between builds, this entire directory may be deleted and rebuilt from scratch.

- `deploy`—This directory contains nothing except those files that will be physically deployed to the server to be run. For this application, this is a single file: `strutsANT.war`.
- `doc`—This file contains the Javadoc for the application when it's generated. Other project documentation may optionally be maintained in this directory.
- `lib`—This directory holds all the `.jar` files and other library files. All these files are later copied into the build directory for inclusion in the `strutsANT.war` file.
- `src`—This is the top of the source directory where all your source code goes. We recommend that you manage check-in/check-out to and from source control from within this directory. In addition to all Java source files, any other files that must be placed somewhere on the classpath (for example, `.properties` files) should be placed here as well.
- `web`—The top of your Web application (`.jsp` files, images, and so on) directory.
- `WEB-INF`—The `web.xml`, `struts-config.xml`, and all Struts and other JSP custom tag library files (`tld` files) reside here.

The following section discusses the structure of the Web application that the build process must create.

The Required Directory Structure for the Deployed Application (and `.war` File)

The structure of a Web application (Web app) is governed by the Java Servlet specifications (which can be reviewed via the Java Community Process site at `http://www.jcp.org/jsr/detail/53.jsp`).

The directory structure required for a Web app is

```
/ --+                          - Web app (JSP) root directory
    |
    +-- META-INF               - Holds the Manifest.mf file
    |
    +-- WEB-INF                - web.xml, struts-config.xml, tld
          |
          +-- lib              - Store all jars, etc here
          |
          +-- classes          - Holds compiled .class files
```

Here's a list of what each is used for and what generally goes in each directory:

- `/`—The top of the Web app directory tree. If you have an `index.jsp` file, it goes here. You'll generally have subdirectories below here for other `.jsp` files, images, and so on.

- META-INF—This directory holds the manifest file, Manifest.mf. The manifest file is generated automatically by Ant.
- WEB-INF—This directory holds the web.xml file, which is the deployment descriptor for the Web app itself. It also holds all TLD files for the Struts and other tag libraries as well as the struts-config.xml configuration file.
- lib—This holds library files (.jar files) that are specific to this particular application.
- classes—This is the top-level directory for all your compiled .class files. As mentioned previously, any of your applications .properties or other files that must be on your classpath must go in this directory structure as well.

This directory structure (except for the META-INF directory, which is created by the ant <war> task) is created in your development area (in the build section) by the Ant build script, and then compressed into the Web archive (.war) file for deployment.

WORKING WITH .WAR FILES

When working with .war files, it's useful to know that they can be treated like .jar files with a different file extension.

To view the contents of a .war file, you can use the jar utility. For example, the command

```
jar tvf strutsANT.war
```

displays the contents of the strutsANT.war file.

Alternatively, you can open, view, and update .war files using the WinZip compression utility. Simply open them as you would any .zip file.

Developing a build.xml File for Building Struts Applications Using Ant

This section is based on the strutsANT.zip file that's included on the CD-ROM accompanying this book. Other sections of this chapter use different archives.

A good Ant build file enables you to build as much or as little of the application as you want. It also lets you pick up where you left off without repeating steps. And—if you want to—it should let you delete everything (hopefully except your source files!) and start over from scratch.

In reality, Ant build files can be created to do virtually anything you can write a program for. People all over the world have added tasks to Ant to do anything that's commonly needed. If all else fails, Ant is completely extendable by using Java to write your own tasks.

This chapter, however, sticks with the basics of how to build a Struts application. Listing 20.1 is the build file used in this sample application. Don't worry about understanding every line right now; each part of it is explained as you progress through this section. The name of the build file is `build.xml` because this is the default name that Ant looks for if you just type **`ant`** without specifying a particular build file by name.

LISTING 20.1 The Ant Build File for the Hello World! Sample Application (`build.xml`)

```
<project name="billing" default="help" basedir=".">

<!-- ===================== Property Definitions ========================== -->

    <!--
         All properties should be defined in this section.
         Any host-specific properties should be defined
         in the build.properties file.

         In this app, the following properties are defined in build.properties:

        o  tomcat.home      - the home directory of your Tomcat installation
        o  webapps.home     - the place to copy the war file to deploy it
    -->

  <property file="build.properties" />

  <property name="app.home"          value="." />
  <property name="app.name"          value="strutsANT" />
  <property name="javadoc.pkg.top"   value="ch20" />

  <property name="src.home"          value="${app.home}/src"/>
  <property name="lib.home"          value="${app.home}/lib"/>
  <property name="object.home"       value="${app.home}/object"/>
  <property name="deploy.home"       value="${app.home}/deploy"/>
  <property name="doc.home"          value="${app.home}/doc"/>
  <property name="web.home"          value="${app.home}/web"/>

  <property name="build.home"        value="${app.home}/build"/>
  <property name="build.classes"     value="${build.home}/WEB-INF/classes"/>
  <property name="build.lib"         value="${build.home}/WEB-INF/lib"/>
```

LISTING 20.1 Continued

```
<!-- ==================== Compilation Classpath =========================== -->

    <!--
         This section creates the classpath for compilation.
    -->

  <path id="compile.classpath">

    <!-- The object files for this application -->
    <pathelement location="${object.home}"/>

    <!-- The lib files for this application -->
    <fileset dir="${lib.home}">
      <include name="*.jar"/>
      <include name="*.zip"/>
    </fileset>

    <!-- All files/jars that Tomcat makes available -->
    <fileset dir="${tomcat.home}/lib">
      <include name="*.jar"/>
    </fileset>
    <fileset dir="${tomcat.home}/common/lib">
      <include name="*.jar"/>
    </fileset>
    <pathelement location="${tomcat.home}/classes"/>
    <pathelement location="${tomcat.home}/common/classes"/>

  </path>


<!-- ==================== Build Targets below here========================= -->


<!-- ==================== "help" Target =================================== -->

    <!--
         This is the default ant target executed if no target is specified.
         This helps avoid users just typing 'ant' and running a
         default target that may not do what they are anticipating...
    -->
```

LISTING 20.1 Continued

```
<target name="help" >
  <echo message="Please specify a target! [usage: ant &lt;targetname&gt;]" />
  <echo message="Here is a list of possible targets: "/>
  <echo message="  clean-all.....Delete build dir, all .class and war files"/>
  <echo message="  prepare.......Creates directories if required" />
  <echo message="  compile.......Compiles source files" />
  <echo message="  build.........Build war file from .class and other files"/>
  <echo message="  deploy........Copy war file to the webapps directory" />
  <echo message="  javadoc.......Generates javadoc for this application" />
</target>

<!-- ==================== "clean-all" Target ============================== -->

   <!--
         This target should clean up any traces of the application
         so that if you run a new build directly after cleaning, all
         files will be replaced with what's current in source control
   -->

 <target name="clean-all" >
   <delete dir="${build.home}"/>
   <delete dir="${object.home}"/>
   <delete dir="${deploy.home}"/>

   <!-- can't delete directory if Tomcat is running -->
   <delete dir="${webapps.home}/${app.name}" failonerror="false"/>

   <!-- deleting the deployed .war file is fine even if Tomcat is running -->
   <delete dir="${webapps.home}/${app.name}.war" />

   <!-- delete the javadoc -->
   <delete dir="${doc.home}"/>

 </target>

<!-- ==================== "prepare" Target ================================ -->

   <!--
         This target is executed prior to any of the later targets
         to make sure the directories exist. It only creates them
         if they need to be created....
```

LISTING 20.1 Continued

```
        Other, similar, preparation steps can be placed here.
   -->

  <target name="prepare">

    <echo message="Tomcat Home  = ${tomcat.home}" />
    <echo message="webapps Home = ${webapps.home}" />

    <mkdir  dir="${object.home}"/>
    <mkdir  dir="${deploy.home}"/>

    <mkdir  dir="${doc.home}"/>
    <mkdir  dir="${doc.home}/api"/>

    <mkdir dir="${build.home}"/>
    <mkdir dir="${build.home}/WEB-INF" />
    <mkdir dir="${build.home}/WEB-INF/classes" />
    <mkdir dir="${build.home}/WEB-INF/lib" />

  </target>

<!-- ==================== "compile" Target ================================ -->

    <!--
        This only compiles java files that are newer
        than their corresponding .class files.
     -->

  <target name="compile" depends="prepare"  >
    <javac srcdir="${src.home}" destdir="${object.home}"  debug="yes" >
        <classpath refid="compile.classpath"/>
    </javac>
  </target>

<!-- ==================== "build" Target ================================== -->

    <!--
        This target builds the war file for the application
        by first building the directory structure of the
        application in ${build.home} and then creating the
        war file using the ant <war> task
```

LISTING 20.1 Continued

```
    -->

  <target name="build" depends="compile" >

    <!-- Copy all the webapp content (jsp's, html, tld's, xml, etc. -->
    <!-- Note that this also copies the META-INF directory -->
    <copy    todir="${build.home}">
      <fileset dir="${web.home}"/>
    </copy>

    <!-- Now, copy all the Java class files -->
    <copy    todir="${build.home}/WEB-INF/classes">
      <fileset dir="${object.home}"/>
    </copy>

    <!-- Now, copy all the properties files, etc that go on the classpath -->
    <copy    todir="${build.home}/WEB-INF/classes">
      <fileset dir="${src.home}">
         <include name="**/*.properties" />
         <include name="**/*.prop" />
      </fileset>
    </copy>

    <!-- Now, copy all the jar files we need -->
    <copy    todir="${build.home}/WEB-INF/lib">
      <fileset dir="${lib.home}" />
    </copy>

    <!-- Create the <war> file -->
    <jar jarfile="${deploy.home}/${app.name}.war"
         basedir="${build.home}"/>

  </target>

<!-- ==================== "deploy" Target ================================ -->

    <!--
         This target simply copies the war file from the deploy
         directory into the Tomcat webapp directory.
    -->
```

LISTING 20.1 Continued

```
  <target name="deploy" depends="build" >

    <!-- Copy the contents of the build directory -->
    <copy todir="${webapps.home}"  file="${deploy.home}/${app.name}.war" />

  </target>

<!-- =================== "doc" Target ==================================== -->

    <!--
         This task creates javadoc. It is dependent upon only the
         'compile' target so it is not executed in a normal build.
         As a result, the target needs to be run on its own.
    -->

  <target name="javadoc" depends="compile">
      <javadoc sourcepath = "${src.home}"
                  destdir = "${doc.home}/api"
             packagenames = "${javadoc.pkg.top}.*"/>
  </target>

</project>
```

The following items summarize each section of the build.xml file:

- **Property definitions**—To make build files more flexible, it's customary to define all directories using properties; for example, src.home. The value of src.home is then retrieved later using the notation ${src.home}. In addition, properties can be read in from a file. The approach demonstrated here is to have the build file contain only *relative* directory references and have any host-specific or hard-coded directory parameters read in from a file. An example of a property that isn't an alias for a directory is app.name, which is the name of the Web app this file builds. Also, remember these properties can't be changed after they're set; Ant doesn't provide variables.
- **Compilation classpath**—Classpaths are built in Ant using <classpath> elements in the build file. This <classpath> definition demonstrates a number of ways of adding elements to the classpath for compiling.
- **Build Targets section**—Ant runs by building targets. All targets in the file are defined below this section. Ant builds a target by executing the tasks within the target. Targets are built in order based on the depends attribute of the

target: Ant traces back through the `depends` attributes of every target and then builds all the targets in the correct order (more on this in the following items).

- **`help` target**—This is the default target for the build file; that is, the target that's executed if no specific target is given on the command line when you run Ant. All this target does is print out the available targets in the build file. This is recommended because it's common for people to simply type **`ant`** at the command line without thinking, and execute whatever the default target is (even if the default target deletes everything and initiates a total rebuild from scratch). This way, it requires the person to indicate on the command line the specific target to be built.
- **`clean-all` target**—This target is executed if you want to remove all `.class` and archive files and initiate a complete rebuild from scratch. An alternative approach is to define multiple clean targets (`clean-object`, `clean-archives`, `clean-source`, and so on) and then have the `clean-all` target simply refer to each of them in its `depends` attribute. This enables you to either selectively clean individual targets or clean everything at once.
- **`prepare` target**—This target performs steps to initialize the build process, including creating any directories that may have been removed by the `clean-all` target. It's best to consolidate all directory creation activities to this section because doing so simplifies maintenance and reduces errors that can creep into the build process over time.
- **`compile` target**—This target compiles all Java files. Note that as with many Ant tasks, the `<javac>` task performs its operations conditionally; it compiles only Java files that need it. Ant compiles a Java file only if there is no class file for it already or if the timestamp on the Java file is newer than the timestamp on the `.class` file (that is, the class file is out of date).
- **`build` target**—This target assembles everything into a build directory in the structure required to build the WAR file for deployment. After everything is copied, it executes the `<jar>` task to create a `.war` file archive for deployment. (There also exists an Ant `<war>` task for this purpose—either approach works.)
- **`deploy` target**—This target simply takes the WAR file created by the build target and copies it to the `webapps` directory of your application server to deploy it. If your application server runs on a different host than the one you perform your builds on, the Ant `<ftp>` task might be useful for you to perform deployments with.
- **`doc` target**—This target builds the documentation for this application. Although for this sample application this consists of generating Javadoc for the application, it's also common to generate other documentation as well. For example, the Ant `<style>` task is often used with XML and XSL files to generate HTML-based docs for an online reference to the application.

Now that you've got a directory structure for developing your application and an Ant build file for building and compiling, it's time to focus on the more "extreme" elements of this chapter: how to make integrated and ongoing testing a part of your everyday development cycle.

Extreme Struts Development with Integrated and Ongoing Testing

Integrating ongoing testing into your development environment doesn't mean you're practicing XP; but on the other hand, you can't practice XP without it. In fact, the approach of integrating ongoing testing into your development process is one of the aspects of XP that's been most widely adopted in mainstream development—even in shops that would never fully embrace XP completely. This adoption has occurred for good reason: It results in better quality code, reduces rework, and helps isolate bugs faster. So, let's get into it.

An Overview of Testing Approaches and Tools

One of the big problems in testing programs that use application servers is that so much of their functionality comes from services the container provides. Put another way, how do you test a Struts `Action` class without actually deploying it and using a browser to test the pages yourself?

There are two ways people solve this problem. The first is to write code that pretends to be an application server and sets up request/response objects and so on to run your code and test it. This is referred to as *mock testing*. (It's also called m*ock object testing* because you have to create mock objects to do it.) This can get complicated, and it's really only a substitute for testing in the container anyway. Just because you pass the tests using mock objects doesn't mean your code is guaranteed to run in the Web container.

The other way this problem can be solved is to do what's referred to as *in-container testing*, or testing your code after it's actually deployed in the container. The challenge with this is writing class-level unit tests and running them in the container. For example, how can you easily test every validation your Struts form bean performs without going to a browser screen and trying to enter every combination of bad data you test for?

Fortunately, the open source developers who came before you have addressed these problems. The options you'll see in this chapter for performing exactly these types of testing are pretty impressive. They're impressive both because of the effort that went into building them and for how amazingly easy they are to use.

The next sections review the tools you'll use for testing and how they work together. Following that you'll set up and run both mock object and in-container tests on the Hello World application you just finished building the Ant script for. You'll also integrate the tests directly into the Ant script so that they can be executed every time you do a build—this is how you build quality directly into your development process. Now that's extreme!

JUnit: The Engine That Drives Ongoing Testing

JUnit is an open source project for software testing developed originally by Erich Gamma and Kent Beck. It's maintained at SourceForge at `http://sourceforge.net/projects/junit` and, in addition, has its own Web site at `http://www.junit.org`. JUnit was developed to provide a simple framework for collecting and performing unit tests on Java code. It's a solid, mature product and is in widespread use.

JUnit has grown into much wider use since the development of Ant tasks that allow JUnit testing to be incorporated directly into Ant build files. Many JUnit users have never seen the original GUI that was delivered with JUnit—they simply write JUnit tests and check them in so that they are run as part of the ongoing build process. This is how the tests developed in this chapter are run.

Honestly, learning much more about JUnit is beyond the scope of this chapter. Because all the tests you create use JUnit under the covers, there's really no need at this point to go into much more detail on JUnit itself.

If you're interested in learning more about JUnit, we recommend that you review the documentation on its site, beginning with the essay, "Test Infected: Programmers Love Writing Tests."

Cactus: A Framework for In-Container Testing

Cactus is a subproject of The Jakarta Project (just as Struts is). Its purpose is to provide a framework for in-container testing. The Cactus project home page is at `http://jakarta.apache.org/cactus`.

This chapter covers both the in-container and mock object approaches to testing; Cactus is used only in the in-container portions of the chapter. You'll actually use an extension to JUnit that enables you to run Cactus tests from JUnit (which means they can be integrated as JUnit tests directly into the Ant build file).

You'll get into Cactus more deeply in later sections of this chapter when you actually write and run in-container tests for the Hello World application. It's important, however, at this point to introduce it and let you know where it fits in the overall picture.

StrutsTestCase: A JUnit Extension for Testing Struts Applications

StrutsTestCase is an extension of JUnit that enables you to easily build JUnit-based test cases using both mock object and in-container testing for Struts applications. StrutsTestCase is hosted at SourceForge (at `http://sourceforge.net/projects/strutstestcase`) and is distributed under an open source license.

StrutsTestCase was developed specifically to provide developers the ability to develop JUnit-based tests for Struts applications. It implements a series of classes that allow for mock object testing of Struts applications. In addition, it provides the ability to implement the same functionality using in-container testing with Cactus.

A copy of StrutsTestCase is provided on the CD-ROM accompanying this book (in addition to versions of Ant, Cactus, JUnit, and the other packages required for this chapter).

Before diving into the details of configuring your system to allow you to run all this software, let's begin by first writing a test case using StrutsTestCase.

Mock Object Testing Using JUnit, StrutsTestCase, and Ant

This section is based on the `strutsJUNIT.zip` file that's included on the CD-ROM that accompanies this book. Other sections of this chapter use different archives.

The first test you create is a simple mock object test for the Hello World application.

How do you know where to begin and what to test? The easiest way is to look at the code you need to test and just start there. To begin, here's a snippet from the `HelloAction.java` file:

```
// If this is first time, go straight to page
        String action = request.getParameter("action");
        if (action == null) {
            return (mapping.findForward("SayHello"));
        }
```

This code snippet is near the beginning of the `execute` method in the `HelloAction` class. This code implements the logic that if no request parameter with the name `action` exists, the `Action` class should forward processing to the `ActionForward` defined in the `struts-config.xml` file as `SayHello`.

Given that this is a piece of conditional logic that requires processing to continue one of two different ways depending on some condition, this is an ideal candidate for testing. Listing 20.2 is the test case to test it.

LISTING 20.2 `TestHelloAction.java`—A Test Case for Testing the Hello World Struts Application

```
package ch20.hello.mocktest;

import servletunit.struts.MockStrutsTestCase;

public class TestHelloAction extends MockStrutsTestCase {

    public TestHelloAction(String testName) { super(testName); }

    public void testNoParameters() {

        setRequestPathInfo("/HelloWorld");
        actionPerform();
        verifyForward("SayHello");
    }
}
```

The following are some general observations on this class:

- It's very short. Considering the overall complexity of what's going on, the developers of the StrutsTestCase testing framework have done an excellent job of simplifying the development of test cases for Struts applications.
- The test case simply sets a request path (`/HelloWorld`) that the mock objects should test, and then runs the core Struts `Action` servlet. This invokes Struts, which chooses the appropriate `Action` class based on the entries in your `struts-config.xml` file.
- Setting up request parameters is done using the `addRequestParameter(`*`name`*`,` *`value`*`)` method. As you can see from the listing, no request parameters were set up prior to invoking `actionPerform`. This tells the mock objects to test processing when no request parameters are present. (Other tests are done later in the chapter that demonstrate how to set request parameters correctly.)
- Invoking the `actionPerform` method causes form bean processing to be performed exactly as it would be if you actually were running Struts. The form bean is populated the same way and the `validate` method is called if your `struts-config.xml` indicates it should be.
- All processing after the `actionPerform` statement is for checking results. This is how you test whether the test ran correctly. This test case tests to make sure that the `Action` class sends processing to the `SayHello ActionForward`.

In English, this test case says, "Test whichever `Action` class is invoked when the path `/HelloWorld.do` is requested. Assume that no request parameters are set. Make sure that after processing is complete, the `Action` class forwards to the `SayHello` `ActionForward`."

Configuring Your System to Run the Mock Object Tests

A number of different configuration steps are required for this testing to work correctly. Ant, Cactus, JUnit, and StrutsTestCase must all be installed and/or have their configurations set.

Given the number of packages involved—not to mention Struts and the other packages you've likely already installed—there's ample room for configuration problems here. In fact, we found this to be one of the more challenging chapters in terms of overall configuration.

To address this, we've included working versions of the sample applications in this chapter on the companion CD-ROM for this book. You might be able to get the applications working on your own just by getting the latest versions of all the packages in use here and configuring them according to their instructions. However, if you have trouble, we advise you to use the versions that we supply. They've all been tested by at least two different people to make sure they work.

Configuring Ant for the Mock Object Testing

Your Ant installation must be updated before these tests can be run. That's because the JUnit code is not part of the standard Ant installation.

The easiest approach to upgrading your Ant installation is to use the version that comes on the companion CD-ROM to this book. It's a release of Ant that was put together by the Jakarta Cactus project team. It's actually just a standard release of version 1.5 of Ant, but it comes with all the libraries installed in the correct versions to enable you to run JUnit, Cactus, and so on with no problems.

This approach also has the impact of upgrading your Ant installation to be able to run the in-container testing that comes later in the chapter.

If you choose another route to upgrading, we recommend you refer to the documentation for Ant, JUnit, Cactus, and StrutsTestCase. (As much as we'd like to provide you configuration instructions for your exact environment, it's really impossible.) Generally, the steps include installing the Ant optional task library along with the supporting library files required by the JUnit and Cactus code. The specific library files you need might change depending on the versions of each of these applications you're using.

Adding the Required Libraries to Your Struts Application

Because you'll be adding test cases to the Hello World Struts application, you must add several JAR files to the application to support them. Specifically, these are

- **strutstest.jar**—The StrutsTestCase library file included on the companion CD-ROM.
- **junit-3.7.jar**—This is the version of JUnit that StrutsTestCase extends. It's also included on the CD-ROM.
- **servlet.jar**—Required because StrutsTestCase generates mock objects that impersonate a servlet container. This file comes with Tomcat and is located in the `/common/lib` subdirectory under your Tomcat home directory. This library must be copied to the `${lib.home}` directory to make it available at compile time.

The files must be copied to the directory identified by Ant as the `${lib.home}` for the build process. This ensures that the build process puts them into the `.war` file for the Web app.

Adding the Test Case to the Application and Modifying the Build File

Now that you have Ant itself configured and all the libraries in place, you're almost ready to run the tests. All you have to do is add the Java file for the test case to your source path and then modify your `build.xml` file to execute it.

The Java file for the test case contained the `package` statement:

```
package ch20.hello.mocktest;
```

Putting the test case Java files in a test package directly below the package containing the files being tested, as you're doing here, is a common approach. So, for this step, simply create the directory `${src.home}/ch20/hello/mocktest` in your development area and copy this test case file there. When you run your `build.xml` file, it automatically picks it up and compiles it with the other files.

Now you need to modify the `build.xml` file to run the test case. To do so, edit your `build.xml` file and add the following target:

```
<!-- ==================== "test" Target =================================== -->

    <!--
        This task runs all test cases. It invokes each test case individually.
        The "test-all" target is tied back to the "struts-test" target which
        actually runs the tests. This allows other test targets to be created
        in this section while maintaining the ability to run each test target
        individually. All individual test targets should be added to the
```

```
        "depends" attribute of the "test-all" target to provide a single
        target that runs all tests.
-->

  <target name="test-all" depends="struts-tests" />

  <target name="struts-tests" depends="build" >

      <junit printsummary="yes" >

          <classpath >
              <pathelement location="${object.home}"/>
              <pathelement location="${build.home}"/>
              <pathelement location="${build.home}/WEB-INF/classes"/>
              <path refid="compile.classpath"/>
          </classpath>

          <formatter type="plain" />

          <test name="ch20.hello.mocktest.TestHelloAction" />

      </junit>

  </target>
```

In addition, you should add two lines to the `help` target in the `build.xml` file indicating there are now two more targets that this build file knows how to build.

You should review the Ant documentation for all the options and details of the `<junit>` Ant task, but here are the high points of this particular usage:

- Two targets are defined: `test-all` and `struts-tests`. This is so there can be a top-level testing target as well as lower level targets. This enables you to run all the tests or just a single test if you need to.
- The `struts-test` target depends on the `build` target. This ensures that all Java files are compiled and any changes to properties files or the `struts-config.xml` have been copied to the build directory prior to running the tests.
- The `<classpath>` contains, among other elements, a reference to the `${build.home}` directory, even though there are no class files directly below it. This is on the classpath so that the StrutsTestCase libraries can locate the `struts-config.xml` file. By default, the StrutsTestCase libraries search the classpath for a directory named `WEB-INF` and then look for the `struts-config.xml` file there (although this default behavior can be overridden).

- The `<formatter>` element is used to tell JUnit how to format the output from its tests. This example uses the `plain` type, but there are other types as well. For example, it's common to use the `xml` type to generate XML-based output that can be used with an XSL stylesheet to generate custom results pages. This entails using the related `<junitreport>` Ant task.
- This example shows only a single test case being run. To add additional test cases, you can either add additional `<test>` elements or use a `<batchtest>` element to specify groups of tests to run.

By default, the output for this test is saved in the file `TEST-ch20.hello.mocktest.TestHelloAction.txt`. This filename can be overridden using the `outfile` attribute of the `<test>` task.

Running the Mock Test Case and Viewing the Results

Now that everything is configured, it's time to actually run the test. To do so, you simply type:

```
ant test-all
```

You should then see output from the build file as it makes directories, compiles the code, and copies files around. The lines related to running the tests are

```
struts-tests:
    [junit] Running ch20.hello.mocktest.TestHelloAction
    [junit] Tests run: 1, Failures: 0, Errors: 0, Time elapsed: 2.042 sec

test-all:

BUILD SUCCESSFUL
```

This indicates that a single test was run and that there were no errors. Output from the test is in the default output file (`TEST-ch20.hello.mocktest.TestHelloAction.txt`), which should read

```
Testsuite: ch20.hello.mocktest.TestHelloAction
Tests run: 1, Failures: 0, Errors: 0, Time elapsed: 2.042 sec
------------- Standard Error ----------------
[INFO] ServletContextSimulator - -ActionServlet: init
[INFO] PropertyMessageResources - -Initializing,
➥config='org.apache.struts.util.LocalStrings', returnNull=true
[INFO] PropertyMessageResources - -Initializing,
➥config='org.apache.struts.action.ActionResources', returnNull=true
```

```
[INFO] PropertyMessageResources - -Initializing,
➥config='ch20.hello.ApplicationResources', returnNull=true
[INFO] RequestProcessor - -Processing a 'POST' for path '/HelloWorld'
------------- --------------- -------------

Testcase: testNoParameters took 2.042 sec
```

The output indicates a successful execution of the `testNoParameters` test case.

Note that if the build file output indicated there were errors running the test, these errors would show up here. Virtually any errors you encounter at this point would be related to configuration, classpath issues, or having incorrect JAR file versions. If you run into problems and have trouble resolving them, please follow the instructions earlier in this chapter on configuring your system.

Testing Additional Struts Functionality in the Mock Test Case

Now that you have a working configuration and have run a test case, let's see what other options StrutsTestCase provides for testing Struts components. Listing 20.3 is `TestHelloActionMultiple.java`, a test case containing multiple individual test cases.

LISTING 20.3 `TestHelloActionMultiple.java`—A Test Case Containing Multiple Individual Test Cases

```
package ch20.hello.mocktest;

import servletunit.struts.MockStrutsTestCase;

public class TestHelloActionMultiple extends MockStrutsTestCase {

    public TestHelloActionMultiple(String testName) { super(testName); }

    public void testNoParameters() {

       // Basic test to illustrate functionality
       setRequestPathInfo("/HelloWorld");
       actionPerform();
       verifyForward("SayHello");
       // Test Form Bean validations
       verifyActionErrors(new String[] {"ch20.hello.no.person.error"});

    }
```

LISTING 20.3 Continued

```
    public void testBadPerson() {

        // Now test Talking to the Bad Person ("Atilla the Hun")

        addRequestParameter("action","getName");
        addRequestParameter("person","Atilla the Hun");
        setRequestPathInfo("/HelloWorld");
        actionPerform();
        verifyForward("SayHello");
        verifyActionErrors(new String[] {"ch20.hello.dont.talk.to.atilla"});

    }

    public void testHappyPath() {

        // Now test the "Happy Path"

        addRequestParameter("action","getName");
        addRequestParameter("person","Struts Kick Start Guys");
        setRequestPathInfo("/HelloWorld");
        actionPerform();
        verifyForward("SayHello");
        verifyNoActionErrors();

    }
}
```

As you can see, these three tests perform a pretty good test of the functionality of this application. Although you should refer to the Javadoc and other documentation on StrutsTestCase for more details, the following is a high-level view of the three test cases run here:

- **`testNoParameters`**—This test case tests the condition where `HelloWorld.do` is called with no `name` or `action` request parameters. The response expected is that `HelloAction` should return the `ActionForward` `SayHello` and the form bean should create the `ActionError` `ch20.hello.no.person.error` because no `name` was submitted. (Note: When I first ran this test, I forgot to update the `HelloForm.java` file. It was still using the original `ch03.hello.no.person.error`—the test case flagged this for me and I fixed the problem!)

- **`testBadPerson`**—This test case tests the condition where `HelloWorld.do` is called and the `name` request parameter equals `Atilla the Hun` (the person we aren't supposed to talk to!). The response expected is that `HelloAction` should return the `ActionForward SayHello` and create the `ActionError ch20.hello.dont.talk.to.atilla`.
- **`testHappyPath`**—This test case tests the normal processing of `HelloAction` when all request parameters are appropriate. The expected response is that `HelloAction` should return the `ActionForward SayHello` and no `ActionErrors` should be created.

Now that the test case is created, you can run the test and view the results.

Running the Mock Test Case and Viewing the Results

Just as before, copy this test case to the `${src.home}/ch20/hello/mocktest` directory, go to the directory where your `build.xml` file is, and type

```
ant test-all
```

Again, you should see output from the build file as it makes directories, compiles the code, and copies files around as needed. The lines related to running the tests are

```
struts-tests:
    [junit] Running ch20.hello.mocktest.TestHelloAction
    [junit] Tests run: 1, Failures: 0, Errors: 0, Time elapsed: 1.542 sec
    [junit] Running ch20.hello.mocktest.TestHelloActionMultiple
    [junit] Tests run: 3, Failures: 0, Errors: 0, Time elapsed: 1.793 sec

test-all:

BUILD SUCCESSFUL
```

As you can see, all three of the new test cases added in `TestHelloActionMultiple.java` were run and they all completed successfully. Output from the test is in the default output file (`TEST-ch20.hello.mocktest.TestHelloActionMultiple.txt`), which should read

```
Testsuite: ch20.hello.mocktest.TestHelloActionMultiple
Tests run: 3, Failures: 0, Errors: 0, Time elapsed: 2.013 sec
------------- Standard Error -----------------
[INFO] ServletContextSimulator - -ActionServlet: init
[INFO] PropertyMessageResources - -Initializing,
➥config='org.apache.struts.util.LocalStrings', returnNull=true
```

```
[INFO] PropertyMessageResources - -Initializing,
➥config='org.apache.struts.action.ActionResources', returnNull=true
[INFO] PropertyMessageResources - -Initializing,
➥config='ch20.hello.ApplicationResources', returnNull=true
[INFO] RequestProcessor - -Processing a 'POST' for path '/HelloWorld'
[INFO] ServletContextSimulator - -ActionServlet: init
[INFO] PropertyMessageResources - -Initializing,
➥config='org.apache.struts.action.ActionResources', returnNull=true
[INFO] PropertyMessageResources - -Initializing,
➥config='ch20.hello.ApplicationResources', returnNull=true
[INFO] RequestProcessor - -Processing a 'POST' for path '/HelloWorld'
[INFO] ServletContextSimulator - -ActionServlet: init
[INFO] PropertyMessageResources - -Initializing,
➥config='org.apache.struts.action.ActionResources', returnNull=true
[INFO] PropertyMessageResources - -Initializing,
➥config='ch20.hello.ApplicationResources', returnNull=true
[INFO] RequestProcessor - -Processing a 'POST' for path '/HelloWorld'
------------- --------------- -------------

Testcase: testNoParameters took 1.262 sec
Testcase: testBadPerson took 0.54 sec
Testcase: testHappyPath took 0.211 sec
```

Any errors would've been displayed here as well. Again, if you're having configuration issues, please refer to the earlier section of this chapter on system configuration.

In-Container Testing Using Cactus, JUnit, StrutsTestCase, and Ant

This section is based on the `strutsCACTUS.zip` file that's included on the CD-ROM that accompanies this book. Later sections of this chapter use different archives.

It turns out that every one of the test cases run in the previous section on mock object testing works fine as a mock object test. This is actually good because mock object tests are easier and more convenient to run than in-container tests. Mock object tests are easier because for in-container testing you need a container available for testing, at a minimum. Plus, you must get the code deployed and loaded in the container in order to test it. Many times this involves deploying the application and restarting the container to get the new code running.

Even so, there are some things that simply can't be tested any other way. With Struts applications, these things are generally related to container-based authentication or Model components. For example, if you have a Model component that needs to connect to an EJB container—or even just a database—it might be difficult or impossible to test this using the mock object approach. You might really need the container to be present to accurately test the code.

Fortunately, the developers of Cactus and StrutsTestCase have come to your rescue again. As you'll see in this section, developing and running in-container tests for Struts is almost as easy as developing and running the mock object tests in the previous section.

Modifying the Test Cases for In-Container Testing Using Cactus

The easiest place to begin is to modify the two test case Java files for in-container testing using Cactus. Because the developers of StrutsTestCase wanted to make it easy to use test cases for either kinds of testing, the only change required is that your test case file must extend a different base class in your Java file.

The base class you used for the mock object testing was `servletunit.struts.MockStrutsTestCase`. For in-container testing, you use `servletunit.struts.CactusStrutsTestCase`.

So, as you can see from Listing 20.4, only three lines are changed: the `package` statement, the `import` line, and the class declaration itself.

LISTING 20.4 `TestHelloAction.java`—To Modify for In-Container Testing, Modify Only the `package`, the `import`, and the Class Declaration

```
package ch20.hello.cactus;

import servletunit.struts.CactusStrutsTestCase;

public class TestHelloAction extends CactusStrutsTestCase {

    public TestHelloAction(String testName) { super(testName); }

    public void testSayHello() {

       setRequestPathInfo("/HelloWorld");
       actionPerform();
       verifyForward("SayHello");

    }
}
```

The easiest way to make these changes is to go to the directory `${src.home}/ch20/hello` and copy the entire subdirectory (including both Java files) to a new subdirectory called `cactus`. Then go into the `cactus` subdirectory and make these same changes to both of the test cases there.

When this is complete, you need to make a few changes to your build environment for all these tests to run correctly.

Modifying Your System Configuration for In-Container Testing Using Cactus

The changes you must make to your system configuration include adding some `.jar` library files to the application, inserting the new test cases to your Ant script, adding some configuration files for Cactus to run, and modifying the `web.xml` of your Struts Web app to configure Cactus.

Adding the Required Libraries to Your Struts Application

Because you're running Cactus to connect to Tomcat and run your tests directly in the container, two additional JAR files are needed:

- **`cactus-1.4.1.jar`**—If you're going to run Cactus tests, you should probably add the Cactus library. The version this example application was tested with is Cactus 1.4.1.
- **`commons-httpclient-2.0.jar`**—This JAR file contains HTTP client utilities that allow the JUnit tests run by Ant to connect to Tomcat.
- **`aspectjrt-1.0.5.jar`**—An additional library file required by Cactus.

The files must be copied to the directory identified by Ant as the `${lib.home}` for the build process. This ensures that the build process puts them into the `.war` file for the Web app.

Inserting the New Test Cases into the Build Script

The easiest way to configure Ant to run the two new test cases you just created for in-container testing is to just add two additional lines to the existing `<junit>` task in the `struts-test` target of your `build.xml` file.

The two lines to add are

```
<test name="ch20.hello.cactus.TestHelloAction" />

<test name="ch20.hello.cactus.TestHelloActionMultiple" />
```

In the sample application, these lines are inserted directly after the two existing test cases.

Should you remove the two previous test cases? Of course not! The value of your test cases grows over time—remove only test cases that are no longer valid. This enables you to maintain your code on an ongoing basis and yet rerun every test case whenever you perform a build. This is the real value of integrating the testing process directly into the build process as this chapter demonstrates.

Adding the Required `.properties` Files to Your Application

The Cactus library file you just added requires these three property files:

- **`cactus.properties`**—This file holds the information required by the Cactus client software to help it locate the container that your tests are deployed in. The properties as they are used for this sample application are

  ```
  cactus.contextURL = http://localhost:8080/strutsCACTUS

  cactus.servletRedirectorName = StrutsServletRedirector

  cactus.enableLogging=true
  ```

  The first property identifies the host and Web app your tests are located in. The second property maps to an entry that you'll make in the `web.xml` file of the Web app in the next section. The third property enables logging.

- **`log4j.properties`**—This file contains configuration for the Log4J logging utility as it runs on the server.

- **`log_client.properties`**—This file contains configuration for the Log4J logging utility as it runs on the client (via the Ant `<junit>` task).

Copies of these files are provided. Simply copy them to the top of your source path in your build directory (that is, copy them to `${src.home}`)and the `build.xml` automatically picks them up and deploys them for you.

Modifying the `web.xml` File in Your Web App for Cactus

Cactus runs by adding a servlet to your Web app where it accepts requests. Based on those requests, it then runs tests against the classes and objects running in your application. To allow Cactus to accept requests from inside your Web app, you must add an entry to your `web.xml` file to configure how it will work.

Listing 20.5 is the updated `web.xml` for the `strutsCACTUS` Web app that contains your code and test case files. The lines that were added are **in bold**.

LISTING 20.5 `web.xml`—The Web App Deployment Descriptor Modified for Cactus

```
<?xml version="1.0" encoding="ISO-8859-1"?>

<!DOCTYPE web-app
  PUBLIC "-//Sun Microsystems, Inc.//DTD Web Application 2.2//EN"
  "http://java.sun.com/j2ee/dtds/web-app_2_2.dtd">

<web-app>

   <!-- Cactus Servlet Redirector configuration -->
   <servlet>
      <servlet-name>StrutsServletRedirector</servlet-name>
      <servlet-class>org.apache.cactus.server.ServletTestRedirector</servlet-class>
   </servlet>

  <!-- Struts Action Servlet Configuration -->
  <servlet>
    <servlet-name>action</servlet-name>
    <servlet-class>org.apache.struts.action.ActionServlet</servlet-class>
    <init-param>
      <param-name>config</param-name>
      <param-value>/WEB-INF/struts-config.xml</param-value>
    </init-param>
    <init-param>
      <param-name>debug</param-name>
      <param-value>3</param-value>
    </init-param>
    <init-param>
      <param-name>detail</param-name>
      <param-value>3</param-value>
    </init-param>
    <load-on-startup>2</load-on-startup>
  </servlet>

  <!-- Cactus Servlet Redirector URL mapping -->
  <servlet-mapping>
    <servlet-name>StrutsServletRedirector</servlet-name>
    <url-pattern>/StrutsServletRedirector</url-pattern>
  </servlet-mapping>

  <!-- Struts Action Servlet Mapping -->
  <servlet-mapping>
```

LISTING 20.5 Continued

```
    <servlet-name>action</servlet-name>
    <url-pattern>*.do</url-pattern>
  </servlet-mapping>

  <!-- The Welcome File List -->
  <welcome-file-list>
    <welcome-file>hello.jsp</welcome-file>
  </welcome-file-list>

  <!-- Application Tag Library Descriptor -->
  <taglib>
    <taglib-uri>/WEB-INF/app.tld</taglib-uri>
    <taglib-location>/WEB-INF/app.tld</taglib-location>
  </taglib>

  <!-- Struts Tag Library Descriptors -->
  <taglib>
    <taglib-uri>/WEB-INF/struts-bean.tld</taglib-uri>
    <taglib-location>/WEB-INF/struts-bean.tld</taglib-location>
  </taglib>

  <taglib>
    <taglib-uri>/WEB-INF/struts-html.tld</taglib-uri>
    <taglib-location>/WEB-INF/struts-html.tld</taglib-location>
  </taglib>

  <taglib>
    <taglib-uri>/WEB-INF/struts-logic.tld</taglib-uri>
    <taglib-location>/WEB-INF/struts-logic.tld</taglib-location>
  </taglib>

</web-app>
```

The two additions to Listing 20.5 are 1) Identify a URI where Cactus can be accessed (`/StrutsServletRedirector`) and 2) tell Tomcat which servlet class should be invoked whenever a request is received for this resource (`org.apache.cactus.server.ServletTestRedirector`). This Cactus servlet then receives the test requests, executes them, and returns the response to the Cactus client being run by the Ant `<junit>` task.

Note that the URI /StrutsServletRedirector is the same URI that was identified in the cactus.properties file in the previous step.

Running the In-Container Test Cases and Viewing the Results

Hold on—you're almost done!

Now that everything is configured and in place, you just need to build the application and deploy it, restart Tomcat to get it running, and then run your tests.

Notice that how you run the tests is one of the key differences between mock object testing and in-container testing. With mock object testing, you could run the tests just after building the application. In-container testing requires you to build and deploy the test cases before you can actually run them.

As before, you deploy the application to Tomcat by issuing the following Ant command:

```
ant deploy
```

After this completes and you've deployed the application, you might need to restart Tomcat. (In fact, I've found that I occasionally need to stop Tomcat, delete the old webapp directory, and then restart Tomcat to get the deploy to work correctly—if you have problems, try it.)

Now that your Web application is deployed and running in the container, you can run your tests. To do so, simply type (as before):

```
ant test-all
```

Output from the test-all target should now read

```
struts-tests:
    [junit] Running ch20.hello.mocktest.TestHelloAction
    [junit] Tests run: 1, Failures: 0, Errors: 0, Time elapsed: 2.524 sec
    [junit] Running ch20.hello.mocktest.TestHelloActionMultiple
    [junit] Tests run: 3, Failures: 0, Errors: 0, Time elapsed: 1.973 sec
    [junit] Running ch20.hello.cactus.TestHelloAction
    [junit] Tests run: 1, Failures: 0, Errors: 0, Time elapsed: 2.924 sec
    [junit] Running ch20.hello.cactus.TestHelloActionMultiple
    [junit] Tests run: 3, Failures: 0, Errors: 0, Time elapsed: 0.931 sec

test-all:

BUILD SUCCESSFUL
```

Congratulations! Your in-container tests using Cactus are now working. From here, it's a simple matter to build up more and more sophisticated tests over time. After you've built up a significant library of test cases, you'll find that they make a significant impact on the overall quality of the code you produce.

Conclusions

This chapter introduced a process of developing, building, deploying, and testing Struts applications. The process presented was a basic version of the process used on many Jakarta projects.

This process incorporates many elements of Extreme Programming (XP). XP is an approach to development that, among other things, stresses ongoing, integrated testing as a core part of the development process.

Specific focus areas within this chapter were

- Defining a standard directory structure for development. This allows automating the process of building, deploying, and testing your Struts application. A recommended directory structure was presented.
- Creating a `build.xml` build script to be used by the Ant build tool to automate building, deploying, and testing the application.
- A general approach to integrating ongoing testing into the overall development process was presented. This approach discussed the two primary approaches to testing programs, such as Struts, that require an application server to run.
- The first approach presented was mock object testing. In this testing approach, Java programs are created that emulate a real application server using test objects, or mock objects. Mock objects are created for the request, response, session, and other objects required by your Struts application to allow it to be tested.
- The second approach presented was in-container testing. In this testing approach, your Struts application is deployed into an application server prior to testing. In addition to your Struts application, additional software is deployed into the application server to listen for testing requests made by client testing software which is run via the Ant build tool. The Cactus testing framework was used in this chapter for both the client- and server-based components of in-container testing.
- JUnit was used as the core testing tool in this chapter. It's run using `<junit>` tasks that allow the execution of JUnit tests using the Ant build tool. In addition, the StrutsTestCase extension to JUnit was used for both mock object and in-container testing of the example Struts application.

APPENDIX A

Installing Struts and the Sample Applications from the CD

IN THIS APPENDIX

- Listing of Applications Included on the Companion CD-ROM
- Step 1: Install the JDK and Tomcat
- Step 2: Install MySQL
- Copy the WAR Files to the Tomcat `webapps` Directory
- Restart Tomcat

Included with this book is a CD-ROM containing everything you need to install a working application server running Struts and to run all the examples from the book.

The example applications are stored in directories by chapter. The third-party applications (for example, Tomcat) are located in a separate area.

Instructions for installing example applications that are covered in a single chapter are generally covered in that chapter in the book. Installing other example applications, like the Stocktrack application that covers multiple chapters, is covered here.

The same approach is taken for third-party applications. Installation of Tomcat, for example, is covered here. Installation of JBoss (like other applications that are used in a single chapter) is covered in the chapter where it is used.

Listing of Applications Included on the Companion CD-ROM

Following is a listing of all third-party applications included on the CD-ROM that accompanies this book.

- Java™ 2 SDK, Standard Edition, v 1.4.1 for Windows and Linux
- Jakarta Tomcat 4.1.12
- Jakarta Struts 1.1b2
- MySQL 3.23.52 for Windows and Linux

- Jakarta Torque 3.0b4
- JUnit 3.7
- Jakarta Ant 1.5 (version from Jakarta Cactus project)
- Jakarta Cactus 1.4.1 (for J2EE 1.3)
- JBoss 3.0.3
- XDoclet 1.1.2
- Apache Axis 1.0
- StrutsTestCase for JUnit 1.9 (version 1.1/2.3)

Step 1: Install the JDK and Tomcat

In addition to all sample applications and third-party tools used in the book, the CD-ROM also contains a copy of Sun's Java™ 2 Platform, Standard Edition, v 1.4.1 (also known as J2SE 1.4.1). You should note, however, that while Struts and Tomcat have been pretty well debugged for J2SE 1.4.1, we can't ensure that all the other applications provided on the CD-ROM have. In particular, JBoss 3.0.3 had a few documented issues with it. To be safe, all the sample code and third-party applications have been tested and work with Sun's J2SE v1.3.1.

The first step to getting the application running is to install the Java development environment (if needed) and the Tomcat application server. Follow the installation instructions included with the release that's appropriate for your operating system. You can find the JDK installers for Windows and Linux in the `\apps\J2SE` directory on the CD.

After the JDK is installed (including setting environment variables such as `JAVA_HOME` and placing the `bin` directory in your path), install Tomcat using the Tomcat installer appropriate for your operating system. When Tomcat's installed, make sure that you can connect to the server (which by default will be at `http://localhost:8080/`).

The Tomcat installers can be found on the CD-ROM in the `\apps\tomcat` directory.

Step 2: Install MySQL

Use the appropriate installer to install MySQL on your computer. After MySQL is up and running, run the `init_database.sql` and `populate_database.sql` scripts located in the `\examples` directory on the CD-ROM using the `MySQL \.` command. For example, on a Windows operating system with the CD-ROM in the `G:\` drive (your input is in bold):

```
C:\mysql
Welcome to the MySQL monitor.  Commands end with ; or \g.
Your MySQL connection id is 1 to server version: 3.23.45-nt

Type 'help;' or '\h' for help. Type '\c' to clear the buffer.

mysql> \. G:\examples\init_database.sql
.
.
.
mysql> quit

C:\mysql -u demo -p stocktrack
Password: <type "struts">
Welcome to the MySQL monitor.  Commands end with ; or \g.
Your MySQL connection id is 1 to server version: 3.23.45-nt

Type 'help;' or '\h' for help. Type '\c' to clear the buffer.

mysql> \. G:\examples\populate_database.sql
.
.
.
mysql> quit
```

Copy the WAR Files to the Tomcat webapps Directory

Next, copy the WAR files for the example(s) you want to install from the examples directory on the CD-ROM to the webapps subdirectory of your Tomcat installation. For example, to install the Stocktrack sample application, copy stocktrack.war to webapps. The following WAR files are available:

- stocktrack.war—The sample stock tracking application. Note that three different versions are included. One represents the application at the end of Chapter 11, one represents the application at the end of Chapter 16, and one represents the application at the end of Chapter 17.
- Taglib.war—Contains all the examples and source code from Chapters 12 to 16, which concern the Struts Tag Library.

NOTE

Installation and configuration details for Chapters 18—20 are provided in those chapters. The applications used in those chapters are JBoss, XDoclet, Axis, JUnit, Ant, Cactus, and StrutsTestCase for JUnit.

Restart Tomcat

To complete the installation, stop and start the Tomcat server. The new Web applications will be automatically unpacked and installed.

Note that the stock-tracking application assumes that you're accessing the MySQL database on the same machine on which the Tomcat server is running. If this isn't the case, you must edit the `Torque.properties` file located in the `webapps/stocktrack/WEB-INF/classes` directory to change the entry for `torque.database.stocktrack.url`.

Symbols

A

B

C

D

E

F

G

H

I

J

K-L

M

N

O

P-Q

R

S

T

U

V

W

X-Z

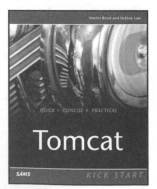